Learning to Negotiate

Negotiating well is hard. Learning to negotiate is even harder. This new textbook offers sound practical advice for doing both. If you are serious about helping yourself – or others – to become better negotiators, this book is for you. The textbook draws from empirical research in fields as diverse as business, law, neuroscience, game theory, and history. It offers a wealth of examples, case studies, and graphic illustrations. And it blends all this into a coherent framework to guide the practitioner. This is an invaluable book for MBA, law, and other professional students, as well as executives seeking to develop and improve their skills in negotiation.

Prof. Dr. Georg Berkel is an attorney and consultant who specializes in the negotiation process. He has practised and taught negotiations in more than twenty countries. Previously he worked in a leading technology company in Germany and Israel. Dr. Berkel earned an MBA at IESE in Barcelona and a PhD at the University of St. Gallen in Switzerland. He has been a regular visiting scholar at the Kellogg School of Management since 2006, a visiting lecturer at the University of Munich since 2008, and professor at IUBH since 2012. He is also a qualified mediator. Visit www.negotiationconsulting.com for more information.

Learning to Negotiate

Georg Berkel
Negotiationconsulting.com

CAMBRIDGE
UNIVERSITY PRESS

University Printing House, Cambridge CB2 8BS, United Kingdom

One Liberty Plaza, 20th Floor, New York, NY 10006, USA

477 Williamstown Road, Port Melbourne, VIC 3207, Australia

314–321, 3rd Floor, Plot 3, Splendor Forum, Jasola District Centre,
New Delhi – 110025, India

79 Anson Road, #06–04/06, Singapore 079906

Cambridge University Press is part of the University of Cambridge.

It furthers the University's mission by disseminating knowledge in the pursuit of education, learning, and research at the highest international levels of excellence.

www.cambridge.org
Information on this title: www.cambridge.org/9781108495912
DOI: 10.1017/9781108863599

First published 2021

Printed in the United Kingdom by TJ International Ltd, Padstow Cornwall, 2021

A catalogue record for this publication is available from the British Library.

Library of Congress Cataloging-in-Publication Data
Names: Berkel, Georg, 1971– author.
Title: Learning to negotiate / Georg Berkel, Negotiationconsulting.com.
Description: 1 Edition. | New York : Cambridge University Press, 2020. | Includes bibliographical references and index.
Identifiers: LCCN 2020029464 (print) | LCCN 2020029465 (ebook) | ISBN 9781108495912 (hardback) | ISBN 9781108811071 (paperback) | ISBN 9781108863599 (epub)
Subjects: LCSH: Negotiation–Study and teaching. | Mediation–Study and teaching. | Conflict management–Study and teaching.
Classification: LCC BF637.N4 B47 2020 (print) | LCC BF637.N4 (ebook) | DDC 302.3–dc23
LC record available at https://lccn.loc.gov/2020029464
LC ebook record available at https://lccn.loc.gov/2020029465

ISBN 978-1-108-49591-2 Hardback
ISBN 978-1-108-81107-1 Paperback

Additional resources for this publication at www.cambridge.org/berkel

Brief Contents

Detailed Contents

Preface

Negotiating well is hard. Learning to negotiate is even harder. There are three challenges to negotiation success, and three challenges to successful learning. One leads to the next, and each is more difficult than the previous one. This book invites you to take a fresh look at an eternal problem. Refraining from quick solutions and drawing on a wealth of examples, it offers empirically valid yet practical advice to see clearly what has been there all along. If you are serious about helping yourself or others to become better negotiators, this book is for you.

We negotiate every day. We do so as managers or lawyers, but also as parents, friends, and citizens. And we are not alone. Just think of what's in the news today. Everybody is constantly negotiating. Decades of research have generated impressive knowledge about *how to do* it. But this research also tells us that we still fall far short of our abilities. Yet much less has been written about *how to learn* it. This book addresses both matters, and takes a very broad perspective. In the first instance, we will look at business transactions, such as buying and selling goods and services, mergers and acquisitions (M&A), joint ventures, venture capital, and investment strategies. We will meet some of history's greatest business minds and explore case studies ranging from Apple to Volkswagen. And we will also dig into legal questions, such as contract law, antitrust, dispute resolution, claim management, and good faith negotiations, in various legal systems across the globe. But the book casts an even wider net. In learning to negotiate we must draw from neuroscience, biology, and psychology, as well as from game theory, history, contemporary politics, artificial intelligence, and even philosophy. So, on our journey, we will not only meet CEOs, executives, and lawyers. We will also encounter brain surgeons, detectives, spies, philosophers, politicians, chess masters, and regular citizens. And more than a dozen Nobel laureates.

The book tells a coherent story that proceeds through nine chapters. Visualizations accompany it throughout. This provides, I hope, a clear structure to our complicated topic. In addition, you can find an individual training plan to print out and use (together with all the figures used herein) at www.cambridge.org/berkel.

Learning lets us see the pattern where others see nothing. Perhaps you know this dialogue between Conan Doyle's master detective and his friend. Dr. Watson: "You have evidently seen more in these rooms than was visible to me." Sherlock Holmes: "No, but I fancy that I may have deduced a little more. I imagine that you saw all that I did."[1]

It is vital that we acknowledge negotiation as the deeply paradoxical process which it truly is. We are tasked with simultaneously creating and distributing value. We must cooperate as well as compete with the other side. And they must do the same. This creates a dilemma for both sides, and makes us deeply ambivalent about the process. But the paradox also provides us with the means to master the challenges of negotiation learning. You may find that because it is so hard, learning to negotiate can become easy.

Acknowledgments

This book offers what I have learned to date. It would be unthinkable without those that have enabled my journey of studying, practicing, and teaching negotiations.

I will forever be indebted to Jeanne Brett and Steve Goldberg, who invited me to Northwestern University's Dispute Resolution Research Center fifteen years ago, to the amazing academics from whom I had the privilege to learn, namely Leigh Thompson, William L. Ury, Holly Schroth, Shirli Kopelman, Adam Galinsky, Brian Gunia, Taya Cohen, Tetsushi Okumura, Lynn P. Cohn, John E. Ward, Lloyd Shefsky, John A. Davis, Africa Ariño, Eric Weber, Francisco Iniesta, and to my mentors at the University of St. Gallen, Ivo Schwander and Martin Hilb.

Outstanding negotiators that I had the pleasure to work with (and from whom I only wish I had learned more) are Florencia Garrido, Grace Alvarez, Harald Hehmke, Barbara Kropp, B. J. Suk, Richy Roberts, Ilan Sharon, Editte Galli Heyne, Jonah Bamberger, Onn Fenig, Yaniv Rogovsky, Orna Bar David, Sharon Kahanov, Avi Nachmias, Moshe Tamir, Vikas Uberoi, Andreas Henke, and Peter Brinkmann.

I am grateful to the students and executives from all over the world that I had the privilege of teaching, and to those who gave me the opportunity to engage in teaching, especially: Manfred Schwaiger, Antonia-Denisa Efron, Avi Primor, Larry Susskind, Michael Wheeler, Sascha Albers, Cynthia Shih-Chia Wang, Ingmar Geiger, Michael Kleinaltenkamp, Christian Essiger, Hans-Uwe Neuenhahn, Ulrich Hagel, Wolfgang Gesslein, Günter Wiedemann, Nadja Müller, Rainer Giebelman, Morten Lindholst, Holger Sommerfeldt, Peter Thuy, Karen Engler, Vito Roberto, Jacqueline Gasser-Beck, Dorette Lochner, and Rainer Stroebe.

I would also like to thank the anonymous reviewers for Cambridge University Press, and especially Valerie Appleby, Rachel Norridge, Tobias Ginsberg, and Llinos Edwards for making this book possible.

First and foremost, my gratitude belongs to my family – Karl, Adelheid, Barbara, Christian, Jakob, Marie, and Johanna – to whom I dedicate this book.

Introduction

Niels Bohr said that profound truths are recognized by the fact that their opposite is also true. Negotiations are full of profound truths. Opposites await at every turn. Negotiation is an essentially paradoxical process. What is good for us can be good for the other side. And it can be its opposite. Or it can be partly one and partly the other. To succeed, we have to do things that are mutually exclusive. Our strength is our weakness. It is no surprise that most of us are deeply ambivalent about it.[1]

In this Introduction I will explain why I wrote this book and provide an overview of what lies ahead. The question of negotiation success and learning has been the focus of my professional life. I will offer the answers that I have found, broken down into small steps and increasing in complexity. While the book's structure is symmetrical, with three parts each containing three chapters, its nine chapters are not of equal size. Rather, they resemble a pyramid. The paradox of negotiation is the crux of the matter and results in two more challenges. These challenges in turn result in the three stumbling blocks of learning – and they can become the three steps that we need to take in order to learn. The Introduction describes this paradox in a nutshell.

So, why another book on negotiation? There are many excellent books on all its facets. We can learn about negotiation and conflict, culture, emotions, improvisation, authenticity, or organizations – and we should. Our understanding of negotiations has substantially advanced in recent years, even if it trickles down to practice with varying speed across the globe. Yet, as hard as negotiation is, learning it is harder still. When we advance on one side, we block our progress on the other. Powerful cognitive illusions bar the way. The good news: When we understand these illusions, they become the very stepping stones of our success.[2]

My own professional training did not provide such an opportunity: It takes half a dozen years to become an attorney in Germany, but hardly any negotiation training is involved. Similarly, only a minority of German managers have been professionally trained in conducting negotiations. So, when I started practicing, I read as much as I could about this fascinating process. Yet, more often than not, something important seemed to be missing. Many books appeared to tell only one side of the story. Trying to put their advice into practice was never satisfying. Perhaps I did not do it right, but it often felt like trying to walk on one leg. Why was this?[3]

I came to realize that every transaction has two sides. Ideally what is good for us is good for the other party as well, but often it is not. So, we have to work with them, as well as against them. Consequently, all contracts are structured along these lines. This is true even where contracts are not explicitly negotiated, which varies across the globe. I have negotiated power plant contracts all over the world for Siemens AG. As part of an interdisciplinary team, I thus contributed to the successful conclusion of transactions worth hundreds of millions of pounds in Europe, Asia, and North America. What drew me to this work is that it is about making deals. We sat and worked with our business partners until we agreed – or agreed to disagree. Forensic lawyers have to focus on the past: Either the plaintiff or the defendant is right. The court room sees mostly zero-sum games. But my corporate team would shape the future.

We did not have to delegate the job to judges or lawmakers: We could do it ourselves. What a privilege! Wherever we were in the world, it was marvelous work, all about trust, open communication, and creative problem-solving. Together with the other side we strove to create the optimal transaction. We often gave the customer more than they had wanted before coming to the table – and often received more ourselves. And we were even getting paid for it! I read and admired the classics of win–win negotiations, such as Roger Fisher, William Ury and Bruce Patton's *Getting to Yes* and Ury's *Getting past No*. And I found what I read to be eminently true: Negotiation is the creation of value for mutual benefit, as shown in Figure 1.

So, what was the problem? It turned out that the opposite of this statement is also true. Yes, value can be created in complex transactions. Yet we live in a world of limited resources. It is a truism, but sometimes what we get must come at the expense of the other side. A win–win solution is not always possible, whether we

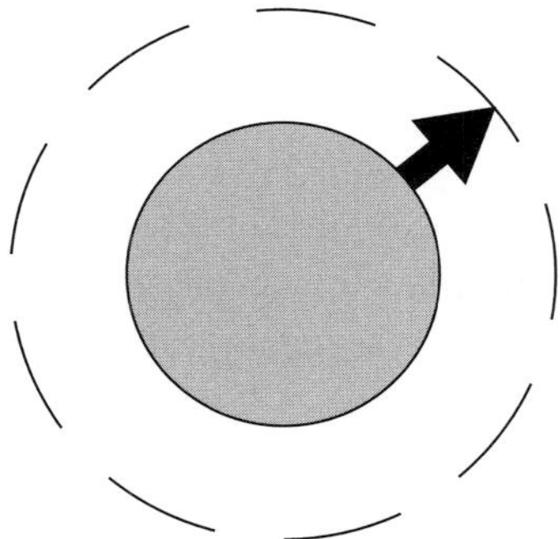

Figure 1 Negotiation as creation of value

like it or not. And initially I did not like it at all. All too often I had to leave the cooperative part to the non-lawyers. My team mates from Engineering could brainstorm all day long. They worked out the optimal project configuration for both sides. But as I put all of it to paper, darker thoughts filled my mind. I had to imagine all the things that could go wrong, and then protect the company from them.

The opposing counsel did exactly the same. Every word counted. What if we delivered late? What if there was a defect? What would happen in the case of a strike, archaeological findings, even war? These risks carried costs. And they also carried probabilities. We calculated the monetary value of our words. Some words impacted our bottom line, which we did not like. Or they impacted the price, which the customer did not like. Nobody wanted those risks, but somebody had to take them. Every now and then we did find a clever trade-off. Occasionally we could sneakily pass a risk on to a third party. But mostly we simply had to determine who would swallow it. And when it came to money, things only became worse. There were no two ways about it: We wanted the price to be as high as possible. They wanted the opposite. It was like having a pie that everybody wanted sitting between us. Even if we could not get all of it, both sides wanted as much as possible. Together we had to decide how to slice it.

This was not at all a noble pursuit of mutually beneficial outcomes. It mostly had a colder, Darwinian feel. We had to approach it with what has been called a "monetary mindset": An I-win-you-lose way of looking at the world. The engineers muttered something about "typical lawyers" and happily left the room. But it was not altogether a bad job. At the best of times, the negotiation could become playful, even light-hearted. There were many things that we never wanted to talk about, such as our horrible alternatives and true walk-away price. There were even things that we hoped they would misunderstand, such as our horrible alternatives and true walk-away price. They knew this, of course, and we knew that they knew. And it was just the same for them.[4]

The whole thing often felt like a game of poker, or chess, or perhaps a judo match. If both sides knew what they were doing, and kept a certain distance, it could turn into a contest of wits. Tongues planted firmly in cheeks, we came to appreciate the adversary's professionalism. Slowly I learned to like this side of the coin. But my win–win books did not help at all. If anything, they made things more difficult. Yes, I did try to understand what the other side really wanted, but often it was simply not compatible with our own wishes. They reached for the biggest slice of the pie. And so did we. The advice I needed now came from a very different stack of books. Books with titles such as *Start with No, Never Split the Difference*, or *Khrushchev's Third Shoe*. I may not have liked everything they suggested, but most of it was undeniably true: Negotiation is the distribution of value for our benefit – and at the expense of the other side: see Figure 2.[5]

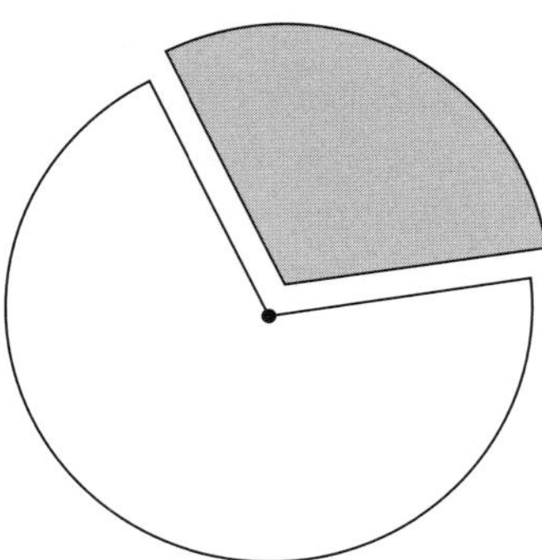

Figure 2 Negotiation as distribution of value

Negotiation is the process by which people with conflicting goals or interests determine how to allocate resources or risks, resolve conflict, or work together. The objective is to achieve the best possible outcome. We can compare, and often measure, how good the result is for both sides. Some negotiations have only one side: If you only haggle about the price of a carpet at a market, all you do is distribute value. But as soon as it becomes more complex, the creation of value becomes possible. Perhaps the carpet can be wrapped or delivered. Perhaps you are interested in other items? Would you like to pay cash or by card? In what currency? Maybe you could recommend the shop to fellow travelers? Or "like" it on social media? We can often break a single issue into multiple issues, or add completely new ones. We can trade things. Rather than being stuck in a purely monetary mindset, we can benefit from what Brian Gunia of Johns Hopkins calls a "bartering mindset." Gunia reminds us that bartering, while almost forgotten in the West, is psychologically sophisticated. And it can be very powerful. A bartering mindset can help to create value. Instead of considering the other side's needs in monetary terms, it encourages us to look directly at their needs. This perspective makes it easier to search for and find mutual interests. Most real-life transactions allow for more than the mere distribution of value.[6]

The reverse is also true: Most transactions are not confined to the creation of value. How wonderful when both sides can get all that they want. You may know the parable of the two sisters that argue about an orange. One wants to drink the juice, the other wants to bake a cake with the rind. In rare situations like these, nobody has to give up anything. No pie must be sliced. Both sides can be made perfectly happy. Alas, a win–win usually comes at the expense of a third party. That's its dirty little secret. Somebody has to pay for it – just not somebody who is at the table. I will explain this more fully later. For now, just think of the neighborhood fruit vendor and the extra orange sale he did not make.

In commercial transactions, perfect compatibility of interests is the exception rather than the rule. Bringing together different interests is the entire point of markets. Typically, everyone wants the juice. Even if you don't, you may pretend otherwise, so that you can ask for a concession. "Oh, you want *all* the juice? Well, I guess then I will need to ask for some apples." You would not do that? Are you equally sure about the other side?[7]

The possible outcomes of a transaction can be plotted on a matrix. The axes denote how good an outcome is for each of the two sides. It visualizes the point that joint gains may be increased and individual gains must be obtained: see Figure 3.[8]

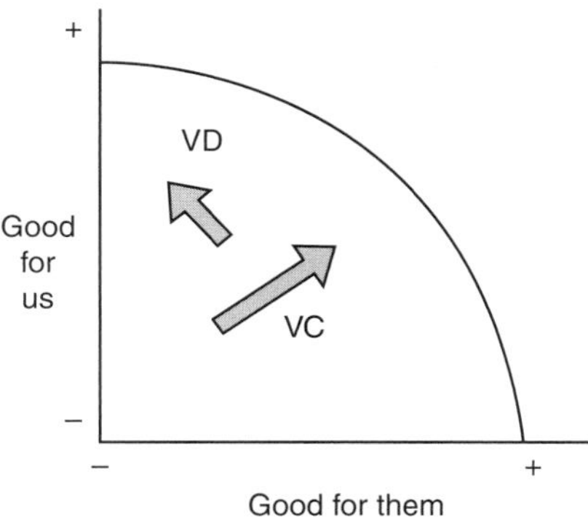

Figure 3 The geometry of the transaction: Value creation (VC) and value distribution (VD)

The Two Sides of the Contract

A pattern emerged when I applied these thoughts to my contract negotiations. A transaction consists of the promises that the parties make to each other. Every promise falls into one of two categories: "the planned" – what the parties plan to do, and "the unplanned" – what they hope they never have to do. This is not only true for power plant contracts. It applies whenever goods or services are exchanged.[9]

"The planned" describes what the parties plan and want to do. It is their reason for entering into the transaction. The builder of a power plant describes its specifications and performance. The buyer promises acceptance and payment in return. This is where the parties strive to expand the pie as much as possible. Conversely, "the unplanned" deals with all the things that can go wrong. Certainly, no one plans for them to happen, and perhaps they never will. But they might, so the parties have to prepare. These are the costly risks that nobody wants to take, so this is where each party strives to do well at the expense of the other side.

Every transaction, by contract or law, also includes some more generic provisions (such as a title, a preamble, a dispute resolution clause, etc.). And there are often technical exhibits that specify the promises made. But the most important part is the promises. Negotiating "the planned" primarily requires the creation of value, while negotiating "the unplanned" primarily requires its distribution. But both sides of the contract require both types of negotiation. We will expand on this later. First, a quick clarification is called for: Contracts depend on law as well as culture (see Figure 4).

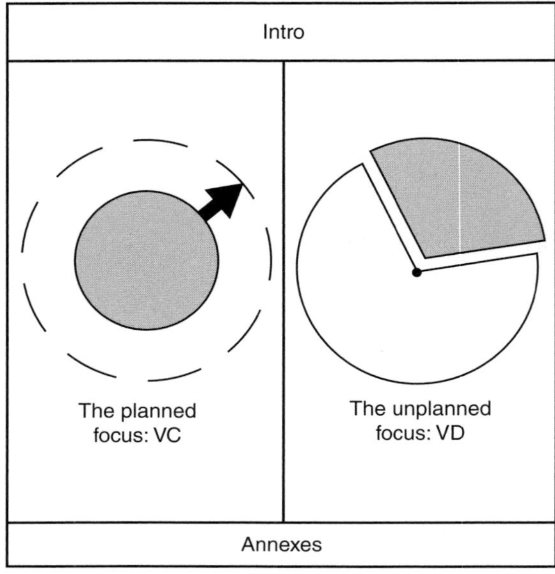

Figure 4 The geometry of the contract: Value creation (VC) and value distribution (VD)

The Law versus Culture

This duality exists even where no formal contract is needed. Of course, not all transactions require an elaborate written document, and actually, not many do. This is both a legal and cultural question. Westerners are accustomed to a long tradition of strong legal systems and the rule of law. They tend to view contracts as solid legal instruments that are strictly enforced if violated. Conversely, there are significant differences in the development of legal systems and the rule of law across Asia.[10]

Even more important may be cultural factors. Notwithstanding the considerable differences in tactical preferences among, for instance, the Chinese, Japanese, and Korean cultures, Asians have a long tradition of doing business without contracts, and of relying more on sincerity and "face." A verbal commitment may be sufficient and binding: Asians can feel insulted when a legalistic Western business partner wants to specify penalties for broken promises.[11]

The situation is different in the West. In sufficiently complex transactions, legal and accounting requirements encourage us to negotiate both the planned and the unplanned. The reason: Even if we do not speak about it, we still distribute the relevant resources and risks. Whether explicitly or implicitly, we are concluding a contract. In the absence of a negotiated document, the law of the land kicks in. So, unless they agree otherwise, the parties settle on the default provisions of the law. Sometimes a party does not realize this, and the other side may secretly capitalize on it. For instance, in many countries the law puts us in a comfortable position when we buy things. Goods usually carry a warranty: The seller is responsible for providing them free of defects – just as the buyer has to make the promised payment. The national law defines what a defect is, and what the seller must do to remedy it. Perhaps the seller has to replace or repair it. Perhaps the replaced part carries another warranty. Perhaps the result is an endless string of "evergreen" warranties.

The point here is that, as long as the parties do not find their own specific agreement, the law provides the "fallback" contract. (At the same time, it is true that in all jurisdictions there are obligations that cannot be amended by the parties. For instance, the parties cannot absolve themselves from binding health and safety regulations or environmental protection laws. But in many of the world's jurisdictions, individuals and companies have a lot of leeway to determine their mutual rights and obligations, should they so choose.) So, we are well protected from any damages that a purchased product or service may cause us. The liability of the seller is usually not limited in any way. Hence it would be a terrible mistake to rely on the default when we are *selling*: We would be exposed to unlimited liability, and the procurement manager on the other side of the table would not believe their luck. In the same way, we would like the default when we are buying.

In other words, we distribute and create value when we negotiate a transaction, whether we do so explicitly (by working with a draft document) or not (by concluding an agreement with a handshake). The only difference is that in the latter case, the content of our transaction is determined by law instead of (our) contract. Which, in turn, determines the economics of the transaction: If a risk is probable, but not excluded by way of contract, the seller must either reduce the profit or increase the price (in order to pass on the cost of the contingency to the buyer).

Not negotiating risk in the hope that it will go away is like a child hoping to disappear upon covering their eyes.

This is not to say that a contract cannot, or should not, be changed after signature. Quite the opposite. As we know, it is difficult to make predictions, especially about the future. Even the best contract cannot foresee all future circumstances. While this is true all over the world, it is especially significant in Asia, where it is assumed that life-changing circumstances cannot be predicted or "contained." In the Asian view, contracts are inherently deficient and can never be completely fair because they cannot deal fully with the future. Instead, a signed contract is but a snapshot of current conditions and thus cannot be final. It should be opened and renegotiated once circumstances change in order to arrive at a new and fair arrangement between the parties.[12]

Beyond these legal and cultural considerations, writing down what is agreed serves a more fundamental purpose. It may sound trivial: Agreements consist of words. Working on these words is the vehicle for agreeing. We need words to formulate positions, interests, rights, and obligations. Only by articulating them can we determine if we do, in fact, agree. What appears to be agreement can fall apart when we go through the trouble of expressing what we really mean. On the other hand, once there is an agreement on the words, we already hold the contract in our hands. They are but the same. We just have to sign.

The Two Sides Are Opposites

So, whether based on law or contract, a transaction consists of both value creation *and* value distribution. As you know, this is the elephant in the room: The behavior that leads to value creation is different from the one needed for value distribution. The first necessitates cooperation, while the later requires competition. The tactics for one are usually the opposite of the tactics for the other, at least in spirit. Yes, sometimes they can be complementary: To reject an unfavorable offer and respond with an aggressive counteroffer is certainly a competitive move. Yet it may also be necessary to encourage the other side to cooperate. (If this seems counterintuitive to you, you are right. But paradoxically it is true. Bear with me here.) However, most of the time, these tactics require the opposite of one another. I will explain the six key cooperative tactics as well as the six key competitive tactics that decades of empirical research have produced.[13]

For now, to make the point, just consider this example: In order to claim value, you should make the first offer. And you should make it as extreme as you plausibly can. Why? Because this is an excellent way to nudge the other side toward giving you a large piece of the pie. The one thing you generally do *not* want to do is to reveal your secret bottom line (there are two exceptions to this rule, as we will see). Even Fisher, Ury, and Patton, the godfathers of cooperative negotiations and the authors of *Getting to Yes*, acknowledge that sometimes the problem is not too little information, but too much. Then you are better off just keeping quiet.[14]

But there is a downside. Think of the sisters and the orange. If they never told each other what they really are willing to accept, they might not have made any agreement at all. This is a structural problem. To create value, we have to expose ourselves. But then other sides might take advantage of us. Or, we might protect ourselves (and perhaps even take advantage of the other side). But then we can only distribute value.

So, what's the big deal? Why don't we just take the contract and look at the clauses? That will tell us what to do: If it is a "planned" clause, it is all about creating value, so we simply use cooperative tactics. If not, it is about the distribution of value, so we just use competitive tactics! If we don't like slicing (or expanding) pies, we have to find another job. Isn't it easy enough? Well, yes. And no.

We usually cannot separate the two sides. Every transaction has a pareto optimal curve – a line of all possible outcomes that cannot be improved upon without making at least one side worse off. But no law of nature dictates that the best result can always be achieved by creating value. One or both parties might be better off by claiming value rather than by creating it. It certainly is true that in many scenarios, we are better off creating value than claiming it. That is the case when we receive a smaller share of a larger pie. But, again, increasing the pie does not necessarily give us better results than seeking to grab the biggest slice. Win–win tactics *can* beat win–lose tactics – but the reverse is also true. The negotiation can be visualized as Yin & Yang: see Figure 5. Not only are the two opposites linked together: Each also needs the other, and each carries a kernel of the other side within. I therefore use the ampersand rather than the conjunction "and," when the two sides appear as a unit, partly deriving their meaning from the polarity. The same rule applies to the terms "Cooperation & Competition" and "Deliberation & Intuition" when we are referring to them as single concepts, which we will explain in the two subsequent chapters.

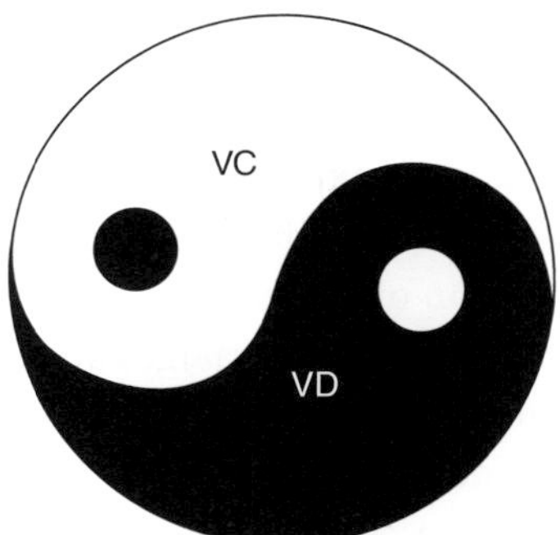

Figure 5 The Yin & Yang of negotiation

Both sides of the contract require both types of negotiation. Planned clauses such as the specifications of the transaction create value. But they also have a cost, such as the contract price, that must be distributed. And unplanned clauses such as warranties and liabilities allot risks. But they also permit the bartering of trade-offs. The two sides are inseparable. And there is an even more profound reason. The tactics of value creation and value distribution, as incompatible as they are, share one common tactic: We must not overdo them. Each tactic becomes too much of a good thing if it does not incorporate a measure of its opposite. And each carries a bit of the other side. Creating value, as I will show, usually requires the claiming of value (just from somebody that is not at the table). And claiming value does often require the unintended surrender of a piece of the pie to the other side.

Behavioral economics and psychology tell us that (at least in the West) our minds hate contradictions. We learned to think in the tradition of Aristotelian logic and have difficulty accepting that opposites may be simultaneously true. Our minds prefer coherence, and there are numerous faulty intuitions (so-called "cognitive biases") that tempt us to see negotiation as more coherent than it really is. Perhaps you know Wittgenstein's animal (shown in Figure 4.1): An optical illusion that lets you see either a duck or a rabbit, but never both at the same time. I argue that this is what happens to us when we observe a negotiation.[15]

In Chapter 1 I will describe the paradox of the negotiation task, and the six key tactics of cooperation and also of competition. Unfortunately, we know from research that most people are not very good at using either set of tactics. There are a number of traps into which negotiators predictably fall. When put to the test, people tend to settle for too little. They walk away from the table when an agreement would have been perfectly possible. They sell themselves short and agree to something that is worse than their alternative. They fail to identify compatible interests. They do not reach mutually beneficial outcomes. And they typically leave money on the table. Most people do not think with sufficient clarity about their own interests and alternatives, or about the other side's alternatives and interests. They fail to grasp what they themselves really want and what they could get out of the other side. But not only do they walk away from the table with much smaller slices than they could, they also habitually fail to realize that a negotiation does not have to be limited to such pie-slicing. Negotiations often do not just involve the distribution of resources and risks; they can often give the parties more than they had originally aimed for. To use a metaphor that is popular with both scholars and practitioners: Not all pies are "fixed"; instead, negotiators can often "expand" them. Yet they frequently fail to realize that in practice. "In short, people's negotiating behavior and decisions are very often suboptimal. And too often this means that value is not created and captured – even by experienced negotiators."[16]

Many negotiators are either too competitive or too cooperative for their own good, often because they see the task as more coherent than it really is. Crucially, these tactics are not wrong. They can just become excessive – even for the most seasoned of negotiators. To illustrate this point, I will turn to the example of two prominent politicians, US President Donald Trump and German Chancellor Angela Merkel. Their politics are almost diametrically opposed, and you might have strong feelings about them. (I certainly do. But this is not our topic.) Intriguingly, they are also diametrically opposed, if we are to believe their words, in their self-professed negotiation styles. To me, they personify competitive versus cooperative tactics. And, in contrast to their politics, I argue that they are both right. And wrong. That is the paradox of negotiation.

Two empirical findings are especially important here. We have a visceral reaction to the success or failure of other human beings. Crucially, this reaction is a result of our perception. When we imagine we are cooperating with the other side, their display of pleasure or distress evokes the same emotion in us. When we imagine we are competing with them, the pattern is reversed: Their smile causes us distress, and their grimace gives us pleasure – "Pleasing frowns, disappointing smiles" is how the researchers put it. Which side of the Yin & Yang we see determines our interaction with the other side. Disturbing? Yes. And it becomes more so when you consider the second research finding: Changing our mind is physically unpleasant: "It is fundamentally unnatural and uncomfortable to change our minds, and this is reflected in the way our brains work."[17]

When I realized this pattern, I could finally make sense of what I observed in practice. I was now on a level playing field with my most admired negotiation partners and adversaries – and realized that they were the same people. And I began to realize our common dilemma.

Facing the Dilemma

In Chapter 2 I will describe "negotiator's dilemma." Negotiators are caught between the demands of value creation and value distribution. But nobody can make the choice by themselves. The outcome is jointly determined by both sides. Whether or not our tactics are successful depends on the tactics of the other side, and vice versa. This is the negotiator's dilemma.

Consider different approaches to information-sharing: Do you want to be upfront and honest, exposing yourself but allowing for sincere dialogue? This would be the cooperative choice. Or do you prefer the competitive choice, playing your cards close to your chest? Will you use the information you obtain from the other party for mutual benefit, or perhaps take advantage of what you have learned? Your answer probably is "Both!" That's exactly my point. You, and they, can only do one thing at a time. The negotiator's dilemma is thus similar to a famous game theoretical model, the "prisoner's dilemma." Game theory is a branch of applied mathematics that analyzes the decision-making of interdependent actors ("players"). Originally employed to analyze parlor games (hence the name coined by Hungarian-American mathematician John von Neumann in his groundbreaking 1928 article, "Zur Theorie der Gesellschaftsspiele" ["On the Theory of Games of Strategy"]), it is widely used for all kinds of social interactions, such as negotiations. It aims to identify optimal solutions in situations where we have to consider the other player's possible decisions. The most famous game is the "prisoner's dilemma," describing the challenge faced by two fictional prisoners. We will get to the details later. What is important here is that the prisoners, just like negotiators, have to decide between cooperating and competing. The outcome depends on the choices of both sides – and puts them into this prototypical dilemma; see Table 1. In 1944 at Princeton University, von Neumann wrote the foundational text of game theory together with another émigré, economist Oskar Morgenstern: *Theory of Games and Economic Behavior.*[18]

Table 1 The negotiator's dilemma

	They cooperate	They compete
We cooperate	Win / Win	We lose / They win
We compete	We win / They lose	Lose / Lose

Each negotiator has an incentive to act competitively, no matter what the other side does. But collectively this will lead to a suboptimal outcome. As Nobel laureate John Forbes Nash Jr. realized, the "lose–lose" result constitutes an equilibrium – neither side can break from it unilaterally. In a negotiation we need the other side in order for us to win. This is why we can still learn from game theoretical insights gained decades ago. How to manage such a dilemma has most famously been studied in the context of the Cold War: The West and the East were caught up in such a dilemma, and the stakes could not have been higher. Then, as now, we can draw valuable lessons from studying it. And it is the classic "tit-for-tat" theorem that will help us develop a simple but effective negotiation strategy: "To negotiate with an iron fist inside a velvet glove" as Keith Murnighan recommends.[19]

Sometimes it is possible to transcend the dilemma. In long-term relationships, we might be able to change the nature of the game. The "stag hunt" scenario first described by Jean-Jacques Rousseau offers a beautiful alternative. Here, cooperating hunters can jointly track down the stag. But those who choose to hunt individually will only catch a hare. In this setting, the win–win outcome is the Nash equilibrium. (From prisoners to stags and velvet gloves, I want to invite you to a journey into game theory that will equip us with some very useful metaphors. We will also take the time to look at the significance of metaphors, because they can be very powerful. For instance, people cooperate more when they are invited to negotiate under a banner of community, rather than individual interest.)[20]

Facing the Ambiguity

This is where the third and deepest challenge awaits. We explore it in Chapter 3: The ambiguity of our thinking about negotiations. To negotiate well, we have to be both intuitive and deliberate. Unfortunately, the two are frequently at odds. Consider this example: "On the way back from the negotiation, the father was driving with his little son in the backseat of the car. They had a horrible accident. The father died on the spot. The son was badly injured and rushed to the hospital. The surgeon on duty hurried to the emergency room, approached the operating table, and turned pale. "I am unable to operate. This is my son!"[21]

If you were puzzled by the appearance of the surgeon, you were misled by your intuition. Congratulations if you were not! (And yes, it is irrelevant that they came from a negotiation. I had to put that in so as not to interrupt your line of thought.) Deliberation might have had to remind you of female surgeons. Intuition & Deliberation represent two different "systems of thinking," a term coined by psychologist Keith Stanovich, and widely popularized by Nobel laureate Daniel Kahneman in his international bestseller *Thinking Fast and Slow*: We can distinguish effortless (and mostly fast) intuition from effortful (and mostly slow) deliberation. Human beings often have to overcome faulty intuitions in order to make rational decisions.[22]

And yet. It is often imperative to rely on gut feelings. A baseball player could theoretically catch the ball by computing its trajectory, if he knew the velocity, projection angle, air resistance, etc. But he relies on an intelligent heuristic instead: "Fix your gaze on the ball, start running, and adjust your speed so that the angle remains constant." A heuristic is a simple procedure to find an adequate answer to a difficult question. (The word has the same Greek semantic root as "Eureka.") This is true in negotiations too, where we will never (legally) have all the information. Like baseball players, we need to hone our intuition.[23]

We have thus stepped into the "Great Rationality Debate," in which scholars argue whether or not humans are fundamentally rational. Thankfully, we do not have to decide. For us it is enough to know that in negotiations, we need both. To visualize the mind, Eric Kandel likens it to an iceberg, with only one-seventh of its bulk floating above water: see Figure 6. Let's use his metaphor.[24]

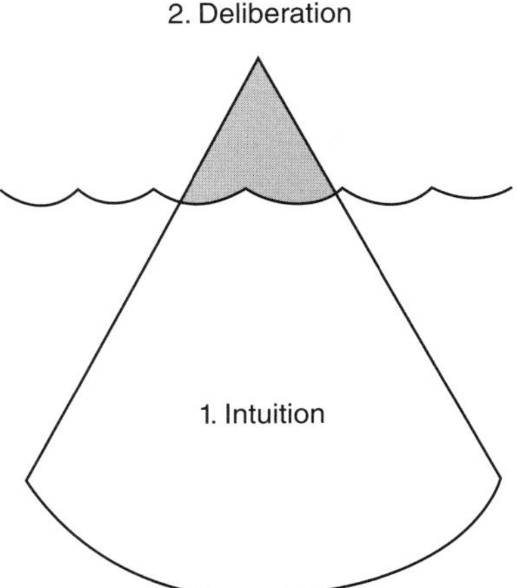

Figure 6 The two systems of thinking as an iceberg

To engage both systems of thinking is the greatest challenge for the negotiator. It is you, not the other side, who is your most worthy opponent, as William L. Ury has stressed.[25]

As we have seen, negotiation is two-sided to its core. It is characterized by opposite truths at all levels: the task, the relationship, and the self. The triple challenge of negotiation success, and how to master it, is described in the first three chapters (Part I) of the book; see Figure 7.

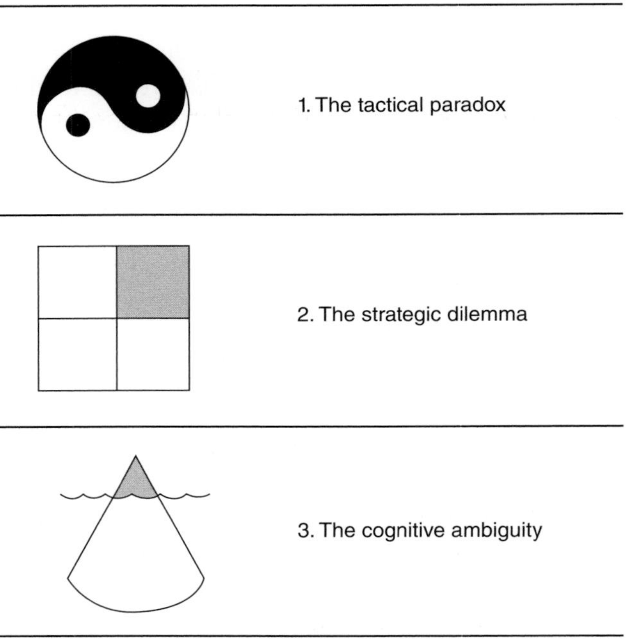

Figure 7 The triple challenge to negotiation success

Building on Part I will allow us to identify the three traps of negotiation learning in Part II (and learn how to overcome them in Part III) shown in Figure 7. It was yet again my personal experience that drove me to this topic, this time as a teacher. I had started teaching negotiations on the side, gradually shifting my professional focus. When I came back to Europe after two years in Israel, I decided to leave the corporate world to concentrate on teaching. I thus came to realize the extraordinary difficulty of learning to negotiate.

My experience as teacher made me painfully aware that even knowing the challenges of negotiation success does not do the trick. Time and again I heard how hard it is to pursue negotiation success in practice. The challenge is epitomized by the case of Michael, a former workshop participant. He was facing one of the most important negotiations of his professional life and asked for advice. Together with a friend he had founded a high-tech company. The venture was successful and had received seven-figure funding. Further growth followed. When he called they had just been approached by a large competitor. Would they be interested in selling the company? Of course they would. This was the opportunity they had been waiting for! They had worked very hard for all these years. Now was their chance to cash in and move on. Michael told me that he had learned a lot in the workshop. Now he just wanted to make sure to get the best possible deal. He would only sell his company once. And he would never see the other side again. Could I give him some advice? Sure. Where was the negotiation at? He explained:

> Things are moving fast. We already had an initial meeting. It seems they really like our technology as well as our people. They quickly ruled out a joint venture – they are only interested in a complete takeover. Exactly what we want. We were pleasantly surprised by the speed of things. But we were a bit surprised when they asked us there and then how much money we want for the company. We had not really gone through the numbers yet! So, we told them that our first-round investors probably would want to multiply their initial investment. By a factor of two, perhaps three. That's the kind of money that we would be looking for. They glanced at each other and seemed content. "Fine," they said, "we can continue on that basis." Now, Georg, what can I do to get the most out of them?

I was taken aback. Michael is one of the most intelligent people I know. He is a great engineer and a successful entrepreneur. The problems he solves in his daily work are much more complex than the negotiation challenge he was facing (even if most of them are not nearly as important). The tactics in a one-off single-issue negotiation are no mystery: If you want to get the most out of the other side, you have to find out their maximum. You then make the first offer slightly beyond that point. There is usually some controversy about this advice, and in Michael's workshop we had covered it at length. The one thing you certainly do *not* want to do is to open with the bare minimum that would be acceptable. But that is what Michael and his partner had done.

So, why is it so hard to learn to negotiate? I believe that it inescapably poses a greater challenge than the acquisition of other social skills. Learning new skills is always hard, but it is often a linear process. The more effort we put in, the better we become (albeit with diminishing returns). Not so with negotiation. There is the danger that negotiating more only makes me better at what I already know how to do. But outside the familiar, my strength becomes a weakness. Due to the nature of our task, learning cannot be coherent.

I will show that each of the three challenges sets up a specific trap for the learner in Part II: Our understanding of the task might be more coherent than it should be (Chapter 4). We might deem our skill set to be more complete than it really is (Chapter 5). And we might mistakenly believe our thinking to be more accurate than it really is (Chapter 6). These three illusions conspire to block the advance of the learner. "Blocking" is a phenomenon originally discovered in the conditioning of animals (think Pavlov's dogs). I believe it is highly relevant for human learning too. There are three types of learning: classical conditioning, instrumental learning, and cognitive learning. I will outline them before we dive into the three traps, and I will also clarify to what extent our success as negotiators is determined by our personality rather than by our actions.

Our learning is further complicated by the "hindsight problem": When looking back it is difficult to determine whether or not a negotiation has been successful. It could be determined by comparing the outcome with the objective that we had a priori. But coming out of the negotiation, we are not the same as when we went in. As our perception of the negotiation changes, we are also changed. Often, we find out what we want only in the negotiation itself. Negotiation is a "transformative experience": Acquiring the experience changes how we value it. It is quite like deciding whether or not to become a vampire. You have to become one to know what it's like. But when you do, your outlook becomes different from what it was before.[26]

Whether or not you are a vampire, to master the challenges of learning you must be humble. "It is a simple yet profound notion: If we realize we don't know everything, we can learn. If we think we know everything, learning is impossible." And, paradoxically, this is especially hard if you are successful. As former US Secretary of State Henry Kissinger observed when reflecting on the strengths and weaknesses of Napoleon Bonaparte: "A man who has been used to command finds it almost impossible to learn to negotiate, because negotiation is an admission of finite power."[27]

Our journey will lead us to the three steps of negotiation learning in Part III: In Chapter 7 we will see how to enhance our understanding by embracing what the ancients called "aporia," focusing on our goal, and using specific techniques to absorb new knowledge. In Chapter 8 we will see how to expand our know-how by perspective-taking, self-control, and deliberate practice – and by enlisting the help of our past and future selves. Building on all of this, in Chapter 9 we will discover how to accurately think about negotiations: Intellectual "bootstrapping" and dialectical thinking are our tools to acquire true expertise.

The key idea of each chapter is illustrated with one of three geometrical shapes (circle, square, or triangle). A picture says more than a thousand words. The popular notion that you learn better when you are instructed in your preferred learning style, for instance as an auditory learner, is not supported by the evidence. Visuals help us all. You learn better when you "go wide." In addition to pictures, I use all manner of examples. Research tells us that we learn better when we are emotionally involved. It is easier for us to learn something if we are involved with, rather than indifferent toward, the topic. I have chosen vivid, sometimes drastic, examples in the hope that you will find them easy to remember.[28]

When we learn, we look for key ideas and organize them into mental models. We now know that learning involves pattern detection, and that the brain changes when this is accomplished.[29]

Decades ago, scientists promoted "errorless learning." They mistakenly believed that when we are allowed to commit errors in learning, we will only remember these errors. As a result, they served up knowledge in small bits and tried to rule out any possibility of error. Today we know that this laudable attempt was wrong. While it might be tempting to believe that learning is better when it is easier, the opposite is true: Research shows that learning sticks better when the mind has to work hard for it. Learners who do not avoid negative information and who direct their attention to difficult aspects of their task do better.[30]

This brings us to the final conundrum: Learning to negotiate can be easy *because* it is so hard. Let's hear it for Niels Bohr: "How wonderful that we have met with a paradox. Now we have some hope of making progress."[31]

PART I
Ambivalence: The Triple Challenge of Negotiation

As negotiators we are challenged on the task, relationship, and personal level – often leaving us ambivalent about the process.

The triple challenge of negotiation is the tactical paradox, the strategic dilemma, and the cognitive ambiguity. One challenge leads to the next. As a result, most people are ambivalent when it comes to negotiations. They might like some aspects but often strongly dislike others. This is perhaps not surprising, given that the Latin root of the word "negotiation" literally means "not fun." And there is a very good reason for this. By its very nature, negotiation is two-sided. There is a duality at every level of the process: The task itself requires us to both create *and* claim value. Figuratively speaking we have to expand the pie and divide it. This means that we face a tactical paradox: We must work with the other side as well as against them – and so do they. Hence our success depends on their choice of tactics just as much as ours.

This pushes both parties into a dilemma: We can only determine the right strategy in light of what the other side does. Put another way, we cannot unilaterally determine whether we will win or lose, and neither can they. Individually, we are often torn between greed and fear. The collective result is all too often lose–lose rather than win–win.

How we handle all of this is a very personal matter, and we have to be both intuitive and deliberate about it. The tactical paradox and the strategic dilemma mean that it is not a priori clear which mode of thinking is the proper one. Thinking about negotiations, therefore, creates cognitive ambiguity.

So, we are faced with demands on every level. Sometimes, these demands are compatible with one another. Often, they are not. Sometimes it is clear which to give preference, but often it is not. And sometimes we intuitively think properly about it all, but often . . . You get my drift. One challenge leads to the next, with each more challenging than its predecessor. We will explore one after the other.

You may want to read Part I even, perhaps especially, if you are an experienced negotiator. The more we know about something, the easier it is to absorb new information and to enhance our understanding. But, as we will soon see, the easier it can also become to box ourselves in. I hope to engage you with a coherent story that develops from one chapter to the next.

1 The Tactical Paradox

The task of negotiation often requires us to use mutually exclusive tactics of creating and claiming value.

Negotiation is the process by which two (or more) parties decide how to allocate resources and risks, resolve conflict, or work together. The decision has two dimensions: How good is the outcome for one side, and how good is it for the other. The result of a negotiation can be plotted in the two-by-two matrix that we saw in the Introduction; see Figure 3. (When there are more than two parties negotiating, additional dimensions have to be added; this rapidly reduces the practicability of the matrix but does not change the substance of the paradox. We shall therefore stick to our two-dimensional mental model.) We "create" value when we realize mutually beneficial outcomes. We "claim" (or "distribute") value when we capture benefit at the expense of the other side. Achieving the best possible deal *must* come at the expense of the other side when we distribute value. This does not have to be the case when we create value.

In this chapter I will describe both aspects and explain the tactics required for each. I will do so in two steps. In the simplest of transactions, there is only one issue on the table. For instance, the buyer and seller at a garage sale just have to determine the price of an item. Unless they throw other issues into the mix, they have no choice but to distribute value: On the table between them sits a pie. They negotiate how to divide it. This can change if the parties identify other issues that they may talk about, such as payment terms, packaging, or delivery. Now the door opens for them to create value: Perhaps they can find ways to enlarge the pie. Having multiple issues on the table is a requirement for the creation of value.

This does not make value-claiming redundant, however. We engage in negotiations in order to obtain the best possible result. Therefore, we cannot stop at expanding the pie. We also have to slice it. We will see that the tactics of value distribution and value creation can be complementary. But often, they are not. They may even be opposites. What allows us to enlarge the joint pie often gets in the way of claiming a larger slice. And the other way around. Yet usually we have to do both. Hence there is a paradox at the heart of the negotiation task: To claim value, we have to use competitive tactics, whereas to create value, we have to use cooperative tactics.

1.1 One Issue: Claiming Value

When the parties decide how to allocate just one resource or risk, they have to do so at each other's expense. Claiming value distribution is similar in transactions large and small. Consider this illustration:

> Shop borders on shop in this seemingly endless labyrinth of alleys. I have now arrived in the carpet seller's alley. Dozens of merchants are standing in front of their small shops and eye the approaching customers. Buyers do not have to go far for price comparisons. After a few steps there is another shop with more merchandise. But there is a catch: Prices are not marked. "This is our mentality. It is a thousand years old. And everybody knows: You have got to haggle!" Celâl smiles. His passion is the carpet business. Dressed in a smart gray suit, he is sitting in front of his shop, drinking tea. Bargaining, of course, is part and parcel of the carpet trade.. . . The centuries-old tradition and its rituals are still very much in evidence at the bazar. Buyers and seller address each other as "brother" or "uncle," even if they are complete strangers. This creates an atmosphere of closeness, almost as if one was doing business in the family. And who would dare to take advantage of a family member? In a skillful exchange of questions and answers, the merchant tries to assess how wealthy, or poor, his counterpart is. He then asks a slightly higher price from rich customers and a slightly lower price from poor ones. Either way: There is a thin line between cleverly negotiating and taking advantage of the other side.[1]

The scene from the Grand Bazar in Istanbul is the perfect stepping stone for us. Call it haggling, bargaining, negotiating, or even arguing – it is the same interdependent decision-making process. We negotiate in many different contexts. Yet the underlying "geometry" and dynamics are often similar. It is true that many negotiations are much more complex. Nevertheless, whenever people decide how to allocate resources or risks, the basic mechanism is the same. We can therefore take from the Grand Bazar our first building block for understanding negotiations. As we go on, we will add layers of complexity. We will follow the principal dichotomy developed by Richard Walton and Robert McKersie in their influential work, *A Behavioral Theory of Labor Relations*. The concept was quickly recognized as relevant beyond labor relations:[2]

> Distributive bargaining is a hypothetical construct referring to the complex system of activities instrumental to the attainment of one party's goals when they are in basic conflict with those of the other party. It is the type of activity most familiar to students of negotiations; in fact, it is "bargaining" in the strictest sense of the word. In social negotiations, the goal conflict can relate to several values; it can involve allocation of any resources, for example, economic, power, or status symbols. What game theorists refer to as fixed-sum games are the situations we have in mind: one person's gain is a loss to the other.[3]

This situation can best be visualized by thinking of a pie that the parties have to share.

1.1.1 The Pie

1.1.1.1 Your Alternative

Imagine you are a buyer at the Grand Bazar (or your local flea market, if you prefer). When you fancy an item, you have a number in mind: The maximum amount of money that you are willing to part with. If there are no other issues to be negotiated, you will conclude the transaction if the seller agrees to less than that number. If he demands more, you will walk away. Because you reserve the right to do so, this number is often called your "reservation price" (RP). Ideally, your RP is a function of the alternatives you have. If you have more than one alternative, it should quantify the best one. In their seminal work, *Getting to Yes*, Fisher, Ury, and Patton coined the acronym "BATNA" to capture this idea. "BATNA" stands for "Best Alternative To Negotiated Agreement." It represents the best choice you have other than closing the deal at hand. It is a straightforward concept when there is a market for what you are buying or selling. You know how much the same item would cost elsewhere. And you can take the additional time and effort required to buy the item elsewhere into account.[4]

Things become trickier when you have no clear alternative. Suppose as a student you receive several job offers upon graduation. The best one becomes the benchmark for the rest. You are in an enviable situation. Using the concept of BATNA will come naturally, even if choosing between good options can be as hard as choosing between bad ones. But what if you have no offers at all? You depend on a job for living and will have to pay back university tuition fees. When you finally receive an invitation for a job interview, you rejoice – but are worried about your bargaining power. If they make you an offer, how will you know if it is acceptable? When there is, in fact, no attractive alternative at hand, it is crucial to acknowledge this.

I can't accept that! You will have to make me a better offer!
HGB.

Figure 1.1 No good alternative

When you acknowledge the lack of a good BATNA, you understand the need to create options. For instance, a company fully dependent on a sole supplier might greatly improve its bargaining power by cultivating a second source. Even mentioning their intent of doing so might prevent the supplier from making over-the-top demands. Such tactical moves can change the game.[5]

We will shortly see that you should even be the one to make the first offer. You have to do this with confidence and ambition, and generally not reveal your lack of alternatives. But in your own mind, you know that you have no good fallback option. You have to weigh the offer against the uncertain prospect of receiving another offer by another company in the future. Negotiation scholars are right when they assert that you always have a BATNA. You might not like it, but there is almost always an alternative. Yet it can be so bad that it is not even realistic.[6]

While this concept might be more or less helpful in a given situation, it is imperative to establish it. It is one of two endpoints between which you can bargain. We must know what happens if we do not reach agreement. But our BATNA is not set in stone. Perhaps you receive another job offer just in time. Perhaps you receive two. Our alternatives are often fluid. Note that they are your source of power. What you have to accept on the table is determined by factors away from it. A potent tactic is to improve your BATNA even as you negotiate. Applying for more than one position is sound advice for job-seeking graduates. They might only be invited to one interview. But at the same time they might be the only qualified applicant that had bothered to apply. Perhaps the recruiter is more desperate than the candidate. This brings us to the other side of the spectrum.

1.1.1.2 Your Target

Your BATNA tells you the worst thing that can come out of the negotiation. But what about the best thing? What should be your target? It might sound trite but it's true: The best you can get out of a distributive negotiation is the least the other side is willing to accept, which is just a bit better than their BATNA. At least, it is if they are rational: A rational negotiator would rather accept this outcome than walk away. So, if you want to maximize your outcome, you should target the RP of the other side. Like your own RP, it is determined by the best alternative of the other side.

This sounds simpler than it is in practice. If you work in a company, you might be incentivized differently. Organizations often fall back on *their* alternative when determining the target. A common approach to selling goods and service is called "cost plus." The seller determines its costs and adds the desired profit to arrive at a price. This means putting the cart before the horse. Cost and profit might be an indicator of the other side's alternatives. But the RP is determined by the buyer, not the seller. Whether or not the buyer can buy these goods from another seller, or actually make them, is a question of their alternatives. It is not a function of the seller's costs! Yet it is natural to focus on your end of the deal – and not only in cases where you are the seller. But we must be careful not to limit ourselves to it.

Looking back to our example in the Introduction, this was Michael's mistake too. Perhaps I should emphasize that it is of course Michael and his co-owners' prerogative to sell their company at any price of their choosing. And their approach might indeed result in a price that they are well and truly satisfied with. But Michael called because he wanted to get "the best possible" price out of the negotiation. And starting to bargain with his walk-away point made this all but impossible. It's true, as he related to the buyer, that his first-round investors were interested in generating a certain return when selling the company. It is no secret that venture capitalists make their money by selling the portfolio company, preferably for a multiple of their initial investment. What Michael told the buyers was therefore neither false nor a surprise. But it set the negotiation off on the wrong foot. It commenced at the wrong end of the spectrum, because the business model of the second investors is very much the same. The interventions of venture capitalists are temporary and linked to the company's future performance. The divestment and subsequent exit of the venture capitalist represent a fundamental step by which they realize their profits. When valuing a company, they seek to determine the amount that can be gained from selling the investment later. Sellers are much better off, as we will explore in more detail below, when they target the RP of the buyer, rather than when they target their own.[7]

Where does all this leave us? We have determined the key concepts of value distribution: Quantifying your BATNA yields your RP; your target should be the other side's RP. And all of this also applies to your counterpart. This brings us to the range within which a rational agreement is possible: The ZOPA. It stands for "zone of possible agreement," and denotes that range of outcomes that is preferable to both sides over no agreement. It is a fancy word for our pie. An agreement outside the ZOPA is irrational for (at least) one of the parties. Hence, the "geometry" of distributive negotiation looks like the diagram in Figure 1.2.[8]

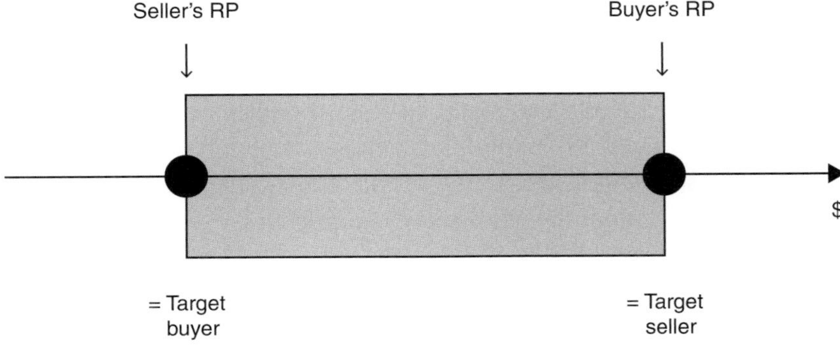

Figure 1.2 The ZOPA ("the pie")

Is there a zone within which agreement is possible? Depending on the situation, the ZOPA might be very large, or very small. There are cases where no ZOPA exists. The size of the zone does not depend on the size of the deal. We find it at the bazar, corporate boardrooms, in a context that is shaped by the intricate computations of finance professionals, and even in the sophisticated world of diplomacy. Let's look at two examples; first, at business M&As and second, at the withdrawal of the United Kingdom from the European Union (commonly called "Brexit"). It is true that both negotiations feature many more issues than just one. But, as in many other transactions, it is possible (if challenging) to aggregate all of these issues into one in order to determine whether or not a deal can be reached. Doing so is, in fact, necessary. The parties must determine whether there is enough room for them to meet: Is there a ZOPA that gives both a better outcome than their alternatives? Specifically: Do buyer and seller of a company have a pie to share? Do the UK and the European Union (EU)? Let's see.

1.1.1.3 The Case of Siemens and Solel

In an M&A transaction, the ownership of a business organization is transferred to other entities. It allows the buyer to expand their activity and the seller to downsize it. But it is often difficult to determine how much a company is worth. There are many definitions of value. One of the factors that determine which standard of value applies in a given situation is the appraisal. Hence, every private company has a number of values simultaneously. In tax and legal matters, for instance, the "fair market value" of a firm is often determined systematically and in accordance with specific rules (such as Revenue Ruling 59–60 in the United States). "Collateral value" measures the amount a creditor would be willing to lend if the company's assets served as security for the loan. In negotiating the acquisition, the "investment value" is key: It describes the value of a business interest to a particular investor. It is different from the theoretical market value, in that it looks at the specific investor and their expected risks and returns.[9]

One would perhaps assume that the price of the target is determined strictly by analyzing the costs and benefit of the transaction. But that is not necessarily the case. Using a sample of acquisitions during 1990–2006, Feng Gu and Baruch Lev have comprehensively investigated the circumstances under which ill-advised acquisitions are being made. A key explanation lies in the share price of the buyer itself: If these shares are valued too highly, the company is tempted to use inflated shares for acquisitions, sometimes overpaying for the target. The researchers document a strong positive association between share overpricing on the one hand and subsequent acquisition intensity as well as goodwill write-offs on the other. In other words, buyers paid more than could be justified by the return they generated from the investment because they had the means to do so, rather than by determining whether these means could be used sensibly![10]

In order to analyze the costs and benefits of the potential acquisition, the buyer musts conduct "due diligence." In doing so, it is common to estimate the future cash flows of the target company and determine their present value (i.e. the amount that would yield the same return if it was invested today at the acquirer's interest rate). By subtracting the cost of the investment, we arrive at the "net present value" of the target. These models quickly become very complex because of a multitude of input factors and assumptions. It is easy to see that the results vary dramatically with the information that is used (such as timeline, discount rate, market development, synergies, etc.). M&A experts such as Robert Bruner caution against the belief that once you have the estimate of values, negotiation outcome will simply follow. Some practitioners even argue that net present value calculations are of mostly academic value and report that they are ironically disregarded in practice: "Bankers take a much more practical and multifaceted approach.... Fair market value is the range in which informed and willing buyers and sellers would buy/sell the business."[11]

If buyers and sellers are rational, that range is nothing else but the ZOPA. (That, admittedly, is a big "if," as we will see.) A strategic investor might be willing to pay a higher price because of synergies and strategic fit than a financial investor. "Since the financial buyer brings no synergies to the deal, the deal itself must supply the earnings and the collateral that enable the transaction to be financed. This effectively creates a boundary around the evaluation, in that there is definable limit of how much a financial buyer can pay for a business." That limit, of course, is the buyer's RP. And strategic buyers have one too, even though it may be higher.[12]

How the ZOPA is perceived determines target-setting. Here is an example. During my time at Siemens AG, I was part of the team that conducted the legal due diligence on an acquisition target, Solel Solar Systems Ltd. of Israel. Siemens eventually made the acquisition in the hope of becoming a world leader in the green energy field.

> In October 2009, Siemens took the Israeli market by surprise, when it offered to acquire Solel Solar Systems for $418 million, after a bidding process that lasted several weeks. Siemens's bid was substantially higher than bids by its French rivals, Alstom SA and Areva SA, and Israel's Shikun & Binui Holdings Ltd., which offered $275 million.... Siemens agreed to pay the huge amount on the basis of its assessment of strong growth in the thermosolar industry, and because Solel Solar was one of the only two companies in the world with the know-how to produce thermosolar energy panels, alongside Germany's Schott AG.[13]

Apparently, Schott AG was not for sale. We do not know the ZOPA of the transaction from the news report. While we do not know the RPs of the parties, we have an idea of their alternatives, and we can make an educated guess about how they set their targets. The expected "strong growth of the thermosolar industry" puts a number on the expected future profits of the buyer. By contrast, the highest bid of the rivals quantifies the best alternative of the seller. Which of the two should a buyer target? This question is hypothetical, of course. To be clear: I do not know what the ZOPA in that acquisition was. I simply was not privy to that level of information. It is perfectly possible that the buyer did, in fact, target the RP of the seller, and paid just a little bit more than the next highest rival, contrary to what the publicly available data might suggest. We cannot, and thankfully don't have to, decide this. But this example illustrates the point we are concerned with here. It is crucial to determine the ZOPA and target the other side's RP. Either way, with hindsight we have 20/20 vision. In the case of Solel, it later turned out that thermosolar technology could not justify the hopes that were set in it. Three years after the purchase, and having reportedly lost an estimated €1 billion on the investment, Siemens exited the solar business again. So did Schott AG shortly thereafter.[14]

1.1.1.4 The Case of Brexit

Whether we like it or not, there are also cases where no positive ZOPA exists. This is straightforward in a bazar setting, when the minimum price requested is above the maximum that the customer is willing to pay. But this limitation also applies in the largest of negotiations. Even when the parties negotiate about dozens or hundreds of items, they reserve the right to walk away if the agreement does not fulfill their minimum requirements.

Consider the case of Brexit, the term used to refer to the withdrawal of the United Kingdom from the EU. The decision to withdraw was made by 52 percent of the participating UK electorate in a referendum on June 23, 2016. The UK Government invoked Article 50 of the Treaty on European Union, thus making the UK due to leave the EU on March 29, 2019. This resulted in complex and controversial negotiations about the modalities of leaving and the nature of the future relationship. Unlike many business transactions, the Brexit negotiations were widely reported on by the international media. Hence they can illustrate a number of important points. The negotiations were special in that they were not about allocating resources. Rather, starting from the UK's full membership in the EU, the parties were resigned to allocating a *reduction* of their joint pie.

In negotiating the "draft agreement on the withdrawal of the United Kingdom from the European Union" (commonly called the Brexit withdrawal agreement), the parties had to benchmark their options against their best alternatives to determine whether a positive bargaining zone did exist. The primary interest of the UK was to regain political sovereignty from the EU; it also had an interest in maintaining access to the common market at the lowest cost possible. The EU's primary interest was to prevent a Brexit that weakened the union politically or economically. The challenge was finding a way forward acceptable to both the EU (which requires the assent of a qualified majority of 72 percent of Member States, representing at least

65 percent of the population of the EU) and a majority of UK Members of Parliament, of the ruling Conservative Party, and of the general population. Right from the start, observers doubted that a deal would be possible unless UK negotiators were able to go back to their constituents and sell a deal that fell well short of the promises made in the referendum. The tentative deal that Theresa May as Prime Minister negotiated with the EU was defeated three times in the UK Parliament before the Brexit date was postponed to October 2019. Shortly thereafter, Boris Johnson took over as Prime Minister. Throughout the negotiations under May, diplomats such as Sir Ivan Rogers, the UK's former representative to the EU, warned that the alternatives to leaving with a transitory agreement were being misjudged. The best the UK could do was to sign May's deal, he argued. Or perhaps the opposite was true? Maybe the deal on the table was worse for the UK than its alternative? It is not for nothing that scholars caution us against the "agreement trap": We fall into it when we agree to a deal that is inferior to our best alternative.[15]

In any negotiation, the parties have to "agree to disagree" if they find that there is no pie to be divided (and unless they find a way to create value instead). If, on the other hand, a ZOPA does exist, the parties have to decide how to slice the pie. As everybody tends to want as large a piece as they can get, this is no trivial matter.

1.1.2 Slicing the Pie

Slicing the pie is an exercise in "win–lose." If both sides settle within the ZOPA, they "win" something. The outcome is better than their alternative. That does not make it a "win–win" though. In a win–win, what one side gets does not have to come (completely) from the pocket of the other side. But in distributing value, what I "win", you must "lose." And vice versa. The parties have no choice but to slice the pie whenever they distribute one resource or one risk.

Most of your transactions are probably more complex than that. A negotiation that covers multiple issues consists of a series of ZOPAs. Having a series of ZOPAs can open the door to the creation of value. But first, and primarily, it means that even very complex transactions consist of a series of pies to be distributed. Every provision that distributes resources, risks, or costs essentially offers its own ZOPA. In our M&A example of Siemens and Solel, all contractual issues boil down to a single item: Price. At the same time, the contractual issues themselves might have their own ZOPAs. For instance, the acquired company might require missing or incomplete contracts (such as confidentiality or invention assignment agreements with key ex-employees) to be remedied. Conversely, the vendor might or might not be able and willing to provide them. Likewise, in the Brexit negotiations, individual issues, such as the question of a physical border on the island of Ireland, have the characteristics of a ZOPA. There are walk-away points and aspired-to targets. The latter might come at the expense of what the other side wants, such as the uniformity of rules governing the UK and Northern Ireland versus the uniformity of rules governing the EU, including the Republic of Ireland.

Since we slice these pies either way, we might as well do it deliberately. This means that we have to quantify them (at least in a business transaction). I will show you the straightforward method to do it, which will bring us to the basic contradiction that sits at the heart of the distribution of value. We will then explore the real-life significance of pie-slicing by looking at the self-professed value-claiming approach of US President Donald Trump.

1.1.2.1 Quantify Risk

It is often necessary to determine the risk that you are shouldering. In business transactions, it is usually possible to monetarily quantify risks. Take the example of a warranty case. The seller might have historical data about the occurrence of defects. The probability that a product will fail during the warranty period is known. And the promised remedy carries a specific cost that can also be quantified, depending on what exactly the contract stipulates. Replacing the defective part might be more or less costly than repairing it. Doing this once will be cheaper than offering an evergreen warranty. Not offering a warranty on the replacement part will be even cheaper. And so forth. Here we have to transform the words of the contract into a monetary amount. Coming up with the correct numbers may not be easy, but the method is simple:

$$\text{Probability of Risk Materializing} \times \text{Resulting Cost} = \text{Monetary Impact of Risk}$$

Either the seller or the buyer has to absorb that risk (if it is not negligible): It will impact either the price that the buyer pays or the contingencies that the seller forms. This assessment should be done for all important risks that accompany the transaction. Every "unplanned" clause in the contract can be quantified like this. The seller has to do this so that he can come up with a valid price in the first place.[16]

For the buyer, it is usually more difficult to assess a risk that originates from the desired product or service. "Rare is the buyer who knows as much about a procedure or a service as the companies that design, produce and market that product or service for a living." This is called the "procurement problem." To overcome it, the procurer has to cleverly infer the supplier's costs. This can be done by offering different projects to choose from, and drawing conclusions from the supplier's choice. It is a more straightforward task when the buyer's costs are comprised of the seller's prices, especially when they are guaranteed by way of contract.[17]

1.1.2.2 Unilateral Benefit

Western reasoning tends to be based on Aristotelian logic, with a tendency to break up problems into separate elements, prioritize, and look for logical rules to explain causality. Abstract linear thinking is so pervasive that people often don't notice its use. For Aristotle, all of philosophy rests on principles. The "principle of non-contradiction" is the most essential. He argues that without it we could not know anything that we know. He offers various definitions of this principle in his work. Most relevant to us is his statement: It is impossible to hold the same thing to be true *and* not to be true.[18]

Aristotle differentiates between "contradictions" and "contraries." We will come back to the latter when we explore value creation. For value distributing, contradictions are vital. Contradictions cannot both be true at the same time, and they have no intermediates. A number has to be either odd or even. It cannot be both. This is, of course, the very principle of distribution. The parties cannot both gain (the biggest slice of) the pie.[19]

The need to distribute value is apparent in the negotiation of prices and risks – but it is not limited to this. Whether in a contract between companies or in a trade deal between nations, all clauses – no matter how much value they can create – constitute a value that must be distributed. This is why Fred Hochberg, former chairman of the Export-Import Bank of the United States, explains international trade under the title, *Trade Is Not a Four-Letter Word*. In many instances, transactions can be boiled down to one value: How much money is left after subtracting the cost of what you give from the benefit of what you receive. To make a profit in business transactions, that number must be positive. Either way, the objectives of the two sides with regard to this number are inverse. The contradiction is between what is good for us and what is good for the other side.[20]

This is not to say that the slices of the pie mean the same to both sides. You might know the story of the banker and the beggar – a variation of a theme from the musical, *Fiddler on the Roof*: On Friday, when he walks by the beggar, the banker gives him a dollar bill.

Beggar: One dollar? Last week you gave me two dollars!
Banker: I had a bad week.
Beggar: So, if you had a bad week, why should I suffer?

Nor is how the resource is divided necessarily equal to how satisfied the parties are. Each has his own utility curve of possible outcomes. The curves do not have to mirror one another. An additional piece of the resource might not have the same utility for both. A rich man might receive a huge slice of the pie, but his satisfaction might be a fraction of his poor counterpart's. The additional gain is of little utility to him. He can afford to risk it. The poor man might be loath to lose whatever little gain might exist for him, and accept a tiny slice.

Not everybody agrees with my assertion that the distribution of value is important but ultimately only one side of the coin. Some define negotiations as zero-sum games entirely. Consider US President Donald Trump. And let me clarify first that

I am not picking his example because I agree, or disagree with his politics; the same is true for Germany's Chancellor Angela Merkel, who will serve us as a second example in a little while. Rather, I am picking these two politicians because their self-described approaches epitomize the two sides of the Yin & Yang. I believe that many readers will, one way or the other, have strong opinions about their politics. I certainly do. But that is of no relevance for our joint purpose. The two, in their own words, offer splendid and memorable examples of prototypical negotiators. Let's not leave these great examples unexploited! Don't let your political views get in the way of your learning.

Donald Trump's negotiation style had caught the attention of negotiation scholars years before he ran for public office. His distributive tactics apparently served him well when he built Trump Inc. on real estate transactions. Once elected as President, one of his first acts in office was to withdraw from the Trans-Pacific Partnership, a trade pact originally conceived by the United States to counter China's growing economic might in Asia. Yale law Dean Harold Koh concludes from Donald Trump's first State of the Union and UN speeches that he views America's interactions with the world as "grimly zero-sum," thereby inevitably promoting reciprocal self-centeredness.[21]

The potential benefit of this approach is clear: By rejecting multilateral agreements, President Trump can pursue one-on-one deals where the US can leverage its overwhelming market power to claim value. Equally clear is the risk. Perhaps nobody comes to the table:[22]

> The president has clearly indicated his desire to break from the past by negotiating trade deals one-on-one, as opposed to sitting down with a bloc of countries. Trump argues that the U.S. has greater leverage bargaining with individual countries, reasoning that America's large market means it has more to offer and that virtually every country is running a trade surplus with the U.S. But . . . since Trump formally withdrew from the Trans-Pacific Partnership, fulfilling a campaign promise on his first day in office, not one of the other 11 Trans-Pacific countries has come forward to express a desire for an individual deal with the U.S. Instead, Japan, Australia and the others are trying to push through the Pacific Rim free-trade agreement without the U.S.[23]

Consequently, critics argue that Trump's "America First" slogan has begun to translate into something more akin to "America alone." If we are to believe his words, Trump's approach to negotiation is quintessentially distributive. This is how he characterized bilateral negotiations at a joint press conference with Angela Merkel: "I believe, you know, when I look at the numbers in Germany and some other countries – people may not like Donald Trump. But you have to understand: That means I am doing a good job, because I am representing the United States." Turning to Mrs. Merkel he added: "Angela is representing Germany. She is doing a fantastic job. My predecessors did not do a very good job. But we will try and catch you." In a nutshell: Only one side can win. Merkel of course holds the exact opposite view. Intriguingly, she expressed this at another White House press conference, as we will see when we explore the creation of value. As I said in the Introduction, it seems to me that they are both right.[24]

1.1.3 The Six Tactics of Value-Claiming

What must we do to succeed at value-claiming? First, as we have just done, we must acknowledge its nature. In the words of Morton Deutsch, another giant of dispute resolution research: It is not about sinking or swimming together. Instead, if the other sinks, you swim, and if the other swims, you sink. Your tactics must influence the other side to give in. These tactics are often called "competitive" because they are antagonistic. Negotiators all over the world use these tactics, albeit with different frequency. Let's look at a beautiful literary illustration of how competitive value-claiming tactics can play out in this excerpt from Thomas Mann's *Confessions of Felix Krull, Confidence Man.*[25]

> And one by one, I took out of my pockets the tortoiseshell comb, the breastpin with the sapphire, the brooch in the form of a little fruit basket, the bracelet with the white pearl, the ruby ring, and, as climax, the string of diamonds, and laid them all, well separated, on the crocheted table cover. Finally, requesting permission, I unbuttoned my vest, took the topaz jewellery from around my neck and added it to the display on the table.
>
> "What do you think of that?" I asked with quiet pride. I saw he could not quite conceal a glitter in his eye and a smacking of his lips. But he gave the appearance of waiting for more and finally inquired in a dry voice: "Well? Is that all?"
>
> "All?" I repeated. "Master, you mustn't pretend a collection like this comes your way every day."
>
> "You'd be happy to get rid of your collection, wouldn't you?"
>
> "Don't overestimate my eagerness," I replied. "If you are asking whether I would like to dispose of it at a reasonable price, I can say yes."
>
> "Quite so," he returned. "Reasonableness is just what you need, my fine fellow."
>
> Thereupon he drew up one of the plush-covered armchairs that stood around the table and sat down to examine the objects. Without invitation I took a chair, crossed my legs, and watched him. I clearly saw his hands shaking as he took up one piece after another, appraised it, and then abruptly tossed it back onto the table. That was probably to cover up the quiver of greed, as was the repeated shrugging of his shoulders, especially when—this happened twice—he held the string of diamonds in his hands and, blowing on the stones, let them slowly slide between his fingers. And so, it sounded all the more ridiculous when he finally said, gesturing at the whole collection: "Five hundred francs."
>
> "What for, may I ask?" "For the whole thing." "You're joking."
>
> "My boy, there's no occasion for either of us to joke. Do you want to leave your loot here for five hundred? Yes or no?"
>
> "No," I said and got up. "Very far from it. With your permission, I'll take my keepsakes, as I see I am being taken advantage of disgracefully."

"Dignity," he said jokingly, "becomes you. And your strength of character is remarkable, too, for your years. As a tribute to it I'll say six hundred."

"That's a step that doesn't get you out of the realm of the ridiculous. I look younger, dear sir, than I am and it won't help at all to treat me as a child. I know the real worth of these things and although I am not simple-minded enough to think I can insist on getting it, I will not permit the payment to differ to an immoral degree. Finally, I know that in this field of business there are competitors and I'll be able to find them."

"You have an oily tongue—along with your other talents. But the idea hasn't occurred to you that the competitors with whom you threaten me are very well organized and may have agreed upon common terms."

"The question is simply this, Master Jean-Pierre, whether *you* want to buy my things, or someone else is to buy them."

"I am inclined to take them and, as we agreed in advance, at a reasonable price." "And what's that?"

"Seven hundred francs – my last word."

Silently I began to stow the jewellery in my pockets, first of all the string of diamonds. With trembling cheeks, he watched me.

"Blockhead," he said, "you don't know your own good luck. Think what a quantity of money that is, seven or eight hundred francs—for me who has to lay it out and for you who will pocket it! What a lot of things you can buy yourself for, let us say, eight hundred and fifty francs—pretty women, clothes, theatre tickets, good dinners. Instead of that, like a fool, you want to go on carrying the stuff around with you in your pockets. How do you know the police aren't waiting for you outside? And don't you take my own risk into account?"

"Have you," I said at a venture, "read about these objects anywhere in the newspapers?"

"Not yet."

"You see? Despite the fact that we are dealing with a total real value of not less than eighteen thousand francs. Your risk is absolutely theoretical. Nevertheless, I will take it into account, as though it were real, since in point of fact I find myself momentarily short of cash. Give me half their worth, nine thousand francs, and it's a deal."

He pretended to roar with laughter, unpleasantly revealing the stumps of decayed teeth. Squeakingly he repeated over and over the figure I had named. Finally, he said solemnly: "You're crazy."

"I take that," I said, "as the first thing you've said since the last thing you said. And you will change that, too."

"Listen, my young greenhorn, this is certainly the very first transaction of this sort you have ever tried to carry on?"

"And suppose that were so?" I replied. "Pay attention to the advent of a new talent that has just appeared on the scene. Don't reject it through stupid miserliness. Try rather to win it over to your side through open-handedness, since it may yet bring you large profits, instead of steering it to another purchaser with a better nose for luck and more taste for the youthful and promising!"

> Taken aback, he looked at me. Doubtless he was weighing my reasonable words in his shrivelled heart while studying the lips with which I had spoken them. Taking advantage of his hesitation, I added: "There's no point, Master Jean-Pierre, in our going on with these offers and counter-offers in lump sums. The collection ought to be examined and evaluated piece by piece. We must take our time about it."
> "That's all right with me," he said. "Let's reckon it up."
> That's where I made a stupid blunder. Of course, if we had kept to lump sums I should never in the world have been able to stick to nine thousand francs, but the arguing and haggling that now ensued over the price of each piece, while we sat at the table and the clockmaker noted down on his pad the miserable valuations he forced on me, beat me down too heartbreakingly. It lasted a long time, probably three quarters of an hour or more. [. . .] The sum total was forty-four hundred and fifty francs and this villain of mine acted as though he were horrified by it and were ruining himself and his whole fraternity.[26]

The novel's protagonist is trying to sell stolen jewelry to Jean-Pierre. Mann began working on the novel in 1910, years before the field of negotiation research had been established. It was published shortly before his death in 1955. Nevertheless, the scene is a realistic description of distributive bargaining. It brilliantly illustrates a number of important moves. And it demonstrates a fundamental rule of competitive tactics, namely that the real cash value of an object is only ever what someone is willing to pay at the time.[27]

How can we increase the others side's willingness to pay more (or less, depending on your role)? Perhaps I should emphasize that the following rules are perfectly valid for shady jewelry deals, but they are also universally applicable, simply because there are ZOPA in almost every transaction. Just think of my poor friend Michael in the Introduction, or the examples from the worlds of M&A and international trade. That is the reason why modern procurement experts still recommend Jean-Pierre's "salami tactics." What Felix Krull called his "stupid blunder" still works for buyers today. If you unbundle prices, you can pick them apart individually.[28]

Now, what are those tactics? And how many of them are there? I am glad you asked.

Table 1.1 The six competitive tactics of value distribution

1	Determine what you do not want
2	Determine what you do want
3	Frame and anchor
4	Be mindful of concessions
5	Be mindful of fairness
6	Don't overdo it

1.1.3.1 Determine What You Do Not Want

Let's start at the beginning. Who would have thought – this German lawyer recommends that we begin with thorough preparation. You need a good planning document and a good contract draft. And you cannot reveal your best alternative to the other side (unless there is one of three reasons for doing so). If the negotiation is not important to you, you might prefer to wing it. In all other cases, you need to determine what you want to achieve. And some of that might only happen as you find out what is possible. Hence I recommend to start with determining what you do *not* want. In other words, what is your plan B? What is the price at which you would rather walk away than close the deal?

Starting with your RP and BATNA, you should visualize the negotiation. Add the information that relates to the subsequent tactics (i.e. the other side's BATNA and RP, probability curves, etc.), and update it as the negotiation develops. Visuals enhance understanding and facilitate communication. Software can help to model decision trees. And images (even comics!) are increasingly used to visualize and draft contracts.[29]

To identify all issues, consult with your stakeholders and inquire with the other side even before formal meetings commence. Quantify your unplanned contract topics. Try to do the same from the point of view of your counterpart. Jeanne Brett has designed a negotiation preparation document that can be extremely useful. Table 1.2 shows part 1 of this document. (We will complete the template when we look at the tactics of value creation.) If there is more than one issue, you should include your assessment of priorities.[30]

We can refine the document as the negotiation progresses, using it on what has been called "post-preparation." The term was coined by Morten Lindholst, who researched how complex negotiations are conducted in the wind power industry. Lindholst was privy to sensitive data because he had been working for Vestas, the global wind turbine market leader at the time. He recommends embracing the

Table 1.2 Jeanne Brett's negotiation planning document (part 1)

	We	They
Issue 1	Our BATNA & RP	Their RP (our Target)
	1. Offer	Their BATNA
Issue 2	Our BATNA & RP	Their RP (our Target)
	1. Offer	Their BATNA
Issue 3	Our BATNA & RP	Their RP (our Target)
	1. Offer	Their BATNA

cyclical nature of multi-round negotiations. Learning from one meeting leads to preparing for the next. Then the cycle repeats after that meeting. Negotiation preparation happens right after meetings as well as before. He found that negotiators often do not (post)prepare sufficiently. One of his key recommendations is for negotiators to allocate sufficient time to be able to do so.[31]

Here is another witness for the case of post-preparation: Gerhard Conrad. He engages in a different kind of business. Conrad is a German spy who became notorious as a mediator in the Middle East. From Ron Arad to Gilad Shalit, German intelligence officers have successfully negotiated prisoner exchanges between Israel and Hamas or Hezbollah. Conrad has been honored for his role by the German and Israeli Governments. It is not easy to glean information about intelligence professionals. But if we research the secret of his success, we find hints of "iron patience," "diplomatic skill," and intimate knowledge of the region. It may surprise you that his peers credit his success to his contracting technique: "In every single session, Conrad drafted a protocol of its results which he had authorized by the side in question before he presented it to the other. This way, he always had concrete results and could confront any party that was trying to evade former concessions with authorized written statements."[32]

Your preparation document is work in progress. You keep adding information to it as you gather it. If at all possible, you should hold the negotiation on the basis of your contract draft; we will shortly explore the power of "anchoring," which you should tap into. If and when you receive a draft from the other side, you can match and compare it to the provisions in your draft. The provisions are likely to be exact opposites, especially when standard contracts or general conditions are used.

Careful with Standard Contracts A note of caution is called for on the use of standard contracts. Shrewd practitioners recommend presenting a fully drafted agreement at the very start of the negotiation. And with good reason: this offers a unique opportunity to shape the process. And it condemns the other side to an uphill battle, against the clock, to gain the upper hand. In every contract clause that distributes a risk or resource, the interests of the parties are contradictory. This is reflected in the standard contracts that their lawyers draft. The decision to base the discussion on one side's draft favors that side. In the limited time available, the other side will usually not be able to reverse the entire contract. They have to focus on what is most important to them, leaving less important issues behind. A proposed distribution of value might not even be addressed, making it, by default, a concession. The party that provides the default solution to all issues will often pick up the spoils.[33]

This brings us to our caveat: The result is often a "battle of the forms" between competing standard contracts. The battle is usually resolved by the courts through determining where the contracts contradict each other. In these cases, neither of them is deemed to be valid: If the parties proceeded to execute the agreement, they have shown that the discrepancies were no condition sine qua non for them. Instead, it is simply the law of the land that determines the rights and obligations of the parties. Consider this very common situation: The general conditions of the supplier severely limit its liability (for instance, by excluding consequential and downstream damages, and capping the overall liability at a fraction of the contract price). Conversely, the general procurement conditions of the buyer explicitly leave the supplier's liability unlimited. How is this contradiction resolved? Neither of these conditions can prevail. Rather, the applicable law determines the seller's liability. This is what the buyer had hoped for from the start. It is not uncommon for buyers to use their general conditions to that end – and to quietly refrain from any negotiations once they have received the general conditions of the seller. It would be difficult to obtain unlimited liability in direct negotiations, but they are afforded by law once the general terms of the seller are "cancelled out."[34]

This caveat brings us to a general rule: Thoroughly consider the other side's situation. You can glean a lot of information by simply asking: "Can you tell us why you are selling?", "What is your timeline?", "Are you considering other vendors?", "Are there other issues that are important to you?", and "What will you do if we don't come to an agreement?" Sure, there might be no answer. Or you might be lied to. But both situations can allow you to draw your own conclusions. Many negotiators refrain from asking such questions. But unless it is really culturally prohibitive to do so, there is no good reason for it. These questions are legitimate. It would be surprising if you did not have them in your mind. So why not ask them? You will almost certainly learn more about the other side than if you do not ask.

Some final words on the preparation document: It is a means to understanding the negotiation, not an end in itself. Paraphrasing Einstein, we can say that it should be as detailed as necessary but not more than that. Remember to keep it fluid, and revise it as you receive new information. As nineteenth-century Field Marshal Helmuth von Moltke, Prussian Chief of Staff famously remarked, no plan of operations survives the first contact with the enemy. Negotiation plans thankfully relate to more peaceful endeavors, but this is true for them too. We don't want to be boxed in by our own thinking. Also, the document might mislead us into thinking that we should negotiate the issues sequentially, one after the other. As we will shortly see, this is not the case. While we cannot cover all issues at the same time, we should keep them all open until the end. Finally, looking at the positions and priorities of both sides, you probably already see issues that might lend themselves to clever trade-offs; we will look at this in detail when we get to the tactics of value creation.

Don't Reveal Your BATNA ... Whether or not you are making the first offer, you don't want to reveal your RP (or probably even your BATNA) to the other side.

Doing so would be a recipe for minimizing your slice of the pie. Why would anyone give you substantially more than they know you would have to accept? But let us be very clear about the implications: It means that you would prefer to be misunderstood. This does obviously not mean that you should lie. Doing so would not only be wrong, it might be illegal, and it would also be unwise because you might get caught.[35]

Depending on your viewpoint, quoting a Jesuit on this occasion might surprise or reassure you. In 1647 Baltasar Gracián published *The Pocket Oracle and Art of Prudence* in Spain. Perhaps the first "self-help" book ever written, it offers 300 witty and thought-provoking aphorisms on how to live wisely. Little of his advice has lost its relevance in the last 350 years:

> Without lying, don't reveal every truth. Nothing requires more care than the truth, which is an opening up of the heart. With a single lie, a reputation for integrity is lost: Deceit is viewed as a fault, and a deceiver as false, which is worse. Not all truths can be spoken: Some because they are important to me, others to someone else.[36]

Personally, I think that the truth of your miserable BATNA qualifies for such concealment.

Of course, if you have no attractive BATNA and the other side knows it, your leverage is rather limited. In that case, different advice is warranted: "Don't bluff. It just makes you look weak, not strong, and it fools no one." But there are two cases where you may have good reasons to disclose your best alternative, to help resolve a dispute or as a last resort. As we will see, you should also reveal a deadline if you have one.[37]

… **Except in a Dispute** … In a dispute resolution negotiation you can reveal your BATNA. In deal-making the alternatives are usually independent of each other – who else I might sell to is not connected to who else you might buy from. But in a dispute, the parties' alternatives are typically linked. They often face one and the same alternative. As William Ury, Jeanne Brett, and Stephen Goldberg explain in their seminal work, *Getting Disputes Resolved*, there are three approaches to resolving conflicts: The parties can focus on either interests, rights, or power.[38]

If the parties cannot reconcile their interests, they might determine who is right or who is more powerful. Interest-based resolution can be pursued by the parties themselves, through negotiation or mediation. Who is right is usually determined by a third party, such as a judge or arbitrator. The solution foreseen by law might or might not be in the best interest of the parties. Often, the parties will try to negotiate their own solution before the judge makes a verdict. In many jurisdictions, the settlement rate (i.e. the percentage of civil cases that are resolved by negotiation between the parties) is rather high. In the US, for instance, there is a common belief among lawyers and judges that 90 percent or more of cases settle. This belief seems to be not entirely accurate; researchers found that 11 percent of tort, 44 percent of contract, 40 percent of "other," and 27 percent of "all" cases were neither tried nor settled in the State of Hawaii, while asserting that "the patterns of Hawaii and federal courts civil filings and trial rates are rather similar." But either way, a large number of cases are settled outside the court room.[39]

Alternatively, the more powerful party just coerces the other side into something they would not otherwise do. In all these cases, both sides face the same choice. Because the interest-based solution is usually best (if it can be found), the rights- and power-based resolutions are sometimes called (tongue-in-cheek) WATNA: Worst alternative to a negotiated agreement. Admittedly, this is not always so. Those of us who live under the rule of law certainly relish the ability to obtain a fair judgment from an independent judiciary if all else fails. Even so, it is often beneficial to save oneself the trouble of going to court.

... or as a Last Resort Similarly, you can reveal your RP as the absolute last resort when, even after making concessions, the other side's best offer is still lower than that. When you are about to get up and leave the table, you might as well make a last attempt: "I am sorry but if that's the best you can do, we won't come to an agreement. If you cannot give me X, then I will have to go with my alternative."

Reveal Your Deadlines On a related note, let's quickly look at deadlines. Should they be revealed or not? Some authors counsel against doing so. A number of popular negotiation books suggest that we should avoid deadlines in the first instance, and if we cannot, we should at least keep them secret. The rationale behind this is intuitive but misguided. Having a deadline does reduce your freedom and puts pressure on you to reach an agreement quickly, but it is often essential for moving stalled negotiations forward. Research by Don Moore and Francesca Gino suggest that if you have a deadline, communicate it. That way you are not the only party that feels its pressure.[40]

This approach only works if the deadline affects everyone equally. Otherwise, it might be better to keep it to yourself. In the case of Brexit, Theresa May's decision to trigger the countdown to the exit date arguably put both sides in a bad position. But some observers warned that leaving without a transition agreement would be worse for the UK than the EU. Threatening a no-deal Brexit hence had "all the conviction of a man pulling a gun in a bank and shouting: 'Give me the money or I'll shoot myself in the heart.'" Later events seem to have confirmed this view. Michel Barnier was the French former foreign minister leading the Brexit withdrawal agreement negotiations for the EU, and was subsequently appointed to head a new taskforce for the completion of the withdrawal agreement and coordination of the various negotiations on the UK's future relationship with the EU. On October 29, 2019 – two days before Brexit would be postponed again, at the request of the UK, and weeks after the UK Prime Minister, Boris Johnson, had famously declared that he would rather "die in a ditch" than not leave the EU on that day, with or without a deal – Barnier declared in an interview with several European newspapers that he deemed the consequences of Brexit as more harmful for the UK than the EU.[41]

Improve Your BATNA Your BATNA is your source of power. Ultimately, what you can achieve "at the table" is determined by your best option "away from the table." Hence, not having an alternative usually puts you in a very weak position. If you desperately need a job but have no job offer, or if you want to purchase a specific item and only know one vendor, then, ultimately, you will have to accept an agreement that is less than ideal. The Kellogg School's Leigh Thompson gives this recommendation: "Think of your BATNA as a beloved plant or pet: you feed it, you water it. BATNAs need care and attention to thrive. If you stop nurturing them, they die."[42]

Here is a case in point. See how the owners of an acquisition target, Dresser-Rand, improved the offer they received from Siemens AG by leveraging a competing bid from Sulzer Ltd. The *Wall Street Journal* reported in 2015 that Siemens Chief Executive Joe Kaeser came under pressure over the price he paid for US oil equipment-maker Dresser-Rand Group Inc.:

> Since Siemens announced the deal, valued at $7.6 billion including debt, many investors and analysts have argued Mr. Kaeser overpaid. The deal values Dresser at roughly 58 times the past year's per-share earnings. Rival U.S. oil-service companies FMC Technologies Inc. and Dril-Quip Inc. trade at less than 16 times earnings.... The transaction drew attention in mid-September, when oil prices were still relatively high, because it involved a competing bid from Sulzer Ltd., a Swiss pump maker chaired by former Siemens Chief Executive Peter Löscher. Siemens ousted Mr. Löscher in July 2013 and Mr. Kaeser, who was then chief financial officer, succeeded him. Some investors have speculated Mr. Löscher only courted Dresser out of spite, to drive up the price for Siemens. But a Dresser-Rand filing with the U.S. Securities and Exchange Commission from October details a long pursuit by both suitors that lifted the offering price and culminated in Siemens's $83-a-share offer.... In September 2011, Siemens—then headed by Mr. Löscher—began negotiations with Dresser about an all-cash acquisition of the Houston firm, according to the filing. Two months later, Siemens tabled an offer of $66 a share. By March 2012, Siemens's offer had reached $74 a share. Talks continued fruitlessly through that December, when Dresser Chief Executive Vincent R. Volpe Jr. terminated them, according to the filing. In September 2013, Mr. Volpe began talks with an unidentified 'Company A' and its largest shareholder, also unidentified, about 'becoming a significant stockholder' of Dresser. The talks fizzled in late 2013, according to Dresser's filing. 'Company A' is Sulzer and the unnamed shareholder is Renova Management AG, the holding company of Russian oligarch Viktor Vekselberg, which owns 32% of Sulzer, according to a person familiar with the negotiations. In February 2014, Mr. Löscher was appointed chief executive of Renova and chairman of Sulzer's board.... But near the end of July, Siemens approached Dresser,

> the filing says. Dresser at the time was still negotiating with "Company A" over a "merger of equals," the filing adds. In early September, Mr. Kaeser–by that point running Siemens for over a year– suggested to Dresser's Mr. Volpe an offer of between $73 a share and $80 a share, according to the filing. Dresser countered that it needed an offer in the $80s. On Sept. 16, Mr. Kaeser made a firm offer of $83 a share.... Throughout the weekend of Sept. 20, both companies continued talks with Dresser. On Sept. 21, according to the filing, Dresser's board concluded that Siemens's all-cash offer "represented superior value" compared with "Company A's" offer of a merger of equals, which would have given Dresser a 51.5% stake in the combined company.[43]

Lax and Sebenius remind us that we negotiate in a "three-dimensional" world: Our success is not only determined by the tactical moves that we make at the table, but also by setting up the most promising situation. They illustrate the point with the example of Thomas Stemberg, the founder of Staples, the original big-box office supply store. After the first round of venture capital financing, his innovative new concept took off. Staples exceeded early sales targets by 50 percent – but now new competitors jumped into the market that Stemberg had started to create. He urgently needed expansion capital and went back to the original venture capitalists. But no matter where he went in the venture capital community, nobody was willing to value Staples as highly as he thought they should. Stemberg felt stonewalled, facing what he called "the venture capitalist cartel." So, what did he do? He went directly to the pension funds and insurance companies that were invested in the funds, as well as high-net-worth individuals, effectively cutting out the middle man. The tactic worked. Not only did he find new investors who agreed with his valuation of the firm, when he went back to his first-round backers with the news he found that they had changed their mind. As Lax and Sebenius emphasize, this approach did not rupture Stemberg's relationships with his venture investors. Bain's Mitt Romney served on the Staples board for years.[44]

A caveat is in order here. Keep in mind that pursuing alternative options *merely* to get a better BATNA can be seen as an act of bad faith. In common law countries, such as the US, there is no general duty to conduct pre-contract negotiations in good faith, unless this obligation is self-imposed (e.g. through a letter of intent). But in many civil law countries, such as those on the European continent, there is a duty to negotiate in good faith. This generally means that the confidentiality of disclosed information must be maintained, received property must be treated properly, and serious intent to make an agreement must exist. The latter would be lacking when negotiations were begun with the specific purpose of withdrawing from them later. Depending on where you are in the world, doing so could be deemed improper by the law. It would be so in Spain, for instance, thus triggering liability. (It might also be difficult for the other party to prove such intent in a court of law, of course.) At the same time, Spanish law does allow withdrawal from a negotiation when one has the chance to achieve a better deal elsewhere. So our caveat here is that, if you don't know how these issues are handled in the legal system in which you are operating, consult a local lawyer. Ordinarily, the problem can be solved by declaring, at the beginning of negotiations, that you reserve the right to walk away at any time – or by including a provision to that effect in your letter of intent.[45]

The Shadow of the Law Just as your BATNA is your source of power, their BATNA is theirs. Just as you should seek to improve your alternatives, you may want to weaken theirs (to the extent that is ethically and legally permissible). This is true in both deal-making and dispute resolution negotiations. It is what lawyers do in preparation for a trial: They are "negotiating in the shadow of the law." Improving one's chances in court, e.g. by collecting evidence, necessarily means worsening the other party's chances. And when you pick a good lawyer and strengthen your case, you are simultaneously improving your BATNA and weakening theirs.[46]

The Case of the Supermarket Buying Groups Let's look at another deal-making example for improving your BATNA. Here, as we saw earlier, the alternatives of the parties are usually not linked. A retailer can buy from a different supplier, and the supplier can sell to a different buyer. Limiting the other side's ability to do so might still increase your leverage. Consider the international buying groups (IBG) that are formed by large European supermarkets. Companies such as Kaufland, Metro, Ahold Delhaize, and Edeka cooperate in IBGs to expand their buying power. A recent report revealed how IBGs operate behind the scenes. "It has been a difficult issue to research," according to one of the authors of the report: "We wanted to hear from suppliers about the situations they encounter when negotiating with IBGs, but only one manufacturer dared to speak to us, anonymously." European retailers fiercely compete for market share. They are continuously expanding the number of stores, developing private label brands, and taking over competitors. And they have gained extensive buying power in the process, which gives them leverage to extract ever lower prices from their suppliers. In the Dutch food supply chain, for instance, 65,000 farmers and 6,500 food manufacturers reach 16.7 million consumers. The food passing through the country's 4,400 supermarkets is sold by only 25 chains – which are organized in just 5 purchasing organizations.[47]

Another case in point is the struggle of the food giant Nestlé with Edeka, a German supermarket chain. When customers came to the stores in early 2018, they found this note:

> Dear Customers, we currently do not have all Nestlé products available. It is our goal to offer you the best quality at the best price. Unfortunately, Nestlé is not in agreement with us on this last issue currently. We hope you understand – and are happy to offer you alternative products from other, including our own, brands. Should you have any questions, please contact our staff.

The action was not limited to Edeka. Similar activities were synchronized across the continent by the Agecore buying group, which includes supermarkets such as Intermarché (France), COOP (Switzerland), and Eroski (Spain). *NZZ*, the Zürich newspaper, speculated that the new CEO of Agecore, who had previously managed a competing buying group, was trying to enforce the attractive prices that he had been granted in the past.[48]

An agreement was reached months later, and Nestlé products returned to the shelves. Unsurprisingly, the parties agreed to keep its content confidential. In a thin-lipped press statement, Nestlé declared: "Our priority remains to ensure our consumers enjoy the Nestlé products they know and love." Industry experts speculated that the food giant had to make significant concessions. Agecore, for its part, continued to use these tactics: Days before Christmas 2018, they stopped ordering goods from Mars, Kellogg, Heineken, and Red Bull, to extract better conditions for the upcoming year.[49]

Negotiators who are reluctant to assert their own interests at the expense of the other side can become much better at it when they imagine negotiating on behalf of somebody else. They don't have to do it for themselves, but for their partner or children who rely on them to "bring home the bacon." It can be similarly helpful to think of your future self: Yes, using this tactic can feel uncomfortable at the moment, but it might be necessary for your (hopefully early) retired self.[50]

1.1.3.2 Determine What You Want

Determining what you want means target-setting based on the other side's RP. For the second step, remember Peter "Yogi" Berra's statement: "If you don't know where you're going, you'll end up someplace else." Admittedly, "determining what you want" sounds a bit obvious. And it is. But unfortunately, that does not mean that it is always done in practice. People typically prepare by thoroughly thinking through their own situation, but, even in very large transactions, not necessarily by pondering the situation of the other side. Even in one-issue transactions, the ZOPA is often not obvious. We can take some comfort in the fact that the most successful businesspeople struggle with this. Consider the case of J. P. Morgan and Andrew Carnegie:

> In 1901, J.P. Morgan wanted to buy the Carnegie Steel Company from its founder, Andrew Carnegie. Carnegie was 65 years old and considering retirement. As Harold C. Livesay recounts in his book "Andrew Carnegie and the Rise of Big Business," when Carnegie finally decided he was ready to sell, he jotted down his estimate of his company's worth in pencil: $480 million. Carnegie had the sheet of paper delivered to Morgan, who took one look and said, "I accept this price." When Morgan arrived at Carnegie's offices to finish the deal, he congratulated Carnegie on becoming the richest man in the world. "I wonder if I could have gotten $100 million more," Carnegie reportedly mused aloud. "I probably should have asked for that." To which Morgan replied: "If you had, you would have gotten it."[51]

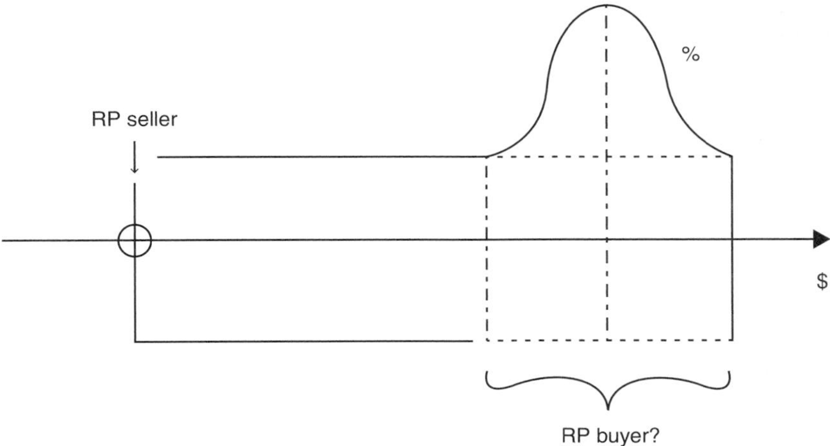

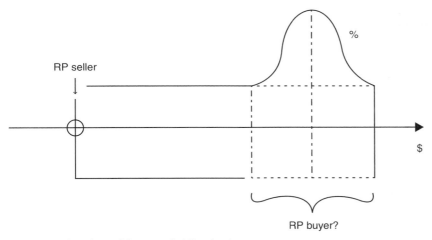

Figure 1.3 The other side's RP: Probability density curve

We can assume that Carnegie would have asked if he had assessed Morgan's RP. Even if your next transaction is smaller than Morgan and Carnegie's, you can benefit from using a probability density function. Imagine you are selling property to a real estate developer. What are their intentions? How high a structure are they allowed? What does their permit say? Are they buying other land as well? After much research, you are not entirely sure about their RP, but you can come up with a good assessment. The resulting curve could look like the diagram in Figure 1.3.[52]

In order to accurately assess the situation, you must consider cost, value, and availability – and know the market well. Depending on your industry, this can be very challenging. When I was negotiating long-term service contracts for Siemens gas turbines, our experts inserted all manner of data into maddeningly complex calculations to emulate the customer's financial situation. As the negotiations progressed, we modified and updated these calculations together. The required level of sophistication is determined by the issues at hand. What is important in any negotiation is the right mindset. We need to slip into the other side's shoes, if only to understand how they look at things.[53]

Nobody says playfulness is not allowed. I remember a negotiation where we faced the other side for weeks across the same, long conference table. Returning to the room after a break, their lead negotiator rolled his chair between myself and our lead negotiator. He did not say a word. We played along. The discussion resumed, and he remained silent for a while. Suddenly he turned to me and said, "Sometimes I really wonder which side you are on!" All with a straight face, of course.

The Case of Spark and Luxturna A much less light-hearted example is the case of Luxturna. It provides a particularly spectacular and controversial example of probing the limits of the other side in setting the price for a new drug.

> The first gene therapy in the U.S. now has a price tag: $850,000 for the one-time treatment, or, more specifically, $425,000 per eye for a retinal disorder. The price is for Spark Therapeutics' Luxturna, approved by the Food and Drug Administration in December to treat a rare, inherited retinal disease that can lead to blindness. The Philadelphia-based biotechnology company also revealed Wednesday morning a set of payment and access programs, including tying payments to how well the therapy works and exploring payment by instalment. The treatment is delivered just once, a facet of gene therapy that poses unique pricing questions in an industry fuelled by steady payments for chronic therapies. "It's wildly expensive but, to be very frank, I think they've priced it what I'll call responsibly," said Dr. Steve Miller, chief medical officer of pharmacy benefits manager Express Scripts, which is partnering with Spark on distribution and specialty pharmacy services for Luxturna. "The product is just phenomenally innovative, and we've been talking about gene therapy for over 20 years. We're now at the threshold of having gene therapy reaching patients." Wall Street expectations for Luxturna's price were around a million dollars, and Spark's $425,000 for each eye comes in under that mark. "It came down to the value we believed was inherent in the therapy," Spark Chief Executive Officer Jeff Marrazzo said in an interview.[54]

In 2018 Spark announced an agreement with Harvard Pilgrim Healthcare, which became the first health plan to cover the treatment. However, some industry experts were wondering whether "sky-high prices must come down before the price is right." The case for the sky-high price is made on the basis of the patient's alternative. They may spend $125,000 a year on medication and incur other costs to treat diseases and injuries because of their condition. Based on these numbers, a $1 million curative treatment might pay for itself in ten years by eliminating those costs. "To cover drugs like Luxturna, payers, providers, and drug makers are facing hard math. A potentially curative therapy can zero out other long-term costs to justify the expense over time, but the drug makers want to get paid as much as they can up front."[55]

Dispute Resolution Preparation Determining what you want looks slightly different in dispute resolution. As discussed, both parties face the same "worst" alternative when they negotiate "in the shadow of the law." Whether or not a lawsuit has already been filed, it serves as our benchmark in these cases. To determine how far the other side is willing to go in the settlement negotiation, we have to determine how they see the outcome of a possible lawsuit. We have to approximate the answers to three questions to do so:

1. What is the worst-case outcome from their point of view at the end of the legal proceedings? If you look at this from the perspective of the plaintiff, you have to assess how the defendant thinks the case will end. How much, when all is said and done, will they have to pay? They will likely appraise this with the help of a

decision tree that shows the flow of the legal arguments and the probability of prevailing at every junction. (Lawyers, of course, often hate this. They are experts in expressing complex matters in words, not in numbers. And they often resent having to allocate a specific probability of success to the available options. It reduces all of their expertise to a two-digit number, and it makes their success more measurable. The old Roman maxim of *iudex non calculat* [the judge does not calculate] is still alive today. A lawyer is often not keen on doing the math.) Add to this the costs that the defendant expects to accrue in pursuing the civil action (court and lawyer's fees), and you arrive at their RP. Perhaps you can add a certain amount on top – to represent the amount they are willing to spend on an earlier and interest-based solution of the matter. At the risk of becoming rather annoying, let me remind you that we are not looking at how *you* see the case here. Contrary to the conceivable protestations of your lawyer, there is probably more than one way to decide the case. And your way might not prevail. The judge and the other party make up their own minds. The other side certainly see things differently, otherwise you would not be in court in the first place. We will explore fairness shortly. We will then discover that the roles we play as plaintiffs or defendants color our perception of the case. So, again, you have to determine the worst-case scenario from the point of view of your opponent. Your own legal assessment might certainly be an indicator of this, but not more. This brings us to the second question.
2. If your assessment of the outcome is different, ask yourself if you can change the other side's mind. Do you have good arguments to adjust their RP upwards? If so, communicate them.
3. Similarly, and lastly, can you improve your BATNA, thereby worsening theirs? For instance, can you collect evidence or introduce witnesses to bolster your case? Out-of-court settlements often stay under the public's radar. Perhaps it is advantageous to the other side if the negative publicity of a verdict is avoided.

These simple, but by no means easy, steps allow you to determine what value you can reasonably want to claim. (There is a fourth step to prepare for settlement negotiations: I would encourage you to explore whether a win–win solution can still be found; you will learn all about this in the second part of this chapter.) The last two steps attest to the fluidity of the situation. Whether in dispute resolution or in deal-making, things change.

It's Alive! Even after having assessed the other side's RP, we must be mindful that it might change. Alternative options are not static. Thompson emphasizes this by presenting her advice under the headline: "It's alive!" Even after having thoroughly prepared, you might be best served by changing your approach, perhaps even dramatically. Michael Wheeler recounts the case of Jay Sheldon, the owner of a small Midwestern cable television. The business was successful, so he decided to buy a second cable company in a neighboring city. However, the (well-prepared) negotiations soon ran into an impasse: The seller asked for at least $15 million, while Sheldon was not willing to pay more than $12 million. No ZOPA existed. This prompted Sheldon to ask this question: "If you think your company is worth fifteen million, how about ours?" It turned out that his counterpart valued Sheldon's company highly too. This led him to turn the deal upside down: Instead of buying another company, he sold his.[56]

1.1.3.3 Frame and Anchor

Frame as Offer Our reference points matter, in all areas of life. To pick an obvious example, consider the world of sports. Why are silver medalists often less happy with their performance than bronze medalists? Because they often focus on the gold medal that they did not win. Bronze medalists, conversely, might focus on how close they were to winning no medal at all. The result? The "silver medal face." For a vivid illustration of this phenomenon, look at the "McKayla is not impressed" meme, created after gymnast McKayla Maroney won silver at the 2012 London Olympics. But even when the whole world is not watching, we might want to be mindful of our expressions, facial and otherwise. Consider the real estate market. Robert Y. Aumann was asked for the advice he could give buyers from game theory. This is the discipline in which he had won a Nobel Prize. His advice is not to express too keen an interest in buying. Doing so needlessly raises the price expectation of the seller. How we communicate obviously influences how we perceive reality. And how we perceive reality influences our decisions. It can "frame" them. Framing means embedding information in a context that gives it meaning. It is difficult not to frame the content of human communication. A seller might be pleasantly surprised by an offer from a buyer that had seemed not very interested. Or they might be frustrated by the same offer from an enthusiastic buyer. The offer might seem high or low in comparison to the seller's expectation. That expectation had been framed by the supposed interest of the buyer. Accordingly, framing can be used strategically in negotiations.[57]

Framing is a technique of "pre-suasion," a coin termed by psychologist Robert Cialdini. Pre-suasion means making someone receptive of the message they are about to receive. As consumers we are constantly subjected to this – just think of sales price tags. The mechanism is comically illustrated in an episode of *The Simpsons* ("Scenes from the Class Struggle in Springfield"), in which Marge ponders purchasing a discounted Chanel suit. She initially balks at the $90 price tag, but changes her opinion drastically when Lisa points out that the suit had been marked down from $2,800.[58]

But framing can exist in more subtle forms too. Background music, for instance, can influence consumer choices. Supermarket customers were found to buy more

French wine when stereotypically French music was playing, and bought more German wine when German music was played. (The study continues to amaze me because "stereotypical" German music, unless it is by Bach or Beethoven, is in my mind linked to beer rather than wine, and not in an entirely good way.) A more recent study by Stanford University of no less than 137,842 diner decisions showed that emphasizing tasty and enjoyable attributes in labeling vegetables increases their intake in situations where they compete with less healthy options. From findings like these, we learn that what is presented first changes the perception of what comes next.[59]

An Invitation to Treat Perhaps you feel that these last examples led us a bit away from our topic. Nothing could be further from the truth. Self-service supermarkets and cafeterias offer insight into what might be the ultimate form of framing in negotiations. Letting the other side have it your way. (If you are slightly uncomfortable about such manipulation, bear with me. Framing is equally useful to help parties realize a win–win.) By exerting free will, the customer makes exactly the offer that the supermarket wants them to make. Wait, is that right? Isn't it the supermarket that makes the offer, and the consumer that accepts it? No, it is the other way around. In the leading case of *Pharmaceutical Society of Great Britain* v. *Boots Cash Chemists Ltd.* in 1952, it was clarified that a customer presenting the goods at the cash desk is making the offer. The seller, by displaying the goods on the shelves, is merely making an *invitatio ad offerendum* [invitation to treat] to the customer. The courts in many other jurisdictions (such as the United States and Germany) come to the same conclusion. That many consumers think otherwise only proves how successful supermarkets have been at framing their customers' perception. When a supermarket chain, such as Trader Joe's, sells more groceries per square foot that the competition ($2,000, versus $1,200 by Whole Foods and $600 by Wal-Mart) *and* consumers lobby the chain to bring a store to their state, then they have clearly mastered the discipline. People, apparently, just like to make the decisions that they are being offered by the store. They like what they get. This brings us to the next point.[60]

Focus on Their Gain As a general rule, we should frame proposals in terms of what the other side gains. We might thus induce a positive frame of reference so that the other side agrees to our offer (or, at least, makes concessions more likely). We can also emphasize the risks faced by the other side and contrast that with the sure gain that we offer. Likewise, we should frame the proposal as offer, not as demand. Don't emphasize what they have to give, but emphasize what they gain. Trötschel, Loschelder, Höhne, and Majer have explored this in various negotiation settings, such as the buying and selling of used appliances. Participants received identical proposals, but some were framed as offers and others as requests. Offers were worded like this: "The seller offers the refrigerator for a price of €160" or "The buyer offers a price of €160 for the refrigerator." Conversely, requests were worded like this: "The seller requests a price of €160 for the refrigerator" or "The buyer requests the refrigerator for a price of €160." Individuals were more likely to concede when the other side gave them an "offer" than when they gave them a "request." This held for both buyers and sellers. What can be inferred from this? We should persuade the other side to focus on what they are going to gain from the negotiation (offer) rather than what they are going to lose (request).[61]

Frame as Option Similarly, we all prefer being able to choose over being pushed. If you give the other side at least two options to choose from, they will not feel stuck with an ultimatum. Humans rarely choose things in absolute terms. When we are given more than one offer, we will often evaluate them relative to one another. As psychologist Dan Ariely points out, we don't have an internal value meter that tells us how much things are worth: "Rather, we focus on the relative advantage of one thing over another and estimate value accordingly." He illustrates this point by another example from the world of consumer marketing, the subscription webpage of *The Economist*. In Table 1.3 I have added the options that were offered to European readers in 2013 and 2018 (in Euros).[62]

Table 1.3 Relative attractiveness of options: Subscription prices for *The Economist*

	Online only	Print only	Print and online
2007 (1 year)	$59	$125	$125*
2013 (51 weeks)	€125	–	€125
2018 (12 weeks)	€20	€20	€20

* plus online access to all articles from *The Economist* since 1997.

As Ariely points out, we might not know whether the internet-only subscription at $59 is a better deal than the print-only option at $125. But certainly "print and online" is a better option than "print only" for the same price! When you look at the options that were offered in subsequent years, it becomes clear which offer *The Economist* would like readers to choose: "Print and online" is always the most attractive option. Perhaps the purpose of the other options is just to provide a frame that will "nudge" the customer toward it? By 2013, the cheaper option had disappeared altogether. The price is fixed, and only a semblance of choice is left.[63]

Frame as Default The 2018 version leads us to our next tactical advice. Previous subscriptions had been for the entire year (or fifty-one weeks – the Christmas editions remains on sale for two weeks), but now the focus is on an "introductory offer" of just twelve weeks. After all, what is €20 for four months? But what happens after the introductory period? Even if it goes up, many people will stick to what is now their default. As Nobel laureate Richard Thaler and his colleague Cass Sunstein explain, people have a strong tendency to stick to the status quo. But if you ever kept an unused gym membership, you already knew that.[64]

The Economist is not the only media outlet that makes use of this mechanism. In July 2018, the website of the *New York Times* announced: "Get the New York Times for just €1 a week. Subscribe now." As I eagerly followed the link and clicked on the advertised "Basic" subscription, I was shown a "friendly reminder" that the rate was valid for the first year only. Thereafter, I would automatically be charged twice as much (€8 instead of €4 every four weeks). I could cancel anytime, of course. Apparently, I had indeed been in need of a reminder. Of my own naivety.

What can negotiators learn from this? We should structure our proposals so that the other side can choose from different options, with our preferred option presented as default. Interestingly, although the "default effect" is very powerful, people are not very good at making use of it: In a recent study, participants were asked to nudge the other side toward selecting a target option by choosing whether to present the target option as default. The researchers found that only half the participants made use of the effect.[65]

Make the First Offer The single most powerful distributive tactic is making an ambitious first offer. Adam Galinsky and Thomas Mussweiler found first offers to correlate with outcomes as much as 85 percent of the time. That may be a surprise to many readers. After all, conventional wisdom has it that a shrewd negotiator should never make the first offer! But that is a myth. If you are prepared, you should make the first offer (if you are not prepared you should go back to the preparation document above). And not only that. Regardless of whether you are buying or selling, you should make the first offer as extreme as you plausibly can! You are skeptical? Let me explain.[66]

We just saw that the other side prefers to be given options (even if there are no real choices). Similarly, nobody likes facing a "take it or leave it offer." In other words, the other side expects you to move toward them. An offer which might have been accepted had it emerged as a result of concession-making, might be rejected when it is thrown on the table and presented as a fait accompli. People might be even more satisfied with an outcome that is worse, just because they had a say in how it was reached. Hence it is wise to leave yourself room to maneuver. "Clever negotiators often get amazing deals for their clients by producing an opening offer that makes their adversary thrilled to pay half that very high amount."[67]

The opening offer acts as a powerful psychological "anchor" in a negotiation, and it usually represents the most you can hope to achieve. Extreme first offers facilitate the claiming of value, because they can anchor the negotiation. The first offer might influence the other party's counteroffer by pulling it toward it and away from what they might have said if they had gone first. Upon hearing your first offer, they have silently negotiated with themselves! And in so doing, they have been anchored. In the series of experiments by Galinsky and Mussweiler, whoever made the first offer obtained a better outcome. At the same time, first offers were a strong predictor of final settlement prices. As Brett puts it, as long as the first offer is not so extreme as to stop the negotiation, there is a "first-mover advantage" for the negotiator who makes it.[68]

So, how can you avoid making the first offer too extreme? We have already seen that the target should be set based on the other side's RP. Your first offer should be just a little bit higher (or lower). Being close to their RP, your offer is by definition not too extreme. Of course, it might look extreme from the point of view of your RP. But, as we have already seen, this is exactly the wrong side of the ZOPA for determining what your target and first offer should be. Often-heard rules of thumb such as "Your first offer should / should not be more / less than a factor X of your walk-away price" completely miss the point. I cannot stress enough that what the other side deem to be reasonable or extreme is determined by *their* alternative, not yours (unless you are in a conflict where the two alternatives typically coincide, as in obtaining a judge's decision).

When selling, don't just take your walk-away price and add a certain margin on top. Instead, take the buyer's walk-away price and add some margin to it. Do it the other way around when you are selling. Your first offer will often not be accepted, especially if you follow this rule. Then making concessions is inevitable. It's best to open with a figure slightly worse than the counterpart's barely acceptable terms. Jean-Pierre knew this, and poor Michael must have forgotten it. But no wonder: While this advice may be easy to formulate, it is not always simple to follow. As we saw in the case of Andrew Carnegie, even the world's richest businesspeople struggle with it. Perhaps your response is: "But I don't know their walk-away price!" I can only reiterate the crucial importance of preparing for the negotiation. If we do not know the size of the pie that we are distributing, we are not acting professionally. We may be lucky, or we may not. And we will probably never find out which of the two it was.[69]

Anchors Can Be Unrelated To round off the topic, let's look at some interesting findings on anchoring. Anchoring leads us to base our assessment of an unknown value on another value, even if it is completely unrelated. For instance, when assessing the value of a company, it is a common error to determine how much profit the company will make in the future by how much profit it has made in the past, or to determine the price of a share based on whether one "likes" the company in question.[70]

Anchoring can take absurd, even disturbing, forms. A series of experiments demonstrated that the sentencing decisions of experienced criminal court judges might be influenced by irrelevant anchors that had obviously been determined at random. The case material studied by the judges included the number of years the public prosecutor demanded as a sentence. But even when this field was left blank and the judges were asked to insert the number by throwing dice, their sentencing appeared to have assimilated that number.[71]

Use Odd Numbers Not only should you make the first offer as extreme as plausibly possible, you should also use an odd, rather than round, number in doing so. Experimental and field evidence from the real estate market suggest that the maker of the first offer might be able to increase the anchoring effect by expressing the offer price in precise terms. The effect has been replicated in various experimental settings. An offer of €14,875 can appear more informative and is likely to lead to a smaller subsequent adjustment than a price of €15,000.[72]

This effect has also been observed in real-world M&A transactions. Petri Hukkanen and Matti Keloharju looked at the initial offers to acquire the majority of the shares of publicly traded US companies. They analyzed a sample of nearly 2,000 cash offers by US acquirers over three decades and found that bidders tend to make round offers – much rounder than the prices at which stocks trade on the market. Such round initial offers were associated with a higher price paid, a lower probability of completing the deal, and a less positive response of the stock market to the offer. In drawing conclusions for practice, the researcher discourages bidders' use on purpose of round offer prices to make the target feel that the bidder left some "meat on the bone" for them, hoping this will improve their chances of winning the deal. Instead, they recommend buyers to use odd numbers in making the first offer: "It is virtually costless to change the offer price from a round number to a precise one, allowing the bidder to signal (or hide) its private information (or lack of it) on the accuracy of its valuation of the target." This simple intervention might increase the chances of a successful offer and yet generate significant cost savings.[73]

You Cannot Avoid It Were you becoming rather melancholic when you learned about all this anchoring and framing research? I certainly did. How comfortable you are with this advice is a personal question. Instead of making an extreme first offer and then haggling about it, many prefer to come in with a "reasonable" offer. Save yourself (and the other side) the trouble, they say. I am not claiming that this will never work, and it's great when it does. Of course, you would not be in bad company either. This is exactly the approach that a famous Vice President of General Electric, Lemuel Boulware, took. This practice was even named after him: "Boulwarism." The problem? Overwhelming empirical evidence shows that usually it does not work.

> Mr. Boulware was vice president of employee and public relations at General Electric from 1956 to 1961, when he retired. He had been responsible for employee relations since 1947, a year after the company went through what it considered a disastrous strike. He helped

> develop practices in the company's relations with employees, unions, stockholders, community neighbours and government at all levels through a program intended to inform these groups that General Electric was trying "to do right voluntarily." In a bargaining policy that came to be known as Boulwarism, the company listened closely to union demands, examined the wages and working conditions of competitors, conducted extensive research on all issues and then put forward a "fair, firm offer," with nothing held back for future concessions. Although General Electric was unhappy with the term "Boulwarism," calling it a "hostile label," the basic bargaining policy that it embraced became the hallmark of the company's dealing with its organized employees in the 1950s and 1960s. Labour's view of the policy was summed up by Paul Jennings, president of the International Union of Electrical Workers. At a convention of the A.F.L.-C.I.O. in Atlantic City in 1969, he called the policy "telling the workers what they are entitled to and then trying to shove it down their throats."[74]

Nobody likes being told what they are entitled to. Hence Howard Raiffa advises us not to embarrass our bargaining partners by forcing them to make all the concessions. Making an extreme first offer spares them the predicament![75]

So now we know why making an ambitious first offer is the single most powerful tactic in distributive negotiation. While the endpoints of the ZOPA are generally independent of each other, the endpoints of the range that negotiators actually talk about often are not. And the parties do not usually backtrack behind their initial offers. This means that by the time the first and second offers are made, parts of the pie have already been distributed. At the same time, once two offers are on the table – one for each party – the final point of agreement can reasonably be predicted to fall midway between those two extremes (the "midway rule"). When combined, the anchoring effect and the midway rule explain the extraordinary power of making the first offer, which itself determines to a considerable extent the outcome of all that haggling.[76]

Don't Be Anchored If you are not making the first offer, you might or might not like the other side's proposal. Here is advice for both scenarios: Even when you really like their very first offer, do not accept it immediately – especially if you really like it! Instead, ask for some concession. Why? You do not want to make them unhappy. And nothing makes them as unhappy as responding, with a broad smile, "Deal!" They would feel what is called the "winner's curse," and you do not want to put it on them. Research shows that when negotiators' first offers are immediately accepted, they are less likely to be satisfied with the outcome than negotiators whose offers were not accepted immediately. This is true even when their outcomes were better.[77]

The second scenario: If you do not like their offer, don't allow yourself to be anchored. The first step is to wipe away extreme offers – do not legitimize or allow them to justify it. Divert the discussion away from the unacceptable anchor, asking questions that focus on the interests and motivations underlying the other side's position. Then put your initial figure on the table, supported by sound reasoning. In doing so, you should focus on information that is inconsistent with the implications of the opponent's first offer. Research shows that the advantageous effect of making the first offer can be eliminated if you think about your opponent's alternatives to the negotiation, your opponent's RP, or your own target.[78]

There is a precondition for effectively (counter-) anchoring: It is obviously impossible if the other side knows your real RP. If your alternative is poor, and the other side knows it, you can still make a high demand. But the other side is not likely to offer you more than your RP – which makes it imperative, as we have seen, not to reveal your BATNA (except in the abovementioned cases).[79]

1.1.3.4 Be Mindful of Concessions

Be mindful about concession-making. Very few negotiations are concluded within one round. The first offer is often not accepted. A back and forth exchange usually ensues that can continue during multiple rounds, just as Thomas Mann imagined in the case of Felix Krull. Just as you should plan in advance the offer you want to open the negotiation with, you should plan for your subsequent concessions. Also, be mindful of the concession patterns you employ. One of the conventions of good faith bargaining is that once a concession is made, it is not reversed.[80]

We should obviously try to concede on issues that are not so important to us but are important to the other side. And we should continually keep their expectations low, by not giving in too often, too soon, or too much. We should also avoid negotiating with ourselves by making subsequent concessions: Before we lower the asking price again, first the other side must have increased their offer. Make them work hard for every concession you make. As we assess the room for concessions, we will discover opportunities for the most potent tactic of value creation: give and take. Because modern negotiation research originates in the United States, a term from the American West is often used to describe it: "log-rolling." It refers to neighbors helping each other with the moving of timber. Assistance in rolling logs was offered in exchange for receipt of the same. Another common expression is quid pro quo ("favor in return" in Latin). We will come back to this later.[81]

1.1.3.5 Be Mindful of Fairness

Being mindful of fairness means understanding that it is a powerful idea, which might nevertheless prove elusive. As Roger Fisher and William Ury emphasize, the parties ideally agree on objective standards for dividing the pie. If possible, cite market prices, business practice, net present value calculations, etc. to support your position. That might not always be possible: No objective criteria might exist. This goes for deal-making as well as dispute resolution. Who is to say if a personal injury case is to be "objectively" settled at $800,000 or $1,000,000? "Any lawyer who has been involved in a personal injury suit will marvel at the capacity of an effective plaintiff's lawyer . . . to give the superficial appearance of certainty and objectivity to questions that are inherently imponderable." The truth is that a fair division of the pie is hardly ever certain or objective.[82]

So, use the power of standards and fairness, but don't become their victim. In value distribution, a degree of mistrust is healthy. Recent research indicates that when trust is low, negotiators will be less anchored than when trust is high. When it is low, first offers are perceived as being too extreme. In addition, low trust might lead the non-trusting party to look for more information, thus also reducing the anchoring effect.[83]

If the other side adopts a position that you believe to be unfair, ask the question: "What makes you believe your position is fair?" Then, after expressing understanding of the other side's perspective, explain why that position seems unfair to you.[84]

Fairness is Subjective A word on fairness. If both sides can agree on what is fair, that is brilliant. But we cannot expect to find such agreement when distributing resources or risks. And perhaps we should not even look for them. Fairness is subjective. It can even come with our role in the negotiation. Loewenstein et al. conducted an experiment in which participants were given identical information about a legal case and were assigned the role of the defendant or the plaintiff. The parties were then asked to negotiate a settlement, basing their approach on the expected outcome of going to trial. Participants were also asked what they perceived to be a "fair" settlement. The researchers found that both aspects were largely influenced by the role that the individuals had been assigned. As a plaintiff, the amount of the expected settlement and the amount of what one deemed "fair" were substantially higher than the amounts given by the participants who were assigned the role of defendant.[85]

Perhaps you have never been a plaintiff or defendant. You can test your fairness judgment with the help of a famous experiment, the "dictator game." You receive $100 and have to decide how to split it between you and your counterpart. If they accept, you do as you propose. If they do not, you both get nothing. Consider – would you like a split of 50:50? Or 70:30? Maybe 90:10? And how would the other side see it? Many people have an amount in their mind that they would rather decline than accept. This is also significant in distributive negotiations: If we push too hard, they may simply walk away.

Who Wants Cucumber? Intriguingly, it is not only humans that are repulsed by what they view as an unfair distribution. Biologists Frans de Waal and Sarah Brosnan have conducted a fascinating experiment with capuchin monkeys which exploited the animals' talent for barter, which they do spontaneously. They are apparently so fond of barter that they will bring you a dried orange peel in exchange for a pebble, both useless items.

> For our experiment, we placed two monkeys in a test chamber sitting side by side with mesh between them. We'd drop a small rock in the area of one of them, then hold up an open hand to ask for the rock back. We'd do this with both monkeys in alternation twenty-five times in a row. If both of them got cucumber slices in return for the rocks, they'd make the exchange all the time, contently eating their food. But if we gave one monkey grapes for the exchanges while keeping the other one on cucumber, we'd trigger some real drama. Food preferences generally match prices in the supermarket, so grapes are far superior to cucumber. Upon noticing their partner's raise, the monkeys who'd been perfectly happy to work for cucumber all of a sudden went on strike. Not only would they perform reluctantly, they'd grow agitated, hurling the pebbles out of the test chamber and sometimes even the cucumber slices. A food that they normally never refused had become less than desirable: it had become distasteful![86]

Throwing away perfectly good food would be called "irrational" by economists – and it is exactly the same behavior that humans display when they are offered an unequitable share in the dictator game. Indeed, as de Waal points out, the one-minute video of the cucumber and grape experiment went viral because people recognized themselves in the cage-rattling protest by the cucumber monkey. Some told the researchers that they had forwarded the video to their boss to let him know how they felt about their salary. (If you have not seen the video, check it out. It is hilarious.)[87]

Whether for humans or monkeys, perceived fairness is a very powerful determinant of satisfaction with an outcome. But the outcome must be perceived as fair by all sides of the agreement. And it is easy to argue about that. Imagine the rich man and the poor man again. How could they fairly split $200? The rich man may suggest a split of $150:$50 in his favor – arguing that it would grieve the poor man more to lose $50 than it would him to lose $150. And he would have a point. (It has been called the "tragedy of bargaining" that those who need a deal the most often receive the fewest of the benefits.) Of course, the poor man, keeping an eye on the different needs of the two, might suggest the reverse apportionment. And he too would have a point.[88]

Equality versus Equity So, what *is* fair division of the ZOPA pie? Some would say the division should be equal, others that it should be equitable. Let's look at both options. Many negotiators intuitively go for 50:50. An equal split appears fair to them. That's the reason why the "midway rule" is so powerful: Experimental studies strikingly bear out that the midpoint between the first offer and the first counteroffer is a very good predictor of the ultimate outcome of the negotiation (if the midpoint is in the ZOPA). But wait! The zone between the first offer and the first counteroffer is seldom the same as the ZOPA! Imagine a ZOPA between $100 and $300. If the first offer is made at $50 and the counteroffer at $450, the midway rule may make a division of $150:$50 look fair. But if the first offer was made at

$250 and the counteroffer at $50, the fair division of the pie would be exactly the other way around. How fair is a rule that can make both versions equally fair?[89]

Maybe an equitable solution would be better? As Peyton Young observed in his classic treatise, *Equity in Theory and Practice*, the key to resolving a distributive bargain is to make a proposal that the other side finds plausible and justifiable: "This is precisely where equity arguments come in: they *coordinate* the expectations of the bargainers by establishing a plausible basis for the agreement. Equity principles are the *instruments* that people use to resolve distributive bargains."[90]

Young describes a problem that was posed nearly two thousand years ago in a "Mishna" from the Babylonian Talmud: "Two hold a garment; one claims it all, the other claims half. What is an equitable division of the garment?" The solution proposed in the Talmud is three-quarters to the first claimant and a quarter to the second. Rabbi Shlomo Titzhaki, known as "Rashi," explained the logic of the division like this: The first claimant concedes nothing to the second claimant; the second claimant, however, is claiming only half of the garment, implicitly conceding the "other half." Since the first claimant is hence entitled to at least half of the garment, only the other half is actually at issue. And what is at stake should be divided equally between the two claimants. Don't be tempted to think that this example might have lost some relevance in subsequent centuries. If you sue a business partner in a German court, you will see this very approach in practice. To arrive at their verdict, judges use the "technique of relation" [*Relationstechnik*] which considers what the defendant puts forward *only* to the extent that it "relates" to what the plaintiff has put forth – i.e. only to the extent that it disputes the plaintiff's claim. What the defendant concedes is not even discussed in court, just as in the garment example. It does not impact the outcome. Only the disputed garment is the subject of the court case.[91]

This approach can, no doubt, lead to a fair and equitable solution. But that rests on at least two conditions. The parties have to know the exact size of the pie. And the rationale for the division is their legal entitlement to the pie's pieces; in other words, they are resolving the dispute by way of law. These conditions might not be applicable in deal-making situations. And they do not consider who is more in need, has more power, or merits more, although these questions might influence what the parties view as fair. And they may have very different ideas. Consider the difficulty of finding a Brexit agreement that is seen as fair by the UK Government, major parties, and the electorate – as well as by the EU Commission, Parliament, and twenty-seven members. Admittedly, an extreme case, which is why it underscores what I consider our main takeaway here: Fairness can be found in the process, but not in the outcome, of value distribution. Treating each other fairly means refraining from lying, bullying, personal attacks, and the like. Beyond that: Use standards of fairness, if you can – but don't expect to find fairness in the outcome.

Advice for Felix Krull Let's use what we have learned to help Felix Krull. Here are some of the things he could have done to improve his outcome:

- When entering into the negotiation, he should have focused more on what he wanted to achieve; he did not have a clear idea about what his target in the negotiation should be, or how he could reach it in the face of resistance.
- Felix could have visited a number of shops to test the waters and develop an understanding of how buyers would evaluate the jewels. And he could have established alternative options.
- Based on his market research, he should have defined his target.
- He then should have made the first offer – which should have been higher than his target. And he should have done so by using an uneven number.
- Alternatively, on hearing the first offer, he should have immediately re-anchored the conversation by making his own counteroffer (instead of discussing the merits of Jean-Pierre's offer).
- He should not have agreed on the salami approach of the buyer, which he was ill-equipped to counter effectively, given the buyer's knowledge advantage.
- When he realized that the negotiation was not going down well, he should have considered breaking off and visiting other purchasers to elicit better BATNAs.

This last piece of advice highlights the risk that is inherent to Jean-Pierre's competitive stance: He might do too much of it, finding himself without a deal altogether. This brings us to the sixth, and last, tactic.

1.1.3.6 Don't Overdo It

The final piece of advice may or may not come as a surprise. As we are closing our exploration of value-claiming, we come back to the idea of the Yin & Yang. Negotiation is not straightforward and simple. It is paradoxical. To succeed at the task of value-claiming, we must also do its opposite: Not claim value. Our success at distributing the pie can become too much of a good thing. When the US Constitution was created at the Constitutional Convention of 1787, Benjamin Franklin cautioned against being too assertive in debate. "Declarations of fixed opinion, and of determined resolution never to change it, neither enlighten nor convince us", he said. "Positiveness and warmth on one side, naturally beget their like on the other." We will return to the Constitutional Convention in the next part of this chapter; Franklin's advice is valid even when we are not negotiating new constitutional frameworks. There are three reasons why we should not claim as much value as we can: Doing so may prevent us from achieving a deal altogether, or we might achieve a suboptimal deal, or we may have to pay for it in the future. We will look at all three in turn. Before we do so, however, let me emphasize that we are still figuring out the tactics of value-claiming. Our objective is still to achieve the best possible deal for ourselves. Doing so, paradoxically, may require some restraint.[92]

You May Not Achieve a Deal First, if we overdo it, the other side might simply walk away. It is true that a rational negotiator should accept even the worst of deals over the no-deal alternative. However, as Nobel laureate Richard Thaler points out, humans are not "econs": This is how he labels "the fictional creature called homo oeconimicus." There is a lot of empirical evidence which shows that people sometimes prefer no deal over what they view as an unfair deal. Just think of the dictator game. If we only look at the numbers, there is no split that anyone should reject. After all, the best alternative to it is naught, zero, zilch. But this is clearly not the case. What would theoretically make us most successful at value-claiming might destroy our success. The prospect of the "dictator" (us) getting most of the pie is precisely what repels the other side. And they might be perfectly willing to forgo their slice if we don't get ours either. What becomes beautifully, even painfully, apparent in the dictator game applies in the real world too. "Cutting off your nose to spite your face" is an expression that has been in use for almost a millennium.[93]

You Might Achieve a Suboptimal Deal The second reason for not overdoing it comes into play even when the other side agrees to a deal. Negotiators who focus on claiming value are ironically often not the ones who succeed at value-claiming! Yes, you read that right. But how can that be? Again, it is because of the two sides of the Yin & Yang. If we put too much emphasis on doing well at the expense of the other side, we typically fail to develop enough insight into their interests and priorities. Yet without such insights, as we will shortly see, negotiators are not able to expand the joint pie. So, they might get a larger share of the pie. But because the pie is smaller, they ironically can end up with a smaller slice for themselves.[94]

You May Have to Pay for it Later The third reason for not pushing too hard is that we may meet the other side again. Even if there is a good deal to be gained now, we may end up having to pay for it in the future. Research into the dynamic pricing of goods purchased on the internet is instructive. Dynamic pricing means that all available on- and offline data is combined to determine the maximum amount that can be extracted from the client. But if the customer's perception of fairness is violated, their purchase satisfaction suffers. They may decide simply not to come back for another transaction.[95]

Many negotiations are not one-off, but go through many rounds. (This is the reason that neither purely distributive nor purely cooperative tactics are typically called for: instead, finding the right strategy usually requires a mix of the two). Customer–supplier relationships, for example, often last for many years. Claiming value too vigorously can backfire. For example, buyers can use reverse online auctions to virtually guarantee the best possible price. The contract is awarded to the lowest bidder. The only way that the seller can make sure they will gain the deal is to push the button when their RP comes up. If they wait longer, a competitor might jump in, leaving them without a deal when they could have achieved one. They might experience a reaction similar to the "winners' curse," albeit in reverse: frustration for being too "greedy." As Harvard's Guhan Subramanian points out, the pressure comes primarily from the same side of the table – from other suppliers who are in exactly the same bind. It is no surprise that researchers found this set-up to have a detrimental effect on the buyer–supplier relationship. How will the supplier respond, when the buyer relies on him at a later point in time? Perhaps procurement was so "successful" in value-claiming that other providers have exited the business, leaving only a sole supplier? Will the supplier be tempted to, literally, turn the table when they can? This problem might arise when the supply of goods and services are negotiated on the basis of contracts, auctions, or a mixture of the two.[96]

The Case of Volkswagen and the Prevent Group Consider the "strange tale of Volkswagen and its Bosnian supplier," as business journalists have put it: The Prevent Group, a little-known company of Bosnian origins has for a long time supplied Volkswagen with various car parts, such as seat covers and gearboxes. Over the years, Prevent bought up various other supply companies. At some point a dispute between the partners arose. Prevent reportedly felt that Volkswagen wanted to pass on the cost of its "Dieselgate" scandal to its suppliers. In 2016 Prevent decided to worsen Volkswagen's BATNA and stopped deliveries of seats and transmission components. As a result, Volkswagen had to halt production lines. It suffered losses estimated to be anywhere between €20 million and €100 million. Thereupon, perhaps not surprisingly, a negotiated solution to the dispute was quickly found. Two years later, and perhaps even less surprisingly, Volkswagen cut ties with the Prevent Group, purportedly in revenge for the manner in which Prevent had stalled Volkswagen production in 2016. Revenge, the journalist pointed out, is a dish best served cold. Was that the end of the story? Not quite. Just a few months prior, and apparently unbeknown to Volkswagen, Prevent had taken over Neue Halberg-Guss, a traditional German foundry that was founded in the eighteenth century. According to the newsmagazine *Der Spiegel*, the new owner now jacked up its prices, tenfold. The customer? Volkswagen, of course.[97]

To conclude: If we push too hard, our tactics can become too much of a good thing (which is also true, as we will see, for the tactics of value creation). Whether or not we go too far in claiming value is – like our target and the plausibility of our first offer – determined by the other side.

The distribution of value constitutes a zero-sum game. To be successful at it we have to employ competitive tactics, optimizing our share at the expense of the other side. But usually, there is more than one issue in a negotiation. In this case, not caring about the counterpart's interest might hurt our chances of claiming value: In non-zero-sum negotiations we might be better off by claiming a smaller piece of a larger pie. It can be in our self-interest to search for agreements that meet our own, *and our counterpart's*, concerns. Doing so is exactly what the creation of value is all about. Let's take a look.[98]

1.2 Multiple Issues: The Creation of Value

Creating value is very different from distributing it. To come back to Morton Deutsch's metaphor: If we swim, the other does not have to sink. Rather, we swim (or sink) together. There are three ways to create value in a negotiation. The parties may align compatible interests, trade on differences in priorities, or agree on a contingent contract. The creation of value is often compared to the expansion of a pie (see Figure 1 in the Introduction).[99]

And there are even more precise analogies. Synchronizing compatible issues is finding out that there are two pies – and that each party wants a different one. Trading off is like taking two pies and sharing one in favor of one party, and the other in favor of the other party. And agreeing on a contingent contract is like deciding how to divide a pie that might or might not materialize. (Because only one party expects that this pie will materialize, some scholars do not consider contingent contracts to be "true" value creation.) Why so many pies? To highlight that we always need at least two issues to create value. Each approach only works if there are at least two items on the table. So, in order to move beyond the mere distribution of value, the parties have to find new issues, or break one issue into two (or more).

1.2.1 Aligning Compatible Interests

When the parties detect compatible issues, they can align them for mutual benefit. It is not always possible for the parties to distribute a fixed pie among them. Think of cases where no positive bargaining zone exists. If the seller's RP is higher than the buyer's RP, there is no ZOPA. In that case, the parties can agree to disagree, or try a different approach: Break the issue at hand into multiple issues, or add new issues to the mix. And, of course, this might achieve better results even when there is a ZOPA! Both parties might be better off by expanding the pie before they divide it (even though each might still prefer to gain the entire pie). In other words, it is often preferable not to play a zero-sum game.

1.2.1.1 Oranges and Leafy Branches

This is most obvious when the interests of the parties are actually compatible. We have already seen the orange parable. I sometimes ask workshop participants what they would do if they were a parent of the two sisters arguing over the fruit. Men sometimes suggest (jokingly, no doubt) to end the conflict by taking the orange for themselves. Many propose to divide the orange between the sisters. Whether or not this is the best course of action depends, as we have seen, on the underlying interests of the girls. (Interestingly, the intuitive response to "split the difference" is not confined to human beings. Biologist Frans de Waal describes an incident he observed in chimpanzees: "I once saw an adolescent female interrupt a quarrel between two youngsters over a leafy branch. She took the branch away from them, broke it in two, then handed each one a part." We will shortly see that some animals, astonishingly, are capable of expanding the pie too.)[100]

The "mother of dispute resolution," Mary Parker Follett, was perhaps the first modern thinker to illustrate the creation of value with a classic example in 1925:[101]

> In the Harvard Library one day, in one of the smaller rooms, someone wanted the window open. I wanted it shut. We opened the window in the next room, where no one was sitting. This was not a compromise because there was no curtailing of desire; we both got what we really wanted. For I did not want a closed room, I simply did not want the north wind to blow directly on me; likewise, the other occupant did not want that particular window open, he merely wanted more air in the room.[102]

Parker Follett also coined the term "integrative" negotiations, for situations where the parties attempt to integrate mutual interests into the agreement. Sometimes it is called "win–win", because the integration of interests can lead to both sides winning. As Richard Walton and Robert McKersie point out, both creating and distributing value are rational responses to different situations:

> Integrative bargaining and distributive bargaining are both joint decision-making processes. However, these processes are quite dissimilar and yet are rational responses to different situations. Integrative potential exists when the nature of a problem permits solutions which benefit both parties, or at least when the gains of one party do not represent equal sacrifices by the other.[103]

In these cases, both parties' interests can be integrated either completely, as in the case of compatible issues, or partially, as in the case of diverging preferences. The creation of value is sometimes confused with the creation of satisfaction. Finding compatible interests *can* lead to a feeling of deep satisfaction, but the two are not the same. Whether or not value can be created is an objective question. The process might feel just as cumbersome and frustrating to the parties as the distribution of value. That's why it can be so tempting to just give in or try to press the other side to do so.

Let's come back to Howard Raiffa's idea of negotiation "geometry" to express this concept visually. Creating value is a two-dimensional exercise. Imagine a matrix in which all possible outcomes are plotted. You can measure the utility of each outcome along two dimensions: the utility of the outcome for party A and its utility for party B. Of course, each utility can conceptually range between 0 and 100 percent.[104]

When we create value, we open up a second dimension. When the interests of the parties are completely compatible (such as at the Harvard Library or in the orange case), the picture looks like Figure 1.4. The orange case represents an ideal case of win–win. Everybody obtains 100 percent of what they want. Nobody has to give up anything. It is easy to see that this result depends on information exchange. If the right information flows, the most desirable outcome can become obvious. A neutral third party, such as a mediator, can be tremendously helpful here. Information can be passed on to them in confidence.[105]

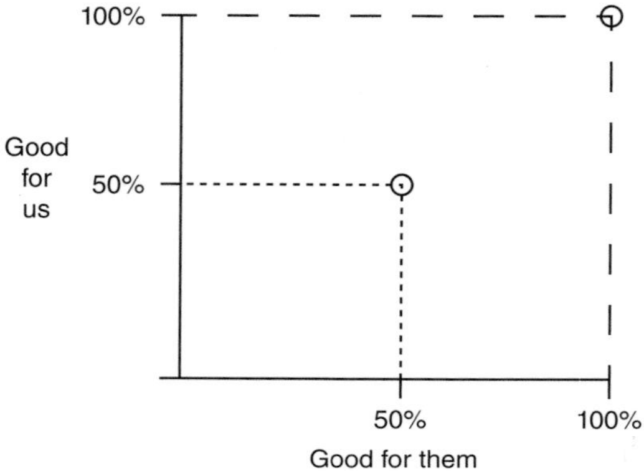

Figure 1.4 Creating value by aligning compatible issues

By exchanging information, the parties can find out, in Parker Follett's words, "what they really want." This is called the parties' "interests." The challenge is to discover the interests behind the parties' demands of each other (called their "positions"). Taking a position means demanding a specific distribution of resources or risks. When I am offering something for sale, the price I demand is my position. When I sue my neighbor, what I demand from the defendant is a position. The position spells out what the party wants: "I want the orange!" versus "No, I want it!" The position does not answer the question why that demand is made: "What I really want is to drink the juice" versus "I just need the rind for making cookies." In order to create value, the parties must move from positions to interests.

Perhaps you are skeptical about the applicability of this idea to the business world. Library windows and orange cookies are all very well, you might say, but how realistic is that? I am glad you ask. Experience shows that compatible interests can be found in all sorts of negotiations. Just consider the buying and selling of a company. The acquirer might want to let go of the staff upon acquisition (to create "synergies"). And the seller perhaps does not care what happens after the sale. Or perhaps the opposite is true: The seller might feel loyal to "their" people and want to protect them by seeking job guarantees from the buyer. And the seller might meet a buyer who is eager to give such a guarantee for fear of losing unique know-how. In both scenarios, the interests of the parties are compatible. If we mix the scenarios, this is not the case. It is not possible to determine the parties' interests categorically and a priori. For value to be created, the parties need to communicate.

So, finding compatible issues requires a crucial step: To identify the true interests behind the positions. With the children allocating the orange rind and the orange juice (rather than splitting it in two), they are really giving each other a pie that only one of them wants.

A Caveat This brings us to an important caveat: Even when interests are perfectly aligned, the creation of value does not necessarily follow. One party will be the first to realize that there are two pies on the table. They might be tempted to have a bite of the other one too. I might not want the peel, but perhaps I can extract a concession by giving it up. Maybe I can get all the orange juice – *and* an apple! The buyer of the company might promise a job guarantee only in return for a lower price. If successful, they will appropriate even more value. Of course, the other side might resent making that concession. Then the parties might not be able to realize an agreement that would have been in their best interest. Usually, not all issues are completely compatible, especially in business transactions. That is the very rationale of markets. And it makes negotiating more challenging. Often, both sides want the juice!

1.2.2 A Trade-Off on Different Preferences

The parties can also have a trade-off on different preferences. This is why they came together in the first place: They do not want exactly the same thing. Parties exchange goods and services for money (in the planned part of the contract), and they allocate risks and costs (in the unplanned part of the contract). And these issues often do not hold the same value for both. A hiring company does not want to shell out a sign-on bonus that would allow the new recruit to buy a car, but giving them one from the company car pool might achieve the same benefit for them at a lower cost.

You might be familiar with the traditional Chinese "36 Stratagems." Developed for warfare, they were soon found to be generally useful in politics and social life. One of them can be translated as "Tossing out a brick to obtain a jade gem." That's the same concept as trading off.[106]

Or, remember the poor man and the rich man. When we looked at the distribution of value, we saw that the parties have different utility functions for their outcomes. This is useful here. We can also apply this thought to the world of value creation. As Lax and Sebenius point out, there are a host of differences that can be used for trade-offs: Differences in risk tolerance (as in payment guarantees), time preferences (as in payment plans), capabilities (as in companies joining forces in an alliance), and costs (as in providing a company car instead of cash to the new recruit).

Let's plot that in our utility matrix. Below complete compatibility, we might find an area where trade-offs are possible. In homage to Fisher and Ury, let's call it "ZOPTO": zone of possible trade-off.

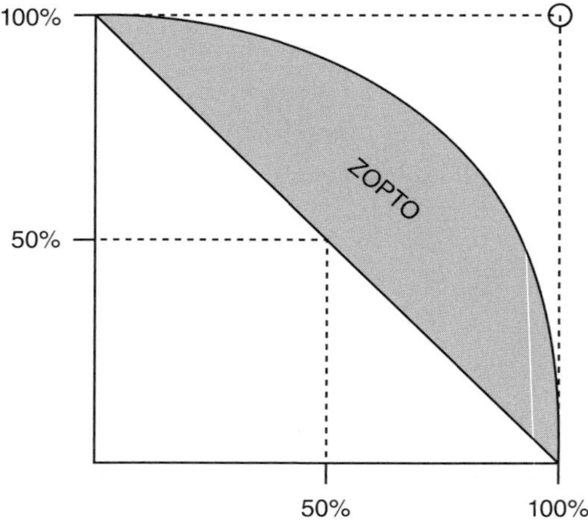

Figure 1.5 The ZOPTO

The prototypical compromise between two positions is to "meet half way." Whether or not a trade-off can actually offer both sides a better outcome than simply splitting both issues down the middle, depends on the actual preferences of the parties. If so, then a ZOPTO exists – a zone within which agreements are better for both sides than a mere 50:50 compromise.

The geometry of every transaction is different, but every transaction has a pareto optimal curve – a line of all possible outcomes that cannot be improved upon without making at least one side worse off. Creating value is the quest for a pareto optimal outcome. The parties can determine where the curve is only by exchanging information. There is no law of nature that dictates the pareto optimal curve to be beyond the compromise point. This means that before the information exchange happens, there is no way of knowing whether or not you would be better off by trying to cooperate or by simply distributing value.

If a ZOPTO does exist, the parties can trade on their differences. Rather than distributing issues sequentially, they can combine them intelligently: Giving something of relatively little value in exchange for something that is more valuable. The brick for the jade stone. This is called "log-rolling," when the preferences of the other side are exactly the other way around. (If no ZOPTO exists, combining two issues does not offer any advantage over distributing them sequentially.)

Even Animals Log-Roll Log-rolling consists of the combination of two activities in one act. They are bound together by an "if – then" mechanism: "If you compromise on issue X, then I will compromise on issue Y." The opportunity for log-rolling can hence be encountered by asking "What if" questions: "What if I compromised on issue Y, would you compromise on issue X?" The subsequent combination of issues requires deliberate effort. Neither finding nor combining different priorities happens automatically in a negotiation. Log-rolling has to be pursued actively and deliberately. To bundle together two future activities (one where the favor is received and one where it is returned) might require a human mind. But the ability to return a favor clearly does not. Recent research with working dogs (Swiss Army Belgian Shepherds) spectacularly revealed that animals reciprocated altruistic help that involved a different task. The dogs were enclosed in separate adjacent kennels. One of the dogs (the "focal dog") received (or not) a food donation from their neighbor who either pulled a rope or pushed a lever. It did not receive a donation when the neighboring dog had not learned how to activate the mechanisms. (In this case, it received the food directly from the experimenter.) The activating dog itself did not receive any food. The next day, the roles were reversed, and the mechanism altered. Now the focal dog could donate food to its neighbor. The researchers found that focal dogs did so significantly more often for neighbors that had helped them the previous day. The animals returned the favor with a different favor. I have met allegedly human negotiators who have yet to master this skill.[107]

The Strange Case of the Broken Turbine So, we have to identify opportunities for log-rolling – and then agree on doing so. These opportunities exist more often than we think. One of the most memorable experiences I have had in negotiating long-term service contracts for large gas turbines revealed an unexpected opportunity for log-rolling. When the customer builds a power plant and has it equipped with gas turbines, their costs and revenues swing dramatically over time. They have to spend hundreds of millions of dollars or euros before the plant starts producing electricity. Once it does, however, the running maintenance and service costs are relatively small when compared to the generated revenues. Many owners purchase a long-term service and maintenance contract from the original equipment manufacturer (OEM) of the turbine over the useful life of the machine, guaranteeing them recurrent inspections and spare-part deliveries at attractive prices. On the other hand, they usually have a very long power-purchase agreement which guarantees them a certain level of income. All this makes their income rather predictable. Once break-even is achieved, they can count on a handsome profit for every hour of electricity production. The worst-case scenario that they fear is that the turbine fails and stops producing electricity. This would not only deprive them of their income but also expose them to harsh penalties and liabilities vis-à-vis their customers.

Because of the layout of a gas turbine, there is one scenario that makes complete shut-down of the plant possible even in the case of a relatively small material failure. As you might know, gas turbines basically generate electricity through three main sections: compressor, combustion chamber, and turbine itself. The compressor feeds pressurized air into the combustion chamber at speeds of hundreds of miles per hour. There the air mixes with the fuel that is also injected in a steady stream. At temperatures beyond 2000° F, the mixture is burned, producing a gas stream that expands through the turbine. The gas turbine itself is an intricate array of alternate stationary and rotating aerofoil-section blades. As hot combustion gas expands through it, it spins the rotating blades. The rotating blades thus perform a dual function: they drive the compressor to draw more pressurized air into the combustion chamber, and they spin the generator to produce electricity.[108]

This means that the blades constantly operate in an environment way beyond their own melting point. It is made possible by a high-tech mix of material and air ventilation systems. Now, what both the OEM and the owner of the power plant fear is for one of these blades to break due to wear and tear. If that happens, the blade is sucked along with the combustion stream, rotating through the turbine and destroying all the blades in its way. Hence a simple defect of one part with relatively little replacement cost can lead to financial damage in the many millions of dollars. In other words, the risk for the buyer of the gas turbine is huge. This, of course, is exactly the reason why the OEM cannot carry it. We have seen this before. Good accounting standards would require the seller to form contingencies for this risk. Even though the risk is small, the contingencies would be substantial – due to the potentially devastating consequential and financial damages. In order to remain profitable, the seller would have to increase the price substantially. This, in turn, would usually price them out of the market. Hence OEMs typically see no other option but to completely exclude any liability for any such damages. This exclusion has to extend even to warranty cases, i.e. cases that lie within the sole responsibility of the supplier. What all this means is that the contractual warranty clauses offered by the OEM typically include a provision that says, effectively: "If there is a warranty defect in one of our blades that destroys the entire turbine and brings you close to bankruptcy in the process, we will certainly give you a crisp new blade. Free of charge. Expect no less!"

It will not surprise you that this clause meets little enthusiasm on the part of the customer. What it does generate, typically, is excitement. "You must be joking. The entire problem arises *because* you have delivered crap – and you want us to relieve you of your responsibility in advance?!" What typically follows is not good-natured brainstorming for a mutually beneficial outcome. Both sides fight tooth and nail to limit their exposure to this very substantial risk. So why am I telling you this? Is that not another example of the dynamics we explored in the distribution of value? Yes, it is. But it can also serve as an example of finding value creation in very unexpected places. The negotiation where I experienced this started off as usual. Opposing counsel went through the contract draft we had provided, clause by clause. He read them out aloud, taking issue with them one by one. He was clearly paid by the hour. When he came to the limitation of liability, he paused. Silence. I mentally picked up my shield, readying myself for the usual outburst of indignation that I knew (and understood) all too well. "We cannot accept this," he said. I sighed, and asked (not entirely sincerely), "Why not?"

To our tremendous surprise, the answer was: "Well, I can accept your exclusion of liability for downstream and consequential damages. We will just buy insurance for that. But our insurance company must then be able to verify that the cause is, in fact, a warranty defect! What we need is an audit right for our insurance company. And your clause does not include that." We were happy to accommodate this request. A give-and-take was found in the most unlikely of places. Even though we had not expected it, it turned out that a ZOPTA did exist.

Significance Beyond Business Log-rolling as a mechanism to create value is significant far beyond business transactions. We find it at the very heart of our democratic institutions and human progress. Two recent studies highlighted the crucial importance of trade-offs and consensus-building within as well as between countries. In *The Narrow Corridor*, Daron Acemoglu and James A. Robinson built on their earlier work, *Why Nations Fail*, to explore why nations also succeed. In their analysis of how liberty has come about in some countries, they are particularly intrigued by Western and Northern Europe, an area that was at best marginal at the times of the great empires. Late to the world stage, it experienced an unprecedented rise of liberty and spectacular technological and economic advances. It became one of only a few places that found the "narrow corridor" between too weak and too strong a state, begging the question of how it got there. What was its advantage?

> The answer to these questions lies in a unique series of historical events 1,500 years ago that created fortuitous balance between the powers of centrally authority and those of common men (not women, unfortunately).... The balance was a consequence of two things. First, the takeover of Europe at the end of the fifth century by democratically organized tribal societies centered on assemblies and norms of consensual decision making. Second, the legacy of critical elements of state institutions and political hierarchy absorbed from the Roman Empire and the Christian church.[109]

The authors think of those two elements as the two blades of a pair of scissors. While both were needed to put Europe on its path, it is only the former that interests us here. It refers to the assembly politics of the Germanic tribes as "a remarkably participatory form of government" and a direct heir to the consensual decision-making that Roman historian Tacitus described in Germania in 98 CE: "On matters of minor importance only the chiefs deliberate; on major affairs, the whole community." Later emperors, such as Charlemagne and his successors, "had to play by the rules of these assemblies, consult the wishes of a diverse cross section of (male) society, and secure a degree of consensus for their major decisions." A direct line runs from these assemblies (via the Magna Carta negotiations) to modern-day parliamentary institutions.[110]

Finding trade-offs and building consensus has played a similarly beneficial role between states. In *Upheaval*, Jared Diamond explored how mankind copes with crisis and change. He traced how six countries have survived "defining catastrophes" (from the Soviet invasion of Finland to Chile's Pinochet regime) to draw conclusions for some of the major crises underway today: Nuclear weapons, climate change, global resource depletion, and worldwide inequalities of living standards. These issues threaten not only individual nations but all of humankind. Diamond argues that we have three avenues to face these challenges. All, remarkably, are based on negotiation. They are agreements: between nations (such as the Paris Agreement of 2016 between the nations that account for 60 percent of worldwide emissions), by regional organizations (such as the EU), and by world institutions (such as the World Health Organization's campaign to eradicate smallpox in 1980). No single nation, it seems to me, will be able to resolve the crises that lie ahead. Nor will even the most powerful nation be able to force its will on everyone else. At the same time, the interests of individual states are far from compatible. So, to overcome these crises, politicians and diplomats the world over will have no choice but to log-roll their way to agreement.[111]

Let's look at how this was done in the past. This will clarify the nature of log-rolling, and it will prescribe ways to employ it in the future. Let's consider three key moments: (1) The Philadelphia Convention of 1787, that laid the foundation for the United States Constitution, (2) The Schuman Plan Conference of 1951 that led to the foundation of the European Community, and (3) The enlargement of the EU in 2004.

1.2.2.1 The Philadelphia Convention of 1787

In his fascinating book, *Democracy: A Case Study*, Harvard University historian David Moss describes pivotal moments in US history to demonstrate the power of productive tension. American democracy, in his analysis, has survived and thrived from one generation to the next on the basis not principally of harmony but of conflict, mediated by shared ideals. And he notes that democratic decision-making has always been rooted in disagreement and tensions. (We will see when we look at tactics that differences, rather than similarities, are what allow us to create value.)[112]

The central question of his book is what makes such conflict either constructive or destructive. His answer (even though he is not using our terminology): The ability of politicians to create value. And it all starts with the willingness of lawmakers to consider conflicting proposals nearly simultaneously. Moss identifies the Philadelphia Convention as a pivotal moment in history. This is where Benjamin Franklin warned against being overly assertive, as we heard earlier. The Convention apparently heeded his call. This is how Moss describes it (Don't be confused by his usage of the word "compromise." Just like Angela Merkel, as we will shortly see, he uses it to describe what we call "cooperation" in negotiation):

> Instead of meeting in the middle or splitting the difference two competing factions or even parties frequently both secured what they most wanted. It was a distinctive form of

> compromise, with the classic American example being the so-called Great Compromise, proposed by the illustrious Connecticut delegation at the Constitutional Convention in 1787. As the convention debated how Congress should be structured, delegates from large states insisted that representation ought to be proportional to population, whereas those from small states favoured equal representation by state, irrespective of population. Instead of meeting in the middle (for example, by adopting a proportional model weighted somewhat toward small states), delegates from both sides agreed to a two-part solution: proportional representation in the House and equal representation in the Senate. Each side, in other words, achieved its preferred option, but had to tolerate the other side also getting what it wanted. Such horse-trading could be explicit, as it was in the Great Compromise, or it could be implicit or even coincidental .... Either way, it was indicative of the productive tension that so often characterized American politics.[113]

1.2.2.2 The Schuman Plan Conference of 1951

Centuries later, on the other side of the Atlantic, a similarly ambitious institution was created – the EU. While seeking consensus in a participatory process may run extremely deep in Europe (as we just saw), so did the disposition to violently pursue interstate goals. Yet zero is the number of times that countries in Western Europe have fought interstate wars since the end of the Second World War. This might seem normal today. But it is truly astonishing if you consider that up until that point, European states had started around two new armed conflicts *per year* since the year 1400. The EU's founding fathers, too, aspired to providing a model of collaborative negotiations between (nation) states: "I was convinced that the union of Europe was not only important for the Europeans themselves: it was valuable as an example for others, and this was further reason for bringing it about," Jean Monnet asserted in his memoirs. He made these remarks at the conference at which the "Schuman Plan" (or "Schuman Declaration") was drafted, which French Foreign Minister Robert Schuman announced on May 9, 1950. The plan led to the creation of the "European Coal and Steel Community," which paved the way for the European Economic Community (and subsequently the EU). It is therefore regarded as a foundational document of European integration – and May 9 has been designated as "Europe Day" in its honor.[114]

Monnet left no doubt as to what would be required to succeed:

> "We are here," I said, "to undertake a common task – not to negotiate for our own national advantage, but to seek it in the advantage of all.... Only if we eliminate from our debates any particularist feelings shall we reach a solution. In so far as we, gathered here, can change our methods, the attitude of all Europeans will likewise gradually change."[115]

Master negotiator that he was, Monnet made use of some shameless framing tactics to reach his honorable goal: "I therefore asked that the word 'negotiations' should not be used to describe our meetings. Instead, for ourselves as well as for the public, they should be known as the 'Schuman Plan Conference.' It was on that same day, I think, that I first used the term 'European Community' to describe our objective." Whether or not it was Monnet who came up with the term, the European Community was born. It thrived and expanded, providing us with another historic moment of value creation.[116]

1.2.2.3 The Enlargement of the EU in 2004

In her analysis of the historical negotiations that led to the enlargement of the European Community (EC) and later the EU, Christine Schneider asserts that the undertaking was never particularly popular. Each wave of expansion has led to political tensions and conflict. Existing members fear that their membership privileges will diminish, and candidates are loath to concede the expected benefits of membership. The very first attempt at widening the EU culminated in the Community's very first crisis in 1963 when Charles de Gaulle, then President of France, rejected the British accession in a dramatic press conference at the Elysée Palace. In de Gaulle's view, Britain's conditions for joining would undermine French dominance in both Europe and the Common Agricultural Policies.[117]

Serious tensions arose again thirty-five years later with another EU enlargement – the accession of Central and Eastern European countries from the former Soviet bloc: Estonia, Latvia, Lithuania, Czech Republic, Slovakia, Poland, Hungary, and Slovenia joined in 2004, Romania and Bulgaria in 2007. A major concern of German and Austrian workers was that the mass influx of cheap unskilled labor from the East could cause major market disruptions:

> The German government, which faced elections at that time, responded to these fears and insisted that the migration problem would have to be solved before accession negotiations could proceed. Echoing domestic public debates and the opinion of major labor organizations, the government claimed that the EU could not cope with immigration any more. Consequently, the acceding states would have to be excluded from labor market integration until there was structural and economic evidence of declining migration pressure.[118]

Fearing large migration flows, the majority of the old Member States imposed transitional rules for the free movement of labor from the new Member States when they joined. Only three countries chose to open their labor markets from the date of the EU enlargement in May 2004: Sweden, Ireland, and the UK. The rest of the EU decided on restrictions on their employment and welfare systems to the new EU entrants for a five-year period (which could be prolonged for an additional two years in the EU Member States where "migration might threaten to cause serious disturbances on the labor market"). The decision of the UK Labour Government was largely uncontroversial and met with bipartisan support in Parliament at the time.

Migration from Eastern Europe would later play a central role in the lead-up to the Brexit referendum.[119]

As Schneider states, European enlargement has always succeeded despite the conflicts surrounding it. But why does the EU continue to admit new states even though current members might lose from their accession? Combining political logic with statistical and case study analyses, she argues that it is the result of how EU members and applicant states negotiate the distribution of enlargement benefits and costs. Schneider explains that EU enlargement happens despite distributional conflicts if the overall gains of enlargement are redistributed from the relative winners among existing members and applicants to the relative losers: "If the overall gains from enlargement are sufficiently great, a redistribution of these gains will compensate losers, making enlargement attractive for all states." The British public, voting in the 2016 Brexit referendum to leave the EU, of course decided that their gain no longer outweighed the cost of membership.[120]

This brings us to a sometimes overlooked but crucial point. Even when there is a ZOPTO, this does not mean that a competitive approach loses its appeal. As Neale and Lys make clear, the process of value creation can have a detrimental effect, leaving one party worse off than it would have been had less value been created. Even when an agreement within the ZOPTO is possible, we would still be better off by achieving one from our ZOOA (zone of our advantage). They, on the other hand, would be better off with an agreement within their ZOTA (zone of their advantage): see Figure 1.6.[121]

This mechanism is perhaps easiest to observe in companies which cooperate with each other in some areas while competing in others. This is typically the case when firms form strategic alliances or joint ventures (such as Star Alliance in the airline industry, or the joint development of commercial pick-up vans announced by Volkswagen and Ford in 2019). Strategic management has labeled this relationship

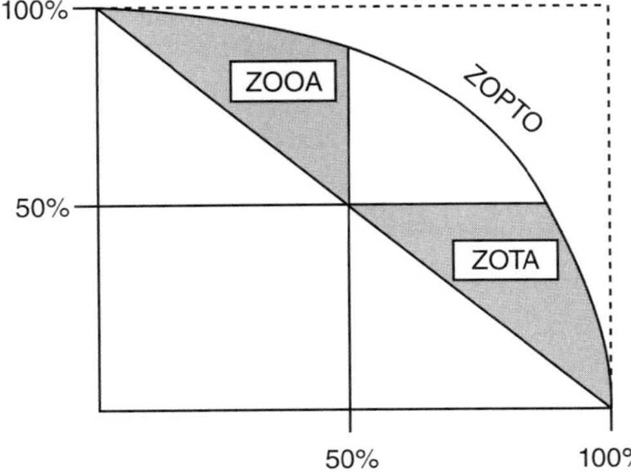

Figure 1.6 The ZOOA and the ZOTA

"co-opetition," and companies engaged in it face a magnified need to have a trade-off between value creation and value distribution.[122]

We will return to the study of co-opetition in a while; it is important here because it epitomizes a general problem: Even when we have an incentive to create value, we would still profit from (and have to defend ourselves from) distributive moves. To put it figuratively: Maximizing your slice of the pie might serve you better than maximizing the entire pie. And even if we both agree to stay clear of both ZOOA and ZOTA, we still would have to determine where exactly within the ZOPTO we meet.

1.2.3 Using Alternative Scenarios

The third and last possibility for creating value in a negotiation is uncovering the parties' different expectations of the future. This allows both sides to produce "contingent contracts" that include two alternative scenarios for the future. For instance, the production company of a television series might expect it to achieve a much larger market share than that expected by the television channel with which it is negotiating the sale of broadcasting rights. In such a case, the parties might include two alternative clauses in their contract.[123]

There is a base case scenario on which the parties unconditionally agree. And then there is the "contingent" clause which only kicks in if the alternative scenario were to materialize. The parties then agree how to address that scenario, based on the notion that only one of them anticipates it will become reality. In the television example, the base scenario determines the price in accordance with the market share (and therefore advertising revenues) that the television station expects for the future. In a second, contingent clause, the parties might agree on a somewhat higher price if the expectations of the seller materialize, in which case the buyer would generate higher revenues from the series. This solution gives both sides more of what they want. The seller can live with their expectations "only" being included in the contingent clause because they believe that the clause will come into force anyway. And the buyer can live with the contingent clause, which they do not expect to come into effect. But, if it should, they would be happy to comply with it because they would then be making more money than originally anticipated.

Contingent contracts can be found in many areas: In sports, where soccer clubs will receive extra cash after the transfer of a player who wins the championship with the new club; and in energy production, where utility companies might be willing to pay more if politically-determined public subsidies turn out to be larger than were originally anticipated. Contingent contracts are also common in venture capital. Investors can employ a "participating preferred" structure to recoup their money in a sale ahead of the other shareholders – as well as a share of the remaining cash. And a final example from the context of M&A: Contingent contracts are often used to protect the acquirer from overpaying. Part of the price is subject to an "earn-out" clause which promises the seller additional consideration if certain financial metrics – such as earnings or gross revenue milestones – are achieved in the future.[124]

Figuratively speaking, agreeing on a contingent contract is like dividing an extra pie that might or might not materialize in the future. (Because only one of the two scenarios will, in fact, become reality, it can also be argued that a contingent agreement does not actually create value.)

1.2.4 Joint Benefit

Which of the three types of value creation, if any, is possible can only be determined by negotiation. That, after all, is its purpose: To decide if and how resources and risks can be allocated, disputes be resolved, or work be jointly undertaken.

This is the side of the Yin & Yang that features prominently in Angela Merkel's negotiation philosophy. As I have already mentioned, to me she personifies one of the two sides of negotiation, with the other side personified by US President Donald Trump. We have already observed what Trump sees as the purpose and nature of negotiation. Let's now hear what she has to say. Merkel, like her German post-war predecessors, has clearly adopted Henry Kissinger's dictum that "a nation situated in the centre of Europe cannot find security save in a world in which negotiations is the normal pattern of relation."[125]

At another press conference with Donald Trump, Merkel laid out her philosophy: "I would say that the success of Germany in the economic area, but also on security and peace – that the success of Germans has always been one where the German success is one side of the coin, and the other side of the coin has been European unity and European integration. That's something of which I'm deeply convinced."[126]

Regarding trade between the two countries, she said:

> I'm here as Chancellor of the Federal Republic of Germany. I represent German interests. I speak with the President of the United States, who stands up for, as is right, American interests. That is our task, respectively.. . . We held a conversation where we were trying to address also those areas where we disagree, but to try to bring people together, try to show what is our vantage point, what is the American vantage point, and then try to find a compromise which is good for both sides.. . . That's the purpose of concluding agreements – that both sides win. And that is the sort of spirit, I think, in which we ought to be guided in negotiating any agreement between the United States of America and the EU.[127]

Note that the word "compromise" in general use has a very broad meaning. The Cambridge Dictionary defines it as "an agreement in an argument in which the people involved reduce their demands or change their opinion in order to agree." If we take a closer look at how that reduction of demands can happen, we find two familiar tactics: It can mean the distribution of value by meeting in the middle (if only one issue is on the table). And it can mean creating value by trading off on different interests. The "Great Compromise" is, as we saw, one of the most important trade-offs in American history. (When negotiation scholars use the word "compromise" in a technical sense, they mean only the former. They prefer to call the latter "cooperation.") So, what is meant depends on the context. This is also true in German, the native language of Angela Merkel, in which she delivered her comments. When we look at the entire quote, her meaning is clear: She aims to find a trade-off that is in the interests of both sides. At the 2019 Munich Security Conference, Merkel elaborated on her view in a speech addressing numerous heads of state and a large US delegation that included the US Vice President and the Speaker of the House of Representatives. In making the case for international cooperation, she acknowledged the weakness of her country to achieve good negotiation results by distributing value:

> Ladies and gentlemen, all these issues [of the international order] that are coming at us like puzzle pieces and which are too many for me to refer to here, are ultimately the expression of a fundamental question. Because we are noticing how great the pressure is on our traditional and, to us, familiar order, this raises the question of whether we are going to break up into a lot of individual puzzle pieces and think that each of us can best solve the problem single-handedly. As German Chancellor, I can only respond: if so, our chances are poor. For the United States of America has so much more economic clout and the dollar as a currency is so much stronger, that I can only say: obviously it holds the better hand. China, with more than 1.3 billion people, is so much larger. We can be as hard-working, as impressive, as super as we like – but with a population of 80 million we won't be able to keep up if China decides that it no longer wants to maintain good relations with Germany. That's how it will be all over the world.
>
> So the one big question is this: Are we going to stay with the principle of multilateralism, which was the lesson we learned from the Second World War and the National Socialism caused by Germany, even when multilateralism is not always fun, but often difficult, slow, complicated? I am firmly convinced that it is better to put ourselves in one another's shoes, to look beyond our own interests and to see whether we can achieve win–win solutions together rather than to think we can solve everything ourselves.
>
> That is why, ladies and gentlemen, I was so pleased yesterday evening when I was preparing my speech and read a quotation by Lindsey Graham, who declared yesterday evening: "Multilateralism may be complicated, but it's better than staying at home alone." I think that is the right response to the motto of this conference "The Great Puzzle: Who Will Pick Up the Pieces?": Only all of us together.[128]

Let's revisit Aristotle before we turn to the tactics of value creation. Drawing from the logical system that he developed, we find that, in value creation, there may be both complementary issues and contraries. In contrast to the distribution of value, the notions that "We have got the best possible deal" and "They have got the best possible deal" can both be true. And when they are not, the two notions are not

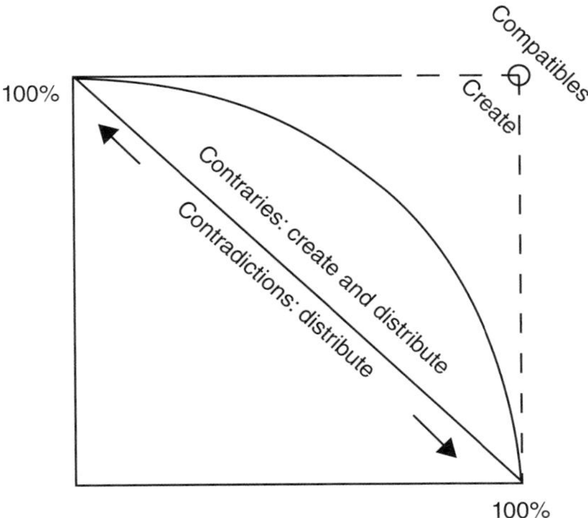

Figure 1.7 Aristotle's logic in the creation and distribution of value

contradictions, but mere "contraries": see Figure 1.7. Aristotle points toward color and temperature: "It was not every subject that *may* be receptive of black and of white that must, therefore, *be* black or *be* white. And the same, with coldness and heat. That is, something or other intermediate between black and white may be present, between hot and cold and the like." Intermediaries between the two are possible, so that each can be true to some extent. In a negotiation we may not both gain all we want, but we might gain most of it.[129]

1.2.5 The Six Tactics of Value Creation

To create value, negotiators have to work together ("co-operate") to exchange information. How information is exchanged differs across the world. In Western countries, the approach is linear. Jeanne Brett calls it "Q + A" for asking questions and answering them. In light of the value distribution tactics that we have already seen (and as we will see in more detail when we look at the dilemma), this tactic requires trust. But it is quite straightforward: After some preparation, ask, tell, build trust, and problem-solve (but don't overdo it). In some East Asian countries, negotiators have developed a different approach that requires less trust. Experiments by Brett and her colleagues show that Japanese negotiators use different tactics to reach the same level of insight: They treat multiple issues holistically and use the pattern of offers, counteroffers, and substantiation to infer information about each other's priorities. As a result, they create as much value as their American counterparts who use the direct Q + A approach (and much more than negotiators who pursue only competitive tactics).[130]

These findings tie in with the broader observation of recent decades that there are cultural differences in perception and judgment. East Asians generally attend to the context more than do Westerners, and Westerners pay more attention to focal objects. For instance, Westerners attend more to what is in the foreground of a photograph, whereas East Asians attend more to the entire scenery.[131]

Indeed, researchers found that the eye movement of Americans and Chinese differ when they observe a picture. As a result, context is more extensively processed by Asians, while some important information might be lost on Westerners. When confronted with incongruent images (e.g. of a cow standing in an elevator lobby), Chinese participants were significantly more likely to process this information than Americans, as evidenced by fMRI scans.[132]

There might be very practical consequences of these differences. A recent study found that Koreans make significantly better judgments of the size of a room than their German counterparts. The researchers argue that making accurate assessments requires the taking in of information relating to all the dimensions of the room – and the Koreans looked around much more than did the Germans.[133]

I will focus on the Western tactics of cooperating through Q + A. Why? First, because most of the empirical research that we rely on to understand value creation has been conducted in the West. But more importantly, the Western approach is my own – the story of this book is determined by it. I am not capable of explaining the world from a point of view other than my own. There are principally six tactics of value creation that are used in the West. We can also call them "cooperative" tactics, because they only work if the parties engage in them together.

The tactics shown in Table 1.4 have to be used together with the six distributive tactics shown in Table 1.1, because the pie must not only be expanded, but also captured.

Table 1.4 The six (Western) tactics of value creation

1	Identify and frame all issues
2	Acknowledge the other side
3	Ask
4	Tell and build trust
5	Generate solutions and problem-solve
6	Don't overdo it

1.2.5.1 Identify and Frame All Issues

It can be difficult to negotiate about only very few issues: Consider a police negotiator who is entrusted with the life of a hostage. But often transactions have many issues. Only if they are identified can they be put on the table. Consider another example: In June 2015, Siemens AG was awarded a record energy order by Egypt with the aim of boosting the country's power generation by 50 percent. The transaction, worth €8 billion, included high-efficiency natural gas-fired power plants and wind power installations. The projects would add an additional 16.4 gigawatts (GW) to Egypt's national grid in an effort to support the country's rapid economic development and meet the growing population's demand for power. The signing ceremony in Berlin was witnessed by Egyptian President Abdel Fattah al-Sisi and German Vice Chancellor Sigmar Gabriel. Siemens committed to supplying on a turnkey basis three natural gas-fired combined cycle power plants, each with a capacity of 4.8GW, for a total combined capacity of 14.4GW together with local Egyptian partners Elsewedy Electric and Orascom Construction. The company also promised to deliver up to twelve wind farms in the Gulf of Suez and West Nile areas, comprising around 600 wind turbines and an installed capacity of 2GW. Significantly, it would also build a rotor blade manufacturing facility in Egypt's Ain Soukhna region, thus also providing training and employment for up to 1,000 people.

The transaction expanded on the memorandums of understanding (MoUs) announced at the Egypt Economic Development Conference held in Sharm El Sheik in March 2015. Joe Kaeser, President and CEO of Siemens AG, who had negotiated the MoU with the Egyptian President, said: "The Egyptian people can count on Siemens. This was true more than 150 years ago when Siemens first started working in Egypt, and it remains our commitment today at this historic signing."[134]

A few weeks later, Kaeser had this to say about the negotiations in an interview with the Bavarian Broadcasting Corporation:

Interviewer: Mr. Kaeser, you have won the largest order in the history of Siemens in Egypt.... This came as a surprise. Can you tell us how you accomplished it?

Kaeser: Well, it was very interesting. It was the first time in my life that I directly negotiated with a head of state. It was a first for me but the Egyptian president takes many things into his hands, not only government business. We were in Sharm El Sheik, a business summit not unlike Davos, for the Middle East. And I had offered the President our help in building up his country. Ninety million people, who do not really have very much in the way of electricity generation capabilities or infrastructure. I offered a package worth €2.5 bn.

He says "Yes, yes. Yes, yes. But it cannot cost more than €2 bn." And I thought: "Well, €500 m difference is quite a lot." So, I said: "What if we build three gas turbines? Then the order value would be around €6 bn and we could consider a discount of perhaps €300 m." But, no, he insisted on a €500 million discount.

Well, I replied: "With three power plants, a discount of €500 m is simply not possible. But – you should really also buy some wind parks from us, you can't just buy gas turbines. A modern country also needs

> renewable energy solutions. What about us building a factory for you in Egypt? We'll train young people, give them a professional education. Add €2 bn for 2 gigawatts, and then I can give you the discount of €500 m." And this is essentially what happened.[135]

To identify the issues that are important to both sides, you can use Jeanne Brett's prep sheet again, adding interests, priorities, and framing to it: see Table 1.5.[136]

Importantly, the document needs to be modified as you glean more information in the course of discussions. We may only come to understand our own interests through discussions with the other side. And, as we will see in the next chapter, we cannot play the game without changing it. Perhaps most captivating, playing the game changes us too. For instance, our expectation of what is fair might be influenced by the role we play in the transactions, and our feelings toward the other side might vary with the role of the other side. This is why negotiation ought to be seen as a quintessentially transformative experience. This of course makes it very difficult to look back and determine whether what we wanted a priori has been reached. You can make it easier for your future self by using the preparation sheet and keeping a log of your moves.

Table 1.5 Jeanne Brett's negotiation planning document (part 2)

	We	They
Issue 1	Our BATNA & RP	Their RP (our target)
	1. Offer	Their BATNA
	Priority	
	Underlying interest	
	Framing	
		Priority
		Underlying interest
Issue 2	Our BATNA & RP	Their RP (our target)
	1. Offer	Their BATNA
	Priority	
	Underlying interest	
	Framing	
		Priority
		Underlying interest

The negotiator's choice of how to describe the situation influences the subsequent process. Framing orientates the parties, encourages them to look at the situation from a specific point of view, and can therefore influence how they choose to behave. Mr. Kaeser framed the transaction not as the mere buying and selling of commercial goods, but as modernizing a country and providing education for its youth.[137]

Experiments show that, depending on the frame that is offered, individuals behave differently in situations that are otherwise identical. In a seminal experiment, Morton Deutsch demonstrated that individual choices in a prisoner's dilemma depends on whether they are induced to feel cooperative or individualistic. We will take a detailed look at the prisoner's dilemma in the next chapter (section 2.1.3.1) because it has much in common with the dilemma that negotiators face. Deutsch's early insights are therefore just as valuable for our context. These were his instructions (which sound rather loaded today):

> In the cooperative condition, the beginning of the instruction was: "Before you start playing the game, let me emphasize that in playing the game you should consider yourself to be partners. You're interested in your partner's welfare as well as in your own." In the individualistic condition, the beginning of the instruction instead was: "Before you start playing the game, let me emphasize that in playing the game your only motivation should be to win as much money as you can for yourself. You have no interest whatsoever in whether the other person wins or loses or in how much he wins or loses."[138]

This effect has been demonstrated many times since, even when the framing is more subtle. For instance, when other individuals were asked to play a prisoner's dilemma game, their decisions were influenced by the name assigned to the game! Remember Jean Monnet's ingenious invention of the term "European Community?" Later research confirms the power of emphasizing joint, as opposed to individual, gains. Individuals playing prisoner's dilemma games under the headline the "Community Game" were found to cooperate much more than individuals who played the same game under the name of "the Wall Street Game." Similar results have been shown when the name of the game was "stock market game" or "community game," and with the instructions for the players being otherwise neutral. It is safe to say that people cooperate more when the name of the game emphasizes the community rather than the individual's interest.[139]

In order for the parties to overcome a purely distributive mindset, we should choose and establish the proper mental frame. We can, for instance, emphasize the "common road" that the parties have already traveled together, the interests they share, and the merits and advantages of their relationship. An experiment by Solomon Asch was described by Daniel Kahneman as "an enduring classic of psychology." People were asked to form impressions and write brief characterizations of the person to whom a short list of trait adjectives applied. For instance, Asch presented descriptions of two people, Alan and Ben, and asked for comments on their personality. What do you think?[140]

Alan: intelligent, industrious, impulsive, critical, stubborn, envious
Ben: envious, stubborn, critical, impulsive, industrious, intelligent

Most people view Alan much more favorably than Ben. This tells us that the initial traits in the list change the very meaning of the traits that appear later.

1.2.5.2 Acknowledge the Other Side

The second tactic is to acknowledge the other side. Taylor Swift's negotiation with Apple Inc. provides an impressive case in point. Apple Inc. had just announced plans to step into the market for streaming audio. In advance of the upcoming release of Apple Music, it had negotiated countless agreements with musicians and studios. The subscription service synchronizes streaming music and radio to a host of programs and devices marketed by the $750 billion Palo Alto company. Buried in the fine print, however, Apple determined that musicians would not be paid for any music streamed during the first three months after the debut. In an online letter entitled "To Apple, Love Taylor," Swift took the company to task. With 59.3 million Twitter followers and over 40 million album sales, Swift called out Apple for taking money away from upstart musicians and hard-working producers. Acknowledging Apple as one of "my best partners in selling music," the musician expressed disbelief at the company's "shocking" policy. Swift explained that she would withhold her multi-platinum album *1989* from Apple Music in return.[141]

> "To Apple, Love Taylor"
>
> I write this to explain why I'll be holding back my album, *1989*, from the new streaming service, Apple Music. I feel this deserves an explanation because Apple has been and will continue to be one of my best partners in selling music and creating ways for me to connect with my fans. I respect the company and the truly ingenious minds that have created a legacy based on innovation and pushing the right boundaries.
>
> I'm sure you are aware that Apple Music will be offering a free 3-month trial to anyone who signs up for the service. I'm not sure you know that Apple Music will not be paying writers, producers, or artists for those three months. I find it to be shocking, disappointing, and completely unlike this historically progressive and generous company. This is not about me. Thankfully I am on my fifth album and can support myself, my band, crew, and entire management team by playing live shows. This is about the new artist or band that has just released their first single and will not be paid for its success. This is about the young songwriter who just got his or her first cut and thought that the royalties from that would get them out of debt. This is about the producer who works tirelessly to innovate and create, just like the innovators and creators at Apple are pioneering in their field . . . but will not get paid for a quarter of a year's worth of plays on his or her songs.

> These are not the complaints of a spoiled, petulant child. These are the echoed sentiments of every artist, writer and producer in my social circles who are afraid to speak up publicly because we admire and respect Apple so much. We simply do not respect this particular call. I realize that Apple is working towards a goal of paid streaming. I think that is beautiful progress. We know how astronomically successful Apple has been and we know that this incredible company has the money to pay artists, writers and producers for the 3-month trial period . . . even if it is free for the fans trying it out.
>
> Three months is a long time to go unpaid, and it is unfair to ask anyone to work for nothing. I say this with love, reverence, and admiration for everything else Apple has done. I hope that soon I can join them in the progression towards a streaming model that seems fair to those who create this music. I think this could be the platform that gets it right.
>
> But I say to Apple with all due respect, it's not too late to change this policy and change the minds of those in the music industry who will be deeply and gravely affected by this. We don't ask you for free iPhones. Please don't ask us to provide you with our music for no compensation.
>
> Taylor.[142]

This is what she received in response: In less than twenty-four hours, Apple Vice President Eddie Cue reversed the company's policy, tweeting: "We hear you @taylorswift13 and indie artists. Love, Apple."

Publishing the letter was a shrewd move in a negotiation between the artist and the technology company – but in a negotiation that did not take place face to face. According to reports, Apple Vice President Eddie Cue and Taylor Swift did not personally meet during the twenty-four hours that the negotiation lasted; they did not even talk on the phone. The case thus serves as a reminder that a negotiation does not have to take place with everybody sitting around a table, or even with everyone in the same room. In fact, much of Taylor Swift's success stems precisely from the fact that the negotiation did not take place behind closed doors but in front of an audience of millions.

The case also offers a splendid example of a situation in which it pays to reveal one's BATNA to the other side. Swift mentions her BATNA – touring, playing music, and recording without an agreement with Apple – thereby indicating to Apple that she is not reliant on their terms of agreement and cleverly focuses attention on one of her interests: Independent artists.

Using Positive Emotions Taylor Swift used her acknowledgment of the other side to drive a hard bargain and invited Apple to think of better ways to cooperate with the artist in the future. And it raised a larger issue: Our emotions play an important role in establishing a trusting, cooperative relationship with the other side. When we meet other people, we connect with them mentally and even physically. Neuroscientists can uncover more of what happens in our brains when we communicate with others. In their fascinating book, *Beyond Reason: Using Emotions as you Negotiate*,

Harvard's Roger Fisher and Daniel Shapiro have identified five core concerns that should be acknowledged in order to generate positive emotions. Taylor Swift's letter provides a textbook example of how this can be done in practice. The five core concerns are appreciation, affiliation, autonomy, status, and role. Fisher and Shapiro argue that when they are addressed, adequately strong negative emotions are minimized and positive emotions fostered. Table 1.6 shows Fisher and Shapiro's five core concerns and what happens when they are met (or ignored).[143]

Table 1.6 Fisher and Shapiro's five core concerns

Core concerns	When the concern is ignored ...	When the concern is met ...
Appreciation	Your thoughts, feelings, or actions are devalued.	Your thoughts, feelings, and actions are acknowledged as having merit.
Affiliation	You are treated as an adversary and kept at a distance.	You are treated as a colleague.
Autonomy	Your freedom to make decisions is impinged upon.	Others respect your freedom to decide important matters.
Status	Your relative standing is treated as inferior to that of others.	Your standing, where deserved, is given full recognition.
Role	Your current role and its activities are not personally fulfilling.	You so define your role and its activities that you find them fulfilling.

The central premise put forward by Fisher and Shapiro is that these five core concerns motivate people in a negotiation; if both sides feel their concerns are met, the relationship will be enhanced and the negotiation outcome improved. As a negotiator attempting to create a positive negotiation environment, we want to be respectful and appreciative of the other party's ideas, interests, thoughts, and behavior. We also want to be respectful of their autonomy – including the ability to make their own decisions. Looking at Taylor Swift's letter, it becomes apparent that she has addressed every single one of these concerns. She has done so in no uncertain terms – and some of them multiple times.

Acknowledging the concerns of the other side is a great move to create value. In this example, addressing the emotional concerns of the recipients at Apple Inc. *also* provides a powerful canvas for Swift's uncompromising position on the issue (I am holding back my new album until you meet my demand; I have an excellent BATNA and do not need to work with you; I actually speak for other artists too; and I have millions of fans who are watching this). The letter therefore offers a case in point for what we are about to study in more detail: the paradoxical nature of the negotiation task that requires *both* the creation and distribution of value.

Table 1.7 Fisher and Shapiro's five core concerns in Taylor Swift's letter to Apple

Core concerns	When the concern is met ...	... and how it is met in Taylor Swift's letter
Appreciation	Your thoughts, feelings, and actions are acknowledged as having merit.	"who works tirelessly to innovate and create, just like the innovators and creators at Apple are pioneering in their field."
Affiliation	You are treated as a colleague.	"Apple has been and will continue to be one of my best partners in selling music and creating ways for me to connect with my fans." "we admire and respect Apple so much."
Autonomy	Others respect your freedom to decide important matters.	"I realize that Apple is working towards a goal of paid streaming." "I think that is beautiful progress." "But I say to Apple with all due respect, it's not too late to change this policy."'
Status	Your standing, where deserved, is given full recognition.	"We know how astronomically successful Apple has been." "this historically progressive and generous company."
Role	You so define your role and list activities that you find them fulfilling.	"I hope that soon I can join them in the progression towards a streaming model."

Finally, I would like to point out a phenomenon to which we will return. It is true that approaching the other side in a positive and acknowledging manner might lead them to reciprocate in kind. Our emotions will often provoke similar responses in others. But this is not always the case. In fact, the opposite can happen. In some situations, we encounter an effect that has been labeled "counterempathy": Seeing the other side happy makes us unhappy, and the other way around. The Germans have a word for it, of course. You probably know it (*Schadenfreude*), just as you probably know which situations we are talking about (win–lose).[144]

1.2.5.3 Ask

Epictetus is said to have remarked that nature has given us one tongue but two ears, so that we may hear twice as much as we speak. Log-rolling requires the parties to simultaneously consider at least two different issues. In doing so, it can be advantageous for the parties to focus on different issues. Recent research indicates that it is beneficial for the parties not to focus on the same resource. Focusing on *different* issues instead can help us to realize trade-offs across resource dimensions, resulting in lower impasses.[145]

Get Inside Their Head, not Their Heart In exploring what the other side truly wants, it is important to engage in perspective-taking. Adam Galinsky and his colleagues have explored the two related yet distinct social competencies. They found that perspective-taking (the cognitive capacity to consider the world from another individual's viewpoint) and empathy (the ability to connect emotionally with another individual) led to different outcomes in negotiations. Perspective-taking increased individuals' ability to discover hidden agreements and to both create and claim resources at the bargaining table. Empathy, on the other hand, did not prove nearly as advantageous, and at times was detrimental to discovering a possible deal and achieving individual profit. They concluded that although empathy is an essential tool in many aspects of social life, perspective-taking appears to be a particularly critical ability in negotiations. It is better to "think for" than to "feel for" one's adversary. Or, put differently, to get inside their head rather than inside their heart.[146]

Permit Yourself to Understand the Other Side To get into somebody else's head is difficult. Just how much of an effort it requires from an experienced negotiator becomes apparent when we read the notes of Carl R. Rogers (1902–87), *On Becoming a Person*. American psychologist Rogers was among the founders of the client-centered approach to psychology and is widely considered to be one of the founders of psychotherapy research. It seems fair to say that he spent his life listening to others, and surpasses most of us in his ability to understand other people. Yet, this is how he describes one of his life's central learnings:

> *I have found it of enormous value when I can permit myself to understand another person.* The way in which I have worded this statement may seem strange to you. Is it necessary to *permit* oneself to understand another? I think that it is. Our first reaction to most of the statements we hear from other people is an immediate evaluation, or judgement, rather than an understanding of it. When someone expresses some feeling or attitude or belief, our tendency is, almost immediately, to feel "That's right"; or "That's stupid"; "That's unreasonable"; "That's incorrect"; "That's not nice." Very rarely do we permit ourselves to understand precisely what the meaning of his statement is to him. I believe this is because understanding is risky. If I let myself really understand another person, I might be changed by that understanding. And we all fear change. So as I say, it is not an easy thing to permit oneself to understand an individual, to enter thoroughly and completely and empathically into his frame of reference. It is also a rare thing.[147]

Take Your Time Understanding another individual is not only a rare thing, it also takes time. This is a key reason why an early offer won't benefit from information gleaned during the negotiating process. It can be premature. If you are the buyer, such information could, for example, alert you to other potentially beneficial items or terms that you might include in a proposal. Don't be tempted to close the deal too quickly, especially when the first acceptable proposal is on the table but little information has been exchanged. Spend more time finding a deal that is better for both sides. Signal that the proposal on the table is worth considering, but also state that it might be improved by learning more about your respective interests and concerns.[148]

1.2.5.4 Tell and Build Trust

Explain why you want to make a deal. Talk about your real interests, preferences, and constraints. Before you can tell them what it is that you want (and why they may want that too), you have to know what it is. This might sound trivial, but in most negotiations it is not. Very often it is only in discussions with the other side that we understand and flesh out our own interests. And it requires us to develop the ability to listen to ourselves. This can be tricky, especially when the negotiation is not merely about a business transaction. As Carl Rogers stated: "I find I am more effective when I can listen acceptantly to myself, and can be myself." Then build a bridge to what is important to the other side. Reveal any additional capabilities or resources you have that could be added to the deal.[149]

The basis of all such efforts is a trusting relationship between the parties. Having a reputation for honesty in business is crucial for sustained success. As an illustration: For Li Ka-Shing, the self-made Hong Kong magnate who was reported to have been the second richest man in Asia in 2017, this is key to building a good business relationship:

> The most important thing is to build the best reputation. Anytime I say "yes" to someone, it is a contract. I'll give you a case as an example. In 1956, when I was in the plastics business, my first order was for a three- to six-month production. I calculated a profit of 20%. My competitors were making 100% profit. A large U.S. competitor of my buyer approached me and offered to pay me an extra 30% profit for the merchandise my buyer had ordered. He said that with the extra profit, I could expand my factory.
>
> I said, "Look, I am also a businessman. I'll make a deal with you. I will start another factory in nine months' time, a much bigger one, and I will take your order. But this time, I have already promised this buyer, and I will finish the order for him, as I am his only supplier."
>
> I did not tell my buyer this story, but he learned it from elsewhere. So, when the buyer came to Hong Kong, he humored me and said that he thought I would be bankrupt by now. He said, "Why didn't you take the extra profit from my competitor?"
>
> I said, "I already promised you." He said, "But at least you could have told me and requested a price increase." I said, "Next time, I will increase the price."
>
> After that, we became even better friends, even after I quit the plastics business. Reputation is the key to success.[150]

Recent research confirms the advantages of enjoying a good reputation in negotiations. A negotiator that is perceived as honest is often offered bigger pieces of the pie. And the other side will respond more favorably to being offered a smaller piece of the pie. When we are perceived as honest, we are trusted more. Yet, when the other side realizes that we offer a much smaller piece than we could, that trust may suffer. This is another paradox: The more we are trusted, the easier it is to maximize our outcome at the expense of the other side – but the more we maximize our outcome, the less trust we will be given. To that end it can be beneficial to use objective criteria for the distribution of resources and risks. Fisher et al. suggest basing the envisioned agreement on criteria such as "market value," "precedent," "tradition," or "reciprocity": "At a minimum, objective criteria need to be independent of each side's will. Ideally, to assure a wise agreement, objective criteria should not only be independent of will but also both legitimate and practical."[151]

A word of caution is in order. In the absence of a third party (such as a mediator) introducing the objective criteria to each of the parties, a human tendency called "reactive devaluation" can make it very difficult for the parties to actually agree on such criteria. In its narrowest sense, reactive devaluation describes the natural tendency of a negotiator to devalue the other party's concession – simply on the basis that it comes from the other party. This same problem can occur when discussing objective standards: "Oh, if it comes from you, then it cannot possibly be objective!" or "I don't think this is fair, otherwise you would not have suggested it in the first place!" (We will come back to these biases when we discuss the challenge of thinking accurately about negotiations in Chapter 3.)[152]

1.2.5.5 Generate Solutions and Problem-Solve

A consistent finding over the years is that intelligence and creativity allow negotiators to generate joint problem solutions. Lax and Sebenius use the metaphor of a "drawing board," on which the successful negotiator "designs" the best deal:

> Smart people working at the drawing board can sometimes discovers hidden sources of economic and noneconomic value, then craft agreements – design deals – that unlock the value for the parties involved. For example: Is it *really* a pure price deal? Does some sort of trade between sides make sense and, if so, on what terms? Can we unbundle different aspects of what looks like a single issue and give to each side what it values most? Should it be a staged agreement, perhaps with contingencies and risk-sharing provisions? If there's a contract involved, should it be an unusual kind of contract – one with a more creative concept and structure than we've used before? One that meets ego needs as well as economic ones?"[153]

We have to try to give the other side the best deal, and to help them sell it to their back table (their boss, constituents, and other stakeholders). We want to attend closely to their needs and interests, and incorporate value-creating benefits for them. Susskind summarizes this approach under the headline: “Write their victory speech.” Make concessions to create goodwill and invite reciprocity: Improve the value of the deal to them. One method for generating alternatives, no matter how wild or impractical, is brainstorming.[154]

Michael Wheeler describes the creativity that enabled American diplomat Richard Holbrooke to mediate a truce between Serbs and Bosnians in the former Yugoslavia in the 1990s. Serbian gunmen were shooting at cars with Bosnian-issued license plates. The plates used Latin letters, while Serbs used the Cyrillic alphabet. There was no way that either side would buckle under and accept the other’s alphabet for its license plates. Holbrooke’s solution? Use only the ten letters that the languages have in common. Have a look at the following letters. The ones that are used in both alphabets are marked in bold. These are the ones that Holbrooke focused on:[155]

А Б **В** Г Д **Е** Ж З И **J** К Л **М** **Н** **О** П **Р** **С** **Т** У Ф Х Ц Ч Ш

Do Not Decide Sequentially Don’t deal with issues one after the other. If we negotiate only one issue at a time, we tend to agree on the easy issues and set aside the harder ones. Then, when we get to the end of the agenda, we might find ourselves with nothing left to trade. Nor should we engage purely in creating value and only thereafter attempt to distribute it. Negotiators can become greedy when they see how large the joint pie is. So we risk impasse and may fail to agree on mutually beneficial terms.[156]

Having said this, it is advisable to keep an eye on the number of issues that are on the table simultaneously. In theory, including as many issues as possible to be able to enlarge the pie would seem attractive. But, as Ingmar Geiger of Freie Universität Berlin and Joachim Hüffmeier of Dortmund University found, fewer issues lead to greater judgment accuracy about the counterpart’s priorities, to greater satisfaction, and to more efficient economic outcomes. Rather than “the more, the merrier”, “less is more” in negotiations.[157]

1.2.5.6 Don’t Overdo It

There are limits to cooperative bargaining: It is not always in our self-interest to engage in the tactics of cooperation. So, don’t overdo it. “Don’t be completely dove-like” is how Baltasar Gracián put it:[158]

> Let the craftiness of the snake alternate with the simplicity of the dove. There’s nothing easier than deceiving a good person. The person who never lies is more ready to believe, and one who never deceives is more trusting. Being deceived is not always the result of stupidity, but sometimes of simple goodness. Two types of people often foresee danger: those who have learnt from experience, very much to their own cost, and the astute, very much to the cost of others. Let shrewdness be as versed in suspicion as astuteness is in

> intrigue, and don't try to be so good that you create opportunities for someone else to be bad. Be a combination of the dove and the serpent; not a monster, but a prodigy.[159]

Modern research findings support this advice. Der Foo and his collaborators found that individuals with high levels of emotional intelligence often give their counterparts a positive experience. They cooperative to create value – but then leave most of it to the other side. In order to do well for themselves, these negotiators, like all of us, need to use the tactics of value distribution as well.[160]

Giving *and* taking is the most promising approach in many negotiations. Research shows that in non-zero-sum situations, negotiators on average achieve a larger piece of pie when they have created value with the other side, than when they have not. In other words, focusing on expanding the pie often beats slicing it. But not necessarily! There is no law of nature that dictates this. The opposite can also be true. This brings us to the paradox of negotiation.[161]

1.3 The Paradox

In a comprehensive analysis of twenty-eight different studies led by Dutch psychologist Carsten De Dreu, the best negotiators were the ones that tried to maximize *both* their own and the other side's outcome. These negotiators are said to have a proscocial motivation: they were found to engage in more problem-solving behavior, engage in less contentious behavior, and achieve higher joint outcomes than those with an egoistic motivation (i.e. those negotiators that sought to maximize their own outcomes, with little or no regard for the outcomes obtained by their opposing negotiator).[162]

To create value, we have to cooperate with the other side. To distribute value, we have to compete with them. These tactics are partly compatible with one another. Both creating and claiming value requires setting high goals and sticking to them, uncovering the other side's priorities, and making low priority concessions in exchange for getting high priority concessions in return (while holding firm on your own high priority issues).[163]

But these tactics are also partly incompatible with one another – especially when the enlarged pie must be divided. And very few negotiations require only one set of tactics. As Lax and Sebenius assert, there is a central, inescapable tension between cooperative moves to create value jointly, and competitive moves to gain individual advantage: The tactics for claiming value can impede its creation, and tactics for creating value are vulnerable to distributive tactics. For instance, each side might strenuously resist any concessions, hoping that only the other side will move. Even if they find a compromise of some sort, these determined efforts to claim value might block the two sides from even realizing the potential for joint gains. Similarly, in order to identify value creation opportunities, we need to disclose information – but disclosing information can expose us to value-claiming tactics by the other side, as Subramanian warns. (Figuratively speaking, the two sides pull the negotiator into different directions, which can be illustrated graphically as in Figure 3.)[164]

Richard Walton and McKersie describe the paradoxical nature of the negotiation task:

> If distributive bargaining is pursued too vigorously, then the negotiator may gain the greater share but of a smaller set of joint gains, or worse, may generate an outcome in which both parties lose. Similarly, if the negotiator pursues integrative bargaining in a single-minded manner, for example, being completely forthcoming with information, he or she can be taken advantage of by the other party.[165]

We have seen that Aristotle distinguished between compatibles, contraries, and contradictions. In a negotiation, we typically have all of them: "What is good for me is good for you" can be, depending on the situation, either true or false. So can its opposite, as well as pretty much any statement in between the two! But how can this be? It seems to defy common sense.

We have arrived at the paradox of the negotiation task. Negotiation is often less of a problem that can be "solved" than a paradox that must be managed. What is a paradox? The original Greek "parádoxos" (παράδοξος) means "against common opinion," and it was long used in this sense only. For example, the reformer Martin Luther called one of his tracts against prevailing Catholic teachings *Theologica Paradoxa* in 1518. Today we use the word slightly differently. It usually refers to something that is seemingly contradictory, or opposed to common sense, and yet perhaps true. (The other way in which it is commonly used is to express something that runs against an expectation. We will explore this variety too, when we look at the negotiator's intuition.) The paradox can be visualized as the Yin & Yang of value creation and value distribution, as we saw in Figure 5.

It is no coincidence that we resort to an East Asian concept here. As we saw, contradictions are perceived differently from the West:

> In the Chinese intellectual tradition, there is no necessary incompatibility between the belief that A and *not A* both have merit. Indeed, in the spirit of the Tao or yin-yang principle, A can actually imply that *not A* is also the case – the opposite of a state of affairs can exist simultaneously with the state of affairs itself.[166]

Note that the use of Yin & Yang to convey the complex reality of negotiations does not imply that Asian negotiators are generally better at negotiating than their Western counterparts. As empirical research has shown over the years, this is not the case. Asian negotiators leave money on the table, too. Mastering the paradox is apparently equally challenging for negotiators from all over the world.[167]

The two contrary elements of Yin & Yang are interconnected, interdependent, and even complementary.

1.3.1 Cooperation and Competition are Interconnected

We cannot really separate the two tactics. Negotiations often go through different stages in which cooperative and competitive behaviors wax and wane. We have seen that issues should not be addressed sequentially, but simultaneously. Trade-offs between the different issues would be impossible otherwise.[168]

This interconnectedness is perhaps best expressed by the term we mentioned earlier in the chapter, "co-opetition." This can be defined as simultaneous Cooperation & Competition among firms with value creation intent. The concept has been developed by Barry Nalebuff and Adam Brandenburger in their pioneering 1996 book, *Co-opetition*. Recent years have seen a renewed interest in this concept, which builds on the insight that interorganizational collaborations have become an important part of corporate strategy to cope with faster dynamics and higher uncertainties. Nalebuff and Brandenburger suggested that managers overcome traditional competitive thinking by cooperating with competitors in order to create value. Prominent examples of this approach are General Motors and Toyota, who used each other's resources, competencies, and knowledge to jointly develop fuel cell-powered cars, while maintaining competition in other market segments; or tourism companies that collaborate in order to promote a tourist destination, but compete to increase the size of their individual, local business.[169]

Cooperation and competition are also inseparably linked outside the world of interorganizational collaborations. It is not necessary for the concerned parties to be actual competitors in the market place in order for them to have to distribute value (competitively) in their negotiations. We saw the same connection when we look at the different parts of a contract: Its parties do not need to be competitors in order to experience this tension. In fact, the term "co-opetition" could be fittingly used to describe the paradox which is inherent in most negotiations.

1.3.2 Cooperation and Competition are Interdependent

Often enough, the two sides cannot even be separated. Each also carries a kernel of the other inside. We might work out the power plant configuration that is optimal for both sides, but the fact remains: You would like to pay as little as possible – and I would like to charge as much as possible. On the other hand, not all risks mean the same to both parties. We might differ in our expectations and in our preferences. While our differences might be a source of frustration, they are also an opportunity for cooperation. We can bundle issues and make trade-offs. Let's find things that are important to you, but not so important to me. And the other way around. Let's barter! Not all slices of the pie have the same significance for both of us. We may not gain all that we want – but perhaps most. No matter how much value creation enlarges the pie, it also must be divided. And no matter how much the pie must be sliced, it also might be expanded. As Susskind succinctly puts it, we should strive for a deal that is good for the other side – and great for us. And they, reasonably, will strive for the same. There is no escaping the paradox of negotiation.[170]

1.3.2.1 The Dark Side of Value Creation

When initially presenting the idea of Yin & Yang, I proposed that each side carries a kernel of its opposite. This is graphically expressed by the two little dots. Another way is to think of them as the "dark little secrets" of value creation and value distribution. Yes, the thought that both sides can win is uplifting and optimistic. To many it is much more attractive than mere mundane pie-slicing. I qualified as a mediator – the third party with the noble aim of helping both sides win – before I came to negotiate contracts for Siemens. And I certainly am not alone in my admiration of this concept. In fact, "win–win" has gained tremendous popularity beyond the confines of negotiation itself. Stephen Covey has captured its allure in one of his *7 Habits of Highly Effective People*: "Think win–win": "Win–win is a frame of mind and heart that constantly seeks mutual benefit in all human interactions." In his provocative treatise of social change, Anand Giriharadas points to the "tantalizing promise" of the win–win approach to social change: "The idea of doing well for yourself by doing good for others is a gospel." It presumes harmony between what is good for winners and good for everyone else.[171]

> In an ideal version of these endeavors, the winner could enjoy an enticing combination of making money, doing good, feeling virtuous, working on hard and stimulating problems, feeling her impact, reducing suffering, spreading justice, exoticizing a resume, traveling the world, and gaining a catchy cocktail-party spiel.... What threads through these various ideas is a promise of painlessness. What is good for me will be good for you.[172]

Yet Giriharadas alerts us to the uncomfortable truth that "social venture capital," "social enterprises", or "impact investing" might sometimes merely cement a problematic status quo rather than change it. "It is fine for winners to see their own success as inextricable from that of others. But there will always be situations in which people's preferences and needs do not overlap, and in fact conflict." Labeling a win–lose situation as win–win is not only inaccurate; it might also masquerade the fact that "winners take all", the title of Giridaradas's book. Changing the world for better, he argues, might require a measure of wealth redistribution. He quotes Vinod Khosla, a billionaire venture capitalist, as saying "to put it crudely, it's bribing the population to be well enough off." Designating something as win–win that is not, can gloss over the problem and make its solution harder. This, of course, comes as no surprise to my European readers. Public systems of social security and health care, such as the UK's National Health Service, have been created *precisely because* it does not pay for entrepreneurs to pursue them.[173]

My own skepticism of win–win goes even further. I believe that it almost always has a dark side. Creating value has a lot in common with the distribution of value: It does require the egoistic capturing of value at the expense of somebody else – just not somebody that sits at the table. Similarly, claiming value actually requires us to accommodate the wishes of the other side at our own expense, because we have to lie to ourselves to reach an agreement. Let me explain.

On the one hand, there is what I call the "dirty little secret of value creation": Sure, expanding the pie sounds great. But where exactly does this extra pie come from? The generation of quantitative monetary value does not happen by photosynthesis. It usually comes out of somebody else's pocket, just not somebody who sits at the table. In the orange example, the agreement that is reached by the sisters makes the otherwise necessary trip to the local fruit merchant obsolete. In trading off on different priorities, the parties often walk a thin line between legitimate and illegitimate forms of cooperation. Companies forge strategic alliances in order to pursue opportunities for joint wins. A price-fixing cartel represents the perfect win–win. And it is perfectly illegal too.[174]

While it is fine to conclude an agreement for the benefit of a third party (just think of a life insurance), it is illegal in many jurisdictions to conclude one to the detriment of a third party. Whether or not a win–win agreement violates the rights of a third party is a legal question. A case in point would be agreements between companies not to poach and hire employees from one another. The 2010 High-Tech Employee Antitrust Litigation alleged that Silicon Valley firms such as Apple, Google, and Intel did do just that. If true, this would no doubt have constituted a win–win for them. But would such behavior have been legal? The answer to this question depends on the applicable jurisdiction. In Germany, for instance, the right approach had long been disputed until the highest court in the system of ordinary jurisdiction, the Federal Court of Justice (*Bundesgerichtshof*) in Karlsruhe decided the matter. It is the supreme court in all matters of criminal and private law in the country, and ruled that companies are allowed to agree with each other not to poach and hire each other's employees – but, if violated, such an agreement is not enforceable. In other words, it is about as useful as an agreement that would not have been allowed in the first place, because such an agreement would infringe upon the individual right of employees to pursue the career of their choice. The court established an important exception though. The agreement is fully enforceable if it is only incidental to another purpose that the parties genuinely pursued. Most relevant here are contracts that allow a potential buyer to conduct due diligence on the potential target.[175]

But even when no antitrust laws are violated, the pie is often expanded at somebody else's expense. If the supplier grants more lenient payment terms in exchange for payment security, the buyer expands the pie with the money that they do not have to borrow from their bank. And the seller does not have to buy insurance against payment default.

Another possibility is that the pie is expanded at the expense of the "former self" of one of the parties. Let me explain. They may have lost value in the past – which now allows the other side to hand it "back" to them. Consider the case which Fisher and Ury use to demonstrate the need to focus on interests, not positions: The Camp David negotiations leading to an Egyptian–Israeli peace treaty in 1978 (and to Nobel Peace prizes for its main protagonists, US President Jimmy Carter, Egyptian President Anwar Sadat, and Israeli Prime Minister Menachem Begin). Israel had occupied the Egyptian Sinai Peninsula since the Six Day War of 1967. When the two countries sat down together to negotiate a peace agreement, their positions were utterly incompatible: Israel insisted on keeping some of the Sinai, while Egypt insisted on the return of every inch to its sovereignty. But it became possible to develop a solution when the parties focused on the interests behind these positions. Egypt's interest lay in sovereignty, while Israel's interest lay in security. At Camp David, the two countries agreed to a plan that would return the Sinai to complete Egyptian sovereignty and, by demilitarizing large areas, would still assure Israeli security: "The Egyptian flag would fly everywhere, but Egyptian tanks would be nowhere near Israel." It is obvious that Israel could return sovereignty over the Egyptian Sinai only because it had previously conquered it.[176]

We find the same structure in a more recent international agreement. After notifying the EU of the UK's intention to leave, Prime Minster Theresa May negotiated an agreement (the "Brexit Deal") on how exactly the exit was going to happen during a transition period until the end of 2020. While May had reached an agreement on the (tentative) Brexit Deal with the EU, the House of Commons rejected it three times, leading to the eventual demise of the Prime Minister. Her successor Boris Johnson took up where she left off and, in renewed negotiations with the EU, reached a new (and equally tentative) deal. In it, the controversial "backstop" provision had been replaced. This backstop was what primarily caused Theresa May's deal to fall through. It had been designed to ensure there would be no border posts or barriers between Northern Ireland and the Republic of Ireland after Brexit: If the transition period passed without the UK and the EU being able to produce a different solution, the backstop would kick in, keeping the UK in a close trading relationship with the EU and avoiding checks altogether until an alternative arrangement was agreed between the EU and the UK. The backstop provided for keeping Northern Ireland in some aspects of the single market as well as for the UK (as a whole) having a common customs territory with the EU. Proponents of Brexit criticized the backstop for keeping the UK in such a close relationship with the EU, and for treating Northern Ireland differently from the rest of the country. On October 17, 2019, Prime Minister Boris Johnson announced that a revised deal had been agreed between the UK and the EU in which the controversial backstop had been replaced with new custom arrangements. If the parties could not seal their main new trade deal by the end of the transition period, the UK would be able to sign and implement its own trade agreements with countries around the world. The revised plan effectively created a customs and regulatory border between Northern

Ireland and Great Britain. Some goods entering Northern Ireland from Great Britain would have to pay EU import taxes (tariffs). In other words, the parties agreed in principle that there would be a customs border down the Irish Sea.

How was this new solution made possible? By a familiar trade-off. Johnson's interest was mainly for the UK "whole and entire" to leave the EU, and for Northern Ireland to be treated equally to the rest. The EU, on the other hand, was primarily interested in preventing a hard border on the island of Ireland and in preserving the integrity of its single market. Their agreement reminds one of Camp David. As one diplomat put it: "Northern Ireland would *de jure* be in the UK's customs territory but *de facto* in the European Union."[177]

I have mentioned before that the Brexit negotiation is really one where the parties have to decide how best to shrink the pie. Accordingly, value is created here at the expense of the parties themselves. The new custom arrangements left both sides with less than they had before Brexit: De facto control by the UK of its entire territory and *de jure* control by the EU over its entire customs area. (Boris Johnson's revised Brexit deal was approved by the UK Parliament after the General Election in December 2019.)

To conclude: In both the Camp David and the Brexit negotiations, as in many other cases, the creation of value required somebody (else) to contribute that value. This does not of course mean that the creation of value is ethically questionable in any way. Israel had won the Sinai in a pre-emptive war that it had not wished for. The EU had wished for the UK to remain. Rather, it just goes to show the complicated reality of most negotiations, and confirms its deeply paradoxical nature. Still, sometimes it seems that this realization is one that many negotiators prefer not to make.[178]

1.3.2.2 The Dark Side of Value Distribution

There is bad news for proponents of win–lose too. It also has its dark side. Competitive negotiators often pride themselves in not being taken advantage of: It is a dog-eat-dog world, but nobody can take them to the cleaners! They came out blazing with an extreme first offer (or equally extreme counteroffer), and are now laughing all the way to the bank. As we have seen, it is good negotiation practice to make the first offer as extreme as is plausibly possible. And indeed, as Nobel laureate Thaler and his colleague Cass Sunstein have pointed out, it is impossible *not* to influence the perception of others in our interactions. So why not do it in a way that is beneficial?[179]

It is easy to overlook the fact that the distribution of value – just like the creation of value – also requires us to accommodate the demands of the other side at our expense! The only difference is just that we are tempted to hide this inconvenient truth from ourselves. How so? You make the first offer, and the other side counters with an equally extreme offer. You both make concessions until you agree (usually by splitting the difference). When exactly do you stop to push for more? Once you have convinced yourself that the deal on offer is pretty much the best you can get. Yet the best you can get is the least the other side is willing to accept. Is it really plausible that you have reached this point? Just like you, they have every incentive to make you believe this precisely when it is not true. They too are well advised to target the other side's walk-away point instead of their own. The mere fact that they have offered a number indicates that this is not, in fact, their last and final number. Yet, if you do not believe so, you can never close a deal. So, unless our counterpart is *completely* (and perhaps naively) honest, reaching an agreement often necessitates a measure of self-deceit. And it is especially tempting for the hard-nosed competitive negotiator not to make this realization. The boss asks: "How did the negotiation go?" The answer: "It was tough. But at the end I got the best possible deal!" Really?

Maybe, deep down, we are aware of this little secret? This might help to explain a puzzling discovery made by Carnegie Melon University's Taya Cohen. In a series of studies, she intriguingly found that empathy discouraged unethical negotiation behavior – such as lies and bribes – but mere perspective-taking did not. Individuals with a greater tendency to feel empathy for others were more likely to disapprove of lying, but people who had a greater tendency to (merely) consider the perspective of others were no more likely to disapprove of ethically questionable strategies than those not inclined to "put themselves in others' shoes." I am going out on a limb here. But perhaps putting myself in their shoes does not prevent me from lying to them, because if they did the same, they would discover that I have to lie to myself too?[180]

Either way: As negotiators we should not idealize either the creation or distribution of value. And we must resist the temptation to wash over their differences. In sum, we can say that the creation of value shares a common core with the distribution of value: Our gain is made at the expense of someone else (just not our negotiation counterpart).

1.3.3 Cooperation and Competition are Complementary

1.3.3.1 They Need Each Other

Just as both sides of Yin & Yang need each other, so the creation of value requires the distribution of value – and the other way around. What do I mean? Without cooperation there can be no competition. And without competition there can be no cooperation. The two stand in a dialectical order. Let's turn to Aristotle again. He held that all virtues are dialectical: They exist in balance with a counter-virtue. A value can only achieve its constructive impact if it incorporates a measure of its counter-value. Braveness needs caution so that it does not become recklessness. And caution without braveness becomes cowardice.

Returning to our two politicians, it is not surprising that the critics of both Angela Merkel and Donald Trump often bemoan that they pursue their favorite approach too excessively. Consider this opinion piece in the *New York Times*, entitled "If Trump Wants to Take On China, He Needs Allies. And he should start with Europe" by Julianne Smith:

> This would make the countries of Europe, historically among America's closest allies, well placed to work with Washington to confront China over trade, its destabilizing policies in Asia, and the authoritarian political model it is promoting around the world.... The best way for the United States and Europe to compete with China would be to resolve their own bilateral trade disputes.... Mr. Trump is right to claim that America finds itself in an era of great power competition with China. Where his administration has repeatedly missed the mark, though, is in its determination to deride the very "global" community that could help America in its challenge. If the president were serious about competing with China, he would be doing more to get as many allies on his side as possible.[181]

Or take Jerrold Post, the long-standing head of psychological profiling for the CIA. Coincidentally, what he sees as the highlight of his agency career was taking the lead on the Camp David profiles of Menachem Begin and Anwar Sadat, preparing President Jimmy Carter for the negotiations. After two decades in the agency, Post continued his work in academia. One of the characteristics of Donald Trump that Post highlighted in a recent profile of the President is a lack of empathy: "Donald Trump has continuously over the years demonstrated an incapacity to empathise with others, including his own family."[182]

I suspect that Angela Merkel shares the view that Donald Trump is too competitive in his negotiations. She did not mention him explicitly in her 2019 Harvard Commencement Speech. But it seems to me that she was not only addressing the audience when she pleaded for more cooperation:

> Protectionism and trade conflicts jeopardize free international trade and thus the foundation of our prosperity .... Changes for the better are possible if we tackle them together. Individual countries cannot achieve much on their own.... More than ever, our way of thinking and our actions have to be multilateral rather than unilateral, global rather than national, outward-looking rather than isolationist. In short: we have to work together rather than alone.[183]

Similarly, Merkel has been castigated for failing to assert what her critics see as non-negotiable positions (such as NATO defense spending). For instance, Donald Trump, in his infamous telephone call with President Volodymyr Zelensky of Ukraine said that "Germany does almost nothing for you. All they do is talk.... When I was speaking to Angela Merkel she talks Ukraine, but she doesn't do anything." To her opponents, Merkel can appear overly cooperative. This is how George Packer described the critique in his widely referenced profile of Angela Merkel in *The New Yorker*:[184]

> Throughout her Chancellorship, Merkel has stayed as close as possible to German public opinion. Alan Posener (of the conservative newspaper *Die Welt*) said that, after nearly losing to Schröder, she told herself "I'm going to be all things to all people." Critics and supporters alike describe her as a gifted tactician without a larger vision.. . . The pejorative most often used against her is "opportunist." When I asked Katrin Göring-Eckardt, the Green leader, whether Merkel had any principles, she paused, then said, "She has a strong value of freedom, and everything else is negotiable.[185]

We can safely assume that Donald Trump shares the view that Angela Merkel should be less cooperative in some negotiations. In his view, certain issues are not negotiable, but rather require the asserting of one's position – for instance when it comes to defense spending goals.[186]

Of course, the leaders' public announcements are part of their negotiation strategy, so we have to take them with more than a pinch of salt. And they are only partly addressed to the other representatives of state that they sit at the table with. They are also meant for "domestic" consumption. As Jeswald Salacuse of Tufts University explains in *Real Leaders Negotiate!* leaders constantly negotiate with their followers, too. And here, Angela Merkel and Donald Trump appear to have a lot in common. In dealing with potential challengers, Salacuse credits Merkel's "ability to exploit the weakness of her challenger" and "her patience in waiting for the right moment to strike." This is what a former US ambassador said about her: "If you cross her, end up dead. There's nothing cushy about her. There's a whole list of alpha males who thought they would get her out of the way, and they're all now in other walks of life." Trump's leadership philosophy, after all, can be summarized in his quote: "Leadership is not a group effort. If you're in charge, then be in charge." At the end of the day, Angela Merkel might be closer to Donald Trump than may be comfortable for either of them.[187]

To be sure, politics is about much more than negotiation. There are not many people on the planet that have to make and implement decisions of such staggering complexity and far-reaching significance as these two heads of governments. Citizens, parliamentarians, ministers, party members, think tanks, allies, friends (and foes) far and near are affected by them, and many will, rightly or wrongly, never agree with either Angela Merkel or Donald Trump. Negotiation is only a part of their monumental responsibility, and I, for one, am astonished at any high-ranking politician that stoically soldiers on, despite the daily onslaught they have to endure in public. Which is of course not to say that we should not learn from observing them. And one important takeaway from analyzing and comparing their approaches to negotiation is that both could arguably become (even) better at it by incorporating some of the behaviors that the respective other seems to possess in abundance.

***

To conclude our deliberation of the Yin & Yang of negotiation, we can say that the dots in each half remind us that our tactics can become too much of a good thing. These considerations lead us to the final thoughts of this chapter. As negotiators we must understand the paradox of the task, and embrace the dialectical order of Cooperation & Competition. Once we master creating and claiming value, we can choose the right tactic for the situation at hand. But which one to pick?

When it comes to specific action, we cannot have it both ways. We have to decide what to do. The Latin root of the word "decision" tells us as much: "Cīdere" means "to cut off, to kill"; it is also the root of the English word "homicide." Why? Because when we decide in favor of one option, we usually have to decide against other options – which we therefore have to cut off. Equally drastically, the German word for "decision" – "Entscheidung" – comes from the Germanic "skaipi" which developed into the English "scabbard": Separating options is linked to drawing a sword.

This brings us to the second challenge of negotiation: The strategic dilemma. In order to determine the right strategy, we have to look at the other side. After all, we have defined it as "joint decision-making process." In other words, the right answer depends on the other side, because whether or not our strategy is successful is determined equally by the choices that they make. This leads us into a dilemma, and brings us to the next chapter.

2 The Strategic Dilemma

The success of our negotiation strategy built from value creation and distribution tactics depends on the other side – and so does theirs.

We have explored the tactics which help us to claim and create value. Now we can pick the right strategy. While tactics are the specific actions that we take, our strategy is the high-level plan which determines the correct tactic for the challenge at hand. How can we choose the appropriate negotiation strategy? When we face a one-time zero-sum negotiation, there is not much of a choice. If we really cannot identify any additional material issues, neither side can help it: We just have to use the tactics of value-claiming.

But when there is more than one issue on the table, it is not so simple. In plotting our strategy, should we focus on creating value, seeking a smaller slice of a larger pie? Or should we focus on claiming value, seeking a larger slice of a smaller pie? What makes the choice between cooperative and competitive tactics so difficult is that we cannot determine its success by ourselves. It depends just as much on the choice of the other side. And they face the same tactical paradox. As a result, we find ourselves caught up in a dilemma with the other side.

How to address this strategic dilemma is the topic of this chapter. The answer is different for a (multi-issue) negotiation that extends over multiple rounds than for a one-time transaction where we will never see the other side again. We will start by exploring the one-off negotiation. It provides valuable insights into the multiple-rounds negotiation.

2.1 One-Off Negotiations

2.1.1 The Negotiator's Dilemma

Both sides face the tactical paradox: They have to decide whether to cooperate or to compete. So, we play out one of four possible scenarios: We might both decide to cooperate, or to compete. Or we might each decide on a different approach.

But let's start at the beginning. As Howard Raiffa and colleagues have pointed out, humans have no natural structure for thinking about deciding. Instead of proactively making decisions, we often just react. Paul C. Nutt has researched decision-making for over two decades. He evaluated hundreds of decisions to measure their success. Citing well-known examples such as the Euro Disney location or the Ford Pinto recall decisions, he concludes that, astonishingly, about half of all decisions fail. He attributes this startling rate of failure to a number of typical "blunders," namely the propensity to enter into premature commitments. He shows that decision-makers often jump on the first idea that comes along, and then spend years trying to make it work. To listen to the other side (*audiatur et altera pars*) is not only a fundamental principle of law. It is also crucial for decision-making: Is there another side of the coin? Is there another decision that I could, or even should, make?[1]

Imagine the joint venture of two companies. If they pooled their knowledge and resources, they could sell more products than each of them individually. Their gains might be even bigger if one side exploited the other's know-how (and the other might be left with less market share). If both seek to take advantage of the other, neither will profit very much from the joint venture.

Consider the example of seller-provided financing that we looked at in Chapter 1. The buyer needs credit to pay for the purchase upfront. The bank offers credit for $3,000. But the seller has access to cheap financing and can provide it for as little as $1,000. Quite an attractive proposition. The buyer could pay the seller almost $2,000 and still be better off than with a bank credit. In other words, the parties have an opportunity to distribute an additional $2,000.[2]

If both the buyer and seller act cooperatively, they will achieve the coveted win–win agreement. But a cooperative negotiator also exposes themselves to the risk of exploitation. If the other side chooses to act competitively, the outcome will be lose–win. By competing, we can protect ourselves from that risk, and might even obtain a great result at the expense of the other side (win–lose). However, if the other side also chooses to compete, both will end up losing (lose–lose). In other words, we need the other side for winning: When cooperating, I can only win if the other side does likewise. When competing, I can only win if the other side does not. In theory everybody loves the win–win, but our fear or greed make it difficult in practice. The negotiator's dilemma is graphically illustrated in Table 1 in the Introduction.

The negotiator's dilemma is similar to the prisoner's dilemma. Each negotiator has an individual incentive to act competitively, but collectively this will lead to both sides losing. The suboptimal outcome represents a "Nash equilibrium," because the parties can only jointly break from it. Before I describe the prisoner's dilemma in all its beauty, I will first describe the significance of metaphors in negotiations.

2.1.2 The Significance of Metaphors

We can easily appreciate the power of metaphors by listening in on a historical conversation. Soviet leader Mikhail Gorbachev and German Chancellor Helmut Kohl regarded their use of metaphors as a turning point in achieving German reunification. We will also look at some more current examples, such as food analogies used in the Brexit negotiations.

We use metaphors to understand one thing with the help of another. Merriam-Webster defines metaphor as a figure of speech in which a word or phrase denoting one kind of object is used in place of another to suggest a likeness or analogy between them. Mental images shape our perception and understanding of the world. Harvard University's Michael Wheeler and his colleagues, Kimberlyn Leary and Juliana Pillemer, studied twenty seasoned negotiators to explore their thoughts and feelings about the process. They asked participants to find and combine pictures that metaphorically depicted those feelings and to describe the collages they'd created during in-depth interviews. (Perhaps you want to pause for a moment and consider your own mental images?) This is what they found: "Most people in our study saw others as predators in the negotiation jungle and themselves as prey. A few, however, identified with the aggressive side of human nature. One acknowledged the wolf within him. Another saw himself as a rifleman taking aim."[3]

Isn't it striking how antagonistic these mental images are? How about your own? However, this aggression is not surprising. Just consider how common the metaphor "argument is war" is in the English language: "Your claims are indefensible"; "their criticism was right on target"; "I've never won an argument with him"; or "If you use that strategy, she'll wipe you out." George Lakoff and Mark Johnson deem metaphors to be fundamental mechanisms of the mind. Because they structure our most basic understanding of our experience, they are "metaphors we live by" (the title of Lakoff and Johnson's seminal 1980 book):

> It is not that arguments are subspecies of war. Arguments and wars are different kinds of things – verbal discourse and armed conflict – and the actions performed are different kinds of actions. But *argument* is partially structured, understood, performed, and talked about in terms of *war*. The concept is metaphorically structured, the activity is metaphorically structured, and, consequently, the language is metaphorically structured.[4]

Perhaps you are more comfortable with another example: Food metaphors. Here are some highlights from Brexit press coverage: *The Economist* has identified "six flavours of Brexit." It has also argued that "the EU offers many menus, from Norwegian to Turkish – but that there is no 'à la carte option.'" French President Emmanuel Macron warned then British Prime Minister Theresa May against "cherry-picking." She vehemently denied doing so, and German Chancellor Angela Merkel was confident that it could be avoided. They all ignored observers that found the entire metaphor to be unhelpful. Meanwhile, Martin Donnelly, the former head of Britain's international trade department, said on BBC Radio 4 that leaving the single market would be like swapping a meal for a packet of crisps: "You're giving up a three-course meal, the depth and intensity of our trade relationship across the European Union and partners now, for the promise of a packet of crisps in the future, if we manage to do trade deals in the future outside the EU which aren't going to compensate for what we're giving up." Little wonder that some observers concluded all this was just "pie in the sky." But as the clock ticked away, the language changed. With the exit date postponed and pressure growing, familiar martial metaphors became more prominent: Judges were called "enemies of the people," ministers "traitors," and parliamentary legislation "surrender acts."[5]

Some estimates suggest that one out of every twenty-five words we encounter is a metaphor. But do metaphors have an impact? Of course, as we have seen, negotiation success depends on a number of objective factors (such as the contractual issues at hand, the strategic goals pursued by the parties, or their alternatives and deadlines). But the human factor often plays an equally important role, if not more so. It is a well-established fact that the way we think of a negotiation will influence our success in mastering it. We have already looked at the importance of framing in both value creation and value distribution. Using metaphors is an excellent way of framing. Consider the following, rather disturbing, research findings.[6]

2.1.2.1 Is Crime a Virus or a Beast?

Psychologist Lera Boroditsky explains: "We can't talk about any complex situation – like crime – without using metaphors. Metaphors aren't just used for flowery speech. They shape the conversation for things we're trying to explain and figure out. And they have consequences for determining what we decide is the right approach to solving problems."[7]

She devised the following experiment with her colleague Paul Thibodeau when they were at Stanford University: Test subjects were asked to read short texts about rising crime rates in the fictional city of Addison and answer questions about what needed to be done about the problem. The researchers gauged how people answered these questions in light of whether crime was described as a beast or as a virus. The five experiments varied slightly. In one of them, for instance, the beast or virus metaphor was instantiated with a single word:

> Crime is a (beast/virus) ravaging the city of Addison. Five years ago Addison was in good shape, with no obvious vulnerabilities. Unfortunately, in the past five years the city's defense systems have weakened, and the city has succumbed to crime. Today, there are more than 55,000 criminal incidents a year - up by more than 10,000 per year. There is a worry that if the city does not regain its strength soon, even more serious problems may start to develop.[8]

The proposed solutions differed greatly, depending on the metaphor that had been used. Of the participants that read "Crime is a beast ravaging the city of Addison", 71 percent called for more enforcement. Only 54 percent of participants who had read the alternative framing ("Crime is a virus ravaging the city of Addison") agreed. Thibodeau and Boroditsky concluded:

> Manipulating the metaphor used to frame the issue of crime influenced how people approached solving the crime problem. When crime was framed as a virus, participants

> were more likely to suggest social reform. Alternatively, when crime was framed as a beast, participants were more likely to suggest law enforcement and punishment. Remarkably, presenting an otherwise identical report with only one word different in the introductory frame yielded systematically different problem solving suggestions.[9]

Significantly, when the 485 participants were asked what they thought was the most influential part of the report, only 15 identified the metaphor! Almost everybody else said that the statistics swayed their decision on how to curb crime. Boroditsky generalizes these findings: "People like to think they're objective and making decisions based on numbers. They want to believe they're logical. But they're really being swayed by metaphors."[10]

The question of whether to treat crime as something to be cured rather than punished is highly relevant in real life. Scotland, which in 2005 was declared one of the most violent countries in the developed world, has since adopted a "public health" model to tackling violence. Police established a Violence Reduction Unit – with the result that the murder rate and number of facial trauma patients in the country had halved by 2018.[11]

People do not only live by metaphors – they (literally) also kill by them. In the early days of advertising, the father of modern public relations (and nephew of Sigmund Freud) Edward Bernays successfully branded cigarettes as feminist "Torches of Freedom" when smoked by women. (When the toxic side of tobacco became clearer, he reversed course and lobbied staunchly against smoking.) As we know, both Adolf Hitler's and Joseph Stalin's ideology and propaganda relied to a large extent on the use of metaphors. Even today, violence might be incited by the metaphoric use of flags or even cartoons.

This danger is certainly not limited to the darkest places in history or on the globe. Metaphors shape our attitudes both at and away from the negotiating table. Consider the change in language which accompanied the repeated delays of Brexit. In autumn 2019, the "Future of England Survey" (conducted by Cardiff University and the University of Edinburgh), which explored people's attitudes to the constitution across England, Scotland, and Wales, was found to make "uncomfortable reading" for those who voted either Leave or Remain in the 2016 EU Referendum. It laid bare the deep divides fueled by the Brexit debate by, among other questions, asking representative samples of electorates in each country what they would be willing to see happen to get their way on Brexit. Most Leave voters across all three countries thought violence toward MPs was a "price worth paying" for Brexit – just as the majority of Remain voters across all three countries thought violence toward MPs is a "price worth paying" to Remain. A (smaller) majority of voters from both camps and across all three countries thought that protests in which members of the public were badly injured were a "price worth paying" to reach their preferred outcome. And most people thought that both violence toward MPs and violent protests in which people were badly injured were "likely to occur" if Brexit takes place. Either way – as observers of negotiations we might want to be mindful of the metaphors that are used. And as practitioners of negotiation, we certainly must.[12]

2.1.2.2 German Reunification and the River Rhine

To illustrate the significance of metaphors, let's look at a historic negotiation before we turn to the prisoner's dilemma. In October 1990, the German Democratic Republic became part of the Federal Republic of Germany. Since the defeat of the Third Reich in 1945, the country had been occupied by the Allies in the West and the USSR in the East. The countries that had overpowered the Nazis had very little desire to see the unification of the Federal Republic of Germany and the German Democratic Republic. This was especially true for the Soviet Union, which had lost 25 million lives in the war. German reunification, especially as part of the West, was anathema in the East. Still, it happened. In 1986, Mikhail Gorbachev became General Secretary of the Communist Party of the Soviet Union. He reformed party and state under the twin banners of *glasnost* ("openness") and *perestroika* ("restructuring"). Change happened in the Eastern bloc during the spring of 1989 with breath-taking speed. Warsaw Pact member Hungary opened its borders and let thousands of East Germans escape to the free West. The "Peaceful Revolution" commenced, leading eventually to the fall of the Berlin Wall in November 1989. It was however by no means clear that East and West Germany would come together. Rather, this was the outcome of negotiations that began with a trip for Helmut Kohl, the West German Chancellor, to Russia. In July 1990, *The Economist* opened a report on what was already being touted as a historical meeting with these words: "The West German chancellor, Mr. Helmut Kohl, will head to Moscow chasing the deal of his life."[13]

The deal slowly took shape over the ensuing months. When asked later what had led to the historic breakthrough, Kohl pointed to a private meeting with Gorbachev. On one of his visits to Bonn, the capital of West Germany, Gorbachev and Kohl went for a nocturnal walk along the river Rhine. They were accompanied only by their faithful interpreter. According to Kohl, their conversation took an important turn, with Gorbachev accepting the idea of unification for the first time. Kohl says he achieved this by employing a metaphor:[14]

> Look at this river. Like history, it flows. It is not static. It may be possible to dam the river. But its water will go over the bank and find another way. It is the same with German unity. It is possible to try to prevent it. And then perhaps the two of us won't live to see it. But as surely as the Rhine reaches the sea, German unity will come. And so will European unity.[15]

Breaking with decades of Soviet protocol, Gorbachev did not renounce the idea out of hand. This was the signal that Kohl had hoped for. Gorbachev later confirmed this account: He emphasized that this meeting transformed them from partners to friends.[16]

The rest is history. Gorbachev and Kohl's meeting in Moscow in February, 1990, produced a sensation: Gorbachev's consent to unified Germany's membership in NATO. The Soviet leader declared:[17]

> I believe that there is no divergence of opinion between the Soviet Union, the Federal Republic, and the GDR about unity and the right of the people to strive for unity and to decide on the further development. There is agreement between you and me that the Germans themselves have to make their choice. The Germans in the Federal Republic and in the GDR themselves have to know what road they want to take.[18]

A few months later, the previously unthinkable happened: Reunification. East Germany voted to become part of the West, thereby also joining NATO. Many factors played a role. American support, for instance, was absolutely crucial. Without it, unification would never have happened. Just like the Soviets, the Americans had to agree. And unlike the Soviets, they could persuade the rest of Western Europe to agree as well. All these agreements were forged in negotiations. And in some of them, metaphors played a role, just as they did in the arguments of the opponents of German unity: Italian Prime Minister Giulio Andreotti professed to love Germany so much that he preferred to have two of them.

2.1.3 Lessons from Game Theory: The Prisoner's Dilemma

The strategic dilemma of which tactic to use is essentially (if metaphorically) captured in the prisoner's dilemma. Much researched during the Cold War, the prisoner's dilemma is back with a vengeance – from TTP to NATO budget negotiations. While it is not completely identical to the negotiator's dilemma, it reveals some crucial insights: Each negotiator has an individual incentive to act competitively, but collectively this means that both lose. The suboptimal outcome represents a "Nash equilibrium," because the parties can only break from it together.

2.1.3.1 The Prisoner's Dilemma

The prisoner's dilemma is a very common metaphor in our field. You may be familiar with it – scholars have written thousands of articles on it. It is perhaps the most famous model of game theory: the mathematical study of games, where games can be defined as "interdependent decision situations whose outcome depends on the choices of all players." In other words, game theorists often explore negotiation situations. Here is a quick recap of the prisoner's dilemma.[19]

There are two criminals, A and B, who have just been arrested on suspicion of burglary. There is enough evidence to convict each suspect of the minor crime of breaking and entering, but not enough evidence to convict them on the more serious felony charge of burglary and assault. The public prosecutor separates A and B immediately after their arrest. They are each approached separately and presented with two options: confess to the serious burglary charges or remain silent (do not confess). The consequence of their decisions depends on what the other decides to do. A and B must make their own choice independently. They cannot communicate prior to making it, and it is irrevocable. The four possible outcomes are shown in Table 2.1. If both choose to cooperate with each other (i.e. to remain silent), then they will both be convicted for the lesser charges and go to jail for one year only. If only one of them chooses to cooperate with the other (i.e. to remain silent), while the other chooses to compete (i.e. to confess), then the confessing prisoner will be released; but the other prisoner goes to prison for the maximum sentence of five years. The most desirable situation from the standpoint of each suspect is to confess but have the other person not confess. If they both confess, there is sufficient evidence to sentence both to ten years in prison.

Table 2.1 The prisoner's dilemma: Actions and outcomes

		B	
		Do not confess (cooperate with A)	Do confess (compete with A)
A	Do not confess (cooperate with B)	A: 1 yr. B: 1 yr.	A: 15 yrs. B: 0 yrs.
	Do confess (compete with B)	A: 0 yrs. B: 15 yrs.	A: 10 yrs. B: 10 yrs.

Imagine you are advising A. Your concern is not morality or ethics; you are simply trying to secure a shorter sentence. What do you advise? If B cooperates, A should compete; then A walks free rather than being jailed for a year. If B competes, it is also advisable for A to compete; thereby limiting A's prison time to ten years, rather than fifteen. Regardless of what B does, it seems best for A to compete. And if we look at the problem from B's point of view, we arrive at the same conclusion. Regardless of what the other side does, each individual has an incentive to compete. Because this holds true irrespective of the other side's choice, competition is called the "dominant strategy." This strategy leads the players to a Nash equilibrium. A Nash equilibrium, named after Mathematician John Nash, captures a steady state of a play in which each player holds the correct expectation about the other players' behaviors, and acts rationally. Given that expectation, the player cannot yield a better outcome by (alone) choosing the alternative action: No player can profitably deviate, given the actions of the other players. In the prisoner's dilemma game, whatever one player does, the other prefers Confess to Do not confess, so that the game has a unique Nash equilibrium: Confess/Confess. In other words, both sides lose.[20]

As Paul Watzlawick and his colleagues point out, as sharp thinkers we cannot stop there: Both sides must see that mutual cooperation is better for both of them than mutual competition. And with that insight the whole cycle starts all over again![21]

We have arrived at the heart of the dilemma. Both sides can do better by cooperating. But our old friends fear and greed make the choice much more difficult: The prisoners fear being exploited – and are tempted to exploit. So do negotiators.[22]

2.1.3.2 Human and Animal Affairs

The tension between cooperation and competition is significant far beyond the negotiation of individual transactions. Some philosophers, such as Avishai Margalit, see in it the basic problem of all human politics. It is easy to recognize the struggle to deal with the dilemma in many contemporary situations: The British public votes to leave the EU, because it deems the benefits of cooperation to be insufficient when compared to its costs. An American President vows to put his country first, believing that he can obtain better trade deals outside systems of collective cooperation. The Catalan public is split on the question of whether the cost of being an autonomous region of Spain exceeds its benefits. And because both cooperation and competition have attractive prospects, the public is evenly split on all these questions.[23]

Neither is the problem confined to human affairs. Astonishingly, as recent research shows, elephants are capable of cooperating as well as free-riding, which arguably puts them into the same dilemma. This is the "loose string task": Two animals have to simultaneously pull the two ends of a long rope that runs around a table on which two pots of food are situated. By doing so, they pull the table closer until they can reach the food. If only one animal pulls the rope, it draws it out. The task cannot be solved unilaterally. A team of researchers led by Joshua Plotnik conducted the test with elephants in the Golden Triangle at the Thai Elephant Conservation Center in Lampang, and found that "elephants know when they need a helping trunk in a cooperative task" (the title of their article). This is remarkable. It had been known that elephants are among the few species that can recognize themselves in a mirror. More recently, they have also passed a "body awareness" test that small children cannot pass (stepping off a mat so they could pull it away). But to jointly solve the loose rope, the animals must be aware not only of themselves and the other, but also of the problem they are facing. However, what I found most intriguing is this: One young elephant, NU, reached a success rate of almost 100 percent by approaching her rope end and firmly placing one foot on it. She thus prevented the rope from being pulled away when her partner arrived and pulled. And it forced her partner to do all the work! Should future experiments reveal other elephants refusing to cooperate with NU, then the "elephant's dilemma" would be complete.[24]

The loose string task has been presented to different species. Chimpanzees and, to a lesser degree, even otters are capable of solving it; ravens are not.[25]

2.1.3.3 Differences Between the Negotiator's and the Prisoner's Dilemma

There are three major differences between the prisoner's and the negotiator's dilemma. Unlike prisoners, negotiators: (1) have the option of not concluding a deal; (2) can communicate; and (3) work on their relationship.

- An unstated assumption of the prisoner's dilemma is that the parties will actually make a deal. However, in many negotiations a party might prefer not to agree to a deal that is barely better than their BATNA, rather than conclude a "terrible" deal.[26]
- Importantly, negotiators are not locked up in separate prison cells, and they can communicate. The prisoners have to make their choices simultaneously and independently of each other. By contrast, in many negotiations, the participants are able to communicate with each other in order to present their preferred strategy transparently. This is exactly what Keith J. Murnighan recommends: "Verbalize your strategy.... Tell the other side how you will negotiate. Many people are anxious at the outset of a negotiation, so make clear to them what your strategy is going to be–and then follow through with that strategy." It is important for the parties to define the situation in a similar way. Hence Murnighan suggests to make your understanding explicit:

  > If we meet and we have a potential sale, or whatever it might be, and I say to you: "I don't want to treat this just as a one-off. I would like us to have a long-term relationship. For us to do that you have to trust me, and it would help if I had trust in you. Let us build some trust. Let us put our cards on the table. Here is why you are attractive to me as a partner – I hope I am attractive to you. Here is what I plan to do – this is what I hope you do. And if that works it will be easy and we will both benefit." Why not say those things?[27]

- Many of our most important relationships are not one-off events. We have ongoing relationships with customers, colleagues, and friends, and we have to repeatedly – and jointly – face the dilemma. We therefore have an opportunity to cultivate cooperation (or its opposite!). It all depends on our motivation.
  Finally, as Fisher and Brown caution, the prisoner's dilemma focuses only on the payoff of the participants. But negotiators also work on their relationship.

  > With regards to relationship issues, a bilateral relationship is not a Prisoner's Dilemma. In the Prisoner's Dilemma, I make myself worse off by being generous if they are stingy.

> But with regards to understanding, for example, if I try to understand you, I am better off regardless of whether you try to understand me. The more I understand you, the better I will be able to anticipate your actions even if they are malicious.... Each of us can be sure that we are better off if we pursue cooperation on the relationship issues, regardless of how the other responds. There is no dilemma.[28]

In sum, the prisoner's dilemma is really just a metaphor for the negotiator's dilemma. We should take it seriously but not literally.[29]

2.2 Multi-Round Negotiations

Before we dive into this part of the chapter, let me give you a quick introduction. When there is more than one issue on the table, and the negotiation is not limited to a single round, we must develop a negotiation strategy: It is not possible to only choose once between competition and cooperation. Rather, this choice must be made constantly – in view of the other side, who must do the same. Many negotiations continue over more than one round. Companies often engage in long-term relationships with customers, suppliers, and stakeholders. Countries seldom change their location and have to constantly distribute resources, resolve conflicts, and determine cooperation with their neighbors. We will henceforth focus on multi-issue multi-round negotiations. We will see that employing the metaphoric strategy of "negotiating with an iron fist inside a velvet glove" – based on the (in) famous tit-for-tat approach – allows us to change the nature of the game.

Many important negotiations are not one-shot transactions. Instead, they deal with a number of issues and take place iteratively over a period of time. We can therefore think of a series of repeated prisoner's dilemma games. One side's choice influences the other side's choice in the next round. This means that in business just as in international relations, negotiations are not necessarily conducted toward stable outcomes. To take an example from international relations, we can turn to Henry Farrell and Abraham Newman. For their book, *Of Privacy and Power*, they researched the interactions of European and North American nations and institutions over the right balance between civil liberties and surveillance (think homeland security, airline passenger data, whistleblowing). The subtitle of their book is *The Transatlantic Struggle over Freedom and Security*, because this is what they found – an ongoing struggle. They encourage us to look beyond the success and failure of actors in bargaining over a specific deal: "When one is not focused on discrete, time-limited outcomes, it becomes easier to characterize the longer-term dynamic processes in which the losers of a first-round often come back to fight another day."[30]

If there is more than one round, choice of strategy becomes more complicated. Think of Angela Merkel and Donald Trump again. There is a policy area where they share the same goal. Both seek to prevent Iran from obtaining nuclear weapons. In April 2018 they expressed their consensus that the Iran nuclear deal – negotiated by the five permanent members of the UN Security Council (US, UK, China, Russia, and France) plus the EU and Germany – is not sufficient to accomplish this goal. But what should they do now? Stick to the deal, continue to cooperate with Iran, and thus try to expand the existing agreement (as Merkel wished)? Or cancel the agreement, impose more sanctions, and thereby try to competitively pressure Iran into conceding to a more stringent agreement (as Trump wished). Is worsening Iran's no-deal alternative by imposing sanctions going to weaken the hawks and empower the doves in the country? Or is it going to do the exact opposite, as argued by University of Chicago sanctions expert, Robert Page? At the time of writing, it is unclear whether the common goal can be reached at all, by negotiation or otherwise. Looking back, historians will be able to connect the dots. But as negotiators, we have to determine our strategy for the future. It can be compared to discovering new territory (for instance, by finding out issues and positions), although that metaphor is not completely accurate. We cannot detach ourselves from the journey.[31]

Heraclitus famously declared that no man steps into the same river twice, for it is not the same river and it is not the same man. Likewise, the negotiation we begin is not the same as the negotiation that we conclude (whether or not with an agreement). For instance, the parties often discover their interests only once they engage with each other. And even more importantly: We change the negotiation, and it changes us. There is a general principle that any time you enter a game, you change it:[32]

> You don't have any choice in the matter. It's a new game because you've joined the cast of players. People often miss this effect. They fail to think through how their coming into a game will change it. They think that what they see is what they're going to get. Not so. The game after you've entered it isn't the same as the one you first saw. In physics, this effect is known as the Heisenberg principle – you can't interact with a system without changing it. There's a Heisenberg principle in business, too; it's the way you change a game by joining it.[33]

We often determine our interests, grasp of fairness, and walk-away points only in dialogue with the other side. So, we can elaborate on our travel metaphor. We create the landscape as we traverse it. And we can do both only together with our travel companions. Hence the journey changes the traveler. How can we make that change a productive one? Game theory, again, provides us with valuable insights.

2.2.1 Lessons from Game Theory: Tit for Tat

We can draw more lessons from game theory as we encounter the renowned tit-for-tat strategy. As we will see, it usually yields the best results in the long run because it encourages the other side to cooperate. We can therefore adapt it for our purposes.

We will be advised to "negotiate with an iron fist inside a velvet glove." This might be a simple strategy, but it is not easy to put into practice. It cannot make the paradox disappear. We still need to master the tactics of both sides of the Yin & Yang – so that we can choose the right one in any situation.

As always, let's start at the beginning. The right strategy might, as Jeanne Brett suggests, "turn takers into sharers." Game theorist and negotiation scholar Keith Murnighan points to Robert Axelrod's seminal work, *The Evolution of Cooperation*, as an encouraging outlook on the grim prospect that people eventually find themselves in non-cooperative equilibria. At the height of the Cold War, Axelrod ran two computer tournaments of repeated rounds of a prisoner's dilemma game. He invited experts all over the world to submit strategies for both tournaments. Each strategy was paired against all other strategies, then the outcomes were calculated and compared. The first tournament included the strategies of sixteen experts, the second of sixty-eight. The winner in both rounds was Anatol Rapoport, an eminent scholar and peace advocate. He had submitted the simplest strategy of all, called tit for tat. This strategy starts the first trial with cooperation and, on all subsequent trials, chooses the other player's previous choice. Because of tit for tat's phenomenal success, Axelrod analyzed it in great detail. He concluded that it encourages the other side to cooperate by being nice, retaliatory, forgiving, and clear. It is nice because it is never the first to defect from cooperation – but it will immediately retaliate when the other side chooses to do so. Yet, as soon as the other person returns to cooperative play, tit for tat does also. Finally, it is clear because it never varies from this simple pattern.[34]

2.2.1.1 Enlarging the Shadow of the Future

Tit for tat thus promotes cooperation by both threatening future retaliation and promising future rewards – thus, in the words of Axelrod, "enlarging the shadow of the future." At the same time, a player using this strategy can never "beat" any other player. As Murnighan cautions, the best it can do, relative to the other party, is to achieve an equal outcome. Relative to the multitude of other players it will come across, it will simply do best on average. The flip side of this is that there is no guarantee for success. Some players will not be induced to cooperate even by tit for tat. Some players will take advantage of it. Game theorists pay much attention to the recent calculations of computer scientist William Press and physicist Freeman Dyson. They indicate that "extortionists" can yield even better results than tit-for-tat players, if they can figure out just how much abuse the other side will take before stopping cooperation completely. The extortionist strategy will resort to competition every once in a while, even though cooperation has previously been established. If, on a whim, the other player decides to return to cooperation, the extortionist can gain a considerably higher payoff. "The situation is reminiscent of a group project in junior high school. If one of the members of the team slacks off, the conscientious students have no choice but to work harder in order to earn a good grade." At this point, the findings appear to be largely theoretical, but they may still alter the way in which game theorists view cooperation. It is not hard to imagine this approach in our context. The annual price reductions "asked" from suppliers in many industries would be an example. The supplier might feel like the proverbial frog which sits in tepid water that is slowly brought to boil – but still prefer making concessions to walking away.[35]

2.2.2 An Iron Fist in a Velvet Glove

How can we make use of what we have learned about tit for tat in our negotiations? Thankfully, negotiators, unlike the prisoners, can communicate. And they should! Twenty-five years after initially describing its usefulness, Keith Murnighan offered another metaphor:

> Always negotiate with an iron fist in a velvet glove. As long as things are going fine, people should feel the velvet. The velvet feels really good. But as soon as things get off track, you have to show people that you are not willing to put up with everything, e.g. with unethical or inappropriate behaviour. You have to show them that you have iron inside, even if it costs you. Because if you let inappropriate behaviour happen, it can quickly ruin your ongoing outcomes.[36]

2.2.3 Mixed Motives and Dual Concerns

As negotiators we have "mixed motives," a term coined by Nobel laureate Thomas Schelling. It refers not to an individual's lack of clarity about their own preferences but rather to the ambivalence of their relation to the other player. It is the natural consequence of the negotiator's dilemma, with its mixture of mutual dependence and conflict of partnership and competition. To pursue these motives has long been regarded as the central element of negotiation, indeed, as its *raison d'être*. For example, a negotiator might prefer an agreement that satisfies their interests over one that favors their counterparts' interests (an incentive to compete), while at the same time preferring any agreement over no agreement (an incentive to cooperate).[37]

We thus have to go beyond even Cooperation & Competition. Many transactions are not one-shot but continue through multiple rounds. And most are not binary, so we have to develop an even fuller spectrum of tools: We need even more skills in our tool kit. Both cooperating and competing allow us to fulfill our own interests (either at the expense of the other side or not). To be able to play tit for tat, we also need the ability to take a step back. We also need two skills that are usually called "acknowledging" and "avoiding." "Acknowledging" means (momentarily) regarding their interests as higher than our own. Typical examples would be making a concession, or apologizing to the other side. "Avoiding" is similar. If the other side is not willing to switch to a cooperative mode, we have to respect this. We cannot unilaterally break from the suboptimal equilibrium of lose–lose. In a case such as this, we might have to refrain from attempting to reach a win–win. This is not especially conducive to either our own or their interests. But it may be our best bet to avoid the game altogether – or at least avoid losing at it by defensively sticking to a competitive mode.

To rise to the challenges of the paradox and the dilemma, we have to be concerned about our own outcome and that of the other side. A well-known model that captures the social motivation of negotiators is the "dual concerns model." The dual concerns are the concern for the "self" and the concern for the "other." They were introduced by Blake and Mouton in 1964, and adapted by various authors. Among them were Pruitt and Rubin, who describe it as follows:[38]

> Concern about own outcomes means placing importance on one's own interests – one's needs and values – in the realm under dispute. People with a strong concern about their own outcomes are highly resistant to yielding; in other words, their aspirations tend to be rigid and high. Concern about the other's outcomes implies placing importance on the other's interests – feeling responsible for the quality of the other's outcomes.[39]

We can plot the concerns in our familiar matrix: see Figure 2.1. Moving upwards denotes an improved outcome for us; moving to the right denotes an improved outcome for the other side. To get a good outcome for ourselves, we need to have high regard for our own interests – which is what the vertical axis shows. The horizontal axis shows the concern we have for the other side. If we regard the concerns of both sides highly, we engage in cooperation. If we only regard our own outcome highly, but not the other side's outcome, we compete with them. If we have low regard for everybody's interests, we avoid the issue. Finally, if we regard the

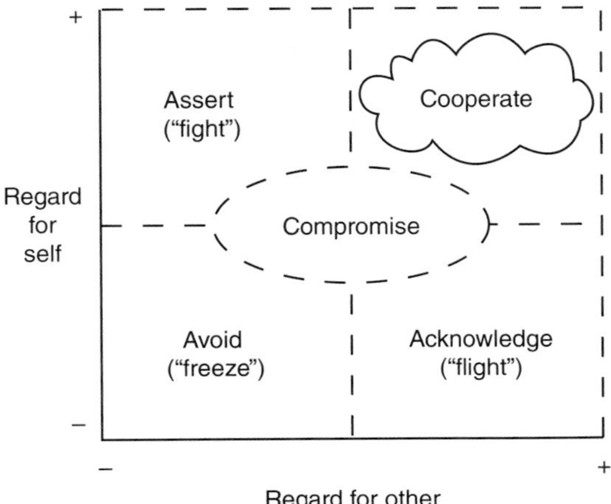

Figure 2.1 Blake and Mouton's dual concerns and the five negotiation tactics

other side's concerns highly but not our own, we acknowledge their interests at our expense.

The dual concerns model makes the following predictions about the antecedents of strategic choice: Cooperation is encouraged when there is strong concern about both our own and the other side's outcomes. Acknowledging (or yielding) is encouraged by a strong concern about the other side's outcome only. Assertiveness is encouraged by a strong concern about our own outcomes only. Finally, inaction (or avoidance) is encouraged when concern about both parties' outcomes is weak. We will also use a fifth category, "compromising." It has been suggested by Richard Shell and sits right in the middle of the figure. This place indicates a moderate concern for both ourselves and the other side. Shell advises negotiators to diagnose their preferences.[40]

Many negotiators perform better in one department than in the other. Most of us are often either overly concerned about ourselves, or about the other side. If you are an experienced negotiator, you probably know where you sit. Which strategy to pursue is a question of the situation and the opponent. It differs, but usually happens under uncertainty. So, what should we do when in doubt? What should be our default strategy in a repeated, multi-issue negotiation? In my view this is almost a philosophical question. I believe that there is no way for us to come up with a general rule for all transactions. This is not a question that can be settled, for the time being at least, empirically. No one has the data of all the world's negotiations. In a few years this may be different. Perhaps then a "HAL 9000"-like supercomputer will draw its conclusions from the commercial transactions of us mortals. (In case you are too young to know the 1968 film classic, *2001: A Space Odyssey*, HAL 9000 stands for "Heuristically Programmed Algorithmic Computer", the artificial intelligence that controls the spacecraft and interacts with the astronauts. Also, watch the film.) We will return to the prospect of artificial intelligence (AI) and learning in the Conclusion. For now, we have to move on without its help. Sometimes it is simply neither practical nor possible to research an item empirically.

Nor is it always necessary. While most of the insights presented herein are based on empirical data, not all of them are. Experiments are not the only way to enhance understanding. Just consider the case of two intellectual giants (that we will come back to later): astronomer Johannes Kepler and philosopher Immanuel Kant. Kepler arrived at his laws of planetary motion by analogical reasoning long before the instruments were invented that would prove the heliocentricity of our solar system. And Immanuel Kant identified the three prerequisites for lasting peace centuries before such a period occurred for the first time in human history – and hence long before the relevant data could be gathered. We only have to consider recent election polling to see that data can also lead to wrong conclusions. Thankfully, we can concern ourselves with lesser matters than the nature of the universe or everlasting peace. I believe our best shot at determining the right strategy in a multi-issue, multi-round negotiation comes from paraphrasing Abraham Lincoln: you can win at the expense of all your negotiation partners some of the time, and at the expense of some all the time. But you cannot win at the expense of all the people all of the time. You can choose the kind of negotiator that you want to be.[41]

Whichever approach you choose, dealing well with the dilemma requires you to step out of it. Two mental models have been found to be useful here.

First model: Negotiators who are reluctant to assert their own interests at the expense of the other side can become much better at it when they imagine negotiating on behalf of somebody else. They don't have to do it for themselves, but for their partner or children who rely on them to "bring home the bacon." It can be similarly helpful to think of your future self: Using this counterintuitive negotiation tactic may feel uncomfortable at the moment, but it might be what is needed to get the best possible deal for your (hopefully early-) retired self.

Second model: Taking the other side's perspective. As Galinsky et al. have stressed, this is not the same as empathizing with them (which can actually diminish your success). But seeing the world with the other person's eyes allows you to better claim and create value.[42]

As fitting as it is, the prisoner's dilemma is only a metaphor. In real negotiations, we need more than just two tactics to deal with the dilemma. Crucially, this means that to be successful, it is not enough to care only for oneself. Rather, we have to care equally for the other side. Only then can we pick and apply the right tactic in a given situation. Why? Recall the mechanics of doing a trade-off. The dots in the Yin & Yang symbol remind us that neither cooperative nor competitive tactics should be overdone. Each needs the other in order to avoid becoming extreme. In the repeated negotiations that interest us most, this means that we sometimes have to do what is good for the other side at our expense, and what is good for us at theirs. So, when we look at the motives of the negotiator, we find a familiar Aristotelean pattern. Having high regard for myself can be contrary to having high regard for you. But the two can also be perfectly compatible with one another! And, of course, they can be contradictory, meaning that they are true to varying degrees. We therefore need to cultivate what has been called "mixed" motives to master the dilemma. Mixed motives are the necessary consequence of the interdependence in which negotiators find themselves.

Above and beyond the six cooperative tactics and six competitive tactics (see Tables 1.1 and 1.4) we must be able to employ the tactics of the lower half of Figure 2.1: Avoiding and acknowledging. Yes, they display only low regard toward ourselves. And they might therefore not immediately improve our outcome. But every time that we seek to create value by trading off on different priorities, we must yield a bit to the other side. Only this will allow us to assert our interest by log-rolling another issue. There are also situations in which we need to give in, in order to get out of a deadlock, or to signal an apology. If both sides are capable of doing this, they can find a way out of lose–lose. Likewise, it is crucial for a negotiator to discern between the battles that should be picked and the ones that should not. We need to know when to avoid a dispute or issue altogether.

The magic happens when the other side also has that capability. As we saw in Chapter 1, Dutch psychologist Carsten De Dreu found that the best negotiators were the ones who tried to maximize both their own and the other side's outcome. They were the ones that reported high concerns for their own interests *and* high concerns for their counterpart's interests. If these negotiators meet like-minded counterparts, they can change the nature of the game. Let's see how.[43]

2.3 Changing the Nature of the Game

As negotiators, we might only be metaphorical prisoners of the situation. But we are in a dilemma nevertheless. Not many people enjoy being stuck in one. Is it really inevitable? Can't we have a neutral or even optimal Nash equilibrium instead? The answer, thankfully, is yes. There are two ways in which we can change the nature of the game: (1) we may attempt to change the payoffs; or (2) we can attempt to morph it into another game: If the prisoner's dilemma is repeatedly played, it can become a "stag hunt" game.

2.3.1 Changing the Payoffs

Robert Axelrod, the originator of the tournament as explained in section 2.2.1, suggests changing the payoffs of the game to promote cooperation. He argues that this is what governments do when they impose sanctions on not paying taxes. Nobody wants to pay them, but it is better to do so than go to jail. Axelrod explains that it is not necessary to completely eliminate the tension between cooperation and competition. It is only necessary to make the long-term incentive for the former greater than the short-term incentive for the latter. When the right probabilities are associated with the different choices, the dominant strategy can become "create value/create value."[44]

We can consciously exit the interaction and negotiate the game itself. By structuring their transactions differently, parties can benefit from creating payoffs that correspond to the stag hunt rather than to the prisoner's dilemma. For example, a great opportunity for this is when two or more corporations decide to work together by establishing a strategic alliance. In his intriguing book, *Game-Changer: Game Theory and the Art of Transforming Strategic Situations*, David McAdams quotes Zhuge Liang, Regent of the Shu kingdom: "The wise win before they fight, while the ignorant fight to win." He argues that the wise win by recognizing all the games that could be played, steering the strategic environment in their favor, and then fighting with confidence in their ultimate victory. The ignorant, by contrast, just play the game that lies before them, their defeat or victory largely out of control and a matter of luck of fortune. In Chapter 1 we saw that by changing your best alternative away from the table, you can greatly change your power at the table. Similarly, as McAdams explains, we can escape the prisoner's dilemma by changing the payoffs of the transaction.[45]

To do so, it can be very useful to engage a neutral third party, such as a deal mediator, who can help the parties create a payoff matrix conducive to cooperation. Consider this case described by Wheeler:

> A neighborhood was alarmed about a landfill operator's application to increase the size of the dump. The residents had long been angry about windblown litter from the site landing all over their lawns. Expanding the facility would only make matters worse, they claimed. They vowed to continue their opposition unless the operator guaranteed payment to an independent contractor who'd clean up future debris to their full satisfaction. The operator refused, convinced that the neighbors would make a sweetheart deal with someone's brother-in-law to fix problems that the landfill hadn't even caused. His business could end up overpaying substantially. The parties were at an impasse: the operator couldn't get his revised permit, and the neighbors still had trash floating into their yards. How could both sides do better? The parties here had a long and antagonistic history, with each side imputing bad motives to the other. The lack of trust stymied creative problem solving. Town officials were caught in the middle. They were sympathetic to the abutters but also valued the landfill business, as it provided tax revenue and an important service to other citizens. When other efforts at peace-making failed, they hired an outside mediator, an environmental lawyer who had no prior ties to the community. He held a public session where people shot accusations back and forth, and then he met privately with individuals. His goal was to find a solution that would address everyone's core concerns. The landfill wanted to grow; that was obvious. And its neighbors wanted their own properties to be cleaner – much cleaner. The mediator then called together key representatives. He told them that he had come up with a possible solution, but he wanted everyone to hear each of its elements before expressing opposition or support. "Point one," the mediator said. "At the start of each fiscal year, the landfill will advance one hundred thousand dollars to the town to cover cleanup costs." The owner started to speak. This was more than he was prepared to pay. But the mediator put up his hand. "Hold on," he said. "Point two. Town officials will control that fund and put the cleanup work out to bid." The neighbors looked at one another. This scenario wasn't quite what they had in mind. "Point three," the mediator continued. "At the end of the year, whatever's left of the fund will be divided two ways. Half will go back to the landfill operator. The town can spend the other half any way it wants." A few people smiled. Others looked confused. "Run that last point by us again,"

somebody said. The mediator explained that whatever was left of the $100,000 would be divided, with the landfill getting a refund, of sorts. The town could spend the other half on the library, a new Little League field, or anything else it needed.

Some people looked sceptical, as they were catching up with the idea that the problem that had long confounded them might have a practical solution. It was as if they were looking for holes in the plan and were perplexed that there weren't any. The up-front guarantee of $100,000 addressed the concerns of even the most pessimistic opponents. In turn, the landfill operator was relieved to see that his exposure would be capped in the worst-case scenario and likely be much lower in the best. After all, the town would now have an incentive to control cleanup costs in order to enjoy a year-end bonus. As for the neighbors, after thinking about it, they actually liked that the landfill could earn back some of its money. Dangling that carrot could make it more careful about keeping trash from blowing off the site in the first place.

It was a simple and elegant solution, one that addressed past problems and created incentives for joint value creation going forward. The only regret was that someone hadn't thought of it earlier. Maybe things had to get bad before they got better. Maybe people would listen only to an outsider with no local political baggage. But often we can't count on a mediator riding in to solve our negotiation problems. Instead, we have to rely on our own creative vision and the capacity to explain it so that it is accepted.[46]

2.3.2 The Stag Hunt Game

The second way to overcome the negotiator's dilemma is by changing its nature so that it morphs into another game: the stag hunt game (sometimes also called the "assurance game" or "coordination game"). The French philosopher Jean-Jacques Rousseau imagined two individuals that go hunting. Each decides whether to hunt a stag or a hare:

> Let us suppose that the hunters each have just the choice of hunting hare or hunting deer. The chances of getting a hare are independent of what others do. There is no chance of bagging a deer by oneself but the chances of a successful deer hunt go up sharply with the number of hunters. A deer is much more valuable than a hare. Then we have the kind of interaction that that is now generally known as the Stag Hunt.[47]

The payoff table of the game is shown in Table 2.2. I have assigned numeric values to the outcomes of the hunt, just as I did when quantifying the possible outcomes of the prisoner's dilemma. Obtaining a stag awards the hunter with a value of 4, and obtaining a hare with a value of 3. Returning from the hunt empty-handed, obviously, has no value to either hunter. Note that these values are not significant as such. They merely express the different preferences both animals carry in relation to one another – and allow us to see the outcome as a result of the interplay between both hunters.

Table 2.2 The stag hunt game

		B	
		Hunts stag (= cooperates)	Hunts hare
A	Hunts stag (= cooperates)	A: 4 B: 4	A: 0 B: 3
	Hunts hare	A: 3 B: 0	A: 3 B: 3

So, the players have a choice to make. And, like in the prisoner's dilemma, their return depends on the other's choice as well. However, the payoff structure is different. As long as each player is convinced that the other player will, in fact, cooperate, it is in their best interests also to cooperate because, in this constellation, cooperation clearly yields the best results for both. In the stag hunt game, what is rational for one player depends on what they believe the other player will decide. In contrast to the prisoner's dilemma, there are two Nash equilibria: hunting stag or hunting hare.

Of equal significance in both dilemmas is the player's reputation if it is repeatedly played. Stag hunters are propelled toward their desired payoffs not so much by greed as by first tenuous and then more robust trust. Each party assumes that the other will cooperate, and, when they do, reciprocate in kind. Defections are usually matched by defections, so that both sides are keen to get back to cooperation. Thus, the players come to establish a positive cycle of cooperation and also break negative cycles of defection. Driven by reciprocity, they arrive at win–win. This is the basis for many long-term private and business partnerships. It makes clear why it so important to establish trust from the very beginning of a negotiation, lest the partnerships be "strained from the start."[48]

Thus, a repeated prisoner's dilemma can "morph" into a stag hunt game. The dilemma is between individual rationality and mutual benefit: Individuals who cooperate choose less rather than more. But if one side is certain that the other will continue to cooperate, mutual cooperation becomes the rational choice. The problem of cooperation in the prisoner's dilemma has not been resolved, but by bringing the future into the picture, its nature has been transformed.[49]

Remarkably, small children already have the ability to work together in stag hunt settings (for instance, when they might receive rice puffs by working on their own, but a bag of gummy bears if they work together). Even more remarkably, so do chimpanzees, such as in an experiment where the "hare boxes" contained a drinking bottle with a weak mixture of fruit syrup and water. The "stag" apparatus consisted of a platform and rope spanning a booth between two cages. When two animals pulled simultaneously on ends of the rope, the platform lifted and the stag rewards

(6 cm of banana for each) became accessible. When the hare was of low value, and the partner's behavior was readily observable, partners of both species were able to successfully coordinate on the higher value stag more than 90 percent of the time. By contrast, when the value of the hare was raised and observing the partner was more difficult, the chimpanzees became less successful, whereas the children compensated (and so remained highly successful) by communicating more often and more specifically.[50]

In the stag hunt, the question becomes whether we can trust the other side. Unfortunately, there is often a lack of trust in other people. For two decades, Karen Walch of the Thunderbird School of Global Management has been asking her students how cooperative and trusting they are personally, and how they feel about their counterparts:

> What we've generally found so far is that 40% of people tend to believe that they are cooperative and trusting. Yet, when asked about the counterpart, people tend to believe that the other party is just looking to win. It's this type of mentality that causes negotiators to take a defensive strategy, which often leaves a lot of value left on the table.[51]

So how can we change the nature of the game from a prisoner's dilemma to a stag hunt? First, as we have seen, both sides need to be willing and capable to negotiate "with an iron fist inside a velvet glove," and they must have mixed motives and the ability to use all five negotiation tactics. After that, there are principally two elements to changing the nature of the game: The negotiators can agree on the right framework within which they operate, and they can cultivate the right attitude. Both promote one another.

2.3.2.1 The Right Framework

Good negotiators agree on the process. They determine the framework in which they work. That framework can facilitate the playing of a specific game, such as the stag hunt game. When a company sets up a procurement price auction, it ensures the best possible price – but makes the creation of a stag hunt game impossible. When the actors are nation states, negotiation frameworks are often institutionalized. The EU, of course, comes to mind again. And indeed, beneficially transforming the nature of negotiations with its neighboring countries might be the primary motivator for countries to join the EU (or EC, its predecessor). Corresponding political declarations are legion. We have looked at Brexit numerous times already, so let's hear what the Prime Minister who took the country *into* the EC, Edward Heath, had to say during the debate in the House of Commons on October 28, 1971, on Britain's application to join the EC:

> It is understandable after 10 years of negotiation and frustration that many in debate and many in the country outside have fought and talked in terms of "we" and "they". Some,

I think, have been overwhelmed by a fear that this country in an organisation such as the Community must always be dominated by "they". That is certainly not how the rest of the Community sees it. But we are approaching the point where, if this House so decides tonight, it will become just as much our Community as their Community. We shall be partners, we shall be cooperating, and we shall be trying to find common solutions to common problems of all the members of an enlarged Community. We have confidence that we can benefit as well as contribute, that we can further our own interests and the interests of the Community at one and the same time.[52]

The creation of a framework that is conducive to a stag hunt game requires a certain mindset. We have already seen that the ability to cooperate necessitates high regard for one's own, as well as the other's, concerns. I believe that overcoming the negotiator's dilemma over time hinges on another, related, quality. To change the nature of the game, both sides need to possess forbearance. And we can look at political science again to appreciate its significance. In this field too, researchers have struggled to identify ways to overcome destructive interactions and safeguard civilization's achievements. They point out the significance of strong institutions, and warn that institutions alone are not enough. Actors must have the right attitude to the game too.

2.3.2.2 The Right Attitude

Daniel Levitsky and Steven Ziblatt have explored what causes democracies to erode, and how such erosion can be prevented. They have identified "forbearance" as a necessary prerequisite. I believe that it is equally crucial in our context, and for the same reasons. Let's look at Levitsky and Ziblatt's reasoning: They show that democracies may not only be dismantled quickly, such as by Hitler in the wake of the 1933 Reichstag fire, but that they can also be eroded slowly, in barely visible steps. They argue that democratic institutions can become political weapons, wielded forcefully by those who control them against those who do not: "This is how elected autocrats subvert democracy – packing and 'weaponizing' the courts and other neutral agencies, buying off the media and the private sector (or bullying them into silence), and rewriting the rules of politics to tilt the playing field against opponents." The researchers hold that institutions alone are not enough to rein in elected autocrats if they could not be kept away from mainstream party tickets. "Constitutions must be defended – by political parties and organized citizens, but also by democratic norms. Without robust norms, constitutional checks and balances do not serve as the bulwarks of democracy we imagine them to be." Levitsky and Ziblatt put it like this:[53]

Historically, our system of checks and balances has worked pretty well – but not, or not entirely, because of the constitutional system designed by the founders. Democracies work best – and survive longer – where constitutions are reinforced by unwritten democratic norms. Two basic norms have preserved America's checks and balances in ways we have come to take for granted: mutual toleration, or the understanding that competing parties accept one another as legitimate rivals, and forbearance, or the idea that politicians should exercise restraint in deploying their institutional prerogatives.[54]

And this is how they defined *forbearance*:

> Forbearance means "patient self-control; restraint and tolerance," or "the action of restraining from exercising a legal right." For our purposes, institutional forbearances can be thought of as avoiding actions that, while respecting the letter of the law, obviously violate its spirit. Where norms of forbearance are strong, politicians do not use their institutional prerogatives to the hilt, even if it is technically legal to do so, for such action could imperil the existing system. Just as divine-right monarchies required forbearance, so do democracies. Think of democracy as a game that we want to keep playing indefinitely. To ensure future rounds of the game, players must refrain from either incapacitating the other team or antagonizing them to such a degree that they refuse to play again tomorrow. If one's rivals quit, there can be no future games. This means that although individuals play to win, they must do so with a degree of restraint. In a pickup basketball game, we play aggressively, but we know not to foul excessively – and to call a foul only when it is egregious. After all, you show up at the park to play a basketball game, not to fight. In politics, this often means eschewing dirty tricks or hardball tactics in the name of civility and fair play.[55]

I believe that this applies not only to the interaction between political players, but to all negotiations. As negotiators, we can ultimately only master the dilemma if we develop the capability to restrain ourselves. Only then can we turn repeated negotiations from a series of individual and unconnected interactions into subsequent rounds of the same transaction. And only then are we able to overcome the negotiator's dilemma.

***

Before we proceed, let's pause for a moment and consider our journey thus far. To recap: The successful negotiator has to be able to master both value creation and value distribution, even though they are paradoxical, so that they can choose and apply the right one in view of the other side. To most of us, some styles come more naturally than others. The same is true for the regard in which we hold ourselves and the other side. All this means that we have to act in accordance with our intuition – as well as against it. So how to properly think about it? This is the third, and deepest, challenge: The ambivalence of rationality and intuition.

Because of our interdependent relationship with the party on the other side of the table, we have to have both high regard for ourselves *and* high regard for them. But we know that the two are sometimes compatible and sometimes not. They can also be direct contradictions of one another, or mere contraries on two ends of a sliding scale that can be simultaneously fulfilled, albeit to differing degrees. The paradoxical task of bargaining puts us in a dilemma that demands equally paradoxical motives from us.

Negotiators have two major worries. The first is that they do not gain all they want. The second is that they do. The same applies to what the other side wants. And the other side has the same worries. How can we think straight about this? This brings us to the third, and deepest, challenge.

3 The Cognitive Ambiguity

Thinking properly about negotiation requires intuition, deliberation – and the ability to choose between the two.

F. Scott Fitzgerald famously remarked that the test of first-rate intelligence is the ability to hold two opposed ideas in the mind at the same time, and still retain the ability to function. It is difficult to deal with the opposed ideas of the tactical paradox and the strategic dilemma. But the biggest difficulty awaits at the personal level. It is parallel to the first two: Just as we have to cooperate and compete with the other side, we have to internally integrate different and conflicting "selves." Negotiators must be simultaneously calm and alert, patient and proactive, practical and creative.[1]

Just as our actions are either deliberate or impulsive, our thinking is deliberate or intuitive. These are the two principal systems of thinking, and both jockey for control. Both forms of thinking have their limitations, and both are needed. Sometimes they lead to the same conclusion, but often they conflict. They can pull us into different directions. In fact, because of the paradox, the two systems of thinking often *should* require two opposing approaches. While we might wish both to eat an apple and keep it for later, we have to make a decision. What we decide to do is determined by our choices and our personality. It depends on who we are – and on who we want to be. Before we can turn toward the other side of the table, we must face whom William Ury calls, tongue-in-cheek, "our most worthy opponent": The biggest obstacle to successful agreement and satisfying relationships is not the other side – it is ourselves, with our natural tendency to (re)act in ways that do not serve our true interests.[2]

Consider this quote by Harvard University psychologist Henry Murray: "A personality is a full Congress of orators and pressure-groups, of children, demagogues, communists, isolationists, war-mongers, mug-wumps, grafters, log-rollers, lobbyists, Caesars and Christs, Machiavels and Judases, Tories and Promethean revolutionists." Perhaps you read the quote and completely agreed. Perhaps you think it a bit over the top but essentially true. Or perhaps you know who Murray was and therefore question what he says. The man who profiled Adolf Hitler and conducted controversial experiments on Harvard undergraduates (one of whom, Theodore John Kaczynski, later became the Unabomber, who orchestrated a bombing campaign in the US between 1978 and 1995) perhaps is not drawing an accurate picture of normal people. My point here is that there may be more than one "voice" in your mind when you think about the world. For instance, you might have agreed with the quote but mistrusted its source. Likewise, in negotiations, we are often torn between the creation and distribution of value, and between regarding our own interests and those of the other side.[3]

Let me draw your attention to the basic duality of our thinking. Sigmund Freud is said to have remarked that the mind is like an iceberg – it floats with one-seventh of its bulk above water. Psychologists and behavioral economists widely follow the dual-process distinction created by Canadian Keith Stanovich. During a sabbatical at Cambridge University in 1991, he began to focus on rationality as mental ability and developed the differentiation between two "systems" of thinking: effortless (and often fast) intuition versus effortful (and often slow) deliberation. Decades after its introduction, dual-process distinction is supported by more recent evidence in cognitive science.[4]

I like to visualize the two systems of thinking by depicting them as the two parts of an iceberg (see Figure 6 in the Introduction): Deliberate thinking corresponds to the observable part above the water, while intuitive thinking is symbolized by the less obvious, but large, part that is under water. Similarly, deliberate thinking takes place in the brain, while emotions and intuitions are often associated with lower parts of the body (the heart, the guts) – even though intuitive thinking, of course, also takes place in the brain. An alternative way of visualizing the two systems of thinking is offered by American psychologist Jonathan Haidt: Our mind is like the rider on the back of an elephant – "The rider is conscious, controlled thought. The elephant is everything else, notably gut feelings, emotions and intuitions that comprise much of the automatic system." Yet another metaphor is offered by British psychiatrist and Olympic consultant Steve Peters, who differentiates between "the Chimp", an emotional machine living in our brain together with our own "Human" selves: "Having a chimp is like owning a dog. You are not responsible for the nature of the dog but you are responsible for managing it and keeping it well behaved."[5]

Please pick the metaphor you find most helpful. And remember that metaphors are not to be taken literally. The two systems of thinking do not stand for specific and separate brain regions, such as the left and right hemispheres. Notably, they are not the same as the two systems of thinking. Instead, each system encompasses a whole bundle of diverse activities that take place all over the brain. Even conceptually, the idea of the two systems is really a simplification that is meant to help us think about thinking. Scientists ceaselessly explore (and endlessly argue about) the right categorizations. When it comes to non-deliberate thinking, Stanovich himself now prefers to use the plural, "because it refers to a *set* of systems in the brain that operate autonomously in response to their own triggering stimuli and are not under higher-level cognitive control."[6]

Our intuition makes decisions based on notions such as fear, lust, hunger, anxiety, disgust, happiness, and sadness. They often provide direct behavioral motivation. When faced with a predator, our ancestors did not carefully weigh different outcomes by calculating risks and expected values. Neither do we. The most natural thing to do when confronted with a difficult situation is to react. In other words – to act without thinking. Note that it is quite human to do so. Eva Ekman, who studies mindfulness at the University of California in Berkeley, emphasizes that she has yet to meet a person who is able to stop unwanted emotions from occurring. And she has studied some of the best emotional regulators on the planet. "Even with my work with . . . the Dalai Lama, he describes the difficulty of feeling angry and responding to anger. He is able to have anger come and go – but not to stop it right in the middle." It seems to me that this idea is generalizable to all intuitions. Our responsibility as human beings is not to suppress emotions, but to manage them adequately and productively.[7]

Importantly, even though many of the errors that we make are the result of our intuitive thinking, this is not to say that it is only intuition that can lead to irrational decisions – or that only deliberate thinking can lead to rational ones. Assuming such a one-to-one relationship would be a mistake. In fact, deliberation can also lead to cognitive errors, and intuitive thinking to rational decisions. To think accurately, especially about negotiation, we need to use Intuition & Deliberation. In this chapter we will look at the benefits of each. We will start with our intuition, which can save us, both in the jungle and at the negotiation table. But it also can lead us astray. Let's explore how.[8]

3.1 Intuition

3.1.1 The Benefits of Intuition

There are a number of benefits that only our intuition can offer us. This has long been acknowledged by creativity researchers such as Graham Wallas and psychologists such as Aaron Beck and Daniel Kahneman. And it is increasingly acknowledged in negotiation research.

In his book, *Mindware*, psychologist Richard Nisbett presents tools for smart thinking. He maintains that you have to help the unconscious help you. While consciousness is essential for identifying the elements of a problem, and for producing rough sketches of what a solution would look like, the necessary conclusions are often reached by the unconscious mind. It is then the job of the conscious mind to elaborate on these conclusions. "The most important thing I have to tell you – in this whole book – is that you should never fail to take advantage of the free labor of the unconscious mind." Neurologist Oliver Sacks concurs: Creativity involves not only conscious preparation but also unconscious preparation. An incubation period is essential to allow the subconscious assimilation of one's influences and sources, to recognize and synthesize them into something of one's own.[9]

London School of Economics co-founder Graham Wallas established his four-stage model of the creative process in 1926, and it still holds sway today: After deliberate preparation, a period of incubation is called for, which might lead to illumination that in turn requires deliberate verification.[10]

Incubation is possible whenever the mind is not deliberately occupied with the problem in question. Inventors often claim that illumination hit them when they were in one of the "3 Bs": In bed, in a bath, or on a bus. Sleep appears to play a particularly important role here. Sleep retains much of its mystery: some scientists stress that despite thousands of experiments, no one has been able to declare with certainty why all life forms sleep. Others wonder whether there are any biological functions that are *not* supported by it. Incubation certainly benefits from it. Researchers such as Deidre Barrett have gathered remarkable examples, historic and modern, of what dreams have brought to invention and art. She quotes French Surrealist poet St. Paul Roux, who said: "It is a common experience that a problem difficult at night is resolved in the morning after the *committee of sleep* has worked on it" (and named her book after that committee). It is a fascinating journey, ranging from the art of Francisco Goya and Samuel Taylor Coleridge to scientific models such as DNA and the atom.[11]

In some situations, we simply have to rely on "gut feeling." This does not have to be a bad thing. Aaron T. Beck, the founder of cognitive therapy, pointed to the benefits of our intuitive thinking:

> In his interpersonal relations, (modern man) is generally able to select the subtle cues that allow him to separate his adversaries from his friends. He makes the delicate adjustments in his own behaviour that help him to maintain diplomatic relationships with people whom he dislikes or who dislike him. He is generally able to penetrate the social masks of other people, to differentiate sincere from insincere messages, to distinguish friendly mocking from veiled antagonism. He tunes into the significant communications in a vast babble of noises so that he can organize and modulate his own response. These psychological operations seem to work automatically without evidence of much cognition, deliberation, or reflection.[12]

Daniel Kahneman draws our attention to our great day-to-day intuition:

> Expert intuition strikes us as magical, but it is not. Indeed, each of us perform feats of intuitive expertise many times each day. Most of us are pitch-perfect in detecting anger in the first word of a telephone call, recognize as we enter a room that we are the subject of the conversation, and quickly react to subtle signs that the driver of the car in the next lane is dangerous. Our everyday intuitive abilities are no less marvellous than the striking insights of an experienced firefighter or physician – only more common.[13]

We can typically determine the gender of a person from observing the way they walk in the distance. Children can quickly learn to differentiate the style of Mozart from that of Handel. Adults can learn to tell hundreds of wines apart. And all of this without our consciously considering it. We often do not even have a vocabulary that would allow us to make these differentiations willfully. This ability becomes all the more important when we talk about the more intangible aspects of negotiation, such as fairness or equity. It cannot always be measured, but the parties often "feel" strongly about it. The situation is similar to finding creative solutions to negotiation problems. We cannot actively will ourselves to be creative; the innovation needs to come to us.

Recent research on the cognitive processes of professional negotiators in the EU institutions, particularly in complex and uncertain task environments, supports this view. Pierre Debaty's study discovered the widespread use of intuition in some key negotiation tasks – namely in "sizing up" the other side and in assessing the dynamics of the negotiation. The author argues that in these tasks, negotiators might not always have a cognitive choice, and suggests "restoring intuition to the negotiation table."[14]

Similarly, a recent study led by Narayanan Kandasamy suggests that gut feeling, as expressed in bodily signals such as a person's heartbeat, contribute to success in the financial markets. It found that traders working on a London trading floor who were better able to perceive their own heartbeats than a control group achieved higher relative profitability, and strikingly, were found to survive longer in the financial markets.[15]

Their review of decision-making in negotiations led Chia-Jung Tsay and Max Bazerman to suggest that intuition – defined here as "gut feeling based on unconscious past experience" – might indeed allow us to arrive at better decisions, particularly when dealing with complex decision problems.[16]

3.1.2 The Limits of Intuition

Our intuition, just like our deliberate thinking, has its limitations. There is voluminous evidence from all areas of life showing that relying only on intuition can lead to irrationality. As a reminder, just consider the last time you were fooled by the "Helmholtz illusion": "Every evening apparently before our eyes the sun goes down behind the stationary horizon, although we are well aware that the sun is fixed and the horizon moves." Even though our rational mind tells us so, our intuitive perception still fools us. On hearing the argument that this illusion was natural, because it just looks like the sun travels around the earth, philosopher Ludwig Wittgenstein dryly asked: "What would it have looked like if it had *looked* as if the earth turned on its axis?" Negotiations provide ample grounds for getting something intuitively wrong. For a start, understanding the paradox of the task usually does not come intuitively, at least to the Western mind. Quite the contrary – our intuition very often prefers ideas to be free of contradictions.[17]

We tend to jump to conclusions, even involuntarily. Just because an explanation occurs to us intuitively, it need not be right. Daniel Kahneman quotes this example from Howard Wainer and Harris Zwerling's article:

> A study of the incidence of kidney cancer in 3,141 counties of the United States reveals a remarkable pattern. The counties in which the incidence of kidney cancer are lowest are mostly rural, sparsely populated, and located in traditionally Republican States in the Midwest, the South, and the West. What do you make of this?[18]

As Kahneman points out, it makes perfect sense to conclude that the low cancer rates are directly due to the clean living of the rural lifestyle: no pollution and access to food without additives. And he proceeds to quote, tongue-in-cheek, the authors of the scenario, Wainer and Zwerling: "It is easy to infer that their high cancer rates might be directly due to the poverty of the rural lifestyle – no access to good medical care, a high-fat diet, and too much alcohol, too much tobacco."[19]

In other words, both low and high cancer rates can easily be attributed to the rural lifestyle and its supposedly beneficial or, as the case may be, detrimental consequences. But in reality, neither the high nor the low cancer rates have anything to do with lifestyle. They are not caused by the lifestyle of the rural population. Instead, the rates are explained by the statistical effect of small numbers. When we look at a small sample size (whether from a rural or an urban population), the result is distorted. Hence the rates are explained by the fact that all of these counties are "sparsely populated." The extreme rates are the result of a statistical rule: Small sample sizes lead to uncharacteristically extreme outcomes. When we toss a coin a few times, it might come heads up all the time. This does not mean that "heads" are more likely than "tails." We are all familiar with the fact that a political poll requires a minimum number of participants to be representative. Turn this insight on its head and you have the explanation why "outliers" inhabit small populations.

In negotiations, depending on our previous life experience, we will intuitively revert to more competitive or more cooperative behavior in a given situation. Some of the five behavioral styles we explored in the last chapter come more naturally to us than others. Because of the dilemma, our intuitive response might be the right one, or the wrong one. Your preferred and intuitive course of action might, for instance, be to cooperate with the other side. But when you have just been subject to a competitive move by them, responding cooperatively might be unhelpful. Instead, analogous to tit for tat, you may now need to take the "velvet gloves" off. Following your intuition in this situation may lead to a lose–win outcome at your expense. If, on the other hand, your default mode is to compete, you may also find yourself losing. You might force the other side to repay you in kind, resulting in the dreaded lose–lose.

Johns Hopkins University's Brian Gunia consequently points to the "unreliability of our gut." Our rapid intuition may tell us *not* to use many of the proper tactics of value creation or value distribution – such as avoiding making the first offer, and dealing with one issue at a time. Similarly, Harvard University's Max Bazerman cautions us to be very careful in "following our gut" in negotiations. While the advice to do so might sound appealing, most people already take their rapid gut instincts seriously and act on them on a daily basis – often to their detriment. He stresses that the past thirty years of behavioral-decision research and its application to negotiation have given us abundant reasons to question our instinctual responses. Psychological research shows that there are a number of harmful biases that are likely to affect our rapid cognitions more than they do our deliberative thought: "After all, it's our rapid cognitions that motivate us to fly off the handle, overeat, drink too much, and gamble away extra earnings."[20]

We will first look at four prominent biases, and then at three examples of how they systematically can get in our way.

3.1.2.1 Biases

As negotiators, we are especially prone to falling into one of four cognitive traps: The idea that a negotiation must be "won"; that "what is good for them must be bad for us"; "if it comes from them it must be bad"; and "we have to strike back."

"A Negotiation Must Be Won" (the Fixed-Pie Bias) That a negotiation "must be won" is a commonly held yet largely unhelpful belief. Many individuals try to win a negotiation in the same way as you might try to win a game or a sports competition. This approach is a logical consequence of the erroneous assumption that every negotiation invariably leads to a winner and a loser. This myth has also been called the "fixed-pie bias": when dividing up a pie, what one side receives, the other side must lose, and vice versa. As we have seen, nearly all negotiations (with the rare exception of the orange case) include elements of winning at the expense of the other side. At the same time, most negotiations are not limited to this. Instead, very often opportunity is present for the parties to "expand the pie."[21]

But, as we have seen, it is often possible for all involved to win. Consider some of the negotiators that were awarded Nobel Prizes:

- Mohamed Al-Sadat and Menachem Begin for bringing about negotiated peace between Egypt and Israel (1978).
- Nelson Mandela and Frederic Willem de Klerk for jointly laying the foundations for a democratic, post-apartheid South Africa (1993).
- John Hume and David Trimble for finding a peaceful solution to the conflict in Northern Ireland (1998).

All of these Nobel Prize-winners had to overcome the fixed-pie mindset that is so prevalent, and natural, in peace- (and deal-)making.

"If It's Good for Them, It Must Be Bad for Us" (the Incompatibility Bias) A variation of this mindset is the "incompatibility bias," which holds that the interests of both sides must be mutually incompatible. In other words, the incompatibility bias assumes that "what is good for them must be bad for us." All too often we erroneously believe that the interests of the other side conflict directly with our own interests, and therefore fail to see that usually more than one issue is at stake. In addition, we also fail to see that these issues are often valued differently by the different parties. We therefore miss the opportunity to jointly maximize our gains by creating a mutually beneficial trade-off.

"If It Comes from Them, It Must Be Bad" (Reactive Devaluation) Often the incompatibility bias has its roots in another cognitive illusion, the reactive devaluation. This occurs when people reactively devalue an idea simply because it comes from another party. Put simply, the reactive devaluation results in the often incorrect assumption that "if the offer comes from them it must be bad for us." An experiment from the Cold War era illustrates this point. At a time when more and more people wished to put an end to the nuclear arms race between the USA and the USSR, individuals were presented with the description of a nuclear weapons reduction plan in the experiment. Respondents were arbitrarily divided into two groups. One group was told that the reduction plan had been drawn up by the Soviets, while the other group was told that the plan originated from the White House. The content of both plans was identical. The respondents were US citizens. When they were asked how they viewed the offer, their assessment varied in accordance with who they thought had made the offer. Respondents who were told that the offer came from Mr. Gorbachev stated that the offer would dramatically favor the Soviets. Practically no respondents from the other group shared that view. Believing that the offer came from their own Government, respondents from this group considered it to be equally beneficial for both sides.[22]

The belief that "the best lawyers are adversarial" is another variation of this myth. This widely held but incorrect belief was conclusively shattered by Andrea Schneider's wide-ranging study, which asked more than 700 practicing lawyers to evaluate the negotiation styles and resulting effectiveness of other lawyers. It was in fact joint problem-solving, rather than stubbornness, arrogance, or egoism, that was widely perceived as the most effective negotiation style among lawyers.[23]

"We Have to Strike Back" (the Irrational Escalation of Commitment) Unchecked intuition can also lead us to irrationally escalate commitment. We intuitively reciprocate the behavior of others. And we might feel that we simply have no choice. But if we respond in kind, the situation can spin out of control. We might never have wanted that. Rather, we might feel that we simply had no choice. In the words of Cambridge University historian Christopher Clark, people can find themselves "sleepwalking" into disaster. (In his book, *The Sleepwalkers: How Europe Went to War in 1914*, Clark explains how a group of well-meaning leaders drove the crisis forward in a few short weeks thorough a series of mutual misunderstandings and unintended signals.)[24]

We do not have to rely on historical examples of intuitive decisions leading to unintended consequences. The irrational escalation of conflicts is a well-documented phenomenon in more recent times (and less dramatic circumstances). It occurs when we continue to take a previously selected course of action even when it is no longer in our deliberate self-interest. Irrational escalation can be observed in price wars and merger battles, when negotiators adopt the attitude of "we will stick to our plan no matter what it costs."[25]

In a price war, each side pursues the goal of beating the other side as opposed to making the industry more profitable. Bazerman and Neale describe a classic example from the early 1980s: The introduction, by American Airlines, of the first "frequent flyer" program. The program was arguably the most innovative marketing program in the history of the airline industry: Customers could earn miles for the flights they took and redeem those miles for travel awards. The incentive plan had been designed to encourage loyalty for American Airlines. But from a negotiations standpoint it was a miserable decision, and soon proved disastrous from a marketing and financial standpoint. Why? All of American Airlines's competitors soon launched their own frequent flyer programs – and even offered double miles to their most frequent passengers. The benefits required to remain competitive quickly inflated out of control and resulted in tremendous liabilities. When Delta announced in December 1987 that all passengers who charged tickets to their American Express card would receive triple miles for all of the following year, analysts estimated that the airlines owed their passengers between $1.5 and $3 billion in free trips.[26]

In 2004, many years after frequent flyer schemes became a standard feature of the industry, Max Bazerman pointed out that the problem remained largely unsolved and had by then turned into a "house of cards":

> Most of us collect our miles and even think of them as an asset that we can rely on using in the future. We think this is optimism. For many U.S. airlines, the debt owed to customers in the form of miles is a value significantly larger than the airlines' market capitalization. This is simply not sustainable. Airlines have already reduced the value of miles by making seats less and less available. But a larger predictable surprise still awaits. We stick by our recommendation: use your miles![27]

A Hostile Environment The reason why these four biases (and others) are so detrimental is that they can fall on fertile ground in negotiations. Keith Stanovich draws our attention to what he calls "hostile environments," which contain other individuals who might (or will) adjust their behavior to exploit your intuitive thinking. It is very clear, especially when we remember the six tactics of value distribution, that a negotiation is the epitome of such an environment. In a zero-sum game, we can only maximize our outcome by minimizing the outcome of the other side. We have to do that, for most part, by trying to exploit the other side's thinking – and so do they.[28]

I will now give three examples where our biases almost automatically lead to suboptimal outcomes: Procurement, claim management and M&A. They may partly explain (1) why companies who have complied with their contractual obligations are in a worse position to negotiate out-of-court settlements than those who have not; (2) why in procurement, sellers often do worse than buyers, and (3) conversely, why in M&A it is often the buyers who do worse.

3.1.2.2 Claim Management and the Fourfold Pattern

Daniel Kahneman and Amos Tversky identified a "fourfold pattern" that emerges when risk preferences are coupled with probabilities. They explain that people are risk-averse for high probability gains and risk-seeking for high probability losses.[29]

The decision weights we assign to outcomes are not identical to the probabilities of the outcomes. What does that mean? Probabilities can range from zero to 100 percent, and every 1 percent decrease or increase represents an identical change. But we do not typically put the same weight on these changes. Consider a lottery in which you can win $1,000,000. Imagine your chances of receiving the price improve by 5 percent. The likelihood increases equally whether the change is from zero to 5 percent, from 5 percent to 10 percent, from 60 percent to 65 percent, and from 95 percent to 100 percent. But of course, these improvements weigh quite differently in our mind. An increase from zero to 5 percent represents a qualitative change, because now the win has become possible. Likewise, the change from 95 percent to 100 percent means that the win is now a certainty.

These examples highlight a general human tendency. We tend to give undue weight to very low and very high probabilities. Overestimating the impact of low probabilities (because it is at least possible) is called the "possibility effect." Underestimating the impact of high probabilities (because it is not quite certain) is called the "certainty effect." Let's combine these findings with another human tendency. When making decisions under uncertain conditions, we value possible positive outcomes differently from negative ones. In general, as Thomas Gilovich and Lee Ross point out, holding objective magnitude constant, bad things hurt us more than good things feel good. Our decision is therefore influenced by the way we frame it. Is it about a gain that is to be made? Or is it about a loss that is to be averted? The answer determines whether we are more, or less, likely to take a risk: People tend to be more willing to take a risk in order to avoid a loss than they are to take a risk in order to make a gain. (This insight sits at the heart of "prospect theory," which we will examine in section 3.1.2.3.) Whether we frame a decision as gain or loss is highly relevant in everyday life, because many outcomes can be equally well described in the language of good or bad, or losses and gains. One example can be found in the realm of claim management. The pattern shown in Table 3.1 emerges from the combination of human thinking about risks and probabilities.[30]

Table 3.1 The fourfold pattern

	Gains	Losses
High probability	95% chance to win $10,000	95% chance to lose $10,000
	Risk-averse	Risk-seeking
	Accept unfavorable settlement	*Reject favorable settlement*
Low probability	5% chance to win $10,000	5% chance to lose $10,000
	Risk-seeking	Risk-averse
	Reject favorable settlement	*Accept unfavorable settlement*

Imagine that the seller of a complex product, such as a power plant, has a claim against the buyer. Suppose the seller is in a strong position and expects to win in a case of dispute resolution. But of course, as in all legal matters, one cannot be entirely certain to prevail in the court of law. German lawyers are fond of saying, “On the high seas and in a court of law, we are in God’s hand.” In the negotiations to settle the claim, the mental frames of the parties might work together to bite the seller. Almost certain of the win, the seller might fear disappointment. His risk aversion could lead him to accept an unfavorable settlement rather than risk being disappointed. On the other side of the table, the buyer is pretty sure that they have to pay up anyway. They are not risking very much. Whether they pay 100 percent of the claim or only 95 percent is almost equally painful. But there is still the hope that they can avoid or minimize the loss. So why not risk rejecting even a favorable settlement? Paradoxically, having a strong legal case may be counterproductive to your settlement negotiations.

3.1.2.3 Procurement and Prospect Theory

Research tells us that buyers tend to outperform sellers in market settings where the balance of power is equal. While the reasons are not entirely clear, I believe the concept developed by Kahneman and Tversky can help explain this success: “Prospect Theory.”[31]

Prospect theory describes how people make decisions under uncertainty. Both buyers and sellers face it. They target the other side’s RP, but they don’t know exactly what it is. In making first offers, concessions, and final moves, they have to decide whether to agree or to continue pushing. They can close the deal – but may leave money on the table. Or they can try to capture it – but might be left without a deal. They cannot have the pie and eat it too. When faced with a choice, a rational decision-maker will evaluate their prospects and choose the one with the highest expected utility.[32]

But people are not always rational in determining the expected utility. Information is not perfect, and the outcome is uncertain. Although we tend to look at the numerical value of different outcomes, we might also be influenced by how we mentally frame the situation. We have just seen that our mental frame influences our risk preferences: We have different preferences when it comes to gains and losses. Prospect theory suggests that our decisions are not the same when we try to avoid a loss than when we try to realize a gain. Even when the numerical values are identical, this mental frame might lead to very different decisions. For instance, patients are more likely to undergo surgery when their doctor says: "Of one hundred patients who have this operation, ninety are alive after five years," rather than saying: "Of one hundred patients who have this operation, ten are dead after five years."[33]

So, as we have seen, the general rule here is that people tend to be risk-averse when it comes to gains and risk-seeking when it comes to avoiding losses. If I focus on what I may receive, I tend to be less willing to risk it by my choices. Conversely, when I focus on avoiding a loss, I might be more willing to take risks to do so. In a negotiation, the risk-averse choice is to accept an offer; the risk-seeking choice is to keep pursuing more concessions. To be sure, individuals have inherently different attitudes to risks. But humans tend not to exhibit consistent risk-seeking or risk-averse behavior. Instead, our attitude depends greatly on the context.[34]

Buying and selling puts us in different contexts. For a seller who focuses on obtaining a high purchase price, the transaction is an opportunity to realize a gain. For a buyer who focuses on spending a low purchase price, the transaction is an opportunity to minimize a loss. This could entice them to behave differently. Sellers would be more risk-averse, leading them to "gamble" less in the negotiation. They would hate to end up empty-handed because of asking for too much. The consequence of this choice is indeed closing more details on average. The flip side is having secured these deals at lower prices on average. Conversely, sellers would push harder for an optimal price. As a consequence, they might lose more deals – but would have to pay lower prices on average. The mental models suggested by both roles conspire to make buyers better off. Even though sellers and buyers face a symmetrical ZOPA, they might evaluate it differently. The greater willingness of buyers to take a risk (to minimize their loss) may explain their greater success.

3.1.2.4 M&A and Overconfidence

For the third practical example of biased perception in negotiations, we return to the field of M&A. Leading M&A expert Robert F. Bruner has analyzed "deals from hell" to draw lessons that "rise above the ashes." One of his key findings is the prevalence of overconfidence. Over-optimism, even hubris, is pervasive at the start of most failed deals. In contrast, the evidence from case studies of successful corporate change suggests that they were based on a sober assessment of the situation.[35]

Behavioral economists have long observed that buyers can become so excited about beating their competitors that they ignore signs that they are overpaying. This happens so frequently that it has a name: deal fever.

> The AOL Time Warner merger, which wiped out $ 200 billions of Time Warner shareholder, is a classic example. There were plenty of warnings that AOL's stock, which was the currency for the merger, was wildly overvalued, yet Time Warner's directors approved the deal unanimously.
> "I did it with as much or more excitement and enthusiasm as I did when I first made love some forty-two years ago," exclaimed Ted Turner, one of those directors and the largest individual shareholder of the company.[36]

What he may have been telling us was that "he was in the same buzzy state of mind as an adolescent who's so excited about spending the night with his new girlfriend that he's not thinking much about the consequences."[37]

The case of Bayer and the Monsanto Company Consider a more recent example: When Bayer, a chemical and drug giant most known for Bayer aspirin, acquired global seed and farm chemicals maker Monsanto, it also bought about 11,200 personal injury cases. *Der Spiegel* estimates that these lawsuits could cost the company $5 billion – and threaten its very existence. Regardless of the final outcome of the suits, the impact was already substantial. Roughly a year after US regulators approved the deal, Bayer (including Monsanto) was worth less than the $63 billion that it had paid to acquire Monsanto. Barron's Robert Teitelman pointed out:[38]

> It looks like Bayer's acquisition of Monsanto is a candidate for the pantheon of terrible mergers and acquisition deals – a crowded club presided over by AOL Time Warner. . . . And that was before Bayer lost two U.S. lawsuits brought by plaintiffs claiming that Monsanto's Roundup weed killer had caused them to contract non-Hodgkin's lymphoma. One received an award of $289 million.[39]

Two months later, *Der Spiegel* of Hamburg reported that a third lawsuit had been lost: A jury in Oakland, California awarded the two plaintiffs damages of roughly $2 billion. This amount was later significantly reduced. But even if it would be overturned completely by a higher court, the lawsuit would still be symptomatic of a larger problem – the remaining personal injury claims.[40]

The question that Barron's asks at the end of the article remains unanswered: "How could Bayer have missed the litigation coming?"[41]

Now, to be sure, they surely saw it coming. And they may have quantified it reasonably. With the sparsity of public information, we bystanders don't know what the ZOPA really was. Also, it might very well be that, in time, the Monsanto acquisition turns out to be the best deal Bayer has ever made, or at least that it was much better than the available alternatives. After all, this is what the company and its advisers have determined. The question that I am raising here, although I'm not able to answer it, is whether the target could have been acquired for substantially less money. In other words, what the next best option of the former owners of Monsanto would have been, and whether it might have delivered a lower price than that which Bayer paid.

It should be noted that buyer overconfidence in M&A deal-making is not an isolated threat. Rather, it is part of a larger struggle to identify and use the right financial indicators of business success. Major corporate decisions, like M&As, are predicated on financial report indicators of profitability and solvency. New York University's Baruch Lev and Feng Gu warn that an "amalgam of guesses and speculations" is increasingly replacing accounting estimates based on solid past experience. They empirically document that the prevalence of accounting estimates in financial reports is increasing. At the same time, they argue that the disclosed financial information no longer reflects the performance and value of business enterprises. They therefore lament the increase in estimates as a major cause of the deteriorating usefulness of financial information, going so far as to proclaim the "end of accounting."[42]

Having dug deeply into the pros and cons of intuition, we can now turn to our second system of thinking, deliberation.

3.2 Deliberation

Our deliberation, like our intuition, is sometimes accurate and sometimes not. Let's look first at when it is beneficial. Thereafter we will explore its limitations and revisit the Great Rationality Debate alluded to in the Introduction.

3.2.1 The Benefits of Deliberation

Successful negotiators deliberately employ the tactics of creating and claiming value that we have explored. Not using a specific tactic can be the result of erroneous intuitions, as we saw in the previous section. But it can also be the result of rational deliberation. Consciously deciding to ask for less than the plausible maximum when selling an item, for instance, can be used as a reputational device. Stefan Povaly of JP Morgan Chase & Co. found that young venture capitalists exited portfolio companies earlier than established firms, and consciously underpriced shares when they took a company public in order to build up a track record of successfully completed exits. This tactic has, rather unflatteringly, been labeled "grandstanding" by private equity researchers.[43]

Others see an even broader problem. *The Economist* recently put forth the idea that initial public offerings (IPOs) are a "racket." The article quotes Ann Sherman, a leading expert on IPO methods at DePaul University, as calling them "legalized bribery," because they allow issuers in effect to buy attention from the market:

> Most of today's IPOs start with a roadshow in which executives of the firm going public and underwriters hit the road – or take private jets – in order to catch the attention of investors and elicit orders from them. The process is part of building the book. For the underwriter, the trick is to find an IPO price that satisfies the company but also stimulates buying – providing a "pop" on the first day of trading. The trouble with the "pop", though, is that it represents money left on the table that should by rights belong to the company's sellers, not its buyers. Jay Ritter of the University of Florida says that during the past decade the underpricing of IPOs in America left a whopping $39bn on that table, or about 14% of the total sum raised. In theory, bankers have an incentive to minimize that amount because they earn fees amounting to as much as 7% of the value of the IPO. In practice, though, they often underprice the listing to favour big investor clients. Money managers pay higher trading commissions, or "soft dollars", he says, in exchange for access to the hottest listings. That makes IPOs look like a racket. But the rub is that until now companies have mostly turned a blind eye. One reason, acknowledges Mr Ritter, is psychological. The sellers usually pocket such a windfall from an IPO that they do not fret about how much more they could have made if it were priced optimally.[44]

(Note that, despite their harsh words, Ms. Sherman is described as "a fan" of IPOs, and *The Economist* argues that there is no good alternative to them.)

Speaking of negotiation in general, we can say that choosing tactics and strategy often benefits from conscious deliberation. Using the iron fist in the velvet glove, for most of us, requires a measure of counterintuition – and therefore only works when we deliberately decide to employ it. And deliberation is also needed whenever we have to keep our own emotions at bay. For instance, a recent study examined the relationship between negative emotions and variables that affect negotiators' profit. The participants' ability to cognitively reappraise negative emotions was found to result in higher profits.[45]

In sum, deliberation is the method of choice to rid ourselves of the numerous biases that threaten our cognition. This is true for all illusions that we have so far explored. But before we look at its limitations, I want to direct you to two additional areas where we can especially profit from deliberation: It can be more accurate than intuition in recognizing emotions, and even in detecting lies.

3.2.1.1 Emotion Recognition and Lie Detection

Some negotiators pride themselves on their intuitive grasp of a counterpart's emotions. They claim that they can observe the other side's feelings by looking at their faces – much like observing an actor. This is an old idea. An actor's face not only expresses emotions vis-à-vis the audience, but also helps the actor to feel that emotion internally. The thoughts of eighteenth-century philosopher Gotthold Ephraim Lessing have been confirmed by later research: "I believe that when the actor properly imitates all the external signs and indicators and all the bodily alterations which experience taught him are expressions of a particular (inner) state, the resulting sense impressions will automatically induce a state in his soul that properly accords with his own movements, posture, and vocal tone." But is the reverse also true? In other words, can we accurately deduce an emotion from a facial expression?[46]

The classical view, still prevalent today, is that each emotion is displayed on the face as a particular pattern of movements – a "facial expression." Hundreds of published experiments have shown that people all over the world match the same words describing emotions (translated into their local language) to meticulously posed photographs of American actors that are meant to exemplify those emotions (such as anger, fear, disgust, surprise, sadness, and happiness). Researchers concluded from this that emotion cognition is universal. They reason that the only way for people to universally recognize (American-style) facial expressions is for them to be universally produced. Thus facial expressions came to be seen as reliable, diagnostic fingerprints of emotions. If this is true, then negotiators are able to accurately intuit their counterparts' emotions by observing their facial expressions.[47]

But more recent findings call this notion into question. When researchers placed electrodes on the surface of the skin to detect the electrical signals that make facial muscles move, a different picture emerged. No facial expressions could be consistently and specifically detected by objectively measuring the muscle movement when people actually felt the emotions. Psychologist Lisa Feldmann Barrett therefore makes the case that there is no "universal fingerprint" that reveals our emotions via our facial expressions. People do not move the same facial muscles in the same way each time they experience a given emotion: "When it comes to emotion, a face does not speak for itself."[48]

She encourages us to consider our own experience: When we feel an emotion such as fear, we might move our face in a variety of ways. When at a horror movie, we might close our eyes or cover them with our hands. When we are not certain if a person directly in front of us might harm us, we might narrow our eyes to see the person's face better. When danger might be lurking around the next corner, our eyes might open wide to improve peripheral vision. "Fear takes no single form. Variation is the norm. Likewise, happiness, sadness, anger, and every other emotion you know is a diverse category, with widely varying facial movements."[49]

As negotiators, we might detect an emotion in a facial expression. But emotions might also lead to quite different, or no, facial expressions. We can therefore not just rely on our observation of the face. Instead, we have to deliberately consider all information that might be relevant in the given situation. It might reveal an emotion that is the opposite of what we were intuiting.

A similar picture emerges when we look at our ability to detect lies in our negotiation partners. It turns out that people's ability to detect lies is no more accurate than chance. This surprising fact is consistently shown by research, and it holds across all types of people – even those whose jobs involve deception detection, such as judges and law enforcement personnel. As the American Psychological Association warns, reliable behavioral indicators of deception (such as posture shifts or gaze aversion) have not yet been identified.[50]

Today's researchers are therefore exploring new methods of deception detection: Instead of visual cues, they look for strategies that interviewers can use to elicit signs of deception. One strategy used by law enforcement (that you might be familiar with from the movies) is to increase interviewees' cognitive load by, for example, asking them to tell their story in reverse chronological order: "Truth tellers can rely on their memory to tell their story backwards, often adding new details, but liars tend to struggle." Unfortunately, this is not very practical in negotiations. Another technique is: Encouraging the other side to say more and listen intently (which is also one of the twelve major negotiation tactics that we have identified). Truth tellers tend not to tell everything immediately, and so can say more. Liars typically have a prepared story with little more to say.[51]

3.2.2 The Limits of Deliberation

While deliberation is often called for, it also has its limitations. We might use it merely to rationalize our decisions; it might not be apt for the question at hand; and when we overthink things, our deliberation can become excessive. Let's look at these three cases.

We all know situations in which our deliberative systems of thinking rationalize our intuitive desires. In one memorable episode of *The Simpsons* already referenced in Chapter 1 ("Scenes from the Class Struggle in Springfield"), Marge ends up buying a marked-down Chanel suit. At first, she struggles to spend so much money on herself. But Lisa insists: "Just buy it! You don't have to rationalize everything!" Marge's response: "All right, I will buy it. It will be good for the economy." It is not only as consumers that we are prone to rationalize our intuition. But not every challenge can be addressed deliberately. Many of the negotiation blunders that we have explored might be justified rather than admitted to by our deliberation. German psychologist Gerd Gigerenzer has been known to start his talks by humorously highlighting the importance of gut feelings by relating the story of a friend. The friend, an Ivy League professor, was struggling over whether to accept an offer from a rival university or to stay in his current position. A colleague took him aside and said, "Just maximize your expected utility – you always write about doing this." The professor, exasperated, responded, "Come on, this is serious."[52]

We might also simply not have enough information, or time, to answer a question deliberately. If you are trying to catch a flying ball, you could theoretically compute its trajectory, but the only practical way is to keep your eyes toward it in a constant angle.[53]

Deliberation can also be inadequate for the question at hand. Even if there is a lot of information as well as time to process it, it might not be wise to make a purely deliberate decision. To paraphrase Oscar Wilde, knowing the price of something is sometimes not the same as knowing its value. Charles Darwin allegedly made a list of pros and cons to decide whether or not to propose to his future wife. But how many people do you know that made the decision of who to marry or what career to pursue based on a SWOT analysis? Does it seem like a good strategy? It might not be when the negotiation transforms our private or business identity (remember the vampire question raised in the Introduction?). And when it comes to determining the right level of forbearance, even experts might find it difficult to put their thinking into words. Consider the master diagnostician who takes a quick glance at the patient to see the symptoms that his less knowledgeable colleagues have missed. As misleading as intuitions can be, they are also the form in which expertise comes. (We will get back to this "paradox of expertise" in the learning part of the book.)

Finally, we can also "overthink" things. There is an inverted-U relationship between performance and arousal: Being either underaroused or overaroused can lead to poor performance. Maximum performance is often achieved in a state of moderate arousal. In negotiation, as in other activities, we can get into a state of "flow" when the requirements of the task perfectly match our abilities. Watching us negotiate in such a state of flow might remind an observer of oriental martial arts. And indeed, Fisher and Ury recommend "negotiation jujitsu": "Use your skill to step aside and turn their strength to your ends. Rather than resisting their force, channel it into exploring interests, inventing options for mutual gain, and searching for independent standards." Conversely, overthinking may lead us to "choke" (underperform) under pressure, a phenomenon well known from professional sports.[54]

Sian Beilock of the University of Chicago explains why we might choke:

> High-pressure environments induce a variety of brain band body reactions. Your heart rate goes up, your adrenaline kicks in, and your mind starts to race – often with worries. When the worries begin, many people do something that seems quite logical on the surface: they try to control their performance and force an optimal outcome. Unfortunately, this increased control can backfire – especially for well-learned skills – because bringing your conscious awareness to skills that once operated outside your working-memory and prefrontal cortex can disrupt them. You cause yourself paralysis by analysis and you choke under pressure.[55]

3.3 A Tripartite Thinking Model

So, if both systems of thinking are equally important, how do you choose the right one for the moment? By reconciling the Great Rationality Debate with a "tripartite thinking model," Keith Stanovich provides an answer. Scientists have been engaged in this debate, in which they argue whether human beings are generally irrational or rational. A notable proponent of the former is Daniel Kahneman, who famously (and pessimistically) noted that in the event of a movie being made about the two systems of thinking, deliberate rational thinking would be a "supporting character who believes herself to be the hero." A notable proponent of the latter is Gerd Gigerenzer, who (controversially) argues that "the trick to making good decisions isn't to amass information, but to discard it – to know intuitively what one doesn't need to know."[56]

Keith Stanovich suggests that both views can be reconciled. He argues that when looking at individuals, it turns out that more sophisticated reasoners tend to be more engaged and reflective. He therefore proposes adding an important differentiation to our understanding of deliberate thinking. It consists, he argues, of both an "algorithmic mind" and a "reflective mind."[57]

Our intuitive thinking will prevail unless deliberately overridden by the algorithmic mechanisms of our analytic mind. But the action of overriding must be initiated by a higher-level control, whose task is to monitor our thinking and call out the analytical mind, if needed. Stanovich labels this higher-level thinking the "reflective mind." We can visualize it by building on our iceberg model: see Figure 3.1.[58]

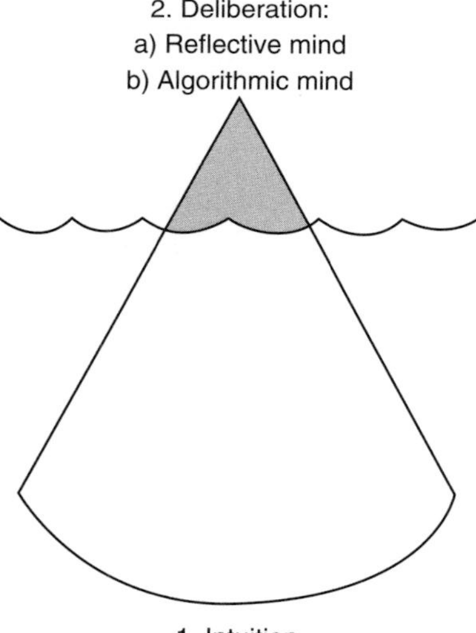

Figure 3.1 A tripartite thinking iceberg model

This may sound more complicated than it is. You can experience these three thinking steps right now. Consider the following problem:

> Jack is looking at Anne, but Anne is looking at George. Jack is married, but George is not. Is a married person looking at an unmarried person?
> A) Yes B) No C) Cannot be determined[59]

The vast majority of people answer "Cannot be determined" when in fact the correct answer is "Yes." Since we do not know whether or not Anne is married, our intuitive response might be to shrug our shoulders and declare that we just don't know. This is where our "reflective mind" should step in. Before we quickly announce the first answer that came to our mind – and despite the fact that it might indeed seem very compelling – we need to pause for a moment and reflect. Is it really significant that we don't know Anne's marital status? Overriding our intuition, that reflection must now task our "arithmetic mind" to do the "calculation": Suppose Anne is married? Then the answer would be "yes", since she is looking at George (who is not married). And suppose Anne is not married? Then the answer would also be "yes," since she is being looked at by Jack (who is married). Our arithmetic system can now confidently report back that, no matter what the underlying scenario is, the correct answer is always "A) Yes."

If you initially thought that the answer to the question could not be determined (like most people), you might now feel rather stupid (like I did). So next time you are faced with a similar problem, it could actually be your intuition that warns you: "Careful! I have made this mistake before. Better calculate all possibilities before I blurt out the wrong answer again." If this was the case, you would have learned something. Paradoxically, it is precisely the realization that you have made a mistake that will have allowed you to do so. Had you not, your faulty intuition would have remained an "unknown" to you, and you would have continued to be "blissfully unaware" of your own ignorance. Such ignorance, as we will shortly see in Part II, is one of the key challenges to learning; we will therefore explore ways to overcome it in Part III.

So, which system of thinking should be chosen by the reflective mind – deliberate or intuitive thinking? The answer: The one that promises success for the task at hand. The paradoxical nature of the task and the dilemma of the negotiator mean that making the smart choice depends on the issue at hand as well as the other side. In choosing, we must also be aware that our choice might impact the outcome: Our way of thinking might preclude the result of that thinking. For instance, if I am very familiar with the tit-for-tat approach, I might intuitively do it right without thinking too much about it. But if I am encountering that strategy for the very first time, in my opponent, then it is only my deliberate mind that can recognize the underlying pattern. Whether or not the other side has verbalized their strategy ("iron fist in a velvet glove"), my assessing their moves and considering my response will at first have to be deliberate. My deliberate response might, in fact, feel very counter-intuitive. Similarly, the question of whether the nature of the game can be changed (by mutually encouraging each other's cooperation through employing a tit-for-tat strategy, or by drawing up a contract that provides a stag-hunt-like payoff schedule) is one that has to be explored deliberately. Finally, a ritual that I have created for myself can put me on an automated and intuitive track, if I have done it enough times. Professional athletes have been known to use rituals (such as the tying of shoes or the placement of a towel) to aid their mental self-control; yet choosing and developing the ritual needs to be a deliberate act. We will come back to the importance of such physical reminders when we look at the three methodical steps of learning.

To summarize: As negotiators we need to think properly about all three challenges: The paradox of the task (so that we use but do not overdo either cooperative or competitive tactics), the dilemma of the relationship (so that we can play tit for tat and develop our skill set), and the ambivalence of thinking itself (so that we can employ the right system for the task at hand). Doing so, however, is tricky, because it is not our default modus operandi. Humans are, as Stanovich warns, "cognitive misers." This description befits the biases that we have already explored as well as the three challenges to learning that we will shortly discover. Cognitive miserliness might keep us from properly using our reflective mind, either by failing to override intuition when it should, or by failing to follow through on such override. Either way, if we do not think properly about the three challenges that we face as negotiators, we will not master them. Our personality plays an important role, as we will discover. But proper thinking, thankfully, can and must be learned. It is the same thinking that allows us to master our learning challenges. And it is the opposite of "miserly thinking." Let's therefore call it "generous thinking."[60]

Before we turn to the subject of learning, a short excursus is called for. How much of our thinking (and learning) is even in our hands? To what extent are negotiators born, not made? Let's clarify.

3.3.1 Excursus: Personality

How important is personality in achieving negotiation success? Different personalities bring different strengths and weaknesses to the table. As a vivid illustration, consider how Susan Cain describes her first client in her book, *Quiet*:

> My very first client was a young woman named Laura. She was a Wall Street lawyer, but a quiet and daydreamy one who dreaded the spotlight and disliked aggression. She had managed somehow to make it through the crucible of Harvard Law School—a place where classes are conducted in huge, gladiatorial amphitheaters, and where she once got so nervous that she threw up on the way to class. Now that she was in the real world, she wasn't sure she could represent her clients as forcefully as they expected.

For the first three years on the job, Laura was so junior that she never had to test this premise. But one day the senior lawyer she'd been working with went on vacation, leaving her in charge of an important negotiation. The client was a South American manufacturing company that was about to default on a bank loan and hoped to renegotiate its terms; a syndicate of bankers that owned the endangered loan sat on the other side of the negotiating table.

Laura would have preferred to hide under said table, but she was accustomed to fighting such impulses. Gamely but nervously, she took her spot in the lead chair, flanked by her clients: general counsel on one side and senior financial officer on the other. These happened to be Laura's favorite clients: gracious and soft-spoken, very different from the master-of-the-universe types her firm usually represented. In the past, Laura had taken the general counsel to a Yankees game and the financial officer shopping for a handbag for her sister. But now these cozy outings–just the kind of socializing Laura enjoyed–seemed a world away. Across the table sat nine disgruntled investment bankers in tailored suits and expensive shoes, accompanied by their lawyer, a square-jawed woman with a hearty manner. Clearly not the self-doubting type, this woman launched into an impressive speech on how Laura's clients would be lucky simply to accept the bankers' terms. It was, she said, a very magnanimous offer.

Everyone waited for Laura to reply, but she couldn't think of anything to say. So she just sat there. Blinking. All eyes on her. Her clients shifting uneasily in their seats. Her thoughts running in a familiar loop: I'm too quiet for this kind of thing, too unassuming, too cerebral. She imagined the person who would be better equipped to save the day: someone bold, smooth, ready to pound the table. In middle school this person, unlike Laura, would have been called "outgoing," the highest accolade her seventh-grade classmates knew, higher even than "pretty," for a girl, or "athletic," for a guy. Laura promised herself that she only had to make it through the day. Tomorrow she would go look for another career.

Then she remembered what I'd told her again and again: she was an introvert, and as such she had unique powers in negotiation–perhaps less obvious but no less formidable. She'd probably prepared more than everyone else. She had a quiet but firm speaking style. She rarely spoke without thinking. Being mild-mannered, she could take strong, even aggressive, positions while coming across as perfectly reasonable. And she tended to ask questions–lots of them–and actually listen to the answers, which, no matter what your personality, is crucial to strong negotiation. So Laura finally started doing what came naturally. "Let's go back a step. What are your numbers based on?" she asked. "What if we structured the loan this way, do you think it might work?" "That way?" "Some other way?" At first her questions were tentative. She picked up steam as she went along, posing them more forcefully and making it clear that she'd done her homework and wouldn't concede the facts. But she also stayed true to her own style, never raising her voice or losing her decorum. Every time the bankers made an assertion that seemed unbudgeable, Laura tried to be constructive. "Are you saying that's the only way to go? What if we took a different approach?"

> Eventually her simple queries shifted the mood in the room, just as the negotiation textbooks say they will. The bankers stopped speechifying and dominance-posing, activities for which Laura felt hopelessly ill-equipped, and they started having an actual conversation.
>
> More discussion. Still no agreement. One of the bankers revved up again, throwing his papers down and storming out of the room. Laura ignored this display, mostly because she didn't know what else to do. Later on someone told her that at that pivotal moment she'd played a good game of something called "negotiation jujitsu"; but she knew that she was just doing what you learn to do naturally as a quiet person in a loudmouth world.
>
> Finally the two sides struck a deal. The bankers left the building, Laura's favorite clients headed for the airport, and Laura went home, curled up with a book, and tried to forget the day's tensions.
>
> But the next morning, the lead lawyer for the bankers—the vigorous woman with the strong jaw—called to offer her a job. "I've never seen anyone so nice and so tough at the same time," she said. And the day after that, the lead banker called Laura, asking if her law firm would represent his company in the future. "We need someone who can help us put deals together without letting ego get in the way," he said.
>
> By sticking to her own gentle way of doing things, Laura had reeled in new business for her firm and a job offer for herself. Raising her voice and pounding the table was unnecessary.
>
> Today Laura understands that her introversion is an essential part of who she is, and she embraces her reflective nature. The loop inside her head that accused her of being too quiet and unassuming plays much less often. Laura knows that she can hold her own when she needs to.[61]

You may have guessed it. The client is the author herself. The story illustrates that we can develop our skills if we work with the personality that we have. So, how is personality relevant?

It is one of the most consistent findings in all of psychology that personality is largely stable in adults. We possess relatively enduring patterns of behavior, thought, and feeling that are markedly consistent across a wide variety of situations and contexts. These traits are not assumed to change at a rapid rate but rather reflect slow processes.[62]

There are three personality traits that have been found to correlate with negotiation success: Positive affect, positive expectation, and high regard for self. The last should not come as a surprise, as we have learned from Blake and Mouton that we need it for cooperating as well as for competing. The good news is that these three personality types are the most malleable ones! We can, to some degree at least, develop our intuition and personality.[63]

Experience in negotiation teaching and consulting suggests a remarkable stability to the predispositions which people report as the foundation of their negotiation style. While there is a strong common belief that personal characteristics influence how effectively we negotiate, this has been supported by few reliable findings over recent decades.[64]

Scientific orthodoxy long held that negotiation skills can and have to be learned – which is what the rest of this book is about. However, there are some personality traits that do influence our negotiation success. Hillary Anger Elfenbein has revived the nearly abandoned pursuit of identifying individual differences in negotiation. She and her collaborators have empirically validated this experience by testing negotiation behavior over a series of simulations. They found that there are indeed some stable individual differences in negotiation performance.[65]

The studies were conducted by researchers from University of California, Berkeley, MIT Sloan, and the Wharton School of the University of Pennsylvania, and concluded that nearly half of objective outcomes were attributable to one of three personality traits. They are: (1) positive beliefs about negotiation, (2) positive affect toward negotiation (both traits lead to better value distribution results), and (3) a strong concern for one's own outcome, which leads to better results in the creation of value (in particular due to log-rolling).

Intriguingly, two traits predicted the negotiator's activities, but not their net results: Intelligence and creativity. Highly intelligent negotiators created more value than others, but they claimed marginally less than others. And highly creative negotiators were also able to create more value, due primarily to uncovering hidden compatibilities.[66]

These findings are in line with similar research into the effectiveness of "emotional intelligence" (EI). This concept entered the cultural imagination in 1995 with the publication of psychologist Daniel Goleman's best-selling book of the same name. While previous research had focused on only one negotiator, Der Foo and his colleagues examined the relationship between the EI of both parties and the results they achieved. As they had expected, individuals high in EI reported a more positive experience. But surprisingly, such individuals also achieved significantly lower objective scores than their counterparts. On the other hand, having a partner high in EI predicted greater objective gain, and a more positive negotiating experience. Thus, individuals high in EI appeared to benefit in affective terms, while creating objective value that they were less able to claim.[67]

Having high EI seems to allow us to expand the mutual pie – but not equip us with the tools needed to appropriate our share. Indeed, Elfenbein argues that our personality is not only what we do, but also what behavior we typically evoke in others. And she found that personality traits also predict how the other side will typically react. Not surprisingly, negotiators that helped enlarge the pie but did not claim this advantage for themselves made the other side feel good. Conversely, counterparts tended to feel worse about negotiators who held strong positive beliefs and expectations, precisely because they were objectively challenging opponents who managed to do well for themselves.[68]

Having reviewed the existing research, Elfenbein reached the optimistic conclusion that the most reliable predictors of negotiation performance are also the most open to personal change: "Namely, positive expectations and comfort with negotiation consistently predict better performance. Another consistent finding is that abilities such as cognitive intelligence and creativity help for win–win agreements."[69]

This fits with something that we discovered earlier: In order for a negotiator to improve their results, they must know how to slice the pie to their advantage. It is not enough to be able to expand the pie if the other side reaps all the benefits. All of this confirms our earlier findings: To be successful our motivation must be mixed, not unilateral. We need to have high regard for ourselves as well as for the other. Mary Parker Follett's dictum stands confirmed decades after she made it: "Mushy people are no more good at this than stubborn people."[70]

The good news is that when we deliberately practice a skill, it becomes a habit over time. As Walter Mischel asserts, habits take the effort out of effortful control. An experienced mediator, for example, might have acquired cooperative negotiation skills in addition to a naturally accommodating style. Over the years, it may have become "second nature." Our intuitions can change, and with it our personality. This means we can improve our skills. The remainder of the book explains how.[71]

***

In view of negotiation's contradictory nature, and the challenges awaiting at each of its levels, it is no wonder that most people are deeply ambivalent about it. Alas, ambivalence has been called "the price for the fruit of the tree of knowledge." It is the necessary consequence of standing up to the paradoxical task of negotiation. Since we have paid the price, it seems to me that we are entitled to the fruit. How can we learn to negotiate? Each of the three challenges that we have seen leads to a specific challenge to our learning. In the next three chapters, we will analyze all of them.[72]

PART II
Blocking: The Three Traps of Learning

The three challenges of negotiation set up traps that can block our learning and box us in (if we are not humble).

To master the triple challenge of negotiation, we must be ambitious. And yet, our learning is all too easily thwarted. Each of the three challenges sets up a specific trap. We might succumb to the illusions of facing a coherent task, of being sufficiently competent, or of having the necessary acumen. One illusion easily leads to the next. Even more annoyingly: We are only deceived when we have already learned something! The illusions cannot occur to a complete novice. We must have acquired *some* knowledge to be fooled into believing we have *all* the knowledge. This is true for all three levels that we have explored in the first part of the book: The task itself, the relationship with the other side, and our own thinking. In this part we will explore why it is so tempting to negate the tactical paradox, the strategic dilemma, and the cognitive ambiguity – but only if we are experienced negotiators. Our strength can certainly *become* a weakness, if we overdo it. But, even more fundamentally, it *is* a weakness: As soon as we have learned something, learning its opposite is very hard to do. As a result, our learning progress is blocked. To overcome this blocking, learners need a degree of humility.

Before we look at the first trap, let's lay some groundwork. We will examine what learning is, and what it is not. To do so we have to dispose of a few learning myths. And we will then discover the three main theories of learning that have developed over the last hundred years.

What Learning Is – and What It Is Not: An Introduction

Psychologists define learning as a process based on experience that results in a relatively consistent change in behavior or behavior potential. How do we know it occurs? It cannot itself be observed. But a change in behavior often can, especially when learning leads to an improved performance of something we do. When the first scientists started to explore learning, they focused on behavior. In our context, learning might refer to the whole spectrum of tactics, choice of strategy, and even our method of thinking. If you improve the way in which you prepare for the negotiation, for instance, you have learned a better behavior. The same goes for your (as such invisible) judgment and decision-making regarding the strategic dilemma.[1]

But learning is not limited to observable behavior. It can also manifest itself in an enhanced understanding that has the potential to change our behavior. The change does not have to be permanent. As with sports, if you do not practice a skill, it will deteriorate. We generally forget what we do not use. However, once we have learned something, it is easier to recall it. Think of riding a bicycle: Even when you have not done it for years, you will quickly get the hang of it again.[2]

When I began to research learning, I found that some of my assumptions were wrong. Apparently, I am not alone. Unfortunately, as with negotiation, we do not seem to understand learning altogether intuitively, and many common lores about learning are mistaken.[3]

Let's explode the most important myths: That it has to be aware, happens on an empty brain, is a question of age, and works best when it is easy.

Learning Does Not Have to be Aware

Perhaps because we think of schools, books, and workshops when we hear the word "learning," many of us believe that it is a process that we have to deliberately engage in. But learning does not have to be aware. Consider classical music. You may never have studied it or even read notes. But after listening to a few pieces by different composers (say Bach or Mozart), you might be able to determine which of the two wrote a new piece that is played to you. How? You would perhaps not even be able to express your reasoning in words (I wouldn't), but still, you would have learned what differentiates their styles. Or consider wine: To the uninitiated, there is no way to tell grapes or *terroir* apart. But if you have grown up in a wine region, you might be unaware that you have absorbed quite a lot of tacit knowledge. The unconscious mind can apparently even learn highly complex patterns. In one experiment, subjects watched a computer screen for hours. It was divided into four quadrants. An "X" would periodically appear in one of the frames. The subjects pressed a button to predict where it would appear next. The actual rule behind its appearance was extremely complicated: The location in the seventh trial of each block was determined by a specific sequence of target locations in four out of the previous six trials. Unsurprisingly, none of the subjects came even close to figuring the pattern out. Nevertheless, their predictions became better with time. The researchers concluded that they had unconsciously acquired an intuitive understanding of the developing pattern.[4]

Lastly, consider the surprising case of Eugene Pauly, an American man who had suffered a virus infection. Viral encephalitis is often harmless, but in rare cases the virus makes its way into the brain. In these cases, it can cause catastrophic damage. This is what happened to the unfortunate Mr. Pauly, who was known simply as "Patient E.P." in his lifetime. The virus had almost completely destroyed his medial temporal lobe, a five-centimeter area near the center of the head. As a result, E.P.'s memory was severely impaired. He could not remember which day of the week it was, or the names of the doctors and nurses, no matter how many times they introduced themselves. While severely amnesic, E.P. was apparently still able to learn new things, albeit unconsciously. Because of the nature of his condition, E.P. offered unique insight into the workings of brain and memory. A team of researchers around Larry Squire, then at MIT, spent more than a decade studying E.P.'s memory loss in detail. They first met seventy-two-year-old E.P. in 1994, two years after he was struck with viral encephalitis, and kept visiting him at the home he shared with his wife until he passed away in 2006. "He never remembered us consciously," Squire explained, "Whereas, initially, he was sceptical, he eventually regarded us as friends and invited us into the house and went right over to the testing table." E.P. not only subconsciously became familiar with the researchers, he also learned new things through habits. E.P. could not draw an accurate floor plan of the house he had been living in for the last ten years. However, right after failing at this test, he startled the researcher:[5]

> Squire took notes on his laptop, and as the scientist typed, Eugene became distracted. He glanced across the room and then stood up, walked into a hallway, and opened the door to the bathroom. A few minutes later, the toilet flushed, the faucet ran, and Eugene, wiping his hands on his pants, walked back into the living room and sat down again in his chair next to Squire. He waited patiently for the next question.

Eugene could not tell the researcher where the restroom was, yet he could go straight to it.[6]

While completely unaware, Eugene had learned new information about the house. Human beings can learn without being aware. We have all learned things about negotiation that we might or might not be aware of. Perhaps some of it is just an unconscious repetition of what we have seen other people doing. It is interesting to consider how we have experienced negotiations over the years. What might you have unconsciously picked up in your family, culture, or workplace?

Learning Does Not Happen on an Empty Brain

Conscious learning, too, is often misunderstood. Contrary to what many believe, it is not like opening up your brain and dumping stuff into it. It is not passive, and it doesn't happen on an empty brain. Learning depends on prior knowledge and assumptions. When we take in new information, we connect it to what we already know. In learning there is no tabula rasa. As an illustration, consider the case of the 'own-race bias': Researchers have found that it is more difficult to learn faces from a different race if we have grown up in a racially homogenous environment. Apparently, the learning of new faces depends on already existing knowledge of faces to which we can connect the new information. When we learn, we do not just consider the material to be learned, but also past experiences and expectations. There is no blank slate.[7]

Learning Is Not a Question of Age

Another enduring myth is that "you can't teach an old dog new tricks." But learning is not only for children and young people. Even very old people are able to learn new things, if in good health. As life expectancy increases, accomplishments such as noted here are increasingly common:[8]

> A 95-year-old man has broken [the] world record for the over-95s 200m at the British Masters Championships. He completed the record-breaking lap in 55.48 seconds before taking a well-earned nap. Dr Charles Eugster took up competitive running only last year and has already broken five records. In the past he has already won 40 gold medals in Rowing and joined a body building club at 87.[9]

As you might suspect, old age learning is not limited to sports. If anything, learning social skills should become easier in old age. And indeed, the argument can be made that "to be a genius, think like a 94-year-old." *New York Times* science writer Pagan Kennedy describes the serendipitous process that drives discovery. She reports on a study on the age of patent holders and Nobel physics laureates by the Georgia Institute of Technology and Hitotsubashi University in Japan. The researchers had systematically gathered data on the demographics of inventors, their motivations, and their careers. In United States the average inventor sends in his application to the patent office at the age of forty-seven. At the same time, the highest-value patents often come from the oldest inventors – those over the age of fifty-five. In a similar study, Jones and Weinberg explored at what age scientists produce their best ideas. It turns out that that age increased over time. During the 1920s and 1930s, the iconic image of the young, great mind making critical breakthroughs was a good description of physics. But apparently this is no longer the case. The researchers found that, since 1980, Nobel Prize-winning achievements were made at the mean age of forty-eight. The study also found that the peak of creativity for Nobel winners is getting higher every year.[10]

Learning Is Not Best When It Is Easy

Decades ago, the method of "effortless learning" was developed, in the mistaken believe that errors are counterproductive. That belief is still widespread today. Learners using the method were spoon-fed new material in small bits and immediately quizzed, virtually ruling out the chance of making any errors. We now know that this retrieval from short-term memory is ineffective. In fact, learning is deepest when it is effortful: "Learning that is easy is like writing in the sand, here today and gone tomorrow."[11]

The Three Types of Learning

Over the years, scientists have identified three main ways in which human beings learn: Classical conditioning, instrumental conditioning, and cognitive learning. Each has an important role to play in learning to negotiate.

- Classical conditioning happens when two stimuli connect with one another, so that one is associated with the other.
- Instrumental conditioning is also called "associative" learning, because an association is formed between a behavior and a reward. The behavior becomes instrumental for reaching the award.
- Cognitive learning requires conscious deliberation, unlike classical and instrumental conditioning.

I would like to encourage you, as we continue, to reflect on how you were influenced (consciously or not) by your own experience.

Classical Conditioning

Our understanding of learning has evolved over the years. Much of this progress has been made through animal studies. This learning process is qualitatively not different in humans and animals, whether the learned behavior is simple or complex.[12]

Classical conditioning happens when two stimuli become connected with each another. It was discovered before the other type of unconscious learning (instrumental conditioning), which is why it is called "classical." The learner makes a new *association* between two stimuli – a stimulus that did not previously elicit the response and one that naturally elicited the response. One of the earliest, and perhaps most well-known, experiments was conducted on dogs: Pavlov's dogs learned to associate the ringing of a bell with the arrival of food.[13]

The Russian physiologist Ivan Pavlov had been conducting research on digestion, for which he won a Nobel Prize, when he (somewhat accidentally) discovered this mechanism. Salivation is a reflexive response to having food placed in your mouth – an effect that occurs both in dogs and humans. Pavlov paired two events to find out whether the dogs could acquire the association. His associates put meat powder into the dog's mouths in order to make the dogs salivate. Pavlov realized that after a few repetitions, the dogs started to salivate at the mere sight of the assistant, and later even at the sound of his approaching footsteps.[14]

Reflex responses are at the core of classical conditioning. Reflexes are naturally triggered by specific stimuli that are biologically relevant for the organism, such as salivation.[15]

More relevant here are the principal reflexes that animals show when faced with a threat. They are commonly labeled the "3 Fs":

- "Fight": The animal may put up a fight to defend itself.
- "Flight": If the threat seems too powerful, the animal may resort to fleeing.
- "Freeze": The animal may also become immobilized.

Each of these reflexes has its merit: The animal might fight back an attacker, it might save itself by escaping the attack, or its lack of response might lead to the attacker losing interest and letting go of it. This might remind you of the dual concerns model that we explored earlier. The 3 Fs of the animal kingdom correspond to the three prototypical tactics that human beings use when responding to a conflict, sometimes dubbed the "3 As" (see Figure 2.1). They are therefore especially significant in negotiations, whether of the conflict resolution or the deal-making kind:

- Asserting: This behavior results from highly regarding ourselves but not the other side. The competitive tactics of value creation are the behaviors by which we assert ourselves at the expense of the other side.
- Acknowledging: Yielding to the other side results from highly regarding the concerns of the other side, but not ourselves. This is a necessary part of any trade-off, where something is ceded to the other side. It is also required, as we have seen, to signal appreciation or as a way to apologize.
- Avoiding: Inaction might be necessary when the concerns for both sides do not require action.

Much like their reflexive cousins, the 3 As seem to have developed early in evolution, and they are often our first impulses in a challenging situation. But, as we have seen, the behavior that we impulsively pull out of our tool kit might or might not be the appropriate one for the challenge at hand. There are many situations in which doing what comes naturally might be the right thing to do. But we have also seen that no tactic should be chosen excessively. In other words: There are situations in which precisely the behavior that does not come naturally to us is required. In these situations we need to override our impulses and deliberately employ a different set of behaviors. We will return to this issue later. What is important here is that our human behavior is also rooted in our biology. And not surprisingly, so is our learning.

More to the point, humans too learn by association. Just remember the last time you watched a horror movie. Gerrig illustrates:

> As the hero approaches a closed door, the music of the movie's sound track grows dark and menacing. You suddenly feel that urge to yell 'Don't go through that door!' Meanwhile, you find that your heart is racing. But why? The answer may be: 'I have learned an association between movie music and movie events – and that's what's making me nervous!'[16]

This learning has unconsciously taken place in the form of classical conditioning.

Perhaps you don't watch horror movies much. But if you pay careful attention to events in your life, you will discover that there are many circumstances in which you can't quite explain why you are having such a strong emotional reaction or such as strong preference for something. You might want to ask yourself, "Is this the product of classical conditioning?" For instance, would you be willing to put on a sweater that was worn by Joseph Goebbels? If your response is an intuitive repulsion, then you have learned, through classical conditioning, to associate the neutral pullover with the disgust that comes from thinking of the Nazi Minister of Propaganda. (Perhaps you also have a strong visceral reaction when you think of an upcoming negotiation? Hang on to this thought.)

Instrumental Learning

Classical conditioning cannot explain everything. Learning is also shaped by another unconscious process: Instrumental conditioning. This is another form of "associative" learning – an association is formed between a behavior and a reward. Instrumental conditioning occurs when a reward is connected with the behavior that led to it. American scientist Edward Thorndike was the first to systematically investigate how animals' behavior might change as a consequence of environmental events. Where Pavlov worked with dogs, Thorndike worked with cats. He observed them figuring out how to open a latch and escape from their cage. Outside waited a large dish of salmon. At first, the cats engaged in trial and error. But once they realized how to open the latch, their latch-opening behavior increased. Thorndike articulated "the law of effect": A response that is followed by satisfactory consequences becomes more probable, and a response that is followed by unsatisfactory consequences becomes less probable.[17]

Burrhus Frederic Skinner followed up on this research. He built boxes in which rats could press a lever to have food ("Skinner boxes"). Skinner developed *behavior analysis*, the area of psychology that focuses on discovering environmental determinants of learning and behavior. He discovered instrumental conditioning (which he called "operant conditioning"): Behavior is learned because it is found to be instrumental to obtaining a reward. Human beings learn many behaviors through instrumental conditioning. Activities are discarded when they do not lead to successful outcomes, and retained when they do. Instrumental conditioning has been used by parents and teachers for millennia, and still is today. It has its place in adult learning too. Just think of the bonus and incentive systems in place in many organizations.[18]

But instrumental conditioning cannot explain everything either. British psychologist Chris Frith argues that studying behavior is not enough:

> It misses out on everything that is interesting about human experience. We all know that our mental life is just as real as our life in the physical world. Rejection by the one we love causes as much pain as a burn from a hot oven. Mental practice can cause improvements in performance that can be measured objectively. For example, if you imagine playing a particular piece on the piano, then your performance will improve.[19]

Cognitive Learning

This brings us to the third form of learning: Cognitive learning. Both classical and instrumental conditioning differ from it in that the latter requires conscious deliberation. It is not necessarily the stimulus itself that teaches us to react in a specific way. Roman philosopher Epictetus pointed out that it isn't the things themselves that disturb people, but the judgments that they form about them. Today, some thinkers would even suggest that our experience of the world might be like a visit to a gallery where the artist is our brain. This pushes the envelope a bit, but it is clear that our minds (consciously or not) appraise the stimuli we receive. Our senses are faced with a "tsunami of information," with just the eye collecting billions of bits each second, but only a few dozen winning our attention. We filter and evaluate the information that we take in.[20]

One of the first modern psychologists to acknowledge this was Magda Arnold. "How does it come about," she asked, "that some experiences have that particular quality we call 'emotional'? Seeing a bear in the zoo arouses nothing but interest and curiosity – but seeing the same animal outside the zoo may arouse violent fear." It is not only the bear but the entire situation that is being appraised. (And it is not only humans that have learned not to fear bears behind bars – the reverse is also true. While scientists debate whether or not animals have consciousness, animals with a long history of being hunted by humans relax in their presence in safe places, such as national parks.)[21]

There are other aspects of learning that cannot be explained by conditioning. We do not only make connections between stimuli, or stimuli and rewards, that we experience. We also learn things that we have never encountered before. For instance, people make up sentences that they have never heard before. How can we generate so many different sentences that are all grammatically correct? Conditioning would have required that we were exposed to those sentences before we could generate them, but this isn't the case. Neither does conditioning explain the innate joy that we often experience when we learn something. Conditioning cannot explain why people would learn without rewards or incentives, although people do. However, we are fundamentally oriented toward making sense of our worlds, and that information is its own kind of reward.[22]

German neurobiologist Gerald Hüther maintains that life – for humans and animals alike – requires learning and that our joy of having learned something is inextricably linked to our joy of being alive. Learning seems to be an innately motivated activity. For instance, infants experience many painful consequences when learning to walk, but that does not deter them from carrying on with the project. Conditioning cannot really explain *why* people want to learn things.[23]

Cognitive learning is based on information-processing and can be willfully pursued. This kind of learning happens as people encounter information, connect it to what they already know, and as a result, experience change in their knowledge or their ability to do certain tasks. "Information-processing approaches to learning give us much more flexibility than classical or instrumental conditioning theories about learning. Information-processing allows us to think about how learning changes depending on who is doing it and how they're going about doing it."[24]

We can easily relate the three types of learning to the two systems of thinking that we have explored in Chapter 3, Intuition & Deliberation. System 1 (intuition) can be linked to conditioned learning. It does not involve any form of deduction or reasoning and allows organisms to (sometimes quickly) change their behavior in a relatively automatic fashion. By contrast, system 2 (deliberation) requires effortful cognitive processes, such as the formation of propositions and the use of logic and decision-making. When we learn deliberately, we look for key ideas and organize them into mental models. We now know that the brain changes when learning is accomplished.[25]

Classical conditioning, instrumental conditioning, and cognitive learning all play important roles in learning to negotiate. They all contribute to the three traps of learning. (The advice in Part III is primarily geared toward your deliberate cognitive learning, even if you may decide to "condition" yourself to do certain things.) So, what are these traps?

4 The Illusion of Coherence

With an incomplete understanding of the paradox, we can only get better at what we already are good at.

The first trap of learning is a direct result of the paradoxical nature of negotiations: We might be under the illusion of a wholly coherent task. It is difficult to appreciate the paradox of value creation and value distribution. It is easy to get the impression that the task is more coherent than it usually is. This can lead to an incomplete understanding of what a negotiator has to do. We might focus on one side at the expense of the other, and we can lose sight of that other side altogether. Look at Figure 4.1: Which animal do you see?

Figure 4.1 Wittgenstein's animal

The drawing in Figure 4.1 was made famous by philosopher Ludwig Wittgenstein. It depicts both a rabbit and a duck. The animals share the eye but look in opposite directions. However, we can see only one at a time. Unless we have learned that the other one is there, we may not see it at all. And even when we know it is, we have to make an effort to overcome our initial perception.[1]

I propose that naming the recognized animal is not merely a metaphor for naming the side of the paradox that catches our eye. If you have been to a zoo recently, you might have observed that many adults, in showing an animal to their youngsters, seem to confine themselves to just that. They often walk up to the enclosure, look at the creature, and ask "What's this?" The instant the question is answered, whether by themselves or the children ("I know, it's a capuchin monkey!"), they apparently lose all interest in the creature and are off to the next cage. All they wanted, it often seems, was the name. (At least this is what I frequently observe at the beautiful Munich Zoo. Then I surreptitiously glance at the animals. If they are underwhelmed by us humans, they are certainly not letting on.)

Recognizing something complicated and naming something in everyday are apparently supported by similar brain systems. In medical practice, for instance, physicians often make diagnostic hypotheses in the first moments of contact with patients, sometimes even before learning about their symptoms. Medical researchers propose that the generation of diagnostic hypotheses in this context is the result of cognitive processes subserved by brain mechanisms that are similar to those involved in naming objects or concepts in everyday life. While being scanned in functional magnetic resonance imaging (fMRI), radiologists were asked to diagnose lesions in chest X-ray images as well as to name animals. The overall pattern of cortical activations was found to be remarkably similar for both types of target.[2]

Whether we look at animals, everyday objects, or optical illusions, our understanding of the world is shaped by a powerful discomfort with ambiguity and confusion. We are wired to see coherence, even when there is none. Often, we just cannot help but fill in the blanks. This is not necessarily bad. The quest for coherence is indispensable for the human experience, as developing a "sense of coherence" is a key determinant for coping with setbacks and is crucial for a healthy life. The visual arts rely on our ability to "see" something that is not there. Think of a romantic movie scene where we imagine more than we see. The Germans have a word for this: *Kopfkino* ["Head Cinema" – because the film is only in your head]. Or think of comics. They have been called "the invisible art" because we have to imagine what happens in the empty space between the panels. Our imagination is what creates much of the magic. Even the most basic cartoon relies on it: Your mind accepts a circle, two dots, and a line as a human face when you look at a smiley.[3]

We see an explanation or a coherent story even when there is none. In his treatise on data visualization, Alberto Cairo points out that charts can "lie" when they do not take people's unease with uncertainty into account. Many people, for instance, understand the size of a hurricane cone to depict the size of the storm or its impact, when it actually shows the storm's probable track. The cone does not become broader because its impact broadens, but because it shows the full range of alternative routes. The error, Cairo argues, arises from the common but unreasonable expectation that forecasts are precise, rather than subject to changes and updates. I would propose that, strictly speaking, it is not the chart that lies, but the human preference for precision and coherence. That desire can have us falsely "remember" elements of a story, words from a list, and even life events (such as a childhood balloon ride) that never happened, just because they would make sense. In extreme cases, this leads to false confessions. There are suspects who have spent years in prison after having convinced themselves of crimes that they had not committed. In less extreme but more frequent cases, negotiators believe an idea to be their own after it was artfully suggested by the other side: "Of course I wanted to drink" said the horse that was led to the water.[4]

The inability to face the sometimes incoherent complexities of the world and the ambivalence of human character can lead to a "cognitive breakdown" that makes the cognitive dissonance disappear. Thus, reducing complexity and paradoxes can also lead us down a destructive path. For instance, an escalating conflict can lead to a dualistic worldview of "us or them" if we do not maintain a measured look at the situation. Dispute resolution expert Bernhard Mayer, in a book published in cooperation with the American Bar Association, warns that the more people succumb to dualistic thinking in response to paradox, the more they become trapped in conflict. It only seems natural that human beings would prefer to have a coherent and non-paradoxical understanding of negotiation – and therefore most do.[5]

H. L. Mencken famously remarked that for every complex problem, there is a solution that is clear, simple, and wrong. When it comes to negotiation, we often do not see the whole picture. The higher the stakes, as the American Bar Association warns, the greater our tendency to view polarities in a more primitive way. We might prefer negotiation models without any paradoxes, dilemmas, or ambivalence altogether. Our desire for coherence can blind us to one of the two sides. Even though both are there, we may see only one, and name one: A duck *or* rabbit. Value creation *or* value distribution. Importantly, what we see is *not* wrong, and neither is the name that we give it. Both are correct! And that is exactly the problem: Recognizing that negotiation is the distribution of value makes it difficult to see that it is *also* value creation, and vice versa, because it is the opposite of what we have come to expect. "Against expectation" is one of the original meanings of "parádoxos" (παράδοξος). (The other is "against common opinion.") Rather than seeing the full picture, it is easy to recognize only that side of the Yin & Yang that we expect to see.[6]

It is easy to fall under the illusion of a coherent task, for three reasons: We might unconsciously, unintentionally, or deliberately acquire an incomplete understanding of the task. First, we might have unconsciously learned an incomplete theory. Humans often simply repeat behavior that they observe in others. Second, we might unintentionally have learned a one-sided theory of the task. Finally, we might have a one-sided "theory in use." The theory that we have learned might have been accurate and comprehensive, but, deep down, we don't really believe it. So, when push comes to shove, we follow the one-sided theory that we really believe in. We follow what is called our "theory in use," in contrast to the "espoused-to theory" to which we pay lip service. Let's look at these three reasons in greater detail.[7]

4.1 Unconsciously Incomplete Theory

We might have inadvertently and unconsciously acquired an incomplete understanding of the task. Our past experience contributes to the way we think about the process, and our general attitude depends partly on how we have been conditioned. A good way to discover our own, potentially unconscious, learnings is to ask ourselves what comes to mind when we think of an important upcoming negotiation. Perhaps a picture, a phrase, or a bodily sensation. It is no surprise that we are often ambivalent about it. We might have mixed feelings. For many, it is a mixture of fear and liking. Let's look at both.

4.1.1 Fear

We saw in Chapter 2 how respondents to the study by Michael Wheeler and his colleagues regarded themselves as prey or predator. I find these mental images remarkable. The participants all painted stark pictures. Pictures may come easier than words, and these were entirely about claiming value. It could not be any more zero-sum: One side has to die, and the other gets to feed on it. There is no mutual interest. With that in mind, how could you think of creating value?[8]

Fear has been one of the most extensively studied products of classical conditioning. Perhaps you have heard of Watson and Rayner's infamous 1920 experiment with Little Albert. The researchers instilled in the infant a fear of a white toy rat by pairing its occurrence with a sudden frightening noise behind the child's head. Even though the boy initially liked the rat, he learned to fear it after just seven instances. Worse, the boy generalized his fear to other furry objects, breaking into tears when encountering a rabbit or Santa Claus. Grown-ups can be conditioned, too. Even a single traumatic event can cause this. Consider the remarkable case of George Foster:

> In the days before email and telemarketing, travelling salesmen went door to door peddling their wares. One day, a particular salesman, George Foster, stood at a front door. The house turned out to be vacant, and unbeknownst to him, a tiny leak had been filling it with gas for weeks. The bell was also damaged, so when he pressed it, it created a spark and the house exploded. Poor George ended up in hospital, but fortunately he was soon back on his feet. Unfortunately, his fear of ringing door bells had become so strong that for many years he couldn't go back to his job. He knew how unlikely a repeat of the incident was, but for all he tried, he just couldn't manage to reverse the (false) emotional connection.[9]

Hopefully, your own experience with business transactions has been less dramatic. In any case, it might be worthwhile to consider how your own adventures have influenced you. What have you observed? What did you do? What have you seen others do? How did this make you feel?

4.1.2 Liking

Let's flip the coin. Just as negative experience can create a condition of fear, a positive experience can induce liking. In fact, the experience does not even have to be positive. It might be enough *not* to have had a negative one. When the repeated occurrence of a stimulus is not followed by something bad, we often develop a mild liking of the repeated stimulus. This effect has been coined "the mere exposure effect" by Stanford University's Robert Zajonc, a psychologist who dedicated most of his career to studying this phenomenon. He found the effect to be true for all sorts of stimuli. Here is an example: Zajonc conducted experiments in which subjects, by virtue of repeated exposure, developed affective preferences for previously novel Chinese ideographs:

> In that experiment the ideographs were first presented under degraded viewing conditions. Later, when given direct recognition memory tests, subjects could not distinguish these old stimuli from new stimuli they had never seen. Yet, despite this lack of overt recognition, when asked which of two ideographs, old or new, they liked better, subjects consistently preferred the previously presented stimulus.[10]

The mere exposure effect does not depend on consciousness. It occurs even when words or pictures are shown so quickly that the observers are not aware of seeing them: They still prefer words or pictures that have been presented repeatedly.

Zajonc argues that the absence of a noxious consequence is a safety signal that is then associated with the stimulus. The repeated-exposure paradigm can be seen as a form of classical conditioning where the absence of aversive events constitutes the unconditioned stimulus. The mere exposure effect means that, on the whole, we like people who are familiar to us. This might explain why many of us value long-standing customer relationships so much. Because we are used to them, we experience less stress. The new customer or sales rep, on the other hand, is perhaps not as bad as we initially think. If we give it time, we might develop a good relationship with them, too.[11]

4.1.3 Conclusion

Whether we primarily fear or like the thought of negotiation, the danger is that this feeling colors the entire process. If our experience is too coherent, then our theory of negotiation may also be. As Mark Twain famously quipped: "Lest we be like the cat that sits down on a hot stove lid. She will never sit on a hot stove lid again – and that is well; but also she will never sit down on a cold one anymore."[12]

4.2 Unintentionally Incomplete Theory

An illusion of coherence might not only be created unconsciously. Regrettably, we might also – deliberately but unintentionally – have acquired an incomplete understanding of the task. As we saw, it is not easy to truly appreciate the task's paradoxical nature.

Unfortunately, not everything we learn is completely accurate, nor can it be. Human knowledge is expanding, yet finite. Science constantly progresses. All theories are incomplete, and some will prove to be erroneous. That we do not know which is which a priori is precisely what defines scientific progress. It thus seems to me that the incomplete theory is more important for advancing knowledge than the "complete" one – because the latter is by definition unachievable. Research relevant to our topic is conducted across the globe and in a wide variety of disciplines. Among them, as you know, are psychology, game theory, sociology, law, management, political sciences, history, biology, and philosophy. Not even the greatest minds in any one of these fields can know all there is to be known. And with scientific progress exploding, the fraction of what is knowable by a person is ever shrinking. However, this cannot stop us from attempting to understand as much as we can about our chosen field of interest. But it has to make us humble. Despite our best efforts, some of what we "know" to be true will not be so. "It ain't what you don't know that gets you into trouble. It's what you know for sure that just ain't so." All books, not only this one, are cases in point – a point to which I will come back in the conclusion.[13]

Like so many other problems, this one was beautifully captured 2,500 years ago by Plato. No wonder some argue that all philosophical questions can in essence be traced back to him. (Alfred North Whitehead famously characterized the entirety of European philosophical tradition as "a series of footnotes to Plato.") In Protagoras, Plato describes Socrates discussing learning with Hippocrates. The dialogue is the origin of the expression "food for the soul." This is how Socrates labels the acquisition of knowledge. He contrasts it with the purchase of regular food, warning:[14]

> There is a far greater peril in buying knowledge than in buying meat and drink: the one you purchase of the wholesale or retail dealer, and carry them away in other vessels, and before you receive them into your body as food, you may deposit them at home and call in an experienced friend who knows what is good to be eaten or drunken, and what not, and how much, and when; and then the danger of purchasing them is not so great. But you cannot buy the wares of knowledge and carry them away in another vessel; when you have paid for them you must receive them into the soul and go your way, either greatly harmed or greatly benefited.[15]

All of us have thus acquired knowledge about negotiations and not all of it beneficial. We could not help it. But what we can and must do, is to revise and improve our knowledge as we progress.

In all of the multi-issue negotiations that we have explored together, we see the tactical paradox. Yet Western minds prefer coherence, not being wired to deal well with paradoxes. Analytical thinking builds on differentiation and avoids contradictions, while holistic thinking prevalent in East Asia often accepts both. This difference is reflected in approaches to negotiation. (Note, however, that while Asian negotiators are often more comfortable with the paradox, they do not reach better results. A key reason is that, when it comes to the dilemma, many have only competitive tactics in their tool kit, hence claiming their share from a smaller pie.)[16]

So, we might deliberately, if mistakenly, have cultivated an understanding that ascribes a greater coherence of the task than is really there. We do not know for sure if statements by Angela Merkel and Donald Trump reflect their true understanding. They were made purposefully and with specific policy goals in mind. Perhaps they were accentuated to have the desired impact. Perhaps both politicians really do view the task as more paradoxical than they reveal. But if we take them by their word, their understanding would seem overly coherent. This does not surprise me at all, and would be in line with my own experience. Wherever I have asked what a negotiation means in the twenty or so countries where I have taught, the answer is typically "a process to get me what I want," or "a process to get both sides what they want." The answers vary greatly, of course, from country to country. But rare is the participant who expresses *both* thoughts equally.[17]

Politicians and business executives are not alone in this. As demonstrated, an overly coherent understanding of the nature of negotiation is found in many domains. Popular theories of social change, for instance, often suffer from it, seeing the potential for win–win but ignoring its distributive side. In the field of international security, it is often the other way around. Many commentators of contemporary transatlantic relations buy into the idea that "Americans are from Mars and Europeans from Venus." Neoconservative historian Robert Kagan coined this phrase in an article from 2007, "Power and Weakness" in *Policy Review*: "[On] major strategic and international questions today, Americans are from Mars and Europeans are from Venus: They agree on little and understand one another less and less." As Washington University's Henry Farrell and Georgetown's Abraham Newman assert, many scholars and policy makers have regarded clashes between the US and the EU over domestic security as battles between a warmongering US and a peace-loving EU. The two gods move in a zero-sum world where ultimately only Mars can get the job done. To say that his success comes at the expense of the other side would be an understatement. He is, after all, the god of war.[18]

But this view offers an incomplete and over-coherent account of transatlantic negotiations. According to Farrell and Newman, for instance, the metaphor misses the point when it comes to agreements on security and privacy. One example they give is the access and exchange of financial data to track suspected terrorist activity. It is true that the original US demand from 2006 to obtain personal financial transaction data in order to track suspected terrorist activity came into conflict with European rules of civil liberty. A five-year period ensued "which swung from pledges of quick cooperation to complete breakdown to the culmination of a final agreement." But the final agreement provides another showcase of a cooperative trade-off: "[It] used the principle of reciprocity to provide security actors in Europe with access to data on financial transactions that they had previously been denied under domestic institutions via an international cooperation agreement." In a nutshell, European data could be gathered directly by the Americans, or by the Europeans and passed on to the Americans. It then was returned to European agencies that could not have gathered it for their own use! A classical win–win. And more support for my argument that trade-offs have to come at *somebody's* expense. Security actors from both sides of the Atlantic achieved it to the detriment of privacy actors.[19]

Indeed, it is sometimes necessary to read negotiation theory *very closely* to truly appreciate the paradoxical nature of the task. Take the best-selling negotiation book, *Getting to Yes*. This book opened the world's eyes to the possibilities and merits of win–win solutions. It is the most significant proponent of the tactics of value creation, and its impact is widely acknowledged. As Kevin Schock emphasized, in his tribute to Roger Fisher: "Focusing on the underlying needs/desires of the parties, treating fellow negotiators with respect, searching for opportunities for mutual gain, and insisting on fair criteria for the resolution of disputes . . . are ideas that are easy to forget when locked in the intellectual and emotional strain of a particularly intense negotiation." It is Roger Fisher and William Ury's singular legacy to have opened the world's eyes to the merits of value creation.[20]

Yet, in doing so, it might unwittingly have inhibited the use of value-claiming tactics beyond reason. This is how James J. White, an early critic of the book, put it: "Had the authors stated that they were dividing the negotiation process in two and were dealing with only part of it, the omission would be excusable. That is not what they have done. Rather they seem to assume that a clever negotiator can make any negotiation into problem solving and thus completely avoid the difficult distribution." In responding to this critique, Roger Fisher rightly stressed that the parties share an overarching common interest, namely to reach a deal. However, this does not eliminate the need to distribute value in order to reach most deals. Hence the book has been criticized for overlooking situations that ultimately require hard bargaining.[21]

Then again, *Getting to Yes* does acknowledge that there are two sides to the task. It explicitly warns that the expanded pie must be sliced; that negotiation can be biased to favor a competitive negotiator; and that we may obtain a favorable result simply by stubbornly claiming value. It just does not follow up on these acknowledgments. The book could (and in my view should) have been more straightforward about the essentially paradox nature of the task.

What applies to the most famous negotiation book certainly applies to all others too. Let me reiterate an unsurprising but crucial fact here. Nobody has a complete and accurate understanding of negotiation. That includes the giants of the field, and certainly the rest of us. I do hope to advance our understanding, but that advance is in itself limited. We will shortly explore the obstacles that can hinder our progress in thinking accurately about learning. We will see then that the very fact that we have learned something can impede further learning – a phenomenon that is called the "curse of expertise." We can easily "box ourselves in" – an image to which I will return later. Yes, I do believe that the tactical paradox, strategic dilemma, and cognitive ambivalence are crucial for our understanding. But in doing so I am missing other important points. Just like you, I am keen on advancing my understanding through the exciting insights that are yet to be generated in the field. Allow me to come back to this idea in the conclusion to the book.[22]

4.3 Incomplete Theory in Use

There is a third obstacle that can get in our way. The theory that we really hold (our so-called "theory in use") is different from the theory that we espouse to. Even if everything that we had learned was accurate and complete, we might choose not to believe all of it. Deep down, we may disagree. We might, for instance, profess to pursue mutually beneficial outcomes. But, when pushed, we might fall back on our true Manichean world view. We may say that the regard of the other side are as important as our own. But if we are honest to ourselves, we might discover that we do not really mean it. Or we might have heard that in order to elevate a prisoner's dilemma scenario to a stag hunt game, we might have to use an iron fist in a velvet glove to punish a competitive move. Yet, we might still believe that more cooperation is the right response.[23]

Note that this is not the same as knowing what to do in order to succeed, and consciously *deciding not to do it.* It is also different from *not knowing* enough about negotiation. *Nobody* knows enough about negotiation. Even the greatest experts cannot absorb the vast and expanding body of knowledge in the sciences that shape the field. Rather, it is about not believing what you know. A gap between our theory in use and our espoused-to theory can occur whether we know a lot or a little. I suppose that the more we learn, the greater the risk of gaps in at least some areas.

We cannot absorb theories about everything that we hear, and not everything is equally important to us. We have to select. And, as we have seen, we tend to be cognitive misers. Furthermore, it takes repeated exposure to a new idea for us to really make it ours. Hermann Ebbinghaus, nineteenth-century pioneer of memory research and discoverer of the learning curve, also revealed the *spacing effect.* In his monumental 1885 book *Über das Gedächtnis. Untersuchungen zur experimentellen Psychologie* [*Memory: A Contribution to Experimental Psychology*], he described how we tend to forget information over time, but are quicker to learn it when exposed to it again. The idea that learning is most effective when it is repeated and spaced out (which you can apply when creating the online learning plans) was robustly confirmed in the twentieth century. The fact that not every message sticks the first time has, not surprisingly, specifically worried advertisers. The *effective frequency*, i.e. the number of times that a person must be exposed to a new message for it to be absorbed, is controversial. A recent meta-analysis points toward no less than ten exposures. Research in advertising and political campaigning reveals that there also has to be *involvement* with the topic. In order to be involved, we have to care about the topic, be interested in it, or believe that it is relevant or salient. But how long will it take to absorb ideas that are incompatible with our existing beliefs? It might be altogether impossible.[24]

People might prefer to stick to incomplete but perhaps coherent theories. The fact that humans are not necessarily great intuitive scientists might aggravate the problem. Scientific theories, as Oxford University's David Deutsch reminds us, are explanations: assertions about what is out there and how it behaves. He argues that they are not really derived from empirical data:

> We do not read them in nature, nor does nature write them into us. They are guesses – bold conjectures. Human minds create them by rearranging, combining, altering and adding to existing ideas with the intention of improving upon them. We do not begin with "white paper" at birth, but with inborn expectations and intentions and an innate ability to improve upon them using thought and experience. Experience is indeed essential to science, but its role is different from that supposed by empiricism.[25]

Empiricism, as Deutsch explains, is the philosophical doctrine that conceptualizes our understanding of reality as being derived from our sensory experiences: "[Experience] is not the source from which theories are derived. Its main use is to choose between theories that have already been guessed. That is what 'learning from experience' is." If we set out to learn from experience, we should, as we will see in Part III, explore our environment, generate ideas about how the world works, and then test those ideas.[26]

Columbia University's Deanna Kuhn explored the prowess of "children and adults as intuitive scientists" in her influential article of the same name. Scientists, as she explains, deliberately examine their theories and assumptions by gathering evidence. The evidence either supports or challenges their models and theories – and they are adjusted accordingly. Is that also how people learn? Of course, we rather prefer to think so. Surely, our learning capabilities go much beyond what, say, Russian dogs or American cats can do. That white lab coat fits us rather well, we think. Unfortunately, it is not quite like that. As Kuhn and her collaborators have found, we are not great intuitive scientists. Why not? Scientists generate knowledge by systematically gathering data to formulate and test hypotheses by looking at the evidence. But people do not do well at distinguishing theories and evidence. We see pictures of smiling faces and we naturally assume that the people we see are happy.[27]

This human tendency is especially problematic because it likes to team up with the various cognitive illusions that we have explored, such as the confirmation bias. Scientific progress is often made when findings do not confirm a theory, but when they falsify it. (Some philosophers, such as Karl Popper, even see falsifiability as the only way to advance knowledge.) But that is something we hardly ever pursue outside the lab. We intuitively look mostly for evidence that would confirm our theories, not evidence that would falsify it. Peter Watson, the British founder of the psychology of reasoning, discovered this for the first time with the help of the 2–4–6 problem. He told subjects that he had a rule in mind for a set of any three numbers. Their task was to detect that rule. He gave an example where the rule applied: "2–4–6." To test their hypothesis, participants could first suggest their own three-number sets. What most people did was to propose only positive examples of their hypotheses. For instance, many thought that the rule was "ascending even numbers." They kept proposing sets of three ascending numbers, such as "4–8–10." While they were informed each time that, yes, their example also concurred with Watson's rule, they did not get any closer to finding it out. Nor could they with the evidence they were seeking. (The rule was simply "any ascending sequence.") To make that discovery, subjects would have had to propose an example that would falsify their hypothesis, such as "6–4–2" or "2–3–4." But hardly anyone did. Instead, most sought to confirm their prior beliefs. It will not surprise you to learn that it was Watson who invented the term, "confirmation bias."[28]

This way of thinking hinders our progress in negotiation as well as in learning, because it might prevent us from really testing our theories in the real world. Especially when we hold strong opinions of complex issues, we are likely to examine empirical evidence in a biased manner. When we receive new information, we quickly accept evidence that confirms our preconceived notions and assess counterevidence with a critical eye. (We will return to this point in more detail when we look at the challenge of learning from feedback in Chapter 6.) As Jonathan Haidt suggests, tongue-in-cheek, we might be more intuitive "lawyers" (defending our intuitions after the fact) than intuitive "scientists."[29]

The same can happen with our theories about negotiation. Couple this unfortunate fact with all the cognitive biases that we have already discussed, and one thing becomes clear. It is very easy to have an incomplete understanding of the negotiation task. And it is very difficult to admit that to ourselves. This is where the first trap awaits us.

***

Whichever way it came about, a mistaken sense of coherence might make negotiation seem simpler than it is. An incomplete understanding of the task can be the consequence. Thinking that we are more knowledgeable about something than we actually are is certainly not unique to negotiations. Brown University's Stephen Sloman and University of Colorado's Philip Fernbach call this the "knowledge illusion." Sometimes, our understanding of even the most mundane objects (such as coffeemakers, cameras, or flush toilets) is much more limited than we readily acknowledge. Many people *feel* they understand how these things work, but in reality, they do not. As Sloman and Fernbach point out, most things are complicated, even when they seem simple:

> We all have domains in which we are experts, in which we know a lot in exquisite detail. But on most subjects, we connect only abstract bits of information, and what we know is little more than a feeling of understanding we can't really unpack. In fact, most knowledge is little more than a bunch of associations, high-level links between objects or people that aren't broken down into detailed stories.[30]

Unfortunately, it is quite human to avoid complexity. Research shows that even the most seasoned scientists often show a tendency to oversimplify when trying to understand a complicated topic.[31]

The illusion of coherence would be bad enough on its own. But it taints all subsequent efforts to become better. Using Abraham Maslow's metaphor, if I think that all I need is a hammer, I will not only see everything as a nail, worse – I will not even have an incentive to acquire additional tools.[32]

This is not an academic problem. Crucially, seeing the negotiation in a one-sided way has very real implications for the way in which reality is perceived and actions are chosen. Remember in Chapter 1 how individuals behaved differently when they were invited to the "The Wall Street Game" or "The Community Game?" Such metaphors can influence our behavior, I would propose, because they shape our expectation of what will happen. Our expectations, in turn, activate specific brain patterns. As a result, we experience cooperation very different from competition.[33]

Let's take a step back to see how. Viewing other people's emotional expressions may induce a mimicry response. Humans have the propensity to resonate emotionally with others. When someone smiles at us, we tend to smile back. Our brains react with joy when we see others smile, and we feel dismayed when we see them frown.

This is the case, when we have common interests. When we work together and cooperate, their gain is our gain. And their joy is our joy. This is what Angela Merkel has in mind, I suppose, when she says: "That's the purpose of concluding agreements – that both sides win."[34]

But this is not always the case. As we have observed, empathy is not an automatic reflex of our brains. There are situations in which our emotional response is the opposite of the other side's response. We frown when we see them smile, and we smile when we see them frown! Which situations? You guessed it: Situations where we view their interests as opposed to our own; where only one side can win; where what one side wins must come at the expense of the other side. You might sincerely regret this, but it remains a fact, and the other side frowning at your success is perhaps regrettable, but unavoidable. This, I believe, is what Donald Trump is thinking when he says (as quoted in Chapter 1): "I believe, you know, when I look at the numbers in Germany and some other countries – people may not like Donald Trump. But you have to understand: That means I am doing a good job, because I am representing the United States."[35]

Early evidence of this phenomenon, called counterempathy, was provided by David Aderman and Gail Unterberger in 1977 and by Lanzetta and his co-workers in the 1980s. Dartmouth College's John Lanzetta and Basil Englis glued electrodes to the faces of participants and led them to believe that they would play an investment game with another person supposedly in another room. How they reacted to that other player's display of pleasure (smiles) and distress (grimaces) varied in accordance with their expectation of what the game was about. When they thought they were cooperating, their emotions were synchronized. When they thought they were competing, their feelings were inverted.[36]

More recent experiments have investigated the neural underpinnings of this phenomenon. Makiko Yamada, Claus Lamm, and Jean Decety of the University of Chicago made high-resolution event-related brain potential recordings (ERP) of participants playing a similar card game. Participants believed that they were playing jointly with another player in an adjoining room. They could observe the other player's smiles and frowns in response to winning or losing on a computer screen. Again, when participants believed that they were cooperating with the other side, a smile elicited a smile, and a frown a frown. When they thought that they were competing, the opposite was the case. "Pleasing frowns, disappointing smiles" is how the researchers entitled their article.[37]

So, let's conclude this chapter by circling back to its beginning. Wittgenstein's animal has served as a metaphor for the two-sided nature of our subject. When it was shown to American adults and children in October, the majority perceived it as a bird. But at Easter, most saw a bunny. Negotiators might see value distribution *or* value creation, likewise in accordance with their expectation. In

Chapter 7 we will see how to overcome the illusion of a coherent task. We will then have to address a problematic finding that neuroscientists have made: Changing our mind is fundamentally unnatural and uncomfortable, and this is reflected in the way our brains work. But first we continue our exploration of learning challenges. At the interpersonal level, negotiators face the strategic dilemma. Learning to address it can be hampered, unfortunately, by the mere illusion of competence. Let's see how.[38]

5 The Illusion of Competence

Without the ability to do the opposite of our impulse, our tool kit remains incomplete – and our strength becomes our weakness.

Just as the first challenge of negotiation success (the paradox) leads to the second (the dilemma), the first challenge of learning leads to the second. And it also brings us from the objective task to our relationship with the other side. In dealing with the other party, we must rely on the complete tool kit of negotiation behaviors. But we can easily be under the mistaken impression that we already possess all necessary tools. This illusion of competence can come from three sources. We might not see the need to expand our skill set because of a mistaken perception of how coherent the negotiation might be. Or, even when we recognize the need for more skills, we might find that knowing does not necessarily lead to knowing *how* to achieve a successful negotiation. Finally, we might possess the necessary know-how, but be unable to access it at the right moment. Let's briefly explore all three problems.

5.1 The Double Curse of Ignorance

The illusion of competence is the unfortunate result of an incomplete understanding of the task. Adequately addressing the strategic dilemma, as we have seen, requires a broad skill set. But why would I seek to expand my tool kit if I do not see the need for more and different tools? I might mistakenly believe that I already have all the skills to master the problem. I might thus feel that I am in control of the process, when in reality it is the other way around: The process controls me.

In all of the multi-issue and multi-round negotiations that we have explored, we can see the strategic dilemma. It is no surprise that those who do see the negotiation process as non-paradoxical and more coherent than it really is, would limit their acquisition of new skills. The tasks of value creation and value distribution paradoxically require us to highly regard our own concerns, and the ones of the other side, even though the two could be contraries, contradictions, or even compatibles. Managing the paradox necessitates, as we have seen, "mixed motives" and "dual concerns" for both sides.

But the motives of the over-cooperative and the over-competitive negotiator are, by definition, not "mixed" enough. They will mostly regard their own interests, or that of the other side. And, for someone who does not truly appreciate the paradoxical nature of the task, that makes perfect sense. The shortcomings of the over-cooperative as well as the over-competitive negotiator are intentional. And it is only natural that they should wish to further hone their existing one-sided skills, rather than expand their tool kit. If I believe that negotiations are essentially only about distributing value, then I have plenty of reasons to improve my competitive skills. But I have little reason to develop my cooperative skills. Worse: I might actively avoid doing so, viewing such skills (correctly!) as potentially detrimental to my competitive efforts.

Without my realizing it, my attempts to become even better at what I already do might make me a worse negotiator – because they pull me ever further away from improving and completing my tool kit.

This is not only a problem with regard to competitive and cooperative tactics. Rather, it is equally true for all five negotiation styles. And it is a hurdle that can only be overcome if we are aware of it. But unfortunately, we are often confused about what we should do and learn.

Especially thorny are ideas that *seem to chime* with something that we already know, when in truth they do not. Perhaps we could say that these ideas merely *rhyme* with one another. This is notably problematic when the ideas are, in fact, incompatible. We might then think, "Ah, I have heard that before," rather than listen properly to the new idea. Sometimes we can thus pick up outright wrong advice – because it "rhymes" with our existing knowledge. Let me give you two examples.

One misleading idea that I frequently encounter in my workshops is about making the first offer. When I explain the power of anchoring, participants sometimes agree but say that their company already has a sales strategy that is based on extreme first offers. When I encourage them to tell us more, it is not uncommon to hear something along the following lines:

> When we prepare for a negotiation, we always do this. We know the profit that we want to make, so we add it to the cost of the product. And then we add a certain negotiation margin on top of that. That way we can make concessions when the customer pushes back and still make the desired profit.

This is of course a valid approach. It does not, however, optimize value-claiming. Such "cost plus" pricing is not based on the RP of the other side. That requires adding the negotiation margin to *the buyer's* walk-away price – not the one of the seller. If this misunderstanding is not clarified, the participant could easily walk away without really absorbing the new tactic, because he seemingly applies it already. One way to effectively counter this misunderstanding is to use a proper negotiation prep sheet, i.e. one that encourages identifying one's own *and* the other side's RP.

A second misleading idea that can dangerously resonate with a learner's pre-existing knowledge is often found in travel guides. Remember the scene from the

Grand Bazar of Istanbul? This is what *The Lonely Planet* travel guide advises under the headline "The Dying Art of Bargaining in Istanbul's Grand Bazaar":

> If you are visiting Istanbul and are keen to buy a carpet or rug in the bazaar, the following tips could be helpful: The "official" prices here have almost always been artificially inflated to allow for a bargaining margin – 20% to 30% is the rule of thumb. Shopping here involves many aspects of Ottoman etiquette – you will drink tea, exchange polite greetings and size up how trustworthy the shopkeeper is. He, in turn, will drink tea, exchange polite greetings and size up how gullible you are. Never allow yourself to feel pressured to buy something. Tea and polite conversation are gratis – if you accept them, you don't need to buy anything in exchange.
>
> It's important to do your research. Always shop around to compare quality and pricing. Before starting to bargain, decide how much you like the carpet or rug, and how much you are prepared to pay for it. It's important that you stick to this – the shopkeepers here are professional bargainers and have loads of practice in talking customers into purchases against their better judgement. Your first offer should be around 50–60% of the initial asking price. The shopkeeper will laugh, look offended or profess to be puzzled – this is all part of the ritual. He will then make a counteroffer of 80–90%. You should look disappointed, explain that you have done your research and say that you are not prepared to pay that amount. Then you should offer around 70%. By this stage you and the shopkeeper should have sized each other up. He will cite the price at which he is prepared to sell and if it corresponds with what you were initially happy to pay, you can agree to the deal. If not, you should smile, shake hands and walk away. These same rules also apply in some textile, jewellery and antique shops in the bazaar, but they don't apply to all.[1]

This, too, is certainly a valid approach. But have you spotted the difference to the corresponding value-claiming tactic explained in Chapter 1? Yes, it is certainly important to "do your research" and to "decide how much you are prepared to pay." But this is of little use when you then follow the subsequent advice of making the first offer "around 50–60% of the initial asking price", bargaining until you reach "around 70%." The basis for everything the traveler does is still the shopkeeper's asking price. *The Lonely Planet* encourages its readers to be anchored. It encourages the opposite of what a traveler should do if they want to haggle effectively, and is not sound bargaining advice. But again, because it superficially seems similar to the real tactical advice, it can easily mislead the learner.

The thinking needed to produce a good result is virtually identical to the one that is needed to accurately evaluate one's actions. This can lead to what has been called the "double curse of ignorance": First, when we have a deficit in expertise, we make mistakes. Second, the same deficit makes us unable to recognize this. As a result, we could be led to think that we were doing quite well when we were doing anything but. Individuals who lack the skill to negotiate successfully are often cursed with the inability to realize it.[2]

5.2 Knowing Is Not Knowing How

Putting theory into practice in the form of behavior change in the real world is another major challenge. Even having an accurate and deep understanding of the negotiation task does not mean that I have the skill to do it in practice. As most of us are painfully aware, "to know" is not the same as "to know how." British philosopher Gilbert Ryle differentiated the two: For instance, I might *know that* a bicycle consists of certain parts and is made of certain materials. And I might know that it is a means of transport which is powered by human effort. But that is not the same as *knowing how* to ride it. This practical knowledge is acquired by a process of trial and error, i.e. learning from the results of my efforts. We could endlessly argue whether or not "knowing how" is really a subset of "knowing that" – but luckily, we do not have to do that. It does not matter here. Either way, the two are connected: The illusion of coherent knowledge can lead to the illusion of already possessing the adequate know-how.[3]

Unlike in the learning of other skills, here the outcomes of our actions are often not clearly predictable. But for skilled expertise to develop, learners need valid feedback. This is the case in many games: There is a very stable relationship between actions and outcomes. Take poker for example. The lessons which the players learn from the outcomes are highly valid. The outcomes, therefore, provide good feedback. They allow the players to enhance their expertise by gaining more experience. Note that the outcomes do not need to be certain for that. Because poker requires skill as well as luck, outcomes are uncertain. Yet they provide valid, high-quality feedback. Negotiation, as we have seen, is different. It makes for a hostile learning environment because it usually does not provide good feedback. In most professions, in contrast to games, we operate in an environment that is both predictable and non-predictable. The feedback that we receive is mixed – part of it is valid, but part of it is not. The expertise that we collect can therefore be called "fractioned." In other words, we acquire know-how in some areas but we lack it in others.[4]

So, we might know very well, in theory, what needs to be done in a given situation. But perhaps we have never had an opportunity to acquire the needed skill to do so. I believe that it is especially difficult to acquire the capability to cooperate. Doing so often requires us to override our first impulse. The behaviors that we impulsively pull out of our tool kit appear to have developed early in evolution. As we have seen, the impulsive 3 As of our human tool kit are not unlike the reflexive 3 Fs of the animal kingdom. As Ury cautions, we are prone to use them (separately or in combination) even when cooperation would be more promising. The ability to cooperate relies on parts of the brain that have developed last. The oldest parts of the brain are sometimes called "the lizard brain" because we share them with lizards and other animals. Some animals also have the ability to cooperate (as we saw in the

Thai elephants example) albeit at a lower level than humans. We humans might be predisposed for cooperation (a finding to which we will come back when we analyze how it can be learned in Chapter 8), but we must cultivate and hone that skill in practice.[5]

Nature gives us the opportunity to do so, but leaves us the choice. Biologist Frans de Waal puts it like this:

> Like other primates, humans can be described either as highly cooperative animals that need to work hard to keep selfish and aggressive urges under control or as highly competitive animals that nevertheless have the ability to get along and engage in give-and-take. This is what makes socially positive tendencies so interesting: They play out against a backdrop of competition. I rate humans among the most aggressive of primates but also believe that we're masters at connecting and that social ties constrain competition. In other words, we are by no means obligatory aggressive. It's all a matter of balance: Pure, unconditional trust and cooperation are naïve and detrimental, whereas unconstrained greed can only lead to the sort of dog-eat-dog world that Skilling advocated at Enron until it collapsed under its own mean-spirited weight.[6]

Yet, while nature leaves us the choice, it has also equipped us with strong impulses. Human beings, as William Ury points out, are reaction machines. This is especially true in negotiations:[7]

> When you are under stress, or when you encounter a NO, or feel you are being attacked, you naturally feel like striking back. Usually this just perpetuates the action-reaction cycle that leaves both sides losers. Or, alternatively, you may react by impulsively giving in just to end the negotiation and preserve the relationship. You lose and, having demonstrated your weakness, you expose yourself to exploitation by others. The problem you thus face in negotiation is not only the others side's difficult behaviour but your own reaction, which can easily perpetuate that behaviour.[8]

I believe that acquiring the know-how to cooperate requires us to possess the other three negotiation styles. Cooperation is, as we have seen, not the same as giving in or accommodating. It does require some elements of these (unless there is textbook-like compatibility of interests, as in the case of the orange), but it primarily requires the ability to assert one's interest. And yet again, having only that tool in your tool kit is not enough. We need to be able, as you know, to equally regard the other side's interests. And, in many situations we need to be able to avoid actions and topics that would only distract us from what is really important.

How can we visualize this idea? I propose using another optical illusion that you are probably familiar with, the "Necker Cube." Swiss crystallographer Louis Albert Necker created his famous cube in the 1980s. It is a wire-frame drawing that can be interpreted to have different front sides because it offers no visual cues as to its orientation. I would like to take three of these cubes, each representing one of the

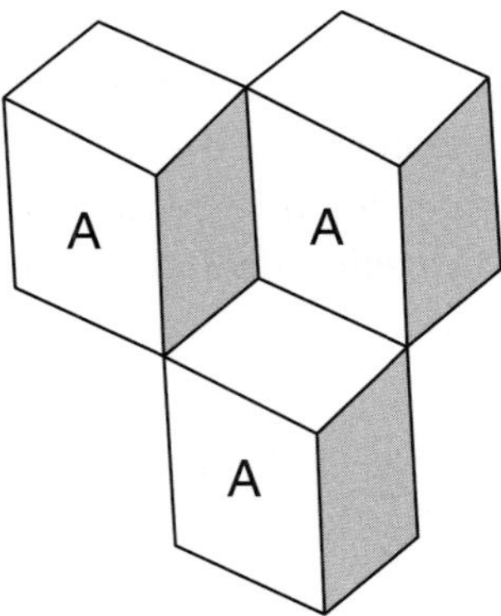

Figure 5.1 Negotiation skills as Necker Cubes

3 As (or 3 Fs, if you prefer): see Figure 5.1. When we are entangled in a negotiation, we can directly observe these behaviors in the other side. And it is one or more of them that come to our mind most readily when we contemplate our own response. Likewise, the 3 As are readily observable in the diagram. What we cannot see directly, is the fourth cube. It is formed only by synthesizing our view of the other three cubes. Likewise, we often cannot observe cooperation as such. It often consists of using different "As" in sequence: In a trade-off we first give the other side what they want (acknowledge) to demand something in return (assert). If an observer saw only the first, or the second part of the move, they would not know what we were attempting to do. Cooperation, in that way, is the "invisible" negotiation style. It is an abstract idea that we create only in our mind. It is therefore aptly depicted by the invisible fourth Necker Cube. It is not in the diagram. But when we look at the conflux of the existing three cubes, we can still see it.

5.3 Inert Know-How

Finally, it is also possible that I generally possess the required skills, but am momentarily not able to exercise them. I might simply be stuck in the heat of the moment, and my knowledge remains "inert." This is typically what happens when the thought of "what I should have said" strikes us. This is when we realize that we should have taken a different approach. Memory is fallible, not because of storage limitations so much as retrieval limitations. The term "inert knowledge" refers to the inability to access relevant information that we possess when we most need to access it.[9]

Significantly, the act of choosing the right approach itself can be problematic. Merely focusing on one strategy can induce tunnel vision. Participants in an experiment were given the task of revising a sales slump within a paint manufacturing company. They were each asked to evaluate the merits of only one of four possible solutions: (1) increasing advertising to raise brand awareness; (2) lowering prices to stimulate demand; (3) hiring personnel to promote sales; or (4) product development to boost quality. Robert Gialdini summarized the outcome: "It didn't matter which of the four ideas the decision makers evaluated: the process of targeting and evaluation one, by itself, pushed them to recommend *it* among the options as the best remedy for the company to adopt."[10]

When we focus on an option there is apparently a risk that we focus only on its positive side. Remember Robert Bruner's "deals from hell" in Chapter 3? He found that M&A transactions are typically launched with confident assertions. So confident, in fact, that hubris is pervasive at the start of most failed deals. Tunnel vision would provide an explanation for many deals that might otherwise seem inexplicable.[11]

Inert knowledge is often caused by "functional fixedness": The human tendency to attempt problem-solving using familiar methods at the expense of using more promising but less salient options. The "candle task" is the classical experiment that illustrates the phenomenon. It was developed by Norman Maier in 1931 and is still used today. This is how Frank and Ramscar describe it:[12]

> Participants must use a box of tacks and a book of matches to mount a candle on a wall so that it can burn normally and without dripping. The optimal solution is to take the tacks out of their box, tack the box to the wall, and place the candle on the box but participants only discover this solution approximately one-quarter of the time.[13]

As we mentioned in Chapter 4, Abraham Maslow suggested that if the only tool you have is a hammer, you may treat everything as if it were a nail. Even when we add new tools to our problem-solving tool kit, our first impulse may still be to use the old hammer. If your default approach is to seek a win–win solution, for instance, you might struggle to claim value, even if you have learned all about it.

***

Whatever the reasons for an incomplete tool kit, we cannot successfully face the negotiator's dilemma with one. If we cannot modify our tactics in view of the situation, we will not be able to control the outcome. And if we do not realize this, we might come under the illusion of controlling the process. Perhaps you have seen the episode of *The Simpsons* where Homer wants to buy a rock from Lisa. Why? He believes the rock keeps the bears away. The reason: Ever since Lisa had it, there have been no bears in sight! Human beings have a strong desire for control, or at least for the illusion of it. Yale School of Medicine professor Steven Novella explains: "We don't like to feel as if we are victims of a capricious universe or as if we are helpless in the face of unseen forces or randomness. We like to think that

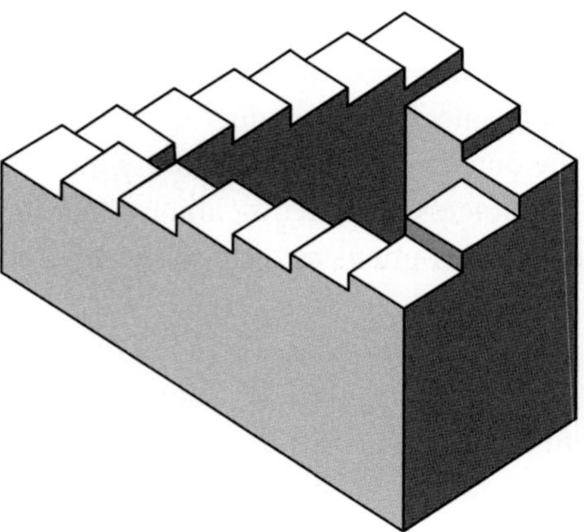

Figure 5.2 The illusion of competence as impossible staircase

we exert some control over ourselves, over the events that happen to us, and over our environment."[14]

We only yield to this tendency when we create the illusion of competence. Its effect, regrettably, might be incompetence. If I am not aware of what skills I am lacking, how can I hope to acquire them? When I am under the illusion of being fully competent to handle the situation, I will naturally continue as I am and just use the skills that I already possess. It might even appear to me that I am advancing my expertise. In reality, I might not be making any progress, as doing the same thing over and over rarely leads to different results. The illusion of competence might be as convincing to us as a Shepard tone. This auditory illusion is named after Roger Newland Shepard, the American cognitive scientist who is considered the father of research on spatial relations. The tone, like our expertise, seems to continually ascend. And yet, like our expertise, it does not. Alas, since this is not an audiobook, I cannot relay the Shepard tone to you. But you probably are familiar with a corresponding optical illusion that we can use instead: The Escher staircase. Maurits Cornelis Escher, the Dutch graphic artist, drew an ever-ascending staircase that likewise resembles the illusion of competence. It is the drawing of a closed path which always seems to go upward. While the viewer sees all stairs going up, the staircase ultimately arrives at its origin again. That is exactly the kind of impression one gets when advancing under the mere illusion of competence. Figure 5.2 is an abstract picture of this idea.[15]

Having an incomplete tool kit is bad enough, especially when we are not even aware of it. But the illusion of control has an even more detrimental effect. It tends to prevent us from thinking accurately about negotiation and its learning. It can thus close down the only avenue we have for escaping from our ignorance: Learning to think properly about negotiations.

6 The Illusion of Acumen

Without the ability to consider the opposite of what our intuition suggests, our experience cannot become expertise.

Learning, as we saw in Chapter 5, is defined as a change in behavior (or behavior potential) based on past experience. The illusions of both a coherent task and a complete tool kit result in an incomplete understanding, preventing us from realizing that we need to expand our behavior repertoire. This remains an "unknown unknown" to us, and as a consequence we might never have a reason to question our intuition. Without questioning our intuition, we cannot improve it. Negotiating well, and becoming better at it, requires the ability to think accurately about the process. We need to apply intuition as well as deliberation in the right measure. And we need to do so looking both forward and back.

There are three obstacles that can get in the way: The curse of expertise, wicked feedback, and an unwillingness to learn. Accurately thinking about the way forward is threatened by the curse of expertise. The curse describes the paradoxical phenomenon that sometimes the very fact that we have learned something can impede further learning. It can turn our strength into a weakness; we have, in a way, learned too much. We have also already touched upon the next, and biggest, obstacle to learning from experience: The unfortunate fact that in negotiations we will receive feedback that is valid mixed up with feedback that is not. This makes it extremely difficult to draw the right lessons, and is the reason why scientists call the kind of feedback that we get in negotiations "wicked." When looking back, it is extremely hard to learn the right lessons in the ambiguous context of negotiations. But it is easy to learn the wrong lessons because of two common biases: The confirmation bias and the egocentrism bias. We will conclude this chapter with an exploration of what is, perhaps, the most challenging obstacle to our accurate thinking: an unwillingness to engage in the difficult task of learning.[1]

These three obstacles can combine to create another illusion. Rather than thinking accurately about negotiation learning, there might only be a semblance of it. We may come under the mere illusion of acumen, just as we are under the illusion to see a triangle or the letter "A" in Figure 6.1.

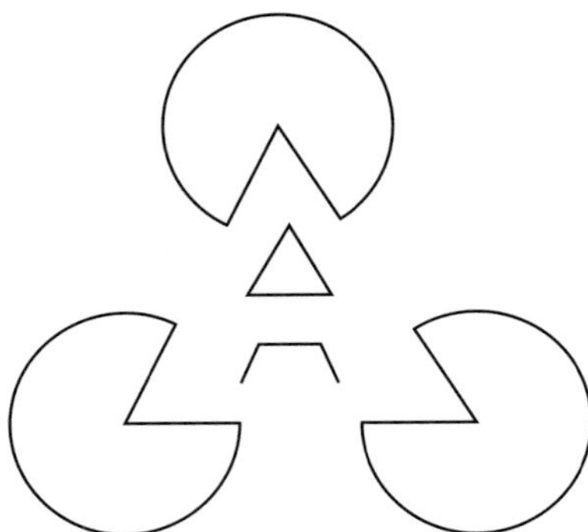

Figure 6.1 The illusion of acumen

6.1 The Curse of Expertise

It is especially easy for intelligent and experienced negotiators to become victims of the illusion of accuracy. In the words of Niels Bohr, an expert is a person who has found out by their own painful experience all the mistakes that one can make in a very narrow field. I like this quip because it nicely contrasts the painful process of becoming an expert with the rather more self-assured status that many experts seem to assign themselves. It is in that self-assurance that the risk lies.[2]

Thinking intelligently earns and merits our self-assurance as experts. Note that it is not the same as rational thinking. The illusion of accuracy is a fallacy of rationality, not intelligence. Based on decades of research into "good thinking," Keith Stanovich warns that intelligence is not a proxy of rational thought. They are two different concepts. People can, at the same time, be intelligent and irrational. In our context, it is easy to embark on an irrational course *precisely because* one has learned the right (but incomplete) thing. In a way, this is a mistake that only intelligent people can make.[3]

This is the curse of expertise. Yes, experts have special abilities and show enhanced performance. But, as cognitive neuroscientist Itiel E. Dror has shown in a wide range of domains, they are also prone to commit specific errors that can lead to *worse* results. Experts acquire schemas, and automatize their performance by categorizing information and honing selective attention. Yet these very mechanisms also restrict the expert's flexibility and control, and might cause them to miss or ignore important information. Despite the brain's limited capacity to process information, experts are able to perform even highly sophisticated tasks with relative ease. As Dror points out, it is exactly the expert's ability to deal with cognitive load by mental representations and efficient thinking. Chunking information and selective attention, for instance, allow expert chess players to quickly detect meaningful patterns that connect the figures on a board. Novices can only see the individual pieces. When quickly shown a chess board, experts detect and remember the underlying patterns within seconds. Novices, on the other hand, hardly remember any pieces at all. Importantly, expert performance depends on the board pattern being meaningful. When trying to remember board positions of pieces placed at random, experts are no better than novices. They might be even worse! Take another example: London taxi drivers. Experienced cabbies develop specific brains that underpin their expertise, making them significantly more knowledgeable about London landmarks and their spatial relationships than novices. But when large parts of the city were re-modeled at Canary Wharf, the experienced drivers did significantly worse at forming and retaining new information than their new colleagues. This paradoxical nature of expertise means that with extraordinary abilities come vulnerabilities and pitfalls. Expertise is a blessing and a curse.[4]

This is what Dinnar and Susskind mean when they warn that "what made you successful can get you in big trouble." We pick up negotiation skills as we gain expertise, and our habits become ingrained through trial and error. Some of them lead to success, and we tend to stick with what has worked in the past. And this is doubly problematic because of the paradoxical nature of negotiation itself. What we have learned is right, but it has its limitations. Sometimes a previously learned behavior is not the right one for the question at hand.[5]

The curse of expertise can be countered by diligently observing the outcomes of our actions and assessing the accuracy of our expertise. We need feedback. Alas, this is exactly where the next trap awaits.

6.2 Wicked Feedback

Learning is most likely to be successful if we receive immediate and clear feedback. It can then be a great tool to prompt reflection and explanation. While we know that feedback is essential for our growth, we often dread and dismiss it. Douglas Stone and Sheila Heen explored the complexity of accepting feedback. They observe, tongue-in-cheek, that people are usually not good at receiving feedback when we give it to them. And when we receive it, we feel that people are not good at giving it! Perhaps we ourselves are the problem? Learning from feedback is never easy. But it is especially difficult in negotiations. Why?[6]

Consider the following story told by Harvard Business School's Michael Wheeler:

> Margaret pushed the down button a third time. "Go ahead," said Richard with a sweep of his hand. "After you." Margaret looked up, half startled that the elevator was already there. She was too deep in her own thoughts to be embarrassed. "Yes," she said absently.

> This was the first time that Margaret and Richard had met, and those were the only words they spoke. This would also be the last time their paths ever crossed. Yet at that particular moment, their fates were intertwined. Unbeknownst to them, Richard and Margaret had been competing against each other for a lucrative contract with ComTX, a major telecommunications company. Each had survived a review process in which dozens of proposals had been winnowed down to two finalists. They each had worked nonstop this past week, trying to negotiate a winning deal.
>
> And here they were, strangers bumping into each other late on a Friday afternoon, having just left different offices on the forty-fourth floor of ComTX's imposing Midtown tower. One of them had just signed a contract with the communications giant. The other had been thanked politely by a company official but told that another bidder had been selected for the project.
>
> Richard rocked back and forth on the balls of his feet, a grin spreading across his face, as the elevator began its descent. He could feel his tension drain. It was all he could do to keep from whistling. Glancing over at Margaret, he was tempted to ask, "Is everything okay?" Her brow was furrowed, and she was shaking her head no, as if she were lost in a difficult internal conversation. Margaret took a deep breath, but that didn't seem to do much good. She was consumed by anxiety and self-doubt.
>
> How, then, is it that Margaret carried the signed contract in her brief-case, while Richard had just been told that his deal was dead?[7]

The fictional story poignantly illustrates the difficulty of drawing the right lessons from our experience. What exactly can we learn from the results we achieve? If we have reached an agreement, just as Margaret had, does this really mean that we did as well as we could have? Or does it mean we sold ourselves short? If we do not close a deal, as in the case of Richard, does this mean that we failed to reach a perfectly possible outcome? Or was it better not to agree? And to what extent is the outcome even due to (1) our actions, (2) the actions of the other side, (3) their lack of alternatives, and/or (4) behind-the-scenes factors that we are not even aware of?

Leigh Thompson and Terri DeHaarport examined the impact of feedback experimentally. They divided participants into three groups. Negotiators in the first group were given complete information about the other side's preferences. Not surprisingly, they were most successful in drawing the right lessons from their experience. Negotiators in the second group were informed only of the value of the deal for the other side after the fact – and consequently were much less able to learn from it. The negotiators in the third group were given no information at all. As expected, they learned the least from the experience. (Unfortunately, receiving complete information is often impossible outside the classroom, which is the key reason why role-play learning is indispensable for learning to negotiate.)[8]

Wheeler concludes: "It is devilishly hard to judge success in negotiation. You may love an agreement you reach or feel lukewarm about it, but either way, results themselves are an imperfect test of how well you've done." He therefore draws on a concept that had originally been developed by Robin Hogarth and calls negotiation a quintessentially "wicked" learning environment. A learning environment is "wicked" when feedback in the form of outcomes of actions or observations is poor, and can be called "kind" when feedback links outcomes directly to the appropriate actions or judgments, and is both accurate and plentiful.[9]

Just think of the kind of environment in which you learn to draw, practice a sport, or speak a foreign language with native speakers. In these contexts, you see what your behavior leads to right away – whether or not you want to. It is easy to measure your satisfaction with the result, and see what should be done to improve. To receive this sort of accurate and immediate feedback in a negotiation is unlikely. The parties often have an interest in *not* revealing the necessary information – and there are good reasons for this. If you assume that you have a good deal, you might prefer not to reveal this. Why risk creating dissatisfaction? Experienced negotiators often work hard to convince the other side that they can barely live with the deal (regardless of whether or not the deal is actually advantageous). If, on the other hand, you suspect that you have a bad deal, you may prefer not to know for sure! You have probably convinced yourself that you achieved what was possible. And this is what you just told your boss, too.

This is the unfortunate reason why Howard Raiffa's ingenious *post-settlement settlement* concept is seldom used. In a post-settlement settlement, parties that have just reached an agreement reveal all relevant information to a neutral mediator, who attempts to create an agreement that would improve the outcome of both parties and suggests this to the parties. If both parties agree, they change their initial agreement. If not, it remains in effect. Despite the fact that a post-settlement settlement can represent a no-risk, mutual improvement over a given deal, it is rarely ever done in practice.[10]

The lack of reliable data is one of the main reasons why many people have an incomplete understanding of the task. In a "wicked" learning environment, experience does not equal expertise. Instead, negotiators can easily find themselves perpetuating the same mistakes that they have always made. The danger is that their confirmation bias kicks in: They see only what they want to see.

6.2.1 Seeing Only What You Want to See

As we saw in Chapter 5, when you provide someone with new information, they quickly accept evidence that confirms their preconceived notions and assess counterevidence with a critical eye. "Our brains are regular belief machines: We are motivated to believe, especially those things that we want to believe." I might prefer to believe that the task at hand is easy for me, and that the results prove I was up for it. In other words, I might become a victim of my *confirmation bias* – the tendency to see what I want to see when I appraise my own performance. People have been found to base their perceptions of performance, in part, on preconceived notions of their skills. Since these perceptions often do not correlate with objective performance, they can lead people to make judgments about their performance that have little to do with actual accomplishment. Unfortunately, people tend to be blissfully unaware of their own incompetence. When we assume that we are good negotiators, we will generally find supporting evidence for this belief. We might after the fact confirm what we had expected a priori. Thus, "we see what we expect to see."[11]

As we saw in Chapter 5, we are likely to examine relevant empirical evidence on complex issues in a biased manner, especially when we hold strong opinions. We are apt to accept "confirming" evidence at face value while subjecting "discontinuing" evidence to critical evaluation. As a result, we might draw undue support for our initial positions from mixed or even random empirical findings. Lord, Ross, and Lepper investigated the impact of new evidence on beliefs about capital punishment. Supporters and opponents were exposed to two purported studies. One confirmed and the other denied pre-existing beliefs about the deterrent effect of the death penalty: "Kroner and Phillips (1977) compared murder rates for the year before and the year after adoption of capital punishment in 14 states. In 11 of the 14 states, murder rates were lower after adoption of the death penalty. This research supports the deterrent effect of the death penalty." Or: "Palmer and Crandall (1977) compared murder rates in 10 pairs of neighbouring states with different capital punishment laws. In 8 of the 10 pairs, murder rates were higher in the state with capital punishment. This research opposes the deterrent effect of the death penalty." The results were sobering: "Both proponents and opponents of capital punishment rated those results and procedures that confirmed their own beliefs to be the more convincing and probative ones, and they reported corresponding shifts in their beliefs as the various results and procedures were presented."[12]

Substantial evidence-based research suggests that when making judgments concerning existing facts and future probabilities, people are likely to do so in ways that confirm their pre-existing belief structures, assume high degrees of personal agency in the world, and create a positive presentation of self. To that end, people often ignore data that contradicts decisions made previously. In the context of negotiation, such overconfidence can cause the individual to overestimate the likely benefits of an agreement, or to underestimate the disadvantages of not reaching the agreement.[13]

And again, even experts are not immune against this bias. To name just one example, let's consider Thorndike's cats again. While the existence of reinforcement learning, which he discovered, is beyond doubt, it might not actually have happened in this experiment. Some biologists proposed that it is not reinforcement learning that enables the cats to escape from the puzzle box. Researchers that replicated the experiment witnessed no behavior that was directed at opening the latch at all. What they did see was the animals' simple but typical greeting behavior. The box was opened by random movements. Accordingly, biologists have argued that Thorndike was observing learning only because he had expected it. "Tripping over the cat" is the title they gave their article.[14]

6.2.2 Egocentrism

The confirmation bias is often accompanied by a certain egocentrism. This is the tendency of individuals to have an over-positive view of their abilities and future. This seems to be a common tendency, at least in the West. *Most* Westerners, when asked how they compare to others, think that they are *better* than average. This, of course, is statistically impossible. For instance, two-thirds of MBA students surveyed at a prestigious American business school regarded their decision-making abilities as above the class average. Astonishingly, when US News & World Report surveyed US citizens about their odds of "going to heaven," most believed they had a better chance than nun and missionary, Mother Teresa.[15]

In a negotiation context, this is dangerous on many levels. Clearly, the better you can see the situation from the perspective of the other side, the better you can optimize the outcome. By contrast, if you are fixated on your own perspective, you will fail to adequately assess the options and alternatives from the point of view of your counterpart. If you do not have the full picture, you cannot hope to reach an optimal result.

In other words, you are only confirming your intuitive thinking – and not learning from experience that you need to try the opposite. As a result, you have no incentive to question and override your intuition. The "reflective mind", as Stanovich calls it, remains unused. And your thinking remains incomplete.[16]

Figure 6.2 Egocentrism

6.3 Unwillingness to Learn

We also have to face the uncomfortable possibility that people may not learn something new simply because they do not want to. Now, when my theory in use is different from my espoused-to theory, as we saw, then I am deceiving myself about what I am learning. Here we look at a different scenario, although admittedly, the result could be much the same. What we are looking at here is the last component of the last trap of negotiation learning.

A related question is how we think about our failure to engage in learning. For example, I am not good at playing musical instruments, but I am fully aware of this. Perhaps your friend decides to engage in a career that does not hinge on her negotiation skills, because this is not something she would like to improve. That would be not only fine, it would be admirably responsible. However, after having explored so many biases together, perhaps you also suspect that this is not always what people tell themselves. Rather, many will tell themselves, as we have seen, that they *do not need to learn more.* They just don't want to. One of the scariest things I have ever heard is an interview with a negotiation consultant. Asked what book on the topic he was currently reading, he responded that he was not reading any more books on his professional field. "All the books that I wanted to read on negotiation" he said, amazingly, "I have already read." And yes, he was planning on a few more decades in the profession.

In the conclusion of their treatise on the illusion of knowledge, Steven Sloman and Philip Fernbach remind us that, yes, by avoiding illusion we are more likely to be accurate. "But illusion is pleasure. Many of us spend a significant part of our lives living in illusions quite intentionally. We entertain ourselves with fictional worlds that offer no pretense of being real.... Is that wrong? Should we really be minimizing our illusions?" Other researchers, such as Donald Hoffman, even make the case that evolution has purposefully shaped our perception precisely in order to hide the truth from our eyes. Similarly, Hugo Mercier and Dan Sperber argue that reason has evolved not to arrive at better beliefs and decisions, but to help us justify our existing beliefs and actions to ourselves as well as others.[17]

Thankfully, that is another question that we do not have to decide here. It is enough to be aware of it for our purposes, although you might want to explore this further. However, you should be aware of the following: If you do try to change your mind, remember that a fear center in your brain will warn you that danger is imminent. Conversely, if you reiterate an idea, your brain's reward centers will be activated. Recent imaging studies show this: You can consciously override the more primitive fear and reward brain centers, but it will take time and require a great deal of determination and effort. This takes us back to Gorman and Gorman's warning (in Chapter 4) that it is "fundamentally unnatural and uncomfortable to change our minds, and this is reflected in the way our brain works." We humans are, as it turns out, extremely resistant to changing our mind. Brace yourself, then, for the conclusion of this part of the book.[18]

***

By learning something, I might inadvertently hinder my further progress. In a way, I have boxed myself in. Perhaps you know the puzzle in Figure 6.3. The task is to connect the dots by drawing four straight and continuous lines without lifting the pencil from the paper. If you have never done it, try it now.

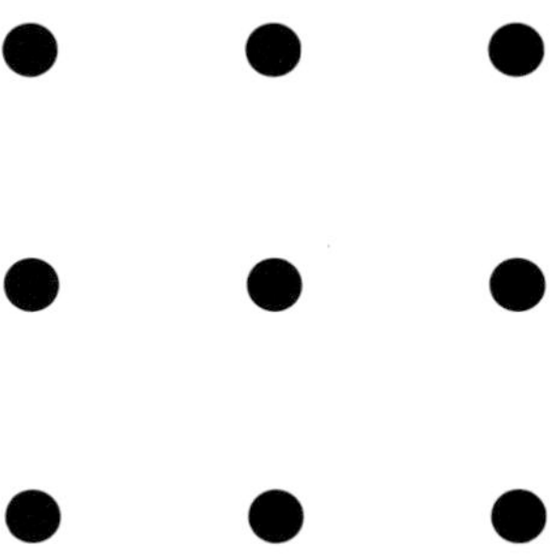

Figure 6.3 The 9-dot puzzle

The lines can pass through the nine dots only if they are drawn outside the confines of the square defined by the dots themselves: see Figure 6.4. However, this square only exists in our intuitive perception! My expectations might prevent me from solving the task. Because I have (correctly!) learned that the nine dots constitute a box, I can find it hard to think outside of this concept.

Likewise, in learning about negotiation, I might have come to understand one side of the task. Because the other side is paradoxically its opposite, I do not reckon with it. I might not even be able to see it. As experiments such as the "Invisible Gorilla" have shown, paying attention to one thing can literally make us blind toward other things. Christopher Chabris and Daniel Simons's experiment (for which they were awarded an Ig Nobel Prize) revealed that people who are focused on one thing can easily overlook something else. They made a video where students in white or black shirts pass a basketball between themselves. Viewers were asked to count the number of times the players of the white team passed to one another. This task bound so much of the viewers' attention, that they often failed to notice a person in a gorilla suit who appears in the center of the image. Similarly, in negotiations, having high regard for one side, or for the other, might prevent us from seeing what else is also there.[19]

The three challenges to learning conspire to block our learning. "Blocking" is a phenomenon that has been discovered in conditioned learning. Remember Pavlov's dogs? Once they had learned to associate the ringing of the bell with the arrival of

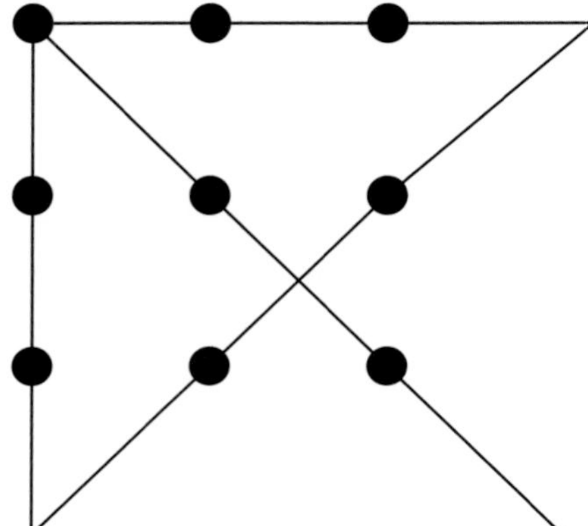

Figure 6.4 The 9-dot puzzle solved: Thinking outside the box

food, something alarming happened: They became incapable of picking up a second, equally valid stimulus (such as a flashing light). Their prior learning had blocked further learning.

Conditioning works partly through dopamine spikes in neurons which predict the reward. Having learned by association means having formed an expectation, and this is where blocking occurs. As Thad A. Polk of the University of Michigan describes:[20]

> If you've already learned an association between 2 stimuli, then that existing association can block the learning of other associations. For example, if you've already learned an association between seeing a red light and hearing a fan, then you might not learn an association between a green light that starts coming on later that also predicts the fan. In that case, the green light does not become associated with the fan, because the red light could already predict it. As a result, there was no prediction error and no new learning.[21]

In one of the most exciting neuroscientific discoveries of the last twenty-five years, biologist Wolfram Schultz of the University of Fribourg found what now appears to be the neural basis of this mechanism. In his experiments, Schultz found that dopamine neurons become very active when the learner receives a reward that they weren't expecting – but the neurons do not fire when the reward had been expected. In other words, the neurons fire in response to a reward prediction error.[22]

I believe that something similar happens in cognitive negotiation learning: Having learned one side of the Yin & Yang, we are essentially "blocked" from appreciating the other side. Because we already have a working, accurate understanding of what a negotiation is, it is now counterintuitive to expect the opposite. The same applies to our understanding of the relationship and of accurate thinking. As we have already seen, having learned something "boxes" us in – and we now only see either the duck *or* the rabbit, not both.

So, when I seemingly have a complete understanding of the task, possess the skills to control the process, and receive the results that I expected, it becomes extremely difficult to question my thinking. I might just follow my intuition. But as we have seen, my intuition might not always recommend the accurate course of action. Sometimes what is required does not come intuitively to me. Hence my "reflective mind" has to monitor my intuition, and sometimes deliberately override it. (Of course, it can also happen that a negotiator overthinks. The error can lie in overriding intuition when it should have been followed. However, the overwhelming empirical evidence suggests that the reverse is a much bigger problem.)

6.3.1.1 Michael's Case

The case that for me exemplifies many of the challenges which learners of negotiation face is the story of my friend Michael, described in the Introduction. After our systematic analysis of these challenges, it becomes clear that he might have stumbled over more than one obstacle. Michael's real theory in use might not have been the much more complex one he espoused to in the workshop. Or his knowledge may have simply remained inert, and his vision tunneled, in the heat of the moment. It is also possible that all of these challenges conspired to form a vicious circle. Michael was thus under the mere illusion of control when he called me. What he had accurately learned before now blocked the completion of the whole picture, giving him no reason to reflect or override his intuition when he responded to the acquirer's tactics.

This changed in the course of our conversation. But what can we generally do to establish a virtuous cycle of learning? First, truly understand the tactical paradox. Second, complete your skill set to manage the strategic dilemma. And for both, learn to properly think about negotiation. How? This is what we will look at now. It all starts with an unpleasant moment, similar to what Michael experienced in our call.

PART III
Ambitious Humility: The Three Steps of Learning

How we learn to better understand, practice, and think about negotiation.

We have now explored the triple challenge to negotiation success, and the corresponding hurdles to negotiation learning. We have seen that the former often leads to ambivalence, while the latter often lead to blocking. We realized that we have to be ambitious *and* humble to succeed.

As we saw at the end of the Introduction, Niels Bohr welcomes the paradox because it can stimulate progress. If we embrace it, it can become our friend in learning. What makes negotiation so challenging is what can make learning it easier. Negotiations are about outcomes. Achieving negotiation success is a practical skill, and its mastery can be measured in many cases. Learning how to negotiate is a much more mundane task than acquiring an understanding of, say, philosophy or art. It is not rocket science, and we can approach it methodically. Luckily, the human mind has an extraordinary capacity to reason and plan. There are three steps that we can take. One step leads to the next, with each overcoming an obstacle: Learning to understand, to acquire the know-how, and to think accurately.[1]

We can thus establish a virtuous cycle. Observable performance improvement requires learning about negotiation theory and then learning how to apply theory adequately to the specific situations we encounter in practice. When you have a proper understanding of the territory you can work on traversing it: You may employ trial and error, observing others, attending training sessions, or reading books. Just keep in mind that, just as you cannot negotiate by yourself, you cannot practice it alone in your room.

Let's start at the beginning. How can you improve your understanding of negotiation?

7 Understanding

How to expand our knowledge by considering the opposite of what we know, with the help of the "torpedo's shock," setting goals, and making sense.

The first step is to polish your understanding of negotiation theory. Learning something complex such as negotiation theory requires what can be called "deep work," an ever-rarer human skill: The uninterrupted concentration on cognitively demanding concepts. To better understand negotiations, we have to embrace all three challenges of negotiation: we have to cooperate *and* compete, have high regard for ourselves *and* the other side, and think deliberately *and* intuitively. To do so, we have to challenge ourselves to embrace the ancient Greek concept of aporia. We can then broaden our apprehension by focusing on specific goals that we set for ourselves. Finally, we can use a number of techniques to truly absorb new knowledge, namely sense-making, exemplifying, analogizing, interleaving, and spacing out. In this chapter we will explore all of these concepts. We will have to start with the somewhat painful truth that our understanding, alas, might be limited.[1]

7.1 Embrace Aporia: The Torpedo's Shock

We are in need of what Socrates called "aporia" (ἀπορῐ́ᾱ), a state of puzzlement that often precedes insight. The puzzlement arises when we realize that we do not (fully) understand the matter at hand. This realization can be very unpleasant. It is one of the reasons why people often prefer to remain ignorant. This has not changed since ancient times: The Athenians put Socrates to death because they would not put up with it anymore. (One would hope that the consequences of this aversion were less drastic today. But thinking of people's attitudes to climate change quickly reminds us otherwise.)

The philosopher Socrates had a clear purpose in life: To facilitate the learning of his fellow Athenians. We know him mainly through the writings of his students, notably Plato, who portray Socrates in the streets of his hometown, engaged in dialogue. Socrates usually steers his unsuspecting counterpart purposefully toward a specific state of mind, the state of aporia. Socrates knew that aporia is a necessary prerequisite for learning.

Unfortunately, being led into such a state is often not welcomed by the other side. His counterpart in the *Meno Dialogue* (written 380 BCE) complained:

> I consider that . . . you are extremely like the flat torpedo sea-fish; for it benumbs anyone who approaches and touches it, and something of the sort is what I find you have done to me now. For in truth I feel my soul and tongue quite benumbed, and I am at a loss what answer to give you.[2]

Socrates agreed, asserting only that he was equally at a loss. Then he proceeded to demonstrate the beneficial effect of aporia. (He also argued that, because our souls are immortal, learning is more like remembering – which is why he refers to it as "recollection" below; but this is none of our concern here.)[3]

Meno Yes, Socrates, but what do you mean by saying that we do not learn, and that what we call learning is recollection? Can you instruct me that this is so?

Socrates I remarked just now, Meno, that you are a rogue and so here you are asking if I can instruct you, when I say there is no teaching but only recollection: you hope that I may be caught contradicting myself forthwith.

Meno I assure you, Socrates; that was not my intention, I only spoke from habit. But if you can somehow prove to me that it is as you say, pray do so.

Socrates It is no easy matter, but still I am willing to try my best for your sake. Just call one of your own troop of attendants there, whichever one you please, that he may serve for my demonstration.

Meno Certainly. You, I say, come here.

Socrates He is a Greek, I suppose, and speaks Greek?

Meno Oh yes, to be sure – born in the house.

Socrates Now observe closely whether he strikes you as recollecting or as learning from me.

Meno I will.

Socrates Tell me, boy, do you know that a square figure is like this?

Boy I do.

Socrates Now, a square figure has these lines, four in number, all equal?

Boy Certainly.

Socrates And these, drawn through the middle, are equal too, are they not?

Boy Yes.

Socrates And a figure of this sort may be larger or smaller?

Boy To be sure.

Socrates Now if this side were two feet and that also two, how many feet would the whole be? Or let me put it thus: if one way it were two feet, and only one foot the other, of course the space would be two feet taken once?

Boy Yes.

Socrates But as it is two feet also on that side, it must be twice two feet?

Boy It is.

Socrates Then the space is twice two feet?

Boy Yes.

Socrates Well, how many are twice two feet? Count and tell me.

Boy Four, Socrates.

Socrates And might there not be another figure twice the size of this, but of the same sort, with all its sides equal like this one?

Boy Yes.

Socrates Then how many feet will it be?

Boy Eight.

Socrates Come now, try and tell me how long will each side of that figure be. This one is two feet long: what will be the side of the other, which is double in size?

Boy Clearly, Socrates, double.

Socrates Do you observe, Meno, that I am not teaching the boy anything, but merely asking him each time? And now he supposes that he knows about the line required to make a figure of eight square feet; or do you not think he does?

Meno I do.

Socrates Well, does he know?

Meno Certainly not.

Socrates He just supposes it, from the double size required?

Meno Yes.

Socrates Now watch his progress in recollecting, by the proper use of memory. Tell me, boy, do you say we get the double space from the double line? The space I speak of is not long one way and short the other, but must be equal each way like this one, while being double its size –eight square feet. Now see if you still think we get this from a double length of line.

Boy I do.

Socrates Well, this line is doubled, if we add here another of the same length?

Boy Certainly.

Socrates And you say we shall get our eight-foot space from four lines of this length?

Boy Yes.

Socrates Then let us describe the square, drawing four equal lines of that length. This will be what you say is the eight-foot figure, will it not?

Boy Certainly.

Socrates And here, contained in it, have we not four squares, each of which is equal to this space of four feet?

Boy Yes.

Socrates Then how large is the whole? Four times that space, is it not?

Boy It must be.

Socrates And is four times equal to double?

Boy No, to be sure.

Socrates But how much is it?

Boy Fourfold.

Socrates Thus, from the double-sized line, boy, we get a space, not of double, but of fourfold size.

Boy That is true.

Socrates And if it is four times four it is sixteen, is it not?

Boy Yes.

Socrates What line will give us a space of eight feet? This one gives us a fourfold space, does it not?

Boy It does.

Socrates And a space of four feet is made from this line of half the length?

Boy Yes.

Socrates Very well; and is not a space of eight feet double the size of this one, and half the size of this other?

Boy Yes.

Socrates Will it not be made from a line longer than the one of these, and shorter than the other?

Boy I think so.

Socrates Excellent: always answer just what you think. Now tell me, did we not draw this line two feet, and that four?

Boy Yes.

Socrates Then the line on the side of the eight-foot figure should be more than this of two feet, and less than the other of four?

Boy It should.

Socrates Try and tell me how much you would say it is.

Boy Three feet.

Socrates Then if it is to be three feet, we shall add on a half to this one, and so make it three feet? For here we have two, and here one more, and so again on that side there are two, and another one; and that makes the figure of which you speak.

Boy Yes.

Socrates Now if it be three this way and three that way, the whole space will be thrice three feet, will it not?

Boy So it seems.

Socrates And thrice three feet are how many?

Boy Nine.

Socrates And how many feet was that double one to be?

Boy Eight.

Socrates So we fail to get our eight-foot figure from this three-foot line.

Boy Yes, indeed.

Socrates But from what line shall we get it? Try and tell us exactly; and if you would rather not reckon it out, just show what line it is.

Boy Well, on my word, Socrates, I for one do not know.

Socrates There now, Meno, do you observe the progress he has already made in his recollection? At first he did not know what is the line that forms the figure of eight feet, and he does not know even now: but at any rate he thought he knew then, and confidently answered as though he knew, and was aware of no difficulty; whereas now he feels the difficulty he is in, and besides not knowing does not think he knows.

Meno That is true.

Socrates And is he not better off in respect of the matter which he did not know?

Meno I think that too is so.

Socrates Now, by causing him to doubt and giving him the torpedo's shock, have we done him any harm?

Meno I think not.

Socrates And we have certainly given him some assistance, it would seem, towards finding out the truth of the matter: for now he will push on in the search gladly, as lacking knowledge; whereas then he would have been only too ready to suppose he was right in saying, before any number of people any number of times, that the double space must have a line of double the length for its side.

Meno It seems so.

Socrates Now do you imagine he would have attempted to inquire or learn what he thought he knew, when he did not know it, until he had been reduced to the perplexity of realizing that he did not know, and had felt a craving to know?

Meno I think not, Socrates.

Socrates Then the torpedo's shock was of advantage to him?

Meno I think so.

Socrates Now you should note how, as a result of this perplexity, he will go on and discover something by joint inquiry with me, while I merely ask questions and do not teach him; and be on the watch to see if at any point you find me teaching him or expounding to him, instead of questioning him on his opinions. Tell me, boy: here we have a square of four feet, have we not? You understand?

Boy Yes.
Socrates And here we add another square equal to it?
Boy Yes.
Socrates And here a third, equal to either of them?
Boy Yes.
Socrates Now shall we fill up this vacant space in the corner?
Boy By all means.
Socrates So here we must have four equal spaces?
Boy Yes.
Socrates Well now, how many times larger is this whole space than this other?
Boy Four times.
Socrates But it was to have been only twice, you remember?
Boy To be sure.
Socrates And does this line, drawn from corner to corner, cut in two each of these spaces?
Boy Yes.
Socrates And have we here four equal lines containing this space?
Boy We have.
Socrates Now consider how large this space is.
Boy I do not understand.
Socrates Has not each of the inside lines cut off half of each of these four spaces?
Boy Yes.
Socrates And how many spaces of that size are there in this part?
Boy Four.
Socrates And how many in this?
Boy Two.
Socrates And four is how many times two?
Boy Twice.
Socrates And how many feet is this space?
Boy Eight feet.
Socrates From what line do we get this figure?
Boy From this.
Socrates From the line drawn corner-wise across the four-foot figure?
Boy Yes.
Socrates The professors call it the diagonal: so if the diagonal is its name, then according to you, Meno's boy, the double space is the square of the diagonal.
Boy Yes, certainly it is, Socrates.
Socrates What do you think, Meno? Was there any opinion that he did not give as an answer of his own thought?

Meno No, they were all his own.
Socrates But you see, he did not know, as we were saying a while since.[4]

Today as then we prefer not to be subject to a torpedo's shock. The Athenians certainly had had enough. They sentenced Socrates to death and made him drink a portion of poison hemlock. (His apology did not help either. He insisted that he was, in fact, god's gift to Athens: "Now therefore, my fellow Athenians, far from making a defense on my own behalf, as one might suppose, I must make it on your behalf to prevent you from making a mistake regarding the gift the god has given you, by condemning me.") But that was then! We certainly have advanced, haven't we? Surely, we are more ready than the ancients to contemplate our own shortcomings. Or are we? Recent research is not encouraging. Robert Wilson and his collaborators explored the state of being alone with one's thoughts. It appears to be an unpleasant experience for many. The researchers found in a series of studies that participants typically did not enjoy spending between six and fifteen minutes in a room by themselves with nothing to do but think, that they enjoyed doing mundane external activities much more, and that many preferred to administer electric shocks to themselves instead of being left alone with their thoughts. If we don't even want to be left alone with our own thoughts, how big is our appetite for aporia?[5]

But it is a myth that when learning goes well it feels confident, successful, and clear. The opposite is true: Moments of confusion, frustration, uncertainty, and lack of confidence are part of the process of acquiring new skills and new knowledge. "Learning is deeper and more durable when it's effortful. Learning that's easy is like writing in sand, here today and gone tomorrow."[6]

The good news is that we do not need to wait for a Socrates to come along in order to benefit from a torpedo's shock. The feeling of aporia is inherent to the negotiation process, because it has an inbuilt complication that will sooner or later puzzle and confuse every serious learner: The inherently paradoxical nature of the task. While we have so far looked at it primarily as a challenge, the paradox (fittingly) is also the very opposite: It is an opportunity to expand and deepen our understanding. If we learn a language, or a sport, we do not enjoy a similar advantage. But when you think about negotiation, sooner or later you will run into the paradox. You may even experience an outright torpedo's shock! Realizing that we do not yet have the full picture is a necessary precondition to completing it.

That's why I propose that our understanding often progresses through two stages. Whether you start with the assumption that negotiation is the creation of value, or with the assumption that it is the distribution of value, you are right. And also, as we have seen, wrong. That realization provides the torpedo's shock which can prompt you to flip the coin. We might experience this when we realize that responding to another competitive move by conceding even more has not led to a more cooperative response. Or when we register that we now need to put our cards on the table to avoid a lose–lose outcome. It is often a moment of aporia that allows us to reverse course.

Aporia thus provides the incentive to switch from the velvet glove to the iron fist – or the other way around. It is what triggers the movement out of our comfort zone, and can facilitate our development. And it may be required for reminding us of the other side of Yin & Yang. Seen in this light, the moment of confusion is a necessary prerequisite for completing one's understanding of what negotiation is.

How can we express the need for aporia visually? The most common representation of learning over time may be the "learning curve." It was first described by Hermann Ebbinghaus in 1885. Even though it has been around for a while, it is not always used properly. When someone says "I just started my new job – and I can tell you that it's a steep learning curve!" they usually mean that it is difficult to learn all the new things that the job requires. If so, they have the curve backward. A steep learning curve, i.e., a curve with a large positive slope, is associated with a skill that is acquired easily and rapidly. This usually requires a long and difficult learning period first, as in the overwhelming new job. We have to slowly build up to the exponential growth of knowledge by laboring through a "shallow" learning curve first.[7]

It seems to me that this is exactly what happens when we first learn about negotiations. As we understand more, we detect the underlying pattern. And we get to see ever more clearly one of the two sides of the Yin & Yang, just as we learn to recognize one of Wittgenstein's animals. Once we do, our understanding of the task grows exponentially until we have captured its essence. Then learning levels off again and the curve becomes shallow once more. It takes longer to substantially increase our understanding – and it becomes harder. Only additional deliberate practice increases our understanding and skill. Once we have reached this level, many of us decide that this is good enough. But we have at that point only learned half of the story. Our understanding of that half is, of course, correct. But, as we have seen, it can also have "boxed us in." In the words of Donald Trump and Angela Merkel, we may see negotiation as creation *or* distribution of value, not both. When we understand that the opposite is *also* true, a new learning curve can commence.

Paradoxically, having learned something makes this second assent more difficult. We might not be looking for a way up anymore. This is when the moment of aporia is needed. Realizing that we do not yet have the full picture opens the door to improving our skill again. The torpedo's shock lets us shift the paradigm. This shift from the first to the second stage of learning through aporia can be graphically depicted, as shown in Figure 7.1.

And we do not even have to wait for the torpedo's shock. Once we acknowledge the paradox, we can just remind ourselves of it. We can at any time decide to consider the other side of the Yin & Yang. (In Chapter 9 we will examine in more detail how to properly think about learning to do this well.)

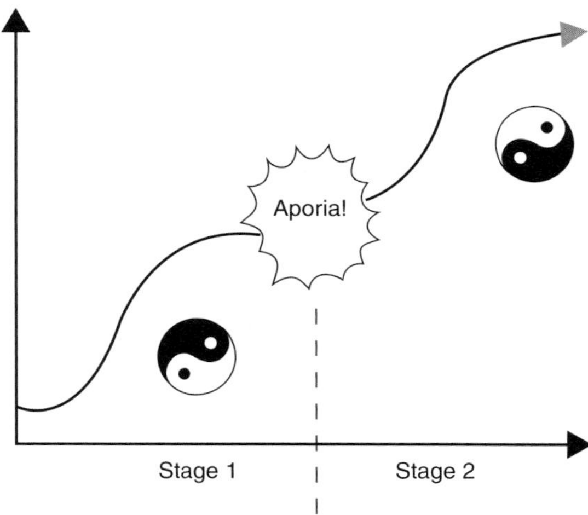

Figure 7.1 Aporia and the two stages of learning

7.2 Focus on the Goal

It is important to pursue a well-chosen goal when learning. We seldom, if ever, learn passively. Our goals affect everything we do along the way. Very few people memorize their friends' phone numbers anymore. The goal is much more easily reached by simply typing them into your cell phone and pressing a button. When we don't need to learn, we might not do so. People experience what has been coined the "Google effect": When they expect to have future access to information, they have lower rates of recall of information and enhanced recall for where to access it.[8]

People are relatively frugal learners, acquiring goal-relevant information while ignoring goal-irrelevant features. What makes people successful is their expertise in categorizing useful versus distracting knowledge. We tend to learn what is relevant to our goals and ignore the rest. Another Sherlock Holmes story comes to mind. In *A Study in Scarlet*, Dr. Watson is startled to find the detective ignorant of Copernican theory. And not only is he ignorant, he appears to be proud of this fact! Having learned that the earth revolves around the sun, Sherlock Holmes tells a shocked Dr. Watson: "Now that I do know it, I shall do my best to forget it." Our literary hero considers this knowledge useless for his pursuits:[9]

> I consider that a man's brain originally is like a little empty attic, and you have to stock it with such furniture as you choose. A fool takes in all the lumber of every sort that he comes across, so that the knowledge which might be useful to him gets crowded out, or at best is jumbled up with a lot of other things, so that he has a difficulty in laying his hands upon it. Now the skilful workman is very careful indeed as to what he takes into his brain-attic.[10]

Is this approach advisable? Wolfgang Köhler, one of the fathers of gestalt psychology, used the same metaphor to arrive at a very different conclusion: "Each science has a sort of attic into which things are almost automatically pushed that cannot be used at the moment, that do not quite fit.... We are constantly putting aside, unused, a wealth of the most valuable materials." Scientific progress requires such seemingly useless material to be seized and reexamined. This is just what Köhler did when he reevaluated the significance of visual illusions. As British neurologist Oliver Sachs explains, they were regarded as trivial at the time. But Köhler would soon show that they constitute the clearest evidence of perception being not just the passive processing of stimuli, but the active creation of configurations (or "*gestalts*"). What we can conclude is this: When you set out to learn something, you will be guided by the goals you set for yourself.[11]

To expand your knowledge and know-how, you should start by identifying a specific goal. Determining how negotiation affects your life is far from a theoretical question: It is the Rosetta Stone of your efforts. Not all messages stick. Advertisers and political campaigners have been especially keen to find out which ones do. There is broad empirical support for the "elaboration likelihood model" (ELM) that was developed by John T. Cacioppo of the University of Iowa and Richard E. Petty of the University of Missouri. Luckily for us, the ELM focuses on how people *learn* a new message. This model is named after the insight that we are more likely to absorb a message (i.e. learn new material) when we *elaborate* on it. This is a fancy way of saying that we truly consider the message and see how it fits with our existing knowledge. This is much more likely with the proper motivation. And we are often motivated to elaborate on new information when it is relevant to our lives – which brings us back to the advantage of having specific goals.[12]

Your goal provides the narrative for what you want to achieve. What is negotiation success to you? What do you want to understand better? What are you already good at? In which aspect would you like to become even better? University of Virginia's Robert Wilson developed "story editing" as a technique to redirect people's narratives. Forming a coherent narrative about ourselves and the world may result in lasting behavior change. A good story possesses four features: It describes what happened, and what the thoughts, desires, and emotions of the protagonists were:[13]

> Stories also do two additional things that we have to learn to do: They convey the way events happened in time, and they make an experience coherent, sensible, and meaningful by putting all the action and consciousness elements in order and by presenting them in such a way that the story has a point, or larger meaning.[14]

7.3 Absorb Knowledge

It is difficult to keep two conflicting ideas in one's head. As human beings we have a strong preference for coherent explanations. We can remember things much more easily if they make "sense" to us. Consider another example from our verbal memory.

> If you ask someone to recall a seemingly random assortment of words verbatim, starting with the first word – "was smelled front that his the peanuts he good hunger eating barely woman of so in could that him contain" – the average person will remember only the first six of those words. If, however, you read the same words rearranged into a sentence that makes clear sense – "The woman in front of him was eating peanuts that smelled so good that he could barely contain his hunger" – some adults will remember all of the words in perfect order, and most people will remember most of the sentence.[15]

The second sentence allows us to make sense of the words by using a mental representation – the vivid description of the scene on the bus.

In fact, the desire to make sense of information that we are presented with is so strong that we may incorrectly remember information that we have never seen. In a series of experiments, Henry Roediger and Kathleen McDermott asked people to memorize word lists. Roughly half of the participants "remembered" a word that was not actually on the list, because it expressed the idea that tied all other words together. For instance, after reading the list "bed, rest, awake, tired, dream, wake, night, blanket, doze, slumber, snore, pillow, peace, yawn, drowsy," people had a false memory of the word "sleep" being included. The mental representation of "sleep" formed in their mind as they read the list. When learning, we use our prior knowledge to make sense of the new information.[16]

7.3.1 Organize Meaning

It has been said that all living organisms organize, and what humans organize is meaning. Negotiation is an intellectual construct. Nobody has ever seen one. What we can observe are actions – the parties perhaps talking, writing, or signing a document. We can also note our own thoughts but we cannot note the thoughts of the other side. Much less can we see "the joint decision-making process to allocate resources and risks, or how to work together in the future", as we defined negotiation in Chapter 1. Cooperation, as well as competition, are cognitive constructs. Our thoughts about the process are embedded in our general view of the world. They are a function of how we believe humans do, and ought to, interact with one another. We might or might not be aware of our beliefs. Either way, they shape how we approach the triple challenge. Drawing inspiration from James Branch Cabell's definition of the optimist and the pessimist, we can say this: The cooperative negotiator proclaims that expanding the pie beats slicing it, and the competitive negotiator fears that this is true.[17]

7.3.1.1 Connect New Theory to Existing Knowledge

We see the world in a way that is commensurate with our prior knowledge. Remember that most people saw Wittgenstein's animal as a bunny at Easter? Their understanding was colored by what was foremost on their mind. When we learn something new, we understand it on the basis of what we already know. This is one of the reasons why metaphors are so powerful: They allow us to understand something new with the help of something that we already understand. What is German reunification? It is like a river flowing to the sea. What is negotiation? It is like enlarging and dividing a pie.[18]

This is also the reason why we find it easier to learn something unexpected. In an experiment, a graduate student's office was filled with typical objects (such as a pencil and a notebook) and atypical objects (such as a harmonica or a toothbrush). After having spent one minute in the room, participants indicated items on a list that they remembered seeing. People's memory was consistently more accurate for what was unexpected. It is easy to relate to this finding. Imagine you travel to a meeting. The motorway takes you through fields and meadows. If you spotted a purple cow, grazing among hundreds of ordinary cows, this would surely grab your attention. And it would be easy to remember it for a long time after you returned home. (This is the flipside of blocking. We may cease to advance if our expectations are always met.)[19]

Similar to the word-list experiment, people may falsely remember things that were to be expected. In another experiment, subjects were led to another graduate student's office and asked to briefly wait for the experimenter to return. About half a minute later, the researcher returned and led the subjects to another room, where they were unexpectedly asked to write down a list of all the items they had seen in the office. You can probably guess what's coming. Almost all subjects recalled common objects, such as the desk, chair, and shelves. But 30 percent also recalled seeing books, and 10 percent recalled seeing a file cabinet – yet the office contained neither.[20]

7.3.1.2 Find the Story Behind the Facts

There's a literary legend that a writer was once challenged in a bar to come up with a story in only six words. What he wrote is this: "For sale: baby shoes, never worn." Whether or not the writer was Ernest Hemingway, as is purported as much as debated, does not have to concern us here. What is significant for us is the meaning-making process that leads us to automatically create a story behind these six words. That story makes the six words unforgettable.

When we learn a new theory, we can use this mechanism. The Australian Science of Learning Research Centre (SLRC) brings together dozens of neuroscientists, psychologists, and education researchers to collaborate on programs to better understand learning. One of the principles that the SLRC recommends for better learning is to "find the story behind the facts." SLRC explains that stories allow us to simulate an experience (much as if we were ourselves their protagonists), leading to higher levels of emotion, engagement, and motivation, thus enhancing memory by up to 60 percent when facts are embedded within a story.[21]

7.3.2 Categorize, Exemplify, and Analogize

7.3.2.1 Categorize

We do not memorize simple "content," but categorized content. More specifically, we memorize configurations of jointly firing neurons. Canadian psychologist Donald O. Hebb is credited with coining the expression "Cells that fire together wire together." Our memories cluster similar objects or experiences together to detect patterns of interaction with our environment. There are, for example, categories for objects, activities, attributes, and abstract ideas. In this book we have been using the categories of value distribution and value creation. And we also made use of "scripts" of how events unfold over time when we studied cooperative and competitive negotiation tactics, or the tit-for-tat strategy.[22]

7.3.2.2 Exemplify

There are two theories explaining how categories find their way into our memory. One is that we encode prototypes – representations of the most central or average member of the category. When we memorize a chair, we memorize the prototypical chair. When we memorize a negotiation, we memorize the prototypical negotiation. According to this view, we recognize objects by comparing them to prototypes in our memory. The alternative theory suggests that we retain memories of the different exemplars we encounter for each category, and recognize objects by comparing them to exemplars which we have stored in our memory. We have a list of chairs in mind, and a list of negotiations. Over the years, researchers have carried out a large number of studies to explore the prototype and exemplar theories. The result? The data appears to support the exemplar view: We categorize new information by comparing it to multiple representations in our memory.[23]

But what constitutes an exemplar list? How do we establish a list of chairs, or one of negotiations? It seems to me that for either theory, we need to have an organizing idea in our mind. Even if we do not use an outright prototype, we must have some sort of definition to determine which objects are on the same list. They have something in common, which is why we have lumped them together. This suggests that in order to commit a negotiation to memory, we have to recognize it as one. Applying the very broad definition of a negotiation that we use herein means that a plethora of situations from all domains of life qualify. But unless we view the heated exchange with our teenager about car keys, or with our spouse about holidays, or with co-workers about project roles, as belonging there, they will not make it to that list. As a consequence, we might never realize that many of the rules that we study in this book apply to all of these situations. And this might contribute to our seeing only part of the picture. We might want to consider which of our interactions fall into the negotiation category, so that we can inscribe them in our mental list.

And we may do so not merely metaphorically. Researchers have found evidence that we do organize our experience into different spaces in our minds. When thinking, we may literally navigate our brain. "We believe that the brain stores information about our surroundings in so-called cognitive spaces. This concerns not only geographical data, but also relationships between objects and experience," explains Christian Doeller. These "cognitive spaces" would effectively be mental lists or mental maps in which we arrange our experience. Brain cells apparently map the dimensions of cognitive spaces:[24]

> In these, each stimulus is located according to its feature values along the relevant dimensions, resulting in nearby positions for similar stimuli and larger distances between dissimilar stimuli. The geometric definition of cognitive spaces allows flexible generalization and inference, and sequential hippocampal activity can simulate trajectories through cognitive spaces for adaptive decision-making and behaviour.[25]

7.3.2.3 Analogize

When we determine whether two objects belong to the same category, or two activities belong to the same script, we look for similarities. But we also look for differences: By coming across dissimilar examples, we learn to differentiate and infer general rules. This brings us to a timeless philosophical question: Where does our ability to think in differences and similarities come from? How do we even know what "similar" means? When we categorize information, we rely on higher order ideas. Plato called this our "knowledge of the forms." He suggested that some of these higher order ideas ("forms") precede our cognitive awareness, as if their knowledge was "built" into us. And indeed, this concept is partly supported by modern-day research. Renée Baillargeon – the researcher whose work has revolutionized our view of infants and how they learn – and her colleagues presented simple demonstrations of movements with physical objects to babies. They found that infants expected objects to be supported in space. This shows that we rely on certain inborn assumptions, for instance that objects are three-dimensional, solid, and need support to be off the ground. Thankfully we do not have to determine which of our ideas are inborn and which are not. For us it suffices to conclude that our learning of new information depends on what we already know. When we understand something new with the help of something we already know, we learn by analogy.[26]

Analogies are powerful tools for expanding our understanding. In remembering, memories have a tendency to activate other memories. If this happens, it can greatly aid the acquisition of new information:[27]

> The ability to apply relational knowledge across different contexts is of central importance in human cognition. One instance of this kind of ability is analogical transfer-mapping knowledge from a prior stored situation to a current situation.... There is abundant research demonstrating, first, that analogical transfer can lead to considerable insights *when it occurs*; and, second, that it very often fails to occur. When people succeed in accessing an appropriate prior example, they typically perform well in mapping the solution to the current problem.... However, people often fail to access prior cases in new contexts.[28]

Let's look at a stellar example (pun intended). Astronomer Johannes Kepler published his three scientific laws of planetary motion between 1609 and 1619. Nicolaus Copernicus had proposed that the planets move around the sun, rather than the other way around. But his helio-centric theory assumed circular orbits. The idea that planets would ride on fixed but invisible spheres in interlocked circles and at constant speed, much like a clockwork, had remained essentially unchanged for millennia. What makes Kepler's break from the inherited tradition so remarkable is that he arrived at this theory not by measuring the solar systems (most means to do so would only be invented much later), but by thinking about it. He arrived at his laws of planetary motion largely by analogical reasoning. One analogy that played a formative note in his thinking was the phenomenon of light from the sun, which travels to the planets and illuminates them as a base domain for a new ontological entity (a precursor to gravity). Kepler pointed out that light appears not to exist between its source and an object it lights up. Perhaps planets were moved by some light-like force? But:[29]

> Planetary motion did not stop during an eclipse, Kepler reasoned, so the moving power could not be just like light, or depend on light. He needed a new analogy.... Each time he got stuck, Kepler unleashed a fusillade of analogies. Not just light, heat, odor, currents and boatmen, but optics of lenses, balance scales, a broom, magnets, a magnetic broom, orators gazing at a crowd, and more. He interrogated each one ruthlessly, every time alighting on a new question.[30]

Dedre Gentner, the world's foremost authority on analogical thinking, emphasizes that when a learner is induced to compare two things, commonalities between the two become more salient and lead to a more abstract understanding of the object at hand. "Analogical reasoning can lead to change of knowledge – not only to enrichment of existing representations but also to true conceptual change." This is how Kepler himself put it: "And I cherish more than anything else the Analogies, my most trustworthy masters. They know all the secrets of Nature."[31]

That power can be harnessed by us mere mortals too. Shirli Kopelman, for instance, encourages us to make use of all the "hats" that we wear in life. We negotiate across different domains in life, and we become better if we can integrate our abilities. (This is also, Kopelman argues, the only way to genuinely be yourself in business and negotiation – hence the title of her book.)[32]

It is useful to accumulate examples and compare across them, thus yielding abstract principles for the learner. For instance, Wheeler suggests that we can improve if we make comparisons between what we are doing now and what we've seen before: "It's something we can do better if we attend to it seriously. While we're negotiating, our minds should turn over clever solutions we've seen elsewhere, no matter how far afield they might seem. We may find lessons, links, or combinations that could be helpful today." Wheeler therefore encourages you, as you read about examples, to stop and ask yourself: "Where have I seen that before? How could I have used that approach in deals that slipped through my fingers? How can I expand my know-how going forward?"[33]

Georg Loewenstein and Leigh Thompson accordingly urge us to actively consider multiple negotiation constellations at once. Merely knowing two examples turns out not to yield the same gains as comparing them. The two researchers showed that when we analyze two cases separately, we overwhelmingly fail to detect the similarities that we would see if we were asked to compare the same two cases. In fact, and rather depressingly, negotiators who analyzed similar cases sequentially were no more likely to use the principles learned from the first case than people who were never shown the cases! "Drawing comparisons across cases as a means of learning them, or analogical encoding, is a route to acquire domain principles that facilitates their later use. Examples may otherwise be inert knowledge." We have to ask ourselves: What is similar, and what is different?[34]

7.3.3 Memorize

There is no known limit to how much you can learn by integrating new material with what you already know. The methods of spacing out, changing context, interleaving, and mixing up all make the learning experience a bit more cumbersome. And that is exactly what makes them so effective. No one can memorize substantial new theory content all at once. We have to allow neutrons to form new connections through repeated stimulation. The experts at the Australian SLRC therefore recommend that we "space out" our learning: We should divide it into several short sessions distributed over a longer time span rather than doing one long session done in a short time span.[35]

In doing so, be mindful that learning is context-dependent. In a remarkable experiment, divers learned lists of words on dry land or underwater. They recalled the words in either the environment of original learning, or in the alternative environment. Words learned underwater were best recalled underwater. The same was true for words learned on land. When the context of learning matched the context of encoding, performance was nearly 50 percent higher than when it did not. Changing where you learn can be beneficial.[36]

7.3.3.1 Interleave

This is a similar method. It does not vary the context, but the object of learning. Rather than studying multiple examples of the same object, and then moving on to the next, we do better when we interleave examples of other objects. For example, people who learned to distinguish different types of birds and artwork by different painters achieved superior results when pursuing this interleaving strategy. Of course, it is more difficult and feels more clunky – which is why learners often prefer to do it the other way around. It seems reasonable to assume that we can profit from interleaving when alternating between the study of competitive and cooperative tactics, for example.[37]

Finally, it is also recommended to "mix up" your practice. We should practice *several* skills in a mixed-up fashion as opposed to the "massed practice" of only *one* skill in a repeated fashion. Peter Brown, Henry Roediger, and Mark McDaniel explain that when we use methods that complicate our immediate learning experience, retrieval is harder and feels less productive. But they emphasize that the effort produces longer-lasting and more versatile application later.[38]

We can conclude from this chapter that it pays to embrace the paradox.

8 Gaining the Know-How

Where we learn how to improve our negotiation skills by moving outside our comfort zone.

8.1 Expand the Tool Kit

Aristotle remarked in his *Nicomachean Ethics* (Book II, 1): "For the things we have to learn before we can do them, we learn by doing them, e.g. men become builders by building and lyre players by playing the lyre; so too we become just by doing just acts, temperate by doing temperate acts, brave by doing brave acts." Negotiation is learned by negotiating. And not only that. Modern psychological research also recommends changing our behavior as a method of changing our narratives: Doing good may lead to being good.[1]

The negotiation skill that is the hardest to learn is the ability to cooperate. It therefore stands out from the five styles that we explored in Chapter 2. There we saw that negotiators need a complete tool kit of cooperation, competition, avoidance, and acknowledgment – as well as the ability to compromise. But in Chapter 5 we encountered the illusion of competence that may prevent us from expanding our skill set. Yet, human beings appear to be predisposed for cooperation: The desire to cooperate (if not the ability) is innate to infants, as is the capability to learn it. Saying that cooperation is not human nature because we have to learn it, would be like saying that it is not human nature to speak.[2]

Although the ability to cooperate appears to be innate, individuals have to cultivate it as they grow up. And collectively, as a species, we evidently still struggle with the challenge. Neurologist Steven Pinker has shown that violence has dramatically declined since the dawn of civilization, calling this the most important thing in human history. Despite unspeakable setbacks, however, the trajectory is clear. He has systematically explored the human faculties that incline us away from violence and toward cooperation. He calls them, in Abraham Lincoln's words, the "better angels of our nature" – which is also the title of his seminal book. There are three faculties: Reason, self-control, and empathy. Let's look at each of them in turn.[3]

8.1.1 Perspective-Taking

The ability to cooperate relies in the first instance on our ability to reason. It requires the ability to see the world through the eyes of another. I believe it is no coincidence that this is a major theme not only in the development of individuals, but of the entire human race. For evidence we need not look further than the foundational text of the Judeo-Christian worldview, the Hebrew Bible. It commences with the (somewhat beast-like) human inability to take perspective. Seeing themselves through the eyes of another (and found wanting) is the very first thought of the first human that gained consciousness. Adam and Eve were not self-conscious before they ate from the appropriately named "tree of knowledge." Genesis 3:7 informs us what happened when they tried the forbidden fruit: "And the eyes of the two were opened, and they knew they were naked, and they sewed fig leaves and made themselves loincloths." These fig leaves have become symbolic, figuratively covering up acts that are shameful in the eyes of others. The human experience apparently starts with taking another's perspective.[4]

Remember tit for tat? It might not allow us ever to beat the other side. But this is precisely why it is so powerful. It succeeds because it can elicit cooperative behavior even from a stranger. How does the other side learn to cooperate? There are two theories. One possibility is that tit for tat is a case of instrumental conditioning. James A. Wall argued that the concession-making response is strengthened over time because cooperative behavior is reinforced while non-cooperative behavior is not. The behavior that is thus reinforced will be repeated. The other possibility is that tit for tat creates a perception of the strategist as both firm and fair: Firm because they made no unilateral concessions and fair because they conceded when the other conceded. This perception then leads to the conscious decision to respond cooperatively. Such learning would be a deliberate cognitive process. It seems reasonable to assume that we learn using the velvet glove in the iron fist the same way.[5]

8.1.2 Self-Control

The second of Pinker's better angels of our nature is self-control. Reason, according to Pinker, was rightly identified by Immanuel Kant as a prerequisite for perpetual, even long peace, because it incentivizes people to cooperate in a dilemma in which they might cooperate or use violence. Reason allows us to delay gratification for the sake of enhancing future benefits. In negotiations this happens all the time: We use self-control to trade one item so that we may gain another, and when we initiate a transaction with a cooperative move (despite our intuitive fear or greed). We use self-control when we have to override our intuitions and impulses, and deal productively with aporia.[6]

8.1.3 Empathy

The most common form of cooperation appears to be helping relatives so that our common genes live on. It is inherent to humans and (other) animals. Evolution encourages it. Your genes will be passed on as long as you have three brothers or sisters, five grandchildren, or nine nieces or nephews that survive you. It makes evolutionary sense to risk your life for them. And indeed, many organisms favor the reproductive success of relatives, even at a cost to themselves. Animals cooperate to facilitate "kin selection." But even unrelated animals frequently cooperate. Wild chimpanzees, for instance, exhibit cooperative behavior to obtain fitness benefits toward kin and nonkin alike. Other examples are fish swarming in a school and birds flying in formation. Meerkats give alarm calls that aid everyone, although this also attracts the attention of the predator. Vampire bats feed each other's babies. Unrelated primates groom one another, share their food, and mob predators. Why do nonrelatives cooperate? "Because many hands lighten the load. School with other fish, and you're less likely to be eaten. Birds flying in a V formation save energy by catching the updraft of the bird in front. If chimps groom one another, there are few parasites." Biologist Robert Trivers laid out the evolutionary logic of such "reciprocal altruism" in 1971: Helping another individual while incurring some cost for this act could have evolved because there is a chance of being in a reverse situation, where the individual who was helped before may now reciprocate the help.[7]

Reciprocity is also a powerful driver of human action. The behavior of others can directly influence our own thinking. There may even be neuronal roots to it. Imagine cooking with family and friends. Everyone is preparing food. Your friend is chopping onions. You watch in horror as she cuts her finger. At this moment the same areas of your brain kick into action as when you cut yourself. Your friend's pain literally *is* your pain. Scientists debate whether the ability to empathize with others is due to the "mirror neurons" first discovered at the University of Parma in the 1990s. Experiments had revealed that when a monkey saw someone else pick up food, particular neurons appeared to respond as if the viewer had also picked up the food. Further studies suggest that humans have significant networks of mirror neurons as well. They might enable us to empathize with others – which is not to say that empathy is an automatic reflex of neurons, as the experiments that revealed "pleasing frowns and disappointing smiles" made clear.[8]

What is not debated is the enormous significance of reciprocity in our lives. Proverbs in many cultures attest to its power. A beautiful Spanish saying is: "*Amor con amor se paga*" [Love is being paid for by love]. In English, somewhat more prosaically, "What goes around, comes around." In German, inexplicably, "*Wie man in den Wald hineinruft, so schallt es auch heraus*" [As you shout into the forest, so it will resound]. Philosopher René Girard argues that essentially all human desire is borrowed from others, and that all conflict arises from such "mimetic" desires. We want something because others want it. More mundane places to find reciprocity in action are American restaurants. It is common practice among servers to give customers a gift in the form of candy when delivering the check. Experiments show that customers who received a small piece of chocolate tipped more than did customers who received no candy. The researchers believe that this is best explained by the power of reciprocity.[9]

Expected reciprocity could also be the reason why having a trustworthy reputation is so beneficial in negotiations. Recent research indicates that there are very tangible advantages to having an honest reputation, which is better than being perceived as either skilled or friendly. Presumably honest negotiators tend to receive better offers in both cooperative and competitive settings. Perhaps being trusted means being trusted with reciprocating in good spirit.[10]

But reciprocal altruism has its limits. Why cooperate with individuals that are not in the peer group? Consider the example of the vampire bats. Yes, even these bloodsuckers can turn into blood donors, as Jonathan Haidt quips: They will regurgitate blood from a successful night of bloodsucking into the mouth of an unsuccessful and genetically unrelated peer. And they keep track of who has helped them in the past – and in return share primarily with those bats. But keeping track of the cooperative or non-cooperative behavior of others is a challenge for bats as well as for people. It only works up to a certain group size, where individuals can recognize each other. Apparently, evolution has not wired us to automatically cooperate with complete strangers.[11]

Some scholars suggest that when groups became too large to recognize each other, religious norms developed to allow for cooperation. Another strategy that deals well with this problem is tit for tat. Even though it is simple, it requires quite some cognitive skill, and has to be learned. As Jeffrey Stevens and Marc Hauser point out, a host of cognitive activities is necessary for employing a tit-for-tat strategy: "Some of the essential psychological ingredients for reciprocation include numerical quantification, time estimation, delayed gratification, detection and punishment of cheaters, analysis and recall of reputation, and inhibitory control; depending on the nature of the reciprocal interaction, some or all of these capacities may be necessary."[12]

Infants acquire the ability to differentiate their own beliefs from beliefs held by others. This ability is a key requirement for trading off on differing interests (and one that might not be shared with non-human primates, even though that discussion is ongoing). What goes on in our brain when we cooperate? To find out, James K. Rilling and his colleagues used functional magnetic resonance imaging (fMRI) to scan thirty-six women as they played an iterated prisoner's dilemma game with other women. They found that mutual cooperation was associated with consistent activation in brain areas that have been linked with reward processing (nucleus accumbens, the caudate nucleus, ventromedial frontal/orbitofrontal cortex, and rostral anterior cingulate cortex). The researchers propose that activation of this neural network motivates humans to resist the temptation to selfishly accept but not reciprocate favors. There seems to be a pattern of neural activation that labels cooperative social interactions as rewarding, and inhibits the selfish impulse to accept but not reciprocate an act of altruism.[13]

Let's look at another foundational text of Western civilization: *The Iliad*. Its first word captures the unrestrained impulsiveness of Achilles:

> Wrath–sing, goddess, of the ruinous wrath of Peleus' son Achilles,
> that inflicted woes without number upon the Achaeans,
> hurled forth to Hades many strong souls of warriors
> and rendered their bodies prey for the dogs,
> for all birds, and the will of Zeus was accomplished.[14]

Crucially, the epic poem does not end, as is often assumed, when Troy is destroyed. After describing a ten-year siege, the poem inconceivably ends just on the eve of Troy's fall! We learn about this, and the Trojan Horse that facilitated the fall, only in the *Odyssey*. But in *The Iliad*, it is a mere afterthought. Irrelevant, apparently, when the poem has reached its true conclusion: our hero has finally learned to empathize. The very last verses conclude what began in the very first ones. Achilles meets Priam, the father of his nemesis Hector. Achilles had slain and mutilated Hector, dragging the corpse behind his chariot for twelve days. When the aging king of Troy enters the enemy camp to ask for the return of the body, Achilles is finally seized by pity and shame. The epic poem closes with these lines:

> Then having come together they duly gave a glorious feast in the house of Priam, king nurtured by Zeus.
> Thus they tended the funeral of Hector, breaker of horses.[15]

What was true for Achilles is still true for us. Humans must learn to empathize with one another. We need not only have high regard for ourselves, but also for the other side. Kant explored the two sides when he formulated the categorical imperative "Act only in accordance with that maxim through which you can at the same will that it become a universal law." Similarly, the best know variation of the "Golden Rule" states "Do unto others as you would have them do unto you." This is included on the Murano glass tile mosaic of Norman Rockwell's drawing at the United Nations headquarters in New York City. All this has, of course, an eminently spiritual dimension: "Thou shalt love thy neighbor as thyself" (Leviticus 19:18) is regarded by both Judaism and Christianity as the most important divine law for human interaction (Talmud, Shabbat 31a:6; Luke 10:25–8).

We have already touched on Aristotle's idea that virtues stand in dialectical order. It can be considered virtuous to have high regard for yourself as well as for others. Aristotle's idea was developed further by German philosophers Nicolai Hartman and Paul Helwig, and was popularized in the 1980s by University of Hamburg psychologist Friedemann Schulz von Thun (whose work remains mysteriously untranslated into English). He developed the "square of values" (*Wertequadrat*). The two

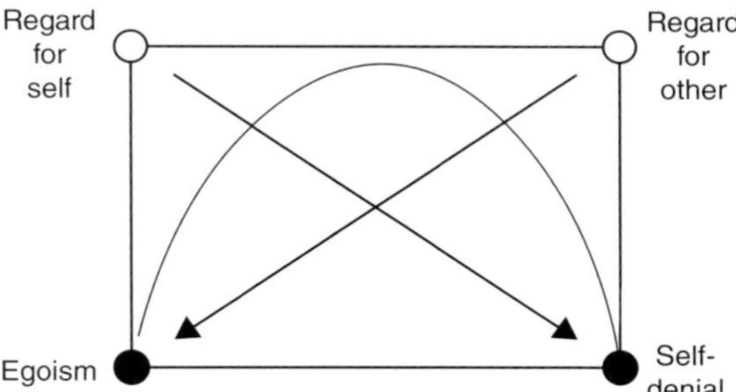

Figure 8.1 The square of values: High regard for self versus high regard for other

sides of the square in Figure 8.1 show the virtue and its dialectic opposite. Below each virtue we see its excess. The diagonals show contradictions (as in the Aristotelean sense, where one is the opposite of the other; see Chapter 7). The square of values is also called the "square of development," because it shows the direction in which capabilities need to be developed. High regard for self in extremis becomes egoism. Conversely, paying regard only to the desires of others in the extreme becomes self-denial.[16]

To develop the right balance regarding self and other, we need to move toward the diagonally opposite point. That right balance does not just require choosing between cooperation and competition. Most negotiations are more complex than that, which is the reason we need all five negotiation styles to succeed. How you define your development is entirely up to you. Your values may or may not coincide with the values of other negotiators. Here is a short story from the *New York Times* that (rather emotionally) makes that point. Writer Firoozeh Dumas describes what her father, who had moved the family from Iran to the US in 1972, valued in negotiations. It is exemplified by the way he sold his beloved car.

> In 1978, my father decided to sell our Chrysler LeBaron. I was 13 years old and a trusted adviser on all things American. It was up to me to write the ad, then call it in to the PennySaver. We had moved to California in 1972 from Abadan, Iran. My father, a mechanical engineer, loved a thousand things in America, including the really big cars, or land yachts, a term we learned from a used-car salesman. He and I visited car dealerships in Southern California the way tourists visited ancient sites in Iran, oohing and aahing at man's ability to create wonder. Our regular pilgrimages had a purpose. As much as my father loved whatever car he owned, he also loved dreaming about the next, bigger one. We also had a weekly routine involving our own vehicle. This being pre-drought days, my dad parked our land yacht on the driveway. On cue, I would unravel the garden hose, fetch two pails, the large, soft, yellow sponges that did not scratch, rags for drying, window cleaner, and dishwasher detergent. We washed the car until it sparkled. I took great pride in my ability to shine the rims to perfection and clean the windows spotless. It may sound

> weird to kids today, but seeing how happy my father was at the sight of our gleaming car made me look forward to this weekly chore.
>
> When it came time to decide on a price, my father wanted $1,000. Luckily for him, my de facto adviser position also included dispensing financial advice, so I suggested that if he wanted $1,000, he should ask for $1,200. My father, with his tendency to agree with all my ideas, good or bad, consented.
>
> A parade of potential buyers started coming to our condo. I made sure to always be there, standing next to my father. My perfect Valley Girl English put people at ease, mitigating my father's thick Persian accent. This was before Iran ever made the nightly news, but I can attest that even back then, a thick Middle Eastern accent had the opposite effect of Maurice Chevalier saying the same thing.
>
> One evening, a man showed up with his two daughters, who were around 8 years old. He checked out the car, while my father rambled on about its great condition and I repeated what I considered to be the key points, but sans accent. After looking under the hood, he decided to buy the car and told us that he would return the next day.
>
> We waited with great anticipation.
>
> As promised, he showed up the following evening, again with his daughters. After exchanging pleasantries, he removed a wad of cash from his pockets and counted twelve $100 bills.
>
> My father took the bills, thanked the man but didn't put the money in his pocket. He kept staring at the wad of cash. After a moment, he peeled off two of the bills and gave them back. "This is for your beautiful daughters. Please take them to Disneyland and buy them whatever they want."
>
> The man looked confused, almost annoyed, like he was being pranked. Even I, with my perfect English, was at a loss.
>
> "Please," my father repeated, pushing the money into the man's palm. "You must take your daughters to Disneyland." The girls started to squeal. The man paused for a moment, then hugged my father vigorously.
>
> As he drove away in his new used LeBaron, I could see the sisters bouncing around the cavernous back seat, pre-mandatory seatbelt laws. They waved furiously at us until their dad turned the corner and we could no longer see them.
>
> That evening, my father could not have been happier. He had gotten exactly what he needed and I learned a simple lesson that I carry with me still, 41 years later. When you have what you need, use the rest to bring joy into someone else's life. That is the best deal you can ever make.[17]

Some negotiators will admire Mrs. Dumas's father. Others may wonder whether he took his own daughter to Disneyland. I invite you to do both. As you ponder your personal values and development potential, however, I must also point you to an inconvenient (if unsurprising) truth: Your development starts with your weakness.

8.1.3.1 See Your Weakness

What keeps us from developing into the desired direction? We have touched on it before: People prefer not to move out of their comfort zone. They might ignore their weakness. But acknowledging it, even just secretly to ourselves, is a necessary precondition for our development. Remember Yogi Berra's saying, "if you don't know where you're going, you'll end up someplace else"? It applies here too. We have to chart a course away from what we want to overcome in order to develop. But how can we overcome our biases and tunnel vision when it is so comfortable to stick to them?

Here is a parable that every law student knows. It's the story of a young lawyer who is asked by a senior partner to prepare for the defense on an important client in an upcoming trial. The young lawyer diligently completes the task. He reports back to the senior partner with a sublime battle plan. But to his surprise, he now learns that the firm is representing the plaintiff! Nothing could have prepared him better for the job – because he already knew the strengths and weaknesses of his side, the defendant. Even if the story is not true, its morale certainly is valid – with one important qualifier.

Linda Babcock and Georg Loewenstein have identified a method to overcome self-serving bias, i.e. the conflation of what is fair with what serves oneself. I believe that this approach can be used to combat all variations of egocentrism and tunnel vision. The researchers developed a tort case based on a real trial that had occurred in Texas, in which the driver of an automobile was sued by an injured motorcyclist with whom he had collided. Participants were randomly assigned to the role of defendant or plaintiff, and asked to negotiate a settlement. Should they fail to reach an agreement, the case would be decided by the court. The researchers found strong evidence that the parties' assessment of their BATNA (i.e. what the judge would decide) was influenced by the role they played; Plaintiffs thought higher verdicts would be fair, while defendants thought lower verdicts would be fair and to be expected.[18]

The researchers then found that merely informing individuals of the bias and its consequences does not protect them from becoming its victim – later participants that received this information had the same assessment of their BATNAs (and consequently the rate of impasse). Apparently, when informed of the bias, we assume that others would be affected by it but believe that *we* are capable of assessing information objectively.[19]

However, Babcock and Loewenstein found that the bias is reduced when people are informed of it *and told that it could arise from the failure to think about the weaknesses in their own case* – and then asked to list the weaknesses in their own case. Conversely, when people are asked to argue their opponent's view as convincingly as possible, there was no significant reduction of the bias. Such preparation could lead to what Tali Sharot calls the "boomerang effect": It might cause people to think of new counterarguments that further strengthen their original view. The qualifier for our young lawyer is that he must be asked to analyze his side's weakness through the eyes of the opponent. It seems to me that this advice is generalizable: To properly realize our weakness, it helps to assess it from our opponents' point of view. This shows us the direction in which we need to develop.[20]

8.2 Enlist the Past and Future Self

We can only ever learn in the present. But in doing so, we rely on our past self. And we do it for the benefit of our future self. We need to take both into account.

8.2.1 The Past and Inert Knowledge

Sometimes we cannot access what our past self has already learned. It might be on the proverbial "tip of our tongue" but just not come out. Our knowledge might be inert. Even when we have a deep understanding of our task and a well-rounded tool kit, we might still not know how to put our knowledge into practice. It happens to the best of us. Alfred North Whitehead even called the problem of preventing knowledge from becoming inert the "central problem of all education." What, if anything, can be done about it?[21]

In a classical study of inert knowledge, students were given a problem about how to use radiation to destroy a patient's tumor. The stream of rays at full strength would destroy the healthy tissue en route to the tumor. The solution: Converge on the tumor with low-strength radiation from multiple directions. After the students had been given this problem and its solution, they were given an analogous challenge: A general needs to capture a fortress but cannot use his entire army to make a frontal attack. One solution is to divide the army and converge on the fortress from many directions. But:[22]

> Even when the tumour problem and the fortress problem are presented in the same session, only about 41 percent of students spontaneously applied the convergence solution to the radiation problem. Though they retained the knowledge about the first solution, they failed to access it. Yet when simply told to think about the earlier problem, a full 85 percent of students applied the convergence solution to the new problem. Simply reminding people of an analogous problem helps them map the solution onto the new problem.[23]

Leigh Thompson and Brian Lucas conclude from this and similar research that analogy training can substantially improve negotiation performance.

Overcoming inert knowledge can quite literally save lives. Standard radiation therapy sends X-rays through the body, damaging healthy tissue both coming and going. By contrast, charged ions slow down and deposit almost all their energy where they stop in the tumor, sparing more healthy tissue. This makes charged-particle therapy ideal for treating children, whose developing bodies are particularly sensitive, and for cancer very close to vital tissues such as the optical nerves. The ion beam can be aimed from a gantry that rotates around a stationary patient, attacking the tumor (much like the castle) from all angles. Gantries can be huge. Heidelberg University Hospital, for instance, operates one that weighs 670 tons and is three stories high. It works exactly according to the principles that can be detected in the fortress problem.[24]

8.2.2 The Future and "If – Then" Plans

The future eventually becomes the present. But like Homer Simpson, we sometimes are tempted to ignore this basic fact of life: When speaking to his loan officer in *The Simpsons* episode, "No Loan Again, Naturally," he claims that he was told that he would not have to repay the borrowed money until the future and then balks at his responsibility, on the grounds that it's still the present rather than the future. We will only have become better negotiators in the future if we plan the right steps today.[25]

We go through the trouble of learning today so that we may live better tomorrow. Human beings can plan what they will do in the future. Since we have already learned from *The Iliad*, we might as well turn to Homer's *The Odyssey*. Ulysses instructs his fellow travelers to tie him to the mast so that he can listen to the Sirens' song without being tempted:

> Race straight past that coast! Soften some beeswax
> and stop your shipmates' ears so none can hear,
> none of the crew, but if *you* are bent on hearing,
> have them tie you hand and foot in the swift ship,
> erect at the mast-block, lashed by ropes to the mast
> so you can hear the Sirens' song to your heart's content.
> But if you plead, commanding your men to set you free,
> then they must lash you faster, rope to rope.[26]

Nobel laureate Thomas Schelling observed that human beings sometimes behave as if two selves are alternately in command. People try to cope with loss of control over themselves in much the same way as they exercise commands over another person. Schelling cites the familiar example of someone who cannot get up when the alarm goes off in the morning. To prevent the future self from sleeping in, the present self might not only set the alarm but put the alarm clock across the room. Schelling's fellow laureate Richard Thaler points out that the forward-looking planner might have good intentions for the future, but the devil-may-care doer lives just for the present. A few years later it turned out that Schelling's idea was very much to the point. Hal Ersner-Hershfield and his colleagues ran a series of fMRI scans to find that the neural patterns seen when subjects described themselves ten years in the future were markedly different from those seen when they described their current selves.[27]

It is no surprise that many people feel disconnected from the individuals that they will be in the future. This seems to be one of the reasons why people value immediate gains over future gains. Undersaving, a well-known problem in the United States, attests to this tendency. Many people will not be able to maintain their pre-retirement standard of living in retirement because they have inadequately saved for the future. In the context of learning, this might explain why we are sometimes unwilling to undergo the effort of learning today for the benefit of having learned tomorrow. Yes, we want our future selves to do things better than we currently do them. But all we ever experience is the present. It is tempting to discount the future rewards. I can go to the gym and get in shape for next summer. This will be great then, but now I am tempted to get some ice cream and head for the sofa.

Just as individuals readily make sacrifices for others to whom they are close, they might make them for their future self – if they feel close. One way of promoting the wishes of the future self is to treat that self like a close other, one for whom present sacrifices are encouraged. Bryan and Hershfield found that appealing to people's responsibility to their future selves ("Your future self is completely dependent on you") is more effective than an appeal to their rational self ("It is in your long-term interest to save for the future") in increasing their retirement savings. And Hershfield proposed another way to address the challenge. When he showed subjects aged images of themselves, their subsequent decisions showed markedly less disconnect between the current and the future selves. When the future self shares similarities with the present self, when it is viewed in vivid and realistic terms, and when it is seen in a positive light, individuals are more willing to make choices today that might benefit them in the future.[28]

Walter Mischel calls the fundamental principle of self-control: "Cool the now, heat the later." We can use the method that he describes in his "Marshmallow Test": Making "if – then" plans. Such plans have the following format: "If the critical situation A is encountered, then I will perform the goal-directed response B!" While goals specify the desired end states, "if – then" plans specify a critical future event and the desired response. Such plans have been found to help people in a whole array of different domains. In our context, it can help us to determine the specific situations in which we typically behave over-cooperatively (or over-competitively), then formulate the more appropriate behavior that we resolve to employ instead.[29]

Here is an intriguing example of an "if – then" plan. Japanese writer Haruki Murakami owned a Jazz bar when he was young, and used to be a chain smoker. In his fascinating book *What I Talk About When I Talk About Running*, he tells the story of how he completely changed his life, gave up smoking, took up running, and became the most successful writer of post-war Japan. He says that he is running six days a week, and he has completed over twenty marathons. Nevertheless, he occasionally has to remind himself of why he is doing this:

> Whenever I feel like I don't want to run, I always ask myself the same thing: *You are able to make a living as a novelist, working at home, setting your own hours, so you don't have to commute on a packed train or sit through boring meetings. Don't you realize how fortunate you are? (Believe me I do.) Compared to that, running an hour around the neighborhood is nothing, right?* Whenever I picture packed trains and endless meetings, this gets me motivated all over again and I lace up my running shoes and set off without any qualms."[30]

Whether or not we are marathon runners, we can make use of Murakami's tactic. Imagine you are getting ready for a negotiation that you know will become heated. Experience tells you that the other side will, sooner or later, attack your team members personally. Experience also tells you that your likely response is to explode. This time, however, you are determined not to let that happen. You make a promise to yourself to respond rationally: "When Mr. X starts shouting again at my team members, I will not shout back. Instead, I will calmly assert that I understand his frustration but that this behavior is not acceptable. I will declare that we all would benefit from clearing our heads, and declare a break."

8.2.2.1 Physical Objects as Reminders

Following through with our plan can be made easier by using reminders. Physical objects can help our mind to extend into the world. In their influential article "The Extended Mind," Andy Clark and David Chalmers addressed the question of where the mind stops and the rest of the world begins. They propose that the environment can be an active part of the human cognitive process – what is mental does not have to be internal:

> First, consider a normal case of belief embedded in memory. Inga hears from a friend that there is an exhibition at the Museum of Modern Art and decides to go see it. She thinks for a moment and recalls that the museum is on 53rd Street, so she walks to 53rd Street and goes into the museum.... Now consider Otto. Otto suffers from Alzheimer's disease, and like many Alzheimer's patients, he relies on information in the environment to help structure his life. In particular, Otto carries a notebook around with him everywhere he goes. When he learns new information, he writes it down in his notebook. When he needs some old information, he looks it up. For Otto, his notebook plays the role usually played by a biological memory. Today, Otto hears about the exhibition at the Museum of Modern Art, and decides to go see it. He consults the notebook, which says that the museum is on 53rd Street, so he walks to 53rd Street and goes into the museum. Clearly, Otto walked to 53rd Street because he wanted to go to the museum and he believed the museum was on 53rd Street. And just as Inga had her belief even before she consulted her memory, it seems reasonable to say that Otto believed the museum was on 53rd Street even before consulting

> his notebook. For in relevant respects the cases are entirely analogous: the notebook plays for Otto the same role that memory plays for Inga. The information in the notebook functions just like the information that constitutes an ordinary non-occurrent belief; it just happens that this information inheres in a physical state located beyond the skin.. . . In both cases the information is reliably there when needed, available to consciousness and available to guide action, in just the way that we expect a belief to be.[31]

It would be very strange if we did not make use of cues in the physical world to help our future thinking. Even God himself, according to the Bible, uses this technique. After the Flood, he promises Noah never to flood the earth again. But, apparently, He expects that His future self will find it difficult to comply with this promise. In Genesis 9: 12–17, and in order not to do the wrong thing at the spur of the moment, He creates a physical reminder to aid his thinking: The rainbow.

> So, when I send clouds over the earth, the bow will appear in the cloud. Then I will remember My covenant, between Me and you and every living creature of all flesh, and the waters will no more become a Flood to destroy all flesh. And the bow shall be in the cloud and I will see it, to remember the everlasting covenant between God and all living creatures, all flesh that is on the earth.[32]

As mere mortals we can certainly use this technique too, whether or not we are religious. A current example: Michel Barnier, who led the Brexit withdrawal agreement negotiations for the EU, claimed that he wanted to remove emotions from the negotiation. He used a coffee mug bearing the slogan "Keep Calm and Negotiate." (Showing the mug to reporters might not have helped in that endeavor. A British reporter commented: "The over-exposed "Keep calm and carry on" poster was intended for distribution if Nazi troops invaded Britain during the Second World War. Michel Barnier, lead negotiator for the other 27 Member States in the Brexit talks, used it cheekily this week as a challenge to the British from across the English Channel. The gauntlet was being thrown down.") Nevertheless, using a physical reminder to prevent yourself from boycotting your own endeavors is a wise move (that you might also prefer to keep to yourself).[33]

8.3 Deliberate Practice

Creating enduring behavior change is difficult. Finding out how it can be done is at the cutting edge of research. Unfortunately, there is no "magical bullet." Practice is important. But the old adage that "practice makes perfect" is rarely true. Rather, research has shown that, generally speaking, once a person reaches a level of acceptable performance, even additional years of practice in the absence of deliberate efforts to improve do not lead to any improvement. Practice does make permanent. And, whether in education, sports, medical training, or negotiation, in the words of legendary American football coach, Vince Lombardi, perfect practice can make perfect. Learning from practice means drawing the right lessons from the outcomes that we achieve. We will now look at the importance of good feedback for improving our understanding and know-how, and the need to deliberately practice our skills.[34]

We have already seen the importance of feedback for drawing the right lessons about our behavior. Learning is most likely if we receive immediate feedback after each attempt. Pamela Casey and her colleagues stressed the need to learn from results to improve future performance: "Competitive athletes improve performance through constant coaching and feedback, and judges can improve performance by getting objective feedback too."[35]

In a classical metaphor by Harvard University's Chris Argris, learning is like a thermostat, and it occurs in two feedback loops:

> Single loop learning can be compared with a thermostat that learns when it is too hot or too cold and then turns the heat on or off. The thermostat is able to perform this task because it can receive information (the temperature in the room) and therefore can take corrective action. If the thermostat could question itself about whether it should be set at 68 degrees, it would be capable not only of detecting error but of questioning the underlying policies and goals as well as its own program. That is a second and more comprehensive enquiry, hence it might be called double loop learning.[36]

In our context: When you learn from the result of a negotiation that you should enlarge your skill set, you are learning in the first loop. If the results also persuade you to reflect upon and amend your underlying understanding of negotiation theory, then you engage in double loop learning. If you do not encounter challenges, you cannot learn.

You know that your real-world negotiations take place in a hostile learning environment and provide only wicked feedback. So, if you are serious about assessing your performance, you have to go back to school. Don't panic, I mean only for a few days! Because only in the safe space of the classroom can you receive accurate feedback from peers. You can even measure what your behavior leads to. And you can test your skill in role plays that allow you to compare your results. Even more importantly, this will enable you to benchmark your skill and see what would have been possible. There is nothing to beat realistic role plays for professional learning. They let you easily identify the things you should do more of – and the things that you should change. If you are ready for it, use the opportunity. If you don't, in future you might be lucky or unlucky, but chances are, you won't really know what you are doing.

Top performance in many fields of human endeavor is not so much the result of predetermined talent, but of the right kind of practice over time. As Goethe remarked, "whatever we nourish in ourselves grows; that is the eternal law of nature." Malcolm Gladwell popularized this idea in his bestseller, *Outliers. The Story of Success.* According to his "ten thousand hours rule," it takes ten thousand hours of practice to become a master in most fields. This assertion was inspired by one of the most influential papers on expertise, published in 1993 by Anders Ericsson (then at the University of Colorado at Boulder), Ralf Krampe and Clemens Tesch-Römer (then at the Max Planck Institute for Human Development and Education, Berlin). They studied a group of violin students in a Berlin music academy and found that the most accomplished of those students had completed an average of ten thousand hours of practice by the time they were twenty years old. While Ericsson sees the ten thousand hours rule as an over-simplification, he and Robert Pool agreed that "becoming accomplished in any field in which there is a well-established history of people working to become experts requires a tremendous effort exerted over many years."[37]

Ericsson carried out extensive empirical research with top performers in areas as diverse as sports, music, and chess, drawing our attention to what he calls "deliberate practice": Practice that is characterized by the conscious pursuit of well-defined, specific goals, which takes us outside our comfort zone by using feedback to continuously modify our efforts, carried out with the help of mental representations and often under the tutelage of a coach. Ericsson points to the example of perfect pitch. It occurs so rarely that it was long assumed to be a gift you were born with. Wolfgang Amadeus Mozart had it, as do one in a thousand people. Yet, when Japanese psychologist Ayako Sakakibara set out to teach perfect pitch to two- to six-year-old children, it turned out that he could: Within a year and a half of training, all children had acquired perfect pitch.[38]

Deliberate practice drives physical changes in the brain that makes it possible for experts to do things they could not otherwise do. Just as we can strengthen our muscles by training with weights, we can foster these brain changes with the right kind of practice over time. Ericsson highlights a wide array of human behavior where extraordinary ability has been developed that would have been deemed impossible for most of human history. For instance, the record-breaking winning time of the 1908 Olympic marathon was two hours and fifty-five minutes. Today, thousands of young people competing in the Boston Marathon practically match this time as a prerequisite for even participating – the qualifying time for men is three hours, and for women three-and-a-half hours.[39]

8.3.1 Practice Changes the Brain

As Ericsson points out, these dramatic improvements are not due to an evolutionary development of human biology in the last decades. Rather, they are the result of much improved training methods, i.e. learning. Learning changes the brain at a molecular level, an insight for which Eric Kandel received the Nobel Prize in 2000.

Magnetic resonance imaging proves the changes that take place in the learner's brain. When we explored the curse of expertise in Chapter 6, we looked at the case of London taxi drivers. In order to be licensed, would-be cabbies have to memorize some 25,000 streets and all potential sites of interest within a six-mile radius of Charing Cross. Brain scans were taken of drivers both before and after training. There was a marked difference between the scans of those who passed the test and those who failed: The volume of the part of the brain that stores geographical information (the posterior hippocampus) had grown significantly in the successfully licensed taxi drivers. This data suggests that the brain stores a spatial representation of the environment and can expand regionally to accommodate elaboration of this representation in people with a high dependence on navigational skills. Similarly, musicians have more developed "musical maps" than non-musicians. And violinists have more room for violin sounds, while trumpeters have more for trumpet sounds. The brain can even "repurpose" neutrons to take on altogether new functions. For instance, the part of the brain used to process visual information in people who can see, does not become idle when a person becomes blind. When people without sight learn to read Braille writing, this part of the brain takes on the new job of processing the sensory information taken in by the fingertips when reading. The brain is impressively flexible and adaptable. It might even learn to compensate for a missing half: In 2002 *The Lancet* reported on the case of a seven-year-old girl that grew up to be bilingual in Turkish and Dutch after her right hemisphere (the seat of language centers) had to be surgically removed because of severe encephalitis.[40]

So, what changes when we acquire expertise? This is how Ericsson summarizes it:

> The main thing that set experts apart from the rest of us is that their years of practice have changed the neural circuitry in their brains to produce highly specialized mental representations, which in turn make possible the incredible memory, pattern detection, problem solving, and other sorts of advance abilities needed to excel in their particular specialties.[41]

8.3.2 Focusing on Your Weaknesses Is Not Pleasurable

Here is a conundrum. Even when people have the same level of perceived competence, those whose motivation is authentic typically have more interest, excitement, and confidence – and therefore enhanced performance, persistence, and creativity – than those whose motivation is merely externally pressured. In other words, to become an expert at something it helps to really like what you are doing. Ideally, we are intrinsically motivated to engage in an activity, meaning that we feel inherent satisfaction, interest, and enjoyment from the activity itself. This is especially important if we want to attain mastery of that activity. Consider how American novelist and screenwriter John Irving describes his work:[42]

> It was the first thing that I wanted to be good at, to the degree that I was willing to make sacrifices and have a kind of dedication and discipline that certainly has been helpful to me as a writer, especially of long novels that need to be revised and rewritten many times. So, the idea that repetition – doing some small thing over and over again – is not boring but is essential at becoming good at anything, any craft, any sport, I learned first from wrestling – before I saw myself seriously as wanting to be a writer. The idea that the process of writing is a lot like the practicing of a sport. No one sees you do it, no one is clapping, there is no win, there is no lose, it's just repetition, it's just a kind of drilling – and it's where you will spend most of your life as an artist, or as an athlete. The moment when a book is published, the window when it's available to the public, and people are talking to you about it, is very small. It's over in a couple of months. But the book might have taken four, five, six, seven years. And the next book will take a comparable amount of time. So, I learned, I think, from wrestling, that you better love the process itself. You better love the practicing, the repeating the same move a hundred times with the same boring sparring partner. An inch at a time, and crossing something out, and moving this sentence here, and taking that sentence and putting it there – it's slow! People would fall asleep watching a writer write or a wrestler in practice. It was very important for me, you know, to learn those things.[43]

But what if you don't "love the practicing"? Deliberate practice often requires repetition that hardly seems pleasurable at all. In fact, Ericsson and Pool emphasize that deliberate practice nearly always involves focusing on a particular skill that is being improved incrementally: The most effective and most powerful types of practice in most fields work by harnessing the adaptability of the human body and the human brain to create, step by step, the ability to do things that were previously not possible. In her best-selling book *Grit*, Angela Duckworth clarifies what that means:[44]

> Rather than focus on what they already do well, experts strive to improve specific weaknesses. They intentionally seek out challenges they can't yet meet.... As soon as possible, experts hungrily seek feedback on how they did. Necessarily, much of that feedback is negative. This means that experts are more interested in what they did *wrong* – so they can fix it – than what they did *right*.... And after feedback, then what? The experts do it all over again, and again, and again. Until they have finally mastered what they set out to do.[45]

If that doesn't sound like a lot of fun, it's because it isn't. That is what makes it so hard. Deliberate practice is for the most part not inherently pleasurable. When Duckworth interviewed American three-time Olympic gold medalist Rowdy Gaines about his practice, he explained that in the years leading up to the 1984 Olympic Games he swam, in increments of fifty-yard laps, at least twenty thousand miles. Here is their exchange:

> "I swam around the world," he told me with a soft laugh, "for a race that lasted forty-nine seconds."

"Did you enjoy those miles?" I asked. "I mean, did you love practicing?"
"I'm not going to lie," he replied. "I never really enjoyed going to practice, and I certainly didn't enjoy it while I was there. In fact, there were brief moments, walking to the pool at four or four-thirty in the morning, or sometimes when I couldn't take the pain, when I'd think, "God, is this worth it?"
"So why didn't you quit?"
"It's very simple." Rowdy said. "It's because I loved swimming. I had a passion for competing, for the *result* of the training, for the feeling of being in shape, for winning, for traveling, for meeting friends. I hated practice, but I had an overall passion for swimming."[46]

This seems to be the solution to the conundrum. Richard M. Ryan and Edward L. Deci of the University of Rochester explain:

> Although intrinsic motivation is an important type of motivation, it is not the only type or even the only type of self-determined motivation. Indeed, much of what people do is not, strictly speaking, intrinsically motivated, especially after early childhood when the freedom to be intrinsically motivated is increasingly curtailed by social pressures to do activities that are not interesting and to assume a variety of new responsibilities. The real question concerning intrinsically motivated practice is how individuals acquire the motivation to carry them out.[47]

The originally extrinsic motivation (such as publishing a book or winning a medal) can be "internalized" and "integrated": "Internalization refers to people's 'taking in' a value or regulation, and interpretation refers to the further transformation of that regulation into their own so that, subsequently, it will emanate from their sense of self." It appears that one becomes an Olympic champion not only by loving the medal, but by learning to love the practice too. If you want to become a better competitive negotiator, you might just have to practice making extreme first offers, or saying "no" to counteroffers for the sake of your goal, but you might never grow to like doing it as such.[48]

Ericsson and Ward stress that deliberate practice is completely at odds with the "rule of least effort," according to which humans strive to perform activities with minimal exerted effort:

> It is clear that skilled individuals can sometimes experience highly enjoyable states ("flow" as described by Mihaly Csıkszentmihalyi, 1990) during their performance. These states are, however, incompatible with deliberate practice, in which individuals engage in a (typically planned) training activity aimed at reaching a level just beyond the currently attainable level of performance by engaging in full concentration, analysis after feedback, and repetitions with refinement. The commonly held but empirically unsupported notion that some uniquely "talented" individuals can attain superior performance in a given domain without much practice appears to be a destructive myth that could discourage people from investing the necessary efforts to reach expert levels of performance.[49]

8.3.3 Desirable Difficulties and Growth Mindset

We can even go a step further. Learners should embrace difficulties – because they are what allow us to learn. This is why Elisabeth and Robert Björk have coined the term "desirable difficulties." Difficulties are desirable for learning because they trigger the encoding and retrieval processes that support learning and comprehension. It can even be argued that the latest neuroscience shows that we learn best when we are confused. As we have seen, learning requires the detection and correction of error. The beneficial effect of difficulties can be compared to going to the gym: We would not hope to build our muscles by lifting the lightest weights.[50]

I believe that this is absolutely true for negotiations too. We have found that they provide a hostile environment for learning from results, rendering feedback wicked. It can only be practiced in an ambiguous and dilemma-laden relationship with one's counterpart. Compare this to the benevolent learning environment in which musicians and athletes practice. For the researcher, it is almost impossible to obtain accurate long-term data on the effects of a negotiator's deliberate practice. Nevertheless, it is clear that to improve at negotiation, we have to embrace the challenge. Researchers found that people who regard an upcoming negotiation as a threat experience more stress and reach lower quality deals than those who view it as a challenge. This is in line with many studies which indicate that positive affect such as happiness can foster cooperation and concession-making as well as problem-solving and integrative agreements, thereby positively influencing the creation of value. The evidence that we have suggests that developing a positive attitude toward negotiation can be beneficial. The same is true for our attitude toward learning. Research suggests we should develop what has been called a "growth mindset." Carol Dweck became interested in her students' attitudes about failure. Some rebounded while others seemed devastated by even the smallest setback. Dweck began to systematically study the behavior of children. Her research led her to differentiate the "fixed mindset" from the "growth mindset" – describing opposite beliefs about learning and intelligence. This is how Brown, Roediger, and McDaniel explain its significance: Dweck's work has shown that people who believe that their intellectual ability is fixed from birth and wired in their genes, tend to avoid challenges at which they might not succeed, because failing would indicate their lesser native competence. But people who are helped to understand that effort and learning change the brain, and that their intellectual abilities lie to a large degree within their own control, are more likely to tackle challenges and persist at them: "They view failure as a sign of effort and as a turn in the road, rather than as a measure of inability and the end of the road." It is important to acknowledge that we are all a mixture of fixed and growth mindsets. Dweck is careful to point out that we all have our own fixed-mindset triggers: When we face challenges, receive criticism, or fare poorly compared with others, we can easily fall into insecurity or defensiveness, a response that inhibits growth.[51]

8.3.4 The Limits of Deliberate Practice

While individual differences in many domains largely reflect the accumulated amount of deliberate practice in many areas, this is obviously not the only contributing factor. In Chapter 3 we looked at Hillary Elfenbein's research that shows the impact of personality on a negotiator's success. Recent meta-analyses remind us that other factors, such as genetic disposition or personality traits, also contribute to the variance in performance. For instance, the personality trait called "grit" – the persistence in accomplishing long-term goals – positively predicts deliberate practice, which in turn positively predicts performance, as Angela Duckworth has shown. People seem to differ in their propensity to engage in deliberate practice, which translates into individual differences in expertise. And once you reach the top level of skill, everyone has practiced a lot. Other factors, such as the quality of your coach, seem to determine who goes on to the super-elite level.[52]

Brooke Macnamara, David Hambrick, and Frederick Oswald systematically reviewed the domains in which deliberate practice has been investigated. The researchers found that engaging in structured activities created specifically to improve performance in a domain made people better at games, music, and sport, but made much less of a difference in education and the professions. A large amount of variation in performance, the researchers argue, is not explained by deliberate practice in any domain. However, it benefited scripted, habitual activities in all fields more than it benefited less scripted activities: "The effect of deliberate practice on performance tended to be larger for activities that are highly predictable (e.g. running) than for activities that are less predictable (e.g. handling an aviation emergency)." In our context, we typically find a mix of predictable and unpredictable activities. There are quite a number of behaviors that we can definitely script and deliberately practice, such as: The words and gestures with which to open, and close, a meeting; how to put together the first contract draft; how to use the velvet glove in repeated interactions; how to use the iron fist; how to make the first offer, and how to respond to one; how to respond when our buttons are pushed; what "if – then" plans to write, and where to practice them. Deliberate practice, it seems to me, lends itself especially to activities that we can cultivate into habits, so that we do them automatically.[53]

There is an inverted-U relationship between performance and arousal: There can be too much as well as too little, especially in high-stakes negotiations where there is a real risk that you might "choke" under pressure. Trying to control our performance to force an optimal outcome can backfire through causing paralysis by analysis. Thankfully, psychologists are using newly discovered information about how the brain supports exceptional performance in order to develop "anti-choke techniques." A key tip is to practice under stress: Practicing under the exact conditions that you will face when it counts is what is needed to perform your best when the stress is turned up. Getting used to the pressure alleviates your fear. (Also, and a bit more sneakily, by understanding when pressure happens, you can create situations that will maximize the other side's stress – if that is what you choose to do.)[54]

But stress, as Stanford psychologist Kelly McConigal points out, also has an upside. Evidence suggests that embracing the challenge, rather than fearing the threat, has a number of upsides. It leads to more effective information-sharing and withholding, as well as smarter decision-making.[55]

Studies indicate that individuals who appraise a prospective negotiation as a threat experience more stress and reach lower quality deals compared to those who appraise it as a challenge. Researchers found that the first group behaved more passively and was less likely to use tough tactics. These negotiators also had relatively inaccurate perceptions of their partners' priorities and interests, which further undermined their efforts. Finally, negotiators who view stress as beneficial, not detrimental, have been found to perform better.[56]

9 Thinking

Where we learn to methodically use Intuition & Deliberation to dialectically build our expertise.

9.1 Build Expertise

Our mightiest tool for both negotiating and learning how to do it is to think about what we are doing. In expanding our knowledge and know-how, we have to be purposeful and take control of our thinking. Only then can we ascend the learning curve. We do so in increments. Expertise is acquired in five stages, as David Robson describes in his fascinating book, *The Intelligence Trap* (see Figure 9.1). Here they are:

1. The beginner is unconsciously incompetent: she does not know what she does not know.
2. After a short while she will become consciously incompetent, realizing what she lacks and what must be learned.
3. With effort, the learner can become consciously competent, but must exert a lot of concentration and deliberation to make the right decisions.
4. The learner becomes unconsciously competent: After years of deliberate practice, these decisions become second nature. At this stage, decisions are quick and intuitive, but often vulnerable to bias. This is where we encounter the curse of expertise.
5. The learner has acquired reflective competence, knowing when to question her intuitions and eliminate error. True mastery is reached in this last step.[1]

In order to learn to negotiate, we have to go through pairs of subsequent learning curves: One for the distribution of value and one for its creation; one for highly regarding one's own interests, and one for regarding the other side's interests; and one for thinking intuitively as well as for thinking deliberately. As we have seen, the two sides of each pair can be complementary, but they can also block one another. Climbing the stages is therefore especially hard to do. Just like we can use physical reminders to aid our thinking, we can sometimes use the help

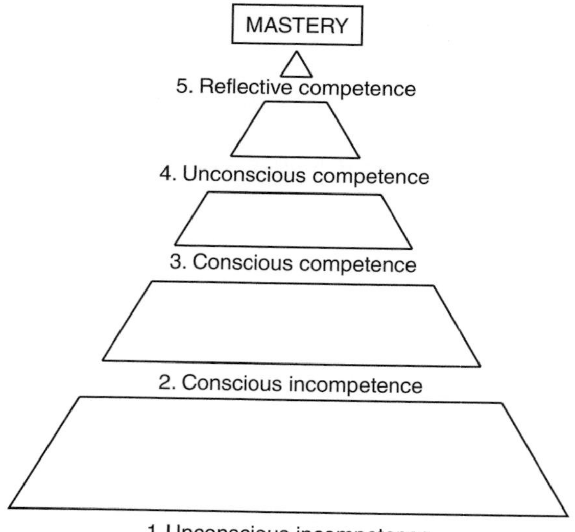

Figure 9.1 The five stages of expertise
Source: Robson, 2019.

of others to do so. Here is a useful example of how such help can even be institutionalized.

The "devil's advocate" (*advocatus diaboli*) played an important role in the Catholic Church's process of canonization (declaration of sainthood). Acting as the counterpart of the *advocatus dei* (God's advocate), his role was to cast doubt on the person's character and present counterevidence. The Israeli Directorate of Military Intelligence (AMAN) drew on this when they established a devil's advocate office. This was one of the reforms instituted after the 1973 Yom Kippur War in which Israel had failed to foresee the impending attacks by Egypt and Syria. General Yosef Kuperwasser, then a Visiting Fellow at the Saban Center for Middle East Policy at the Brookings Institution, described the office:

> The devil's advocate office ensures that AMAN's intelligence assessments are creative and do not fall prey to group think. The office regularly criticizes products coming from the analysis and production divisions, and writes opinion papers that counter these departments' assessments. The staff in the devil's advocate office is made up of extremely experienced and talented officers who are known to have a creative, "outside the box" way of thinking.... The devil's advocate office also proactively combats group think and conventional wisdom by writing papers that examine the possibility of a radical and negative change occurring within the security environment. This is done even when the defense establishment does not think that such a development is likely, precisely to explore alternative assumptions and worst-case scenarios.[2]

9.2 Bootstrapping

We can pursue expertise even when we are not part of an organization. Thankfully, reflective competence is a thinking method. It is entirely within the control of those who are willing to pursue it. Canadian lawyer William Kaplan claims that out of the same Israeli intelligence reform came another role, the tenth man, which he described thus: "The Tenth Man is a devil's advocate. If there are 10 people in a room and nine agree, the role of the tenth is to disagree and point out flaws in whatever decision the group has reached." We can be our own inner "tenth man."[3]

How to do it? Here is a great method (and another great metaphor): Stefan Herzog and Ralph Hertwig, two psychologists at the University of Basel, have proposed a process they call "intellectual bootstrapping" to improve individual judgment. Building on the statistical fact that the average estimates taken by a group of people are frequently more accurate than the typical estimate of an individual, they sought to stimulate "the wisdom of many in one mind." What they suggest is this:

> Originating from the same person, a dialectical estimate has a different error than the first estimate to the extent that it is based on a different knowledge and assumptions. We call this approach to boosting accuracy in quantitative estimation dialectical bootstrapping. "Bootstrapping" alludes to Baron Münchhausen, the fictional character who claimed to have escaped from a swamp by pulling himself up by, depending on who tells the story, his own hair or bootstraps. "Dialectical" refers to the Hegelian process of development, which has three stages: thesis (the first estimate), antithesis (dialectical estimate), and synthesis (aggregation). By means of dialectical bootstrapping, the wisdom of crowds can be simulated by a single mind that averages its own conflicting opinions.[4]

I believe that this technique is extremely helpful in our context, too. Herzog and Hertwig propose "that any technique that prompts people to generate the dialectical estimate using knowledge that is at least partly different from the knowledge they used to generate the first estimate can suffice." Let's turn to the medical field to find the technique that fits our needs best.[5]

9.3 Dialectic Thinking

As we saw when we looked at the curse of expertise, we might be more likely to make certain mistakes *because* we have learned valid but incomplete lessons about negotiation. In general, smart people might be more vulnerable to certain kinds of mistakes, as Robson points out: Intelligent and educated people might be less likely to learn from their mistakes, for instance, or take advice from others. "And when they do err, they are better able to build elaborate arguments to justify their reasoning, meaning that they become more and more dogmatic in their views."

Robson points to the field of medicine, which is at the forefront of exploring better thinking methods. Between 10 and 15 percent of initial diagnoses are incorrect. This means that doctors will make at least one error for every six patients they see. It is thought that in US hospitals alone, around one in ten patient deaths – between 40,000 and 80,000 per year – can be traced to a diagnostic mistake. Robson describes the improvement in diagnostic performance that Silvia Mamede of Erasmus MC, the Institute of Medical Education Research in Rotterdam, has promoted. She teaches doctors a simple approach: Register (and quickly note down) the intuitive "gut" impression. Then pause and reconsider these assumptions. Compare the evidence for your gut impression with alternative hypotheses.[6]

The result: Mamede has found that doctors can improve their diagnostic accuracy by up to 40 percent in taking this simple approach. It is so powerful because it allows the doctors to systematically use both systems of thinking. Thinking both intuitively *and* deliberately about the problem yields better results than doing either one alone. Just following the gut leads to the mentioned diagnostic errors. And trying to bypass the gut, using only analysis *in place of intuition*, often leads to even worse results. As Robson concludes: "You can't just use system 1 or system 2 – you need to use both."[7]

Mamede's approach fits beautifully with the tripartite model of thinking that Stanovich has developed. It is the simple (but certainly not easy) three-step thinking model that we negotiators are looking for:

1. Listen to your intuitive gut reaction.
2. Pause, and deliberately reflect on alternative possibilities.
3. Decide which approach to pursue.

In Figure 9.2, we can visualize the method with the help of our familiar iceberg model.

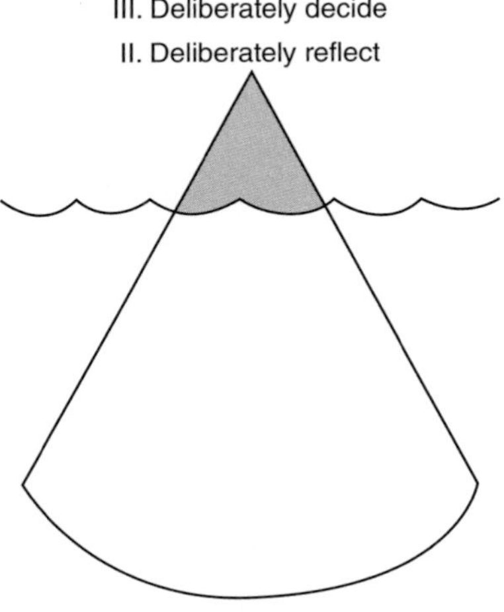

Figure 9.2 Dialectical thinking

Conclusion and Outlook: Humility and Artificial Intelligence

This concludes our journey. Well, almost. It seems to me that a vital ingredient is still missing. Remember Henry Kissinger's remark that Napoleon Bonaparte would have found it hard to learn to negotiate, because it would have required him to face his own shortcomings (no pun intended)? The secret source of learning (about negotiation and everything else) is: Humility. I am ready to call experts to the witness stand for this. In line with the pattern of this book I just can't help but make it three: Benjamin Franklin, Pope John XXIII, and Daniel Kahneman.

One of the historical examples that we have looked at was the "Great Compromise." Notably, the delegates at the Philadelphia Convention rejected it at first. Only when Benjamin Franklin championed the proposal with a rousing speech did the proposal succeed:

> I confess that there are several parts of this constitution which I do not at present approve, but I am not sure I shall never approve them. For having lived long, I have experienced many instances of being obliged by better information, or fuller consideration, to change opinions even on important subjects, which I once thought right, but found to be otherwise. It is therefore that the older I grow, the more apt I am to doubt my own judgment, and to pay more respect to the judgment of others.[1]

Pope John XXIII (born Angelo Giuseppe Roncalli) was elected as Bishop of Rome in 1958. He was known for his down-to-earth style and gentle humor.

> In the first private audience he had been granted, a newly appointed bishop complained to John XXIII that the added burden of his new office prevented him from sleeping. "Oh," said John compassionately, "the very same thing happened to me in the first few weeks of my pontificate, but then one day my guardian angel appeared to me in a daydream and whispered, 'Giovanni, don't take yourself so seriously.' And ever since then I've been able to sleep."[2]

At the end of a recent interview, Daniel Kahneman was asked by Chris Anderson, the head of TED: "If you could inject one idea into the minds of millions of people, what would that idea be?" His answer was: "Don't trust yourself too much. Don't trust in ideas and beliefs just because you can't imagine another alternative to them. Overconfidence is really the enemy of good thinking, and I wish that humility about our beliefs could spread." The interview was aptly published under the headline "Daniel Kahneman wants you to doubt yourself."[3]

I probably should heed my own advice. So, here we go: Perhaps you remember the nine-dot task in Figure 6.3, meant to elicit out-of-the-box-thinking. And maybe you have noticed that this book consists of nine chapters. This is of course a coincidence, but a meaningful one. In trying to find out how learning to negotiate works, I have arrived at my answers – and presented them to you. But: We must not be boxed in by them. What I have presented rests on my current, and very limited, knowledge of an ever-expanding but already vast field. Some of my ideas will be incomplete, even wrong. Some of the research in this book might prove to be non-replicable later. And some of the most important insights into our subject have not even been discovered (at least as far as I am aware)!

The same is, of course, true for every other book on the subject. But that should not discourage us. As Karl Popper stressed, knowledge consists of the search for truth – not the search for certainty. All human knowledge is therefore uncertain. "Since we can never know anything for sure, it is simply not worth searching for certainty, but it is well worth searching for truth; and we do this chiefly by searching for mistakes, so that we can correct them."[4]

***

Negotiation is learning. And learning is negotiating. They are but the same. So, you might find that mastering one makes mastering the other easy. The challenges to negotiation success aggravate the challenges to learning. But they also provide the desirable difficulties that stimulate your mastery of those challenges. If you achieve this, the double curse of ignorance will become the double blessing of your expertise.

AI has developed impressively since its inception in the 1960s. It has started to impact negotiation and its learning. Let's explore the three phases that AI has gone through so far. In the first phase, AI learned to recognize patterns through experience. Today it is better at this than humans in many fields. IBM's "Deep Blue" was the first chess computer to beat a reigning champion in 1996. Having been fed immense data from the Grandmaster Game database, Deep Blue could build on the experience of the best human players in history. Trying to match this processing power now would be like trying to outrun a sportscar. Garry Kasparov, the champion defeated by Deep Blue, said in a recent lecture at Georgetown University: "Anything we can do, and we know how to do it, machines will do it better. If we can codify it, and pass it to computers, they will do it better."[5]

The machine's data processing power is changing business just as much as it changes games. Gregory Zuckerman remarked, in his treatise on Renaissance

Technology's founder Jim Simons, the secretive mathematician who pioneered algorithmic trading and generated unheard of wealth: "MBAs once scoffed at the thought of relying on a scientific and systematic approach to investing, confident they could hire coders if they were ever needed. Today, coders say the same about MBAs, if they think about them at all." This is how Simons himself explains the success of his data-driven investment strategy: "The 'secret sauce' was really, in the first instance, having very smart people working in the firm." Ninety of its 300 employees are PhDs in mathematics, astronomy, etc. Next he mentions the terrific IT infrastructure that processes 9 terabyte of incoming daily data. Then he stresses the open atmosphere that allows for cooperation, and the fact that everybody receives a piece of the profits. There is, he cautions, one overriding rule, however: "The only rule is that we *never* override the computer."[6]

Consider another example, from medical research. Cancer is the second most common cause of death. Most health professionals agree that its early detection offers the greatest chance of a cure or control of the disease. In particular, skin cancers are highly treatable if they are caught early. Because of the fine-grained variability in the appearance of skin lesions, automated classification of skin lesions using images is a challenging task. Researchers at Stanford University trained a system of AI called "CNN" (convolutional neural networks) to do so by feeding it only pixels and disease labels from a data-set of about 130,000 clinical images. As a result, the AI achieves performance on par with a control group of human experts. A dermatologist in full-time practice will see about 200,000 cases during his lifetime. AI is already capable of classifying skin cancer with a level of competence comparable to dermatologists – and it will continue to absorb data equivalent to the lifetime experience of many human experts.[7]

The second step in the evolution of AI was taken by a program called "AlphaZero." It mastered the games of chess, Shogi and Go, and in 2017 began defeating the previous world-champion programs. The difference? AlphaZero's pattern recognition is not based on huge amounts of human data. It is, in fact, not based on human experience at all. The only input it received were the rules of the game. It then trained itself solely via "self-play," itself generating the experience that allowed it to induce patterns. According to Oxford University's Luciano Floridi, it achieved supremacy after just nine hours of practice. While the storage limitations of human memory are unknown, our processing power clearly cannot compete with such algorithms. And, of course, we are mortal. So, as a race, shall we just throw up our arms, and go home?[8]

Certainly not. You will have realized that the games of chess, Go, and Shogi all have one thing in common. They provide the kindest of learning environments. There is a clear and finite set of rules as well as perfect viability between actions and results. The rules literally constitute the game. This is very different from games that are merely constrained by their rules, but don't consist of them, such as football.

Knowing the rules does not make the algorithm a good football player. More generally, AI is a disaster at finding the right strategy in a wicked environment, as Epstein points out: AI may beat humans at *Jeopardy!* But when it was tasked with finding cures for cancer, it spectacularly flopped. Oncologist Vinay Prasad emphasizes that "the difference between winning at *Jeopardy!* and curing all cancer is that we know the answer to *Jeopardy!* questions." MIT's Thomas Malone reassures us that IBM's Watson might be a champion at *Jeopardy!* but it cannot even play tic-tac-toe, much less provide answers to wicked problems. Contrary to what many believe, AI is not like a baby farmer that will eventually grow up to become an adult farmer. Rather, AI is like a tractor – a tool for the human farmer to use. And when it comes to wicked problems, AI is still no match for humans. This brings us to the third phase of its evolution.[9]

The only form of intelligence that can outperform both AI and human intelligence is the combination of the two. Notably, "Cyborg" chess teams, where humans (even mid-level professionals) can outsource certain pattern recognition tasks to AI "team members," beat both types of opponents. Importantly, the human player is the one who controls and decides the game, despite the assistance received from the computer.[10]

In all professions, humans can outsource experience-based pattern recognition to AI to help them work better. Think of the many ways in which machines and algorithms are already used to aid a medical doctor's diagnostic skills. Or, in our context, think of lawyers that nowadays can rely on AI to collect relevant case law, obliterating the need for a room full of junior lawyers or para-legals. This is why globalization expert Richard Baldwin argues that such jobs will disappear quickly from our knowledge economy. Work, and learning, that are easily replicable by algorithms are quickly becoming less valuable. Georgetown University's Cal Newport calls such work "shallow," and contrasts it with the hard-to-replicate "deep work" that will continue to create real value.[11]

This is why I believe that negotiation skills will become even more valuable in the future than they are today. I will go out on a limb here and say it. It seems to me that most of the tactics of claiming value can be performed by AI, and much of it better than human attempts. Algorithms are bias-free. They can be excellent at gathering market data, analyzing BATNAs, quantifying RPs, calculating risks and returns, and even anchoring by throwing out an extreme first offer. And they won't even blush when they do it. Facebook is already experimenting with "negotiation bots" that can bargain simple transactions with one another (although it had to shut the bots down when they also learned to lie). And researchers are now even trying to program empathy and counterempathy into prisoner's-dilemma playing algorithms.[12]

As negotiators, we will be using more and more AI tools to help us size up and slice the pie. And as learners of negotiation, we will incorporate these tools into "cyber-human" learning loops to make our performance more effective. By all means, continue to use Word documents, Excel spreadsheets, and AI to support your efforts.[13]

But what cannot be replicated is the capacity that you, dear reader, have bolstered by reading this book: Facing and mastering the contradictory wickedness of the tactical paradox, the strategic dilemma, the cognitive ambiguity, and the general ambivalence of the process. I believe that, in many ways, negotiations might epitomize what AI *cannot* do.

To conclude our contemplation of AI, let's return to the tractor analogy. When the tractor was invented, its two main effects reinforced each other. Not only could the machine tirelessly bring multiple units of horsepower to bear, it also obviated the need to feed real horses. Remarkably, as much as half of the land on small farms was devoted to providing feed for the animals used to cultivate the rest. Tractors multiplied not only the yield but also the land from which it was taken. What hitherto unused cognitive resources might our modern tractor free for us learners of negotiation?[14]

I hope this book helps you in putting your own resources to use. Take what helps you, and disregard what does not. Make it yours. In a word: Learn to become an even better negotiator. Good luck!

Notes

PREFACE

1 Doyle, 2016 [1892], p. 213.

INTRODUCTION

1 The quote by Niels Bohr is cited in Rozental, 1967, p. 328: "One of the favorite maxims of my father was the distinction between the two sorts of truth, profound truths recognized by the fact that the opposite is also a profound truth, in contrast to trivialities where opposites are obviously absurd."

2 We can learn about negotiation and: conflict (Ury, Brett, & Goldberg, 1993), culture (Brett, 2014), emotions (Fisher & Shapiro, 2006), improvisation (Wheeler, 2013), authenticity (Kopelman, 2014), and organizations (Movius & Susskind, 2009).

3 Fisher, Ury, & Patton, 1999; Ury, 2007. Recent studies found that only a minority of German managers have been professionally trained in conducting negotiations: Voeth, Herbst, Haggenmüller, & Weber, 2020, pp. 21–4.

4 "Monetary mindset": Gunia, 2019, p. 4.

5 Camp, 2002; Voss & Raz, 2016; "Khrushchev's third shoe": Macioszek, 2005. The title of this latter (German) volume came from the author's claim that Khrushchev brought a third shoe to the United Nations so that he could bang it on the rostrum in order to appear mad – a competitive tactic designed to pressure the other side into giving in. While a number of authors have described the "banging of the shoe" episode (for instance, Carlson, 2009, p. 251ff), no footage exists and some people doubt that it ever took place. Either way, the story evokes a vivid picture that is easy to memorize.

6 I have amalgamated two successive definitions created by Jeanne Brett of Northwestern University (Brett, 2007, p. 1; Brett, 2014, p. 1). We can break a single issue into multiple issues, or we can add new issues (Brett, 2014, p. 4). "Bartering mindset": Gunia, 2019.

7 Two sisters argue about an orange: Fisher, Ury, & Patton, 1999, p. 59. The story seems to predate the book. It has been attributed to organizational behaviour pioneer Mary Follett Parker (1868–1933), even though the specific source remains unknown. Kolb concludes that the parable originated only in the 1970s, attributing it to leadership expert Robert House (Kolb, 1995).

8 The possible outcomes of a transaction can be plotted on a matrix. Kenneth W. Thomas of the Naval Postgraduate School seems to have been the first to conceptualize conflicting interests in this way in 1978, modifying Blake and Mouton's now famous "Managerial Grid" to fit the larger context; Harvard's Howard Raiffa then used it in 1982 to analyze negotiations. See Thomas, 1992 and Raiffa, 1982.

9 With a view to project managers I have conceptualized "the planned" and "the unplanned" elsewhere: Berkel, 2016.

10 There are significant differences in terms of the level of development of the legal system and the rule of law across Asia. Singapore has a strong legal system and strict enforcement of laws; the same cannot be said of China: Benoliel, 2013, p. 10.

11 There are considerable differences in tactical preferences among Chinese, Japanese and Korean cultures; the widely held Western assumption of East Asian cultures as fairly homogeneous is not correct: Lee, Brett, & Park 2012. Asians may feel insulted when a Western business partner wants to specify penalties: Benoliel, 2013, p. 17.

12 In the Asian view, contracts are inherently deficient: Benoliel, 2013, p. 10.

13 To reject an unfavorable offer is also required to foster cooperation; see e.g. Hüffmeier & Hertel, 2012, p. 146f (with further references).

14 Make the offer as extreme as you plausibly can: Galinsky & Mussweiler, 2001. Even Fisher and Ury acknowledge this: Fisher, Ury, & Patton, 2011, p. 39.

15 Even seasoned scientists have a tendency to avoid complexity: Gorman & Gorman, 2017, p. 174. As a consequence, unexpected experimental results are often dismissed as errors: Johnson, 2010, p. 138f. In line with the seminal work of Daniel Kahneman and his late colleague Amos Tversky, we will call such faulty intuition "(cognitive) biases" and the shortcuts that are suggested to us by our intuitive system "heuristics" (Tversky & Kahneman, 1974). The article summarizes their work from the preceding five years and was influential in all areas of social science. It laid much of the foundation for our current understanding of "errors of judgment." The two scientists then directed their attention to the subject of "'errors in decision' making" and, five years later, published an equally influential article, "Prospect Theory: An Analysis of Decision under Risk" (Kahneman & Tversky, 1979), which forms the basis for much of their subsequent work and the cognitive biases presented herein. Their insight was honored with a Nobel Prize (posthumously in the case of Amos Tversky) in 2002.

16 Most people are not very good at negotiation: Thompson, 2014, p. 5. They fail to identify and optimize compatible interest: Thompson & Hrebec, 1996; and to reach mutually beneficial outcomes Nadler, Thompson, & Boven, 2003. Traps: Schroth, 2015, p. 3f; Leigh Thompson, 2014, p. 5f. "In short, people's negotiating behavior ... by experienced negotiators": Movius & Susskind, 2009, pp. 171–2.

17 Visceral reaction to the success of failure of others: Lanzetta & Englis, 1989; Yamada, Lamm, & Decety, 2011. "It is fundamentally unnatural and uncomfortable to change our minds, and this is reflected in the way our brains work": Gorman & Gorman, 2017, p. 251.

18 von Neumann, 1928; von Neumann & Morgenstern, 1944.

19 The lessons we have learned at the times of the Cold War have unfortunately not lost their relevance. On the contrary: experienced politicians now warn against the re-emergence of a prisoner's dilemma confrontation between East and West: Shultz, 2018; Gorbachev, 2018. "To negotiate with an iron fist inside a velvet glove": Murnighan, 2015.

20 "Wall Street Game" versus "Community Game": Kay & Ross, 2003. People cooperate more when the name metaphorically emphasizes the community's interest rather than that of the individual's: Ellingsen, Johannesson, Mollerstrom, & Munkhammar, 2012, p. 128.

21 The poor surgeon is of course the son's mother. The example is from a brochure of the Gender Commissioner of the University of Cologne 2009, as cited by Dörfler & Roos, 2016, p. xxii.

22 "Two systems of thinking": Keith E Stanovich, 1999. Popularized by Nobel laureate Daniel Kahneman, see: Kahneman, 2011. It is often imperative to overcome faulty intuitions and make rational decisions: e.g. Bazerman & Neale, 1993.

23 "Heuristic": Kahneman, 2011, p. 98. "Gut feelings": Gigerenzer, 2007, p. 9f. There is a scholarly debate about the merits of intuition, with some favoring it more than others. Kahneman is skeptical, while Gigerenzer has a favorable view: Kahneman, 2011, p. 457, n. 99; versus Gigerenzer & Todd, 1999.

24 "The Great Rationality Debate": Stanovich, 2011, p. 5ff; or J. S. B. Evans & Stanovich, 2013. To visualize the mind, Eric Kandel likens it to an iceberg, with only one-seventh of its bulk floating above water: Kandel, 2018, p. 1. He credits Sigmund Freud with the metaphor, although it is difficult to find evidence that Freud actually used it.

25 Ury, 2015.

26 Laurie Ann Paul uses the vampire example to illustrate the theme of her book on "transformative experiences," and she credits University of Wisconsin Math professor Jordan Ellenberg with suggesting the metaphor: Paul, 2014a, p. 1. See also: Paul, 2014b.

27 "It is a simple yet profound notion: ... learning is impossible": Levitin, 2017, p. xiv. "Napoleon": Kissinger, 2013 [1957], p. 43.

28 There is no better learning when the instruction is in preferred learning style: Brown, Roediger, & McDaniel, 2014, p. 4. Visuals help all of us to learn. Our memory for pictures may even be better than our memory for words and sentences. More than anyone else, Lionel Standing has studied the human capacity to effortlessly process large quantities of pictorial information: Polk, 2018. Standing found that there always seems to be more room to store new information, particularly for pictures. In a classic and ambitious study, he asked participants to remember up to 10,000 pictures that were presented once each for five seconds. In a subsequent test, participants recalled which pictures they had seen more than 70 percent of the time: Standing, 1973. A recent PhD thesis demonstrated that people have superior memory recall when they illustrate words that are presented to them: Wammes, 2017.

29 The brain changes when learning is accomplished: Spitzer, 2002, p. 158f. "Mental model": Brown et al., 2014, p. 6.

30 Brown et al., 2014, p. 90. Learning better when hard: Brown et al., 2014; p. 3 and 67ff. Learners who direct their attention to difficult aspects of their task do better: Ehrlinger, Mitchum, & Dweck, 2016.

31 Niels Bohr, quoted in: Moore, 1966, p. 196.

CHAPTER 1

1 Radio feature of Bavarian Public Radio: *The Grand Bazar in Istanbul* (translated by the author): Mösing & Steiner, 2013.

2 We can find negotiation research and advice under related labels, see for instance: Herring, 2011. The underlying "geometry": This is a term borrowed from: Raiffa, 1982, p. 46.

3 Walton & McKersie, 1965, p. 4.
4 “BATNA”: Fisher, Ury, & Patton, 1999.
5 “Sole supplier”: Lax & Sebenius, 2006.
6 You always have a BATNA: Thompson, 2008, p. 33.
7 Regarding the liquidation preferences of the exiting investor, see: Caselli, 2018, p. 259ff. The interventions of venture capitalists are temporary and linked to the company’s future performance: Caselli, 2009, p. 39. Regarding details of the evaluation method used by investing venture capitalists, see: Alemany, 2018, p. 223ff. For a detailed exploration of private equity exit strategies, see: Povaly, 2007.
8 Underlying “geometry”: Raiffa, 1982, p. 46.
9 Marks, Slee, Blees, & Nall, 2012: “Every private company has a number of values simultaneously”: p. 17. “Fair market value”: p. 22. “Collateral value”: p. 23. “Investment value”: p. 23.
10 Gu & Lev, 2011.
11 Experts, such as Robert Bruner of Darden, caution against the belief that once you have an estimate of values, the negotiation outcome will simply follow: Bruner, 2004, p. 773. “Bankers take a much more practical and multifaceted approach”: Miller, 2008, p. 31.
12 “Since the financial buyer . . . pay for a business”: Marks et al., 2012.
13 Globes, 2012, p. 21.
14 Siemens had reportedly lost an estimated €1 billion on the investment and announced that it would exit the solar business: Berghoff, 2017, p. 26. So did Schott AG shortly thereafter: Schott, 2016.
15 “Observers doubted that a deal would be possible”: Malhotra, 2016. See also: Eidenmueller, 2016. “Leaving with a transitory agreement”: Rogers, 2018.
“Agreement trap”: Cohen, Leonardelli, & Thompson, 2014.
16 If you want to explore these issues in more detail, see: Berkel, 2016.
17 “Rare is the buyer . . . for a living”: Garrett, 2008, p. 15. “Procurement problem”: Bajari & Tadelis, 2006, p. 122.
18 Abstract linear thinking pervasive in the West: Brett, 2014, p. 33. For Aristotle, all of philosophy rests on principles: Gottlieb, 2015. As Gottlieb shows, there are variations of how Aristotle defines the principle across his oeuvre.
19 Aristotle’s “contradictions” and “contraries”: Aristotle, 1938, p. 89.
20 Hochberg, 2020. He stresses that trade has winners and losers, but emphasizes that they do not necessarily win and lose the exact same amounts (p. xxxii).
21 Donald Trump’s negotiation style: Shell, 2006, p. 155. Shell calls Donald Trump “competitive to the core.” Scholars differentiate between negotiators who want to do as well as they can for themselves (they are “individualistically” motivated) from those whose primary motivation lies in doing better than the other side (they are “competitively motivated”). The later motivation focuses on something that is, per se, irrelevant to negotiation as a process of obtaining the best possible result – which is an absolute measure – and has, not surprisingly, been shown by Jeanne M. Brett’s research to be the motivation leading to the poorest results: Brett, 2007, p. 23. In exploring the negotiation style of Donald Trump here, I am not speculating on his *motivation* (competitive or not). Rather I look at his self-expressed *competitive tactics*, which showcase an almost prototypical approach to the distribution of value. Trump Inc. in real estate transactions:

Honig, 2018. Withdrawal from the Trans-Pacific Partnership: Londono & Motoko, 2018. Yale Law Dean Harold Koh concludes that Donald Trump views America's interactions with the world as "grimly zero sum": Koh, 2018, p. 146.

22 Benefit of this competitive approach: Solís, 2017. The risk: Lee, 2017.

23 Nakamura & Parker, 2017.

24 "America alone": Nakamura & Parker, 2017. This is how Trump characterized bilateral negotiations at a joint press conference with Angela Merkel of Germany: Whitehouse.gov, 2018. President Trump's motivation to "try and catch" Chancellor Merkel can also be seen as a testament to Trump's desire to do better than the other side, rather than to do as well as possible for himself. This motivation is commonly called "competitive" (rather than distributive), and scholars have argued that this is the driving force behind his approach to negotiations: Richard Shell, 2006, p. 155 and Stearns Johnson, 2018. When it comes to zero-sum games, the two approaches coincide: If we do as well as we possibly can in dividing the pie, we are also getting more (beating) the other side.

25 It is not about sinking or swimming together: Deutsch, 2014, p. 24. Negotiators all over the world use them, albeit with different frequency: Brett, 2014, p. 53. Brett calls these tactics "Substantiation and Offer" because they help you to generate value for yourself by influencing the other side to make concessions by making an offer (or demand) and then digging your heels in and substantiating it. As we will see, this is very different from the tactics of value creation, where you are actually interested in what the other side has to say.

26 Mann, 1955, p. 156.

27 The real cash value of an object is only ever what someone is willing to pay at the time: Schonfield, 2008, p. 70.

28 Buyers ought to unbundle prices, so that they can pick them apart individually: Schuh et al., 2017, p. 194.

29 Visualizations: Haapio, Plewe, & deRooy, 2017.

30 Jeanne Brett's negotiation preparation document: Brett, 2014, p. 18.

31 "Post-Preparation": Lindholst, 2015, p. 276.

32 German intelligence in Middle Eastern prisoner exchanges: Steinberg, 2011, p. 2.

33 Presenting a fully drafted final agreement: Rosen, 2016, p. 3.

34 For more information on "battle of the forms," standard contracts, and how to use them, see: Berkel, 2016.

35 Lying about your RP is unethical, unwise, maybe illegal: Thompson, 2008, p. 43.

36 Aphorism No. 181: Gracián, 1647, p. 69.

37 A generalizable lesson that Sir Ivan Rogers draws from the Brexit negotiations: "Don't bluff. It just makes you look weak, not strong, and it fools no one": Rogers, 2019, p. 40.

38 Ury et al., 1993, p. 3.

39 Common belief that 90 percent or more of cases settle: Barkai & Kent, 2014, p. 130. Researchers found different numbers for the State of Hawaii: Barkai & Kent, 2014, p. 131; and assert that that they are indicative of whole US: Barkai & Kent, 2014, p. 130.

40 Counsel against disclosing our deadlines, e.g.: Hendon, 2007; p. 135. But often essential for moving stalled negotiations forward: Gino & Moore, 2008, p. 172; Moore, 2004.

41 "Leaving without a transition agreement": Rogers, 2019, p. 41. "Give me the money or I'll shoot myself in the heart": Cohen, 2018; Barnier, 2019.

42 BATNA as beloved plant or pet: Thompson, 2008, p. 36.
43 Alessi, 2015.
44 Lax & Sebenius, 2006, p. 13ff.
45 Marsden & Siedel, 2017.
46 "Negotiating in the shadow of the law" is a phrase coined by Mnookin & Kornhauser, 1979. It originally referred to divorce settlements, but is equally applicable to other contexts.
47 IBG Report: van der Wal & ten Kate, 2017. "It has been a difficult issue to research": ten Kate, 2017.
48 Nestlé and Edeka: Friese, 2018. Speculation about new CEO of Agecore: Aiolfi, 2018.
49 Harvey, 2018. Industry experts speculated that the food giant had to make significant concessions. Agecore, for its part, continued to use these tactics: Horch, 2018.
50 Negotiate on behalf of someone else and "bring home the bacon": Shell, 2006, p. 198.
51 J.P. Morgan and Andrew Carnegie: PON, 2012.
52 From Howard Raiffa's famous case study, "Elmtree House": Raiffa, 1982, p. 38.
53 Accurately assess the RP as well as priorities of your counterpart: Brett, 2014, p. 38.
54 Luxturna: Tirrell, 2018.
55 Kirkner, 2018.
56 It's alive!: Thompson, 2008, p. 35. Jay Sheldon: Wheeler, 2013, p. 1.
57 For a fascinating discussion of the "silver medal face," listen to Yale's Laurie Santos podcast: Santos, 2019; Aumann, 2018. Framing can be used strategically in a negotiation: Bazerman & Neale, 1993.
58 Pre-suasion: Cialdini, 2016, p. 4. Marge Simpson and Chanel suit: Beggs, 2014, p. 173.
59 French and German music and wine: Cialdini, 2016, p. 6. The field study was conducted by: North, Hargreaves, & McKendrick, 1999. A more recent study by Stanford University of no less than 137,842 diner decisions showed that emphasizing tasty and enjoyable attributes in labelling vegetables increases their intake when they compete with less healthy options: Turnwald et al., 2019.
60 Invitation ad offerendum (offer to treat): *Pharmaceutical Society of Great Britain* v. *Boots Cash Chemists Ltd.* [1952] 2 All ER 456 1952. See: Harris, 2015, p. 391; Philippe, 2004, p. 366. Trader Joe's: Dubner, 2018.
61 Trötschel, Loschelder, Höhne, & Majer, 2015.
62 Prefers being able to choose: Aaron, 2007, p. 41. Being given a choice is preferable to having only one option, but, as Barry Schwarz has shown, that does not mean that having more choices is always better: Having too many options paradoxically makes us less happy with our choices: Schwartz, 2004. "Rather, we focus on the relative advantage of one thing over another and estimate value accordingly": Ariely, 2009, p. 2.
63 "Nudging": Thaler & Sunstein, 2009.
64 Strong tendency to stick to the status quo: Thaler & Sunstein, 2009, p. 37ff.
65 "Default effect": Zlatev, Daniels, Kim, & Neale, 2017.
66 Galinsky & Mussweiler, 2001.
67 Offer thrown on the table: Lewicki, Saunders, & Barry, 2003, p. 51. "Clever negotiators often get amazing . . . high amount": Thaler & Sunstein, 2009, p. 27.
68 Opening offer as anchor: Thompson, 2008, p. 12. The first offer might influence the other party's counteroffer: Brett, 2014, p. 54. Series of experiments: Galinsky & Mussweiler, 2001. "First-mover advantage": Brett, 2014, p. 54.

69 Counterpart's barely acceptable terms: Thompson, 2008, p. 13.

70 Unrelated value: Korobkin & Guthrie, 2004, p. 799. For instance, when assessing the value of a company, it is a common error to determine how much profit the company will make in the future by how much profit it has made in the past, or to determine the price of a share based on whether one "likes" the company in question: Kahneman, 2011, p. 12. Thompson describes another experiment: Participants were asked to guess how many physicians were listed in the Manhattan phone book. But they were first asked questions that turned out to influence their guess. Some participants were asked whether they thought the number of physicians was greater or less than 100, while other participants were asked whether they thought it was greater or less than 1,000,000. It is certainly obvious that there are more than 100 doctors in Manhattan, but less than 1,000,000. "However, these two different anchors caused people to make very different guestimates about the actual number of physicians in Manhattan": Thompson, 2008, p. 143.

71 Troubling forms of anchoring: Enough & Mussweiler, 2001.

72 Real estate market: Janiszewski & Uy, 2008. An offer of €14,875: Loschelder, Stuppi, & Trötschel, 2013.

73 Hukkanen & Keloharju, 2015, p. 15.

74 Cook, 1990.

75 Raiffa, 1982, p. 48.

76 "Midway rule": Raiffa, 1982, p. 40.

77 Galinsky, Seiden, Kim, & Medvec, 2002.

78 Wipe away extreme offers: Schroth, 2015. Divert discussion: Aaron, 2007a, p. 40. Think about your opponent's alternatives: Galinsky & Mussweiler, 2001.

79 No anchoring if they know your RP: Brett, 2014, p. 13.

80 Very few negotiations are concluded within one round: Thompson, 2008, p. 66. Convention of good faith bargaining: Raiffa, 1982, p. 50.

81 Keeping the other party's expectations low: Hendon, 2007. This is a key lesson which Hendon drew from his analysis of concession papers of over 10,000 executives from different cultural backgrounds that he collected over a fifteen-year period.

82 Objective standards: Fisher, Ury, & Patton, 1999. Cite market prices, business practice, net present value calculations: Aaron, 2007, p. 43. No objective criteria may exist – or they may be "inherently imponderable": White, 1984, p. 117.

83 Zhang & Brett, 2017.

84 "What makes you believe your position is fair?" see: Aaron, 2007, p. 43.

85 Loewenstein, Issacharoff, Camerer, & Babcock, 1993.

86 de Waal, 2019, p. 210f.

87 People recognized themselves: de Waal, 2019, p. 220.

88 Splitting $200: Raiffa, 1982, p. 53. "Tragedy of bargaining": Spaniel, 2014, p. 206.

89 Midpoint as predictor: Lax & Sebenius, 2006, p. 194.

90 Young, 1994, p. 18 (original italics).

91 The problem was posed in a "Mishna" from the Babylonian Talmud: Young, 1994, p. 65.

92 Benjamin Franklin quoted after: Isaacson, 2003, p. 448.

93 Thaler, 2015, p. 4.

94 The competitive negotiator might end up with a smaller slice: Brett, 2014, p. 53.

95 Customers might not come back: Haws & Bearden, 2006.

96 Pressure comes primarily from the same side of the table: Subramanian, 2010, p. xi. Detrimental effect on the buyer–supplier relationship: Jap, 2007.

97 Sullivan, 2018. Prevent's business history: Kreimeier, 2018. Spiegel, 2018.

98 Better off by claiming a smaller piece of a larger pie: Brett, 2014, p. 22.

99 If we swim the other does not have to sink. Rather, we swim (or sink) together: Deutsch, 2014, p. 24.

100 Chimpanzees: de Waal, 2009, p. 190.

101 The "mother of modern dispute resolution": Menkel-Meadow, Love, & Schneider, 2006, p. 8.

102 Parker Follett, 1994 [1925], p. 5. Parker Follett was perhaps the first modern thinker who illustrated the idea behind the creation of value.

103 Walton & McKersie, 1965, p. 5.

104 Lewicki et al. use a similar figure to depict "Creating and Claiming Value and the Pareto Efficient Frontier": Lewicki et al., 2003, p. 75.

105 On the role of a mediator, especially in deal-making, see: Goldberg, 2015. See my brief overview (in German) of the benefits of deal mediation here: Berkel, 2015.

106 "Tossing out a brick to obtain a jade gem": Taylor, 2013, p. 67. In German: von Senger, 2004, p. 139.

107 Swiss Army Belgian Shepherds: Gfrerer & Taborsky, 2018.

108 The US Department of Energy offers a great explanation of "How Gas Turbine Power Plants Work" at its Office of Fossil Energy webpage; see: www.energy.gov/fe/how-gas-turbine-power-plants-work.

109 Acemoglu & Robinson, 2019, p. 153.

110 "A remarkably participatory form of government", and the quote from Tacitus's *Germania*: Acemoglu & Robinson, 2019, p. 155.

111 Diamond, 2019, p. 418ff.

112 Moss, 2017, p. 3.

113 Moss, 2017, p. 7.

114 Western Europe interstate wars: Pinker, 2012, p. 251. "I was convinced that … for bringing it about": Monnet, 1978, p. 511.

115 Monnet, 1978, p. 323.

116 "I therefore asked that the word 'negotiations' … 'European Community' to describe our objective": Monnet, 1978, p. 323.

117 European Community's "first real crisis": Schneider, 2009, p. 1.

118 Schneider, 2009, p. 2.

119 Restrictions on their employment and welfare systems to the new EU entrants: Pedersen & Pytlikova, 2008, p. 1.

120 "If the overall gains … for all states": Schneider, 2009.

121 Neale & Lys, 2015, p. 226.

122 "Co-opetition": Gnyawali & Ryan Charleton, 2018, p. 2526. Two comments to clarify terminology across fields: In the co-opetition literature, as in this article, "value creation" is referred to as "joint value creation," referring to both partners. "Value distribution" is labelled "firm value creation," referring to a company's individual gains at the expense of the other side. Furthermore, co-opetition researchers refer to

organizations that literally compete for market share when they use the term "competition." When mirrored against negotiation literature, the words evoke "competitive social motivation" (i.e. the motivation to outdo others, as in sports) rather than the motivation to do as well for oneself as possible, which sits at the heart of "competitive" value distribution tactics.

123 The television series example is from Jeanne Brett's popular negotiation simulation, *Cartoon*. The role-play exercise is available at: www.negotiationandteamresources.com/learning-resources/.

124 Venture capitalists "participating preferred" structure: Caselli, 2018, p. 259. For an overview of earn-out clauses as tools to reduce the acquirer's risk, see: Caselli, Gatti, & Visconti, 2006.

125 "A nation situated in the centre of Europe . . . pattern of relation." Kissinger had Austria in mind when he wrote his reflections on Metternich and political equilibriums. Still, it applies just as much to Austria's northern neighbor which shares its position in the centre of Europe: Kissinger, 2013 [1957], p. 43.

126 Whitehouse.gov, 2017.

127 Whitehouse.gov, 2017.

128 Merkel, 2019b.

129 Aristotle, 1938, p. 98.

130 Brett, 2014, p. 60.

131 Westerners attend more to what is in the foreground of a photograph, whereas East Asians attend more to the entire scene: Nisbett & Masuda, 2003.

132 Eye movement of Americans and Chinese: Chua, Boland, & Nisbett, 2005.
Incongruent images: Jenkins, Yang, Goh, Hong, & Park, 2010.

133 Korean and German room-size assessment: Saulton, Bülthoff, De La Rosa, & Dodds, 2017.

134 Siemens, 2015.

135 Kaeser, 2015.

136 Brett, 2014, p. 18.

137 Framing: Aaron, 2007, p. 48.

138 In a seminal experiment, Deutsch demonstrated that individual choices in a prisoner's dilemma depend on whether they are induced to feel cooperative or individualistic: Deutsch, 1960. His instructions as cited by Ellingsen et al., 2012, p. 117.

139 "The Community Game" versus "The Wall Street Game": Kay & Ross, 2003.
People cooperate more when the name of the game emphasizes the community: Ellingsen et al., 2012, p. 128.

140 Emphasizing the "common road": Bühring-Uhle, Eidenmüller, & Nelle, 2017; p. 148.
The experiment devised by Solomon Asch: Kahneman, 2011, p. 82.

141 Sisario, 2015.

142 Swift, 2015.

143 Neuroscientists uncover more and more of what happens in our brains, when we communicate with others. For instance, researchers in Haifa found emotions to directly influence learning and memory: Different emotions cause the brain to work differently and on distinct frequencies: Tendler & Wagner, 2015. The experiments were conducted on animals, yet deemed to be transferable to the workings of the human brain: Rats

were first made to encounter previously unfamiliar rats while electrical activity in their brains was examined. In the second experiment, the rats encountered inanimate objects. At the behavioral level, the rats showed a high level of interest in both cases. But an exceptional level of brain activity arose only in the unfamiliar and exciting social situation. The researchers argued that a similar effect is at work in humans, explaining why people tend to remember in particular their first encounter with a future friend or partner. In another, ongoing research project, researchers in Australia explore how human touch and eye gaze in face-to-face interaction can have positive effects on the brains of the involved people, specifically its effect on therapeutic relationship and healing: Kerr, Wiechula, Feo, Schultz, & Kitson, 2016. Fisher and Shapiro's five core concerns: Fisher & Shapiro, 2006, p. 14.

144 Counterempathy: Cropanzano, Becker, & Feldman, 2012, p. 173.

145 Focusing on different issues: Warsitzka & Trötschel, 2017.

146 Galinsky, Maddux, Gilin, & White, 2008. It is better to "think for" than to "feel for" one's adversary, see: Galinsky et al., 2008, p. 383. Better to get inside their head rather than inside their heart: Grant, 2013, p. 197.

147 Rogers, 1967, p. 18 (original emphasis).

148 Signal that the proposal on the table is worth considering but also state that it might be improved by learning more about your respective interests and concerns: Aaron, 2007, p. 45.

149 Rogers, 1967, p. 17.

150 Li Ka-Shing, 2006.

151 A negotiator that is perceived as honest is often offered bigger pieces of the pie: SimanTov-Nachlieli, Moran, & Har-Vardi, 2017. And the other side will respond more favorably to being offered a smaller piece of the pie: Zhang & Brett, 2017. Objective criteria: Fisher et al., 2011, p. 89.

152 Reactive devaluation: Lewicki et al., 2003, p. 152.

153 Intelligence, positive emotions, and creativity: Elfenbein, 2015. "Drawing board": Lax & Sebenius, 2006, p. 10.

154 "Write their victory speech": Susskind, 2014, p. 115.

155 Wheeler, 2013, p. 210.

156 Negotiators can become greedy . . . mutually beneficial terms: Brett, 2014, p. 95.

157 "Less is more": Geiger & Hüffmeier, 2017.

158 It is not always in our self-interest to engage in the tactics of cooperation: Wetlaufer, 2004.

159 Baltasar Gracián's rule 243: Gracián, 1647, p. 92.

160 Der Foo, Anger Elfenbein, Hoon Tan, & Chuan Aik, 2004.

161 Grant, 2013, p. 213. Negotiators on average get a larger piece of pie when they have created value with the other side, than when they have not: Brett, 2014, p. 22.

162 De Dreu, Weingart, & Kwon, 2000, p. 901ff.

163 Both creating and claiming value . . . high priority issues: Brett, 2014.

164 Inescapable tension: Lax & Sebenius, 2006, p. 131. Subramanian, 2010, p. 24. The deeply ambiguous nature of negotiation has recently been highlighted by Wheeler (2013, pp. 8ff, 10), who stresses that fluidity and ambiguity are missing from the conventional wisdom on negotiation, and by titles such as: *Good for You, Great for Me. Finding the Trading Zone and Winning at Win–Win Negotiation* (Susskind, 2014), *Getting (More of)*

What You Want (Neale & Lys, 2015), or *Friend and Foe. When to Cooperate, When to Compete, and How to Succeed at Both* (Galinsky & Schweitzer, 2015).

165 Walton & McKersie, 1965, p. xxv.

166 Nisbett, Peng, Choi, & Norenzayan, 2001, p. 294.

167 Note that Asian value creation is less linear than in the West. As Brett has shown, Asian negotiators may engage in the complex exchange of multiple simultaneous offers, rather than just state their preferences. While this approach can be considerably more sophisticated than in the West, the creation of value is not sufficiently done in Asia either. Asian negotiators leave money on the table too: Brett, 2014.

168 Stages: Adair & Brett, 2005. Simultaneous addressing: Thompson, 2008, p. 105. Win-win *versus* win-lose mindset, see e.g.: Lax & Sebenius, 2006.

169 Interorganizational business collaborations: Bouncken, Gast, Kraus, & Bogers, 2015, p. 2. For a systematic literature review, see: Dorn, Schweiger, & Albers, 2016. Prominent examples from: Bouncken et al., 2015; Nalebuff & Brandenburger, 2002.

170 Susskind, 2014. "No matter how much creative problem solving enlarges the pie, it must still be divided": Lax & Sebenius, 1986, p. 33. It is not an effective negotiation strategy to focus exclusively on expanding the pie; the negotiator must simultaneously focus on claiming resources: Thompson, 2014, p. 128.

171 Stephen Covey cited after: Giridharadas, 2019, p. 31. "The idea of doing well for yourself by doing good for others is a gospel": Giridharadas, 2019, p. 60.

172 Giridharadas, 2019, p. 38.

173 "It is fine for winners . . . in fact conflict": Giridharadas, 2019, p. 51. Vinod Khosla quoted after: Giridharadas, 2019, p. 58.

174 Companies forge strategic alliances in order to pursue opportunities for joint wins, see e.g. "Negotiating Strategic Alliances Successfully" which I wrote with alliance expert Sascha Albers of the University of Antwerp in Belgium (in German): G. Berkel & Albers, 2015. Re cartels and antitrust laws see also: Brett, 2014, p. 163ff.

175 Federal Court of Justice: *Bundesgerichtshof*, 2014.

176 The Camp David negotiations: Fisher, Ury, & Patton 1999, p. 42f. In addition, the United States rewarded Egypt and Israel for the Camp David Accords by providing economic assistance: Dixit & Nalebuff, 2008, p. 73.

177 See the BBC website for information on the UK leaving the EU: BBC, 2019. As one diplomat put it: "Northern Ireland would *de jure* be in the UK's customs territory but *de facto* in the European Union", according to: Boffey, Henley, O'Carroll, & Mason, 2019.

178 Leigh Thompson calls them "flower-child negotiators," meaning naively idealistic negotiators: Thompson, 2014, p. 129.

179 "[T]he first misconception is that it is possible to avoid influencing people's choices": Thaler & Sunstein, 2009, p. 10ff.

180 Cohen, 2010.

181 "Mr. Trump is right to . . . America in its challenge" (the quoted sentences do not appear in the article in this order): Smith, 2019.

182 Incapacity to empathize with others: Post, 2019, p. 4. The Camp David profiles as the "highlight" of his time at the agency: page x.

183 Merkel, 2019a.

184 Trump, 2019.

185 Packer, 2014.
186 "German Defense Spending Is Falling Even Shorter. The U.S. Isn't Happy": Bennhold, 2019.
187 Former US ambassador cited in: Salacuse, 2017, p. 225. "Leadership is not a group effort. If you're in charge, then be in charge" cited after: Kogan, 2019.

CHAPTER 2

1 Raiffa, Richardson, & Metcalfe, 2002; Nutt, 2002, pp. 4, 35.
2 Seller-provided financing case: Bühring-Uhle et al., 2017, p. 89.
3 Leary, Pillemer, & Wheeler, 2013. "Most people in our study saw . . . himself as a rifleman taking aim": Wheeler, 2013, p. 86.
4 Lakoff & Johnson, 2003, p. 5.
5 Cashmore, 2018; "Six flavours of Brexit": Economist, 2017; "Cherry-picking": Macron, 2018; Kentish, 2017; Cooper & Myfanwy, 2018; Metaphor not helpful: Wyatt, 2016; "Packet of crisps": Elgot, 2018; "Pie in the sky": Walsh, 2018.
6 Some estimates suggest that one out of every twenty-five words we encounter is a metaphor: Gorlick, 2011.
7 Lera Boroditsky quoted in: Gorlick, 2011.
8 Thibodeau & Boroditsky, 2011, p.3.
9 Thibodeau & Boroditsky, 2011, p. 9.
10 Boroditsky generalizes these findings; quoted in: Gorlick, 2011.
11 Shackle, 2018.
12 "Metaphors we kill by": Sapolsky explores this depressing topic in the likewise titled chapter of his book: Sapolsky, 2017; Edward Bernays, see: Mark Crispin Miller: Bernays, 2005, Introduction; "Uncomfortable reading" for both those who voted Leave and those who voted Remain in the 2016 EU Referendum: Wyn Jones, 2019.
13 *The Economist* report as cited in: von Hellfeld & Chase, 2010.
14 Kohl, 2003.
15 Kohl, 1996; p. 44.
16 Gorbachev later confirmed this account: Kuhn, 1993, p. 35.
17 Adomeit, 2006.
18 Kohl, 1996, p. 272.
19 McAdams, 2008; games as "interdependent decision situations": Brams, 2003, p. 5; the recap of the prisoner's dilemma is modelled after: Thompson, 2014, p. 295.
20 Nash equilibrium: Osborne & Rubinstein, 1994, pp. 14, 17.
21 Watzlawick, Beavin Bavelas, & Jackson, 1967 (reissued 2014).
22 It is a veritable dilemma: Bühring-Uhle et al., 2017, p. 90.
23 Margalit, 2011, p. 49.
24 Elephants in the Golden Triangle: Plotnik, Lair, Suphachoksahakun, & De Waal, 2011; "Body awareness": Dale & Plotnik, 2017. "NU": Plotnik et al., 2011, p. 5199.
25 Schmelz, Duguid, Bohn, & Völter, 2017.
26 Prefer not to agree over terrible deal: Subramanian, 2010, p. 26.
27 Murnighan, 2015, p. 164.
28 Fisher & Brown, 1989, p. 200.

29 "Taking the negotiator's dilemma metaphor seriously but not literally" is sage advice (which applies even more to the prisoner's dilemma as metaphor for the negotiator's dilemma), given by: Lax & Sebenius, 1986, p. 41.
30 To take an example from the latter, we can turn to Henry Farrell and Abraham Newman: "When one is not focused on discrete, time-limited outcomes, it becomes easier to characterize the longer-term dynamic processes in which the losers of a first-round often come back to fight another day": Farrell & Newman, 2019, p. xv.
31 Plett Usher, 2018; EFE-epa, 2018; Hirschfeld Davis, 2018; University of Chicago sanctions experts Robert Page argues that worsening Iran's no-deal alternative by imposing sanctions will weaken the doves and empower the hawks: Pape, 2019. Pape draws parallels to the Second World War, when Admiral Isoroku Yamamoto, who led the Japanese attack on Pearl Harbor, flipped his position as a result of US sanctions.
32 Parties often really only find out what their interests are once they engage with each other: Wheeler, 2013, p. 10.
33 Nalebuff & Brandenburger, 2002, p. 69.
34 Brett, 2014, p. 8; Murnighan, 1991, p. 25.
35 "Enlarging the shadow of the future": Axelrod, 1984 (revised 2006), p. 126; Murnighan, 1991, p. 26; Press & Dyson, 2012.
36 Murnighan, 2015.
37 "Mixed motives": Schelling, 1960, 1980, p. 98; *raison d'être*: Carnevale & De Dreu, 2006.
38 Blake & Mouton, 1964.
39 Pruitt & Rubin, 1986, p. 28.
40 Note that Blake and Mouton preferred to use the term "problem solving" over "cooperation" and "contending" over "assertiveness." Nevertheless, they mention these alternative designations without taking issue with them. Note also that they preferred not to use "compromising" as a separate category, arguing that there was no need to postulate a separate strategy for it when it arises either out of lazy problem-solving or from simply yielding to the other side. "Compromising": Shell, 2001, p. 159.
41 Gentner, 2002; Immanuel Kant: Pinker, 2012, p. 290. Pinker credits Bruce Russett and John R. Oneal with this insight from Kant's work in "Perpetual Peace: A Philosophical Sketch," as explained in: Russett & Oneal, 2001.
This is what Abraham Lincoln is quoted as saying: "You can fool all the people some of the time and some of the people all the time, but you cannot fool all the people all the time." Note that there is an ongoing debate on who really said that, and when.
42 Imagine negotiating on behalf of somebody else: Shell, 2006; Galinsky et al., 2008.
43 De Dreu et al., 2000.
44 Axelrod, 1984 (revised 2006), p. 133; Subramanian, 2010, p. 109.
45 Zhuge Liang: McAdams, 2014, p. 13; changing the payoffs: McAdams, 2014, p. 145.
46 Neutral third party can help: Brams, 2003, p. 30; Wheeler, 2013, p. 219.
47 Skyrms, 2001, p. 31.
48 First tenuous and then more robust trust: Young, 2016; establish trust from the very beginning: Child, Faulkner, & Tallman, 2005, p. 123.
49 The shadow of the future has not resolved the problem of cooperation in the prisoner's dilemma. It has transformed it into the problem of cooperation in the stag hunt: Skyrms, 2001, p. 6.

50 Duguid, Wyman, Bullinger, Herfurth-Majstorovic, & Tomasello, 2014.

51 Karen Walch as quoted in: Jensen, 2013.

52 Heath, 1971.

53 Political scientists, like negotiation scholars, have identified many constellations in which actors face prisoner's dilemma situations; e.g.: Cohen, 1994, p. 6ff; "This is how elected autocrats subvert democracy": Levitsky & Ziblatt, 2018, p. 7.

54 Levitsky & Ziblatt, 2018, p. 9.

55 Levitsky & Ziblatt, 2018, p. 106.

CHAPTER 3

1 Integrate different "selves": Kopelman, 2014, p. 46; Simultaneously calm … and creative: Wheeler, 2013, p. 79.

2 Ury, 2015.

3 Henry Murray quoted in: Beck, 1976, p. 24.

4 Sigmund Freud as quoted in: Kandel, 2018; Stanovich began focusing on rationality as mental ability: Robson, 2019, p. 44. Dual-process distinction is supported by much recent evidence in cognitive science, see: Evans & Stanovich, 2013. Stanovich originally suggested this terminology in: Stanovich, 1999. By contrast to the differentiation suggested in Kahneman's book, *Thinking, Fast and Slow*, Stanovich maintains that deliberate and effortful analytical "system 2" can, but does not have to be, "slow" – and system 1 can, but does not have to be, fast: Evans & Stanovich, 2013, p. 229.

5 Haidt, 2006, p. 4; Peters, 2012, p. 6.

6 Stanovich, 2011, p. 19. Brain models differentiating between the left and the right hemisphere have long been discarded, but the fascinating work of British psychiatrist Iain McGilchrist may change this: McGilchrist, 2019.

7 Our intuition makes decisions based on notions: Novella, 2012, p. 13; "Human beings are reaction machines": Ury, 2007, p. 32; Ekman, 2019.

8 Not only intuition can lead to irrational decisions: Evans, 2009, p. 41.

9 Nisbett, 2015, p. 66; Sacks, 2016, p. 140.

10 Wallas, 1926. See also: Sadler-Smith, 2015.

11 Some scientists stress that despite thousands of experiments, no one has been able to declare with certainty why all life forms sleep: Kryger, 2017, p. 5; Others wonder whether there are any biological functions that are *not* supported by it: Walker, 2018, p. 8; Barrett, 2001.

12 Beck, 1976, p. 11.

13 Kahneman, 2011, p. 11.

14 Debaty, 2014.

15 Kandasamy et al., 2016.

16 Tsay & Bazerman, 2009, p. 14.

17 There is voluminous evidence from many areas of social life that relying exclusively on it can lead to irrationality: Stanovich, 2011, p. 31; Helmholtz cited in: Frey, 1998, p. 205; Ludwig Wittgenstein cited in: Hoffman, 2019, p. 19.

18 Kahneman, 2011, p. 119; Wainer & Zwerling, 2006.

19 Kahneman, 2011, p. 109.
20 Gunia, 2018; Bazerman, 2013.
21 Many individuals try to win a negotiation in the same way as you might try to win a game or a sports competition: Brett, 2014. p. xx.
22 Nuclear weapons reduction plan: Ross & Stillinger, 1991.
23 Schneider, 2002.
24 Clark, 2012.
25 Irrational escalation: Bazerman & Neale, 1993, p. 9ff.
26 Bazerman & Neale, 1993, p. 9ff.
27 Max Bazerman, quoted in: Lagace, 2004.
28 Stanovich, 2011, p. 21.
29 Kahneman, 2011, p. 310.
30 Gilovich & Ross, 2015, p. 92. For the most famous study on how numerical framing can influence people's judgments and decisions, refer to Tversky & Kahneman, 1986: Here they showed that people would respond to the outbreak of a potentially lethal disease differently depending on their focus to save lives or avert deaths.
31 Buyers tend to outperform sellers: Bazerman & Neale, 1993, p. 41.
32 Prospect theory describes how people make decisions under uncertainty, see e.g.: Kahneman & Tversky, 1979; Kahneman, 2011, p. 278ff.
33 Prospect theory suggests: Thaler & Sunstein, 2009, p. 39.
34 General rule here: Kahneman, 2011, 358f; risk-averse and risk-seeking choice in negotiation: Bazerman & Neale, 1993, p. 38; instead, our attitude depends greatly on the context: Thompson, 2014, p. 329.
35 Bruner, 2005, p. 347.
36 Cain, 2012; p. 157.
37 Cain, 2012, p. 161. We will return to her research in more detail shortly.
38 Bayer bought about 11,200 personal injury cases: Teitelman, 2019; *Der Spiegel* cited in: Jauernig & Braun, 2019; Bayer was worth less than the $63 billion that it had paid to acquire Monsanto: Teitelman, 2019.
39 Teitelman, 2019.
40 *Der Spiegel* article: Jauernig & Braun, 2019.
41 Teitelman, 2019.
42 Lev & Gu, 2016, p. 97.
43 "Grandstanding": Povaly, 2007, p. 116.
44 *The Economist*, 2019.
45 Yurtsever, 2008.
46 Gotthold Ephraim Lessing quoted in: Beilock, 2017, p. 14.
47 Emotion cognition is universal: Feldman Barrett, 2017, p. 4ff.
48 Feldman Barrett, 2017, p. 9.
49 Feldman Barrett, 2017, p. 11.
50 This surprising fact ... law enforcement personnel: Bond & DePaulo, 2006; As the American Psychological Association warns . . . not yet been identified: Zimmerman, 2016.
51 "Truth tellers can rely on their memory . . . but liars tend to struggle": Zimmerman, 2016.
52 Gerd Gigerenzer also opens his book, *Gut Feelings*, with this story: Gigerenzer, 2007, p. 3.

53 Gigerenzer, 2007, p. 8.
54 Inverted-U relationship: Beilock, 2013; p. 246; "negotiation jujitsu": Fisher, Ury, & Patton, 1999, p. 110.
55 Beilock, 2013, p. 209.
56 Kahneman, 2011; p. 31; Gigerenzer, 2007.
57 Stanovich, 2011, p. 14.
58 Stanovich, 2009, p. 57. In effect, Stanovich is proposing a kind of "tripartite theory of mind," and the title of this article suggests as much.
59 Stanovich, 2011, p. 106. Stanovich and his research group studied this problem taken from the work of Canadian artificial intelligence researcher, Hector Levesque.
60 "Cognitive misers": Stanovich, 2018.
61 Laura's story is described in: Cain, 2012, p. 7. It is an autobiographical story of the author herself: "That was a story about me. I was my own first client": Cain, 2012, p. 15.
62 Allemand, Steiger, & Hill, 2013.
63 Elfenbein, 2015.
64 Experience in negotiation teaching . . . foundation of their negotiation style: Shell, 2001, p. 157.
65 Elfenbein, 2015.
66 Two traits: Elfenbein, Curhan, Eisenkraft, Shirako, & Baccaro, 2008, p. 1470.
67 Der Foo et al., 2004.
68 Personality is not only what we do: Elfenbein et al., 2008, p. 1471; personality traits also predict: Elfenbein, 2015.
69 Elfenbein, 2015.
70 Parker Follett, 1994 [1925], p. 48.
71 The good news is that when we deliberately practice a skill, it becomes a habit over time: Ericsson & Pool, 2016. Anders Ericsson of Florida State University is the expert on deliberate practice. We will return to his work when we identify the three steps of negotiation learning in Part III. Mischel, 2015, p. 67.
72 "price for the fruit of the tree of knowledge": Simon, 2002, p. 83.

PART II

1 "Learning is a process based on experience . . . behaviour potential": Gerrig, 2014, p. 169.
2 Learning is not limited to observable behaviour . . . change your behaviour: Gerrig, 2014, p. 169.
3 Brown et al., 2014, p. 8.
4 The unconscious mind may actually be superior to conscious thinking in learning highly complex patterns: Nisbett, 2015, p. 56. Subjects were exposed for twelve hours to a computer screen: Lewicki, Czyzewska, & Hoffman, 1987.
5 Duhigg, 2012, p. 7; Larry Squire studied E.P.'s memory loss: Ghose, 2013.
6 Duhigg, 2012, p. 10. See also: Bayley & Squire, 2005.
7 Learning is not like opening up your brain and dumping stuff into it: Pasupathi, 2012, p. 6). For an overview of the own race bias, see: Meissner & Brigham, 2001.
There is no tabula rasa, no blank slate: Pasupathi, 2012, p. 19.

8 Even very old people are able to learn new things, given good health: Pasupathi, 2012, p. 7.
9 BBC, March 10, 2015: www.bbc.co.uk/newsround/31815847.
10 "To be a genius, think like a 94-year-old": Kennedy, 2017; study on the age of patent holders and Nobel physics: Walsh & Nagaoka, 2009; Jones & Weinberg, 2011.
11 Brown et al., 2014, p. 3; see also p. 90 for a description of the "effortless learning" myth.
12 Gerrig, 2014, p. 170.
13 Gerrig, 2014, p. 171.
14 See Pasupathi, 2012p. 10ff; and also Gerrig, 2014, p. 173.
15 Reflex responses . . . such as salivation: Gerrig, 2014, p. 171.
16 Gerrig, 2014, p. 169.
17 Edward Thorndike's work with cats: Haselgrove, 2016, p. 16; Thorndike's "the law of effect": Gerrig, 2014, p. 181. See also (in German): Hüther, 2016, p. 69.
18 Instrumental conditioning has been used by parents and teachers for millennia, and still is today: Miltenberger & Crosland, 2014.
19 Frith, 2007.
20 Like a visit to a gallery: Humphrey, 2015. Our senses are faced with a "tsunami of information" . . . winning our attention: Hoffman, 2019, p. 155.
21 Arnold, 1960, p. 91; quoted in McEachrane, 2009; not only the bear but the entire situation that is being appraised: Kalisch, 2017, p. 96. Reverse is also true: Safina, 2015, p. 34. Scientists debate whether or not animals have consciousness; see e.g. the "Cambridge Declaration on Consciousness": Low et al., 2012.
22 As human beings, we also learn things that we have never experienced before: Pasupathi, 2012, p. 22; Fundamentally oriented toward making sense of our worlds, information is its own kind of reward: Pasupathi, 2012, p. 24.
23 Hüther, 2016, p. 67.
24 This kind of learning happens . . . ability to do certain tasks: Loewenstein & Thompson, 2006, p. 90; "Information-processing approaches": Pasupathi, 2012, p. 19.
25 Three types of learning relate to the two systems of thinking, see: Haselgrove, 2016, p. 100; organize key ideas into a mental model: Brown et al., 2014, p. 6;
Brain changes when learning is accomplished: see e.g. Kandel, 2018; Thaler, 2015; Ericsson & Pool, 2016; Duckworth, 2017; Sharot, 2017.

CHAPTER 4

1 The duck–rabbit figure first appeared in the humorous German magazine *Fliegende Blätter* on October 23, 1892; a stylized version of the drawing was made famous by the philosopher Ludwig Wittgenstein, who included it in his *Philosophical Investigations*: McManus, Freegard, Moore, & Rawles, 2010, p. 167.
2 Brazilian researchers propose that the generation of diagnostic hypotheses in this context is the result of cognitive processes subserved by brain mechanisms that are similar to those involved in naming objects: Melo et al., 2011.
3 Our understanding of the world is shaped by the human discomfort with ambiguity: Brown et al., 2014, p. 109f; the quest for coherence . . . a healthy life: As such it sits at the heart of the medical field of "Salutgenesis" which has identified the factors that

contribute to a healthy human life: Sagy & Mana, 2017, p. 77. Israeli American sociologist Aaron Antonovsky (1923–94) was impelled to formulate his "salutogenetic" model by dramatically detecting factors that allowed a group of Nazi concentration camp survivors to retain positive emotional health. Comics, "the invisible art": McCloud, 1993, p. 63ff.

4 Cairo, 2019, p. 142; falsely "remember" elements of a story: Kahneman, 2011, p. 75; falsely remember words from a list: Chabris & Simons, 2009, p. 47; falsely remember life events: Wade, Garry, Don Read, & Lindsay, 2002; in extreme cases, false confessions: Shaw & Porter, 2015.

5 "Cognitive breakdowns" have implications far beyond individual health. For instance, religious scholars such as Jonathan Sacks locate them at the heart of religiously motivated violence, see: Sacks, 2016; p. 55. Mayer, 2015, p. 17.

6 The higher the stakes . . . the greater our tendency to view polarities in a more primitive way: Mayer, 2015, p. 3.

7 Yet another problem might occur when a person changes their mind in a way that they are not comfortable with – as has been found, for instance, when people develop empathy for individuals whose acts they morally deplore. In this case, they might consciously "cancel out" their value-driven intuitions. But, as Harvard University psychologist Steven Pinker, warns, the change of heart might nevertheless reveal itself later: Pinker, 2012, p. 588.

8 Fear cropping up frequently when people are asked what comes to mind when they think of negotiations is also the experience described by Thunderbird professor Karen Walch, in the introduction to: Walch, Mardyks, & Schmitz, 2018, p. xv. Leary et al., 2013; Wheeler, 2013, p. 86.

9 George Foster's story has been described by Swiss science writer (Dobelli, 2011, p. 199) who credits it to: Baumeister, 2005. George Foster, over time, was able to resume his job and even go back to ringing doorbells without having a panic attack. His behavior gradually reverted to its baseline because he experienced no more instances of exploding houses: Baumeister, 2005, p. 283.

10 Murphy & Zajonc, 1993, p. 723. We develop a mild liking of a repeated stimulus that is *not* followed by something bad – an effect coined by Zajonc, who dedicated most of his career to studying it, the "mere exposure effect."

11 The mere exposure effect means that, on the whole, you will come to like more and more the people who are nearby, see: Gerrig, 2014, p. 471. Note that the mere exposure effect does not occur if the first exposure to the stimulus is followed by a negative event, and that it cannot be explained by the stimulus being followed by a positive event (in which case, by definition, the mere exposure effect cannot occur).

12 Twain, 1897, p. 124.

13 "It ain't what you don't know . . .": This quotation is often attributed to Mark Twain, but there is little evidence for this.

14 Alfred North Whitehead cited (in German) in: Fröhlich, 2015, p. 27. Hippocrates, son of Apollodorus is (only) a namesake of the famous Hippocrates of Kos, the father of medicine, who was a contemporary of Plato's and is mentioned in this dialogue by Socrates as an exemplary teacher of physicians.

15 Plato, 1976, p. 52.

16 Western analytical thinking builds on differentiation and avoids contradictions, while the holistic thinking prevalent in East Asia accepts them: Nisbett et al., 2001. For instance, it has been shown that the Chinese seem to be more comfortable with proverbs that contain an apparent contradiction ("too humble is half proud") than are Americans: Peng & Nisbett, 1999. Within East Asia we have to differentiate further: As Lee, Brett, and Park stress, it is not a homogenous region, and the different cultures of China, Japan, and Korea lead to different negotiation tactics: Lee, Brett, & Park, 2012. The ability to accept contradictions unfortunately does not make Asians better negotiators: Brett, 2014, p. 21.

17 How individuals view negotiation is also a function of culture: Brett, 2014.

18 Kagan, 2007.

19 Farrell & Newman, 2019, p. xiv; the access and exchange of financial data: Farrell & Newman, 2019, p. 13ff; "which swung from pledges … final agreement": Farrell & Newman, 2019, p. 13; "[It] used the principle of reciprocity … international cooperation agreement": Farrell & Newman, 2019, p. 14. Farrell describes this case vividly in his "Conversation with Tyler" podcast: Farrell, 2019. It also supports Farrell and Newman's larger point that international negotiations do not simply take place between states anymore, but involve a multitude of public and private actors.

20 Schock, 2013, p. 437.

21 Inhibited the use of value-claiming tactics beyond reason: Reyes, 2015, p. 16. *Getting to Yes* does acknowledge that there are two sides to the task: It explicitly warns that the expanded pie must be sliced (p. 58); that negotiation can be biased to favor a competitive negotiator (p. 10); and that we may obtain a favorable result simply by stubbornly claiming value (p. 12): Fisher et al., 2011. White, 1984, p. 116; Fisher, 1984; the book has been criticized: McKeown, 2013.

22 Note that the term "curse of expertise" is sometimes used with a slightly different meaning. To the best of my knowledge it was first used by Pamela Hinds to describe an expert underestimating the difficulty which novices face and the corresponding difficulty in accurately predicting their performance: Hinds, 1999. See also: Beilock, 2013, p. 9ff. Herein the expression is used, as we will see, to describe what Etiel L. Dror calls "the paradox of human expertise" (2011).

23 Our theory in use can be different from the theory we espouse to: Peppet & Moffitt, 2006.

24 A recent meta-analysis: Schmidt & Eisend, 2015; there also has to be *involvement* with the topic: Benoit & Benoit, 2008, p. 25.

25 Deutsch, 2011, p. 4.

26 Deutsch, 2011, p. 4. If we set out to learn something we should explore our environment, generate ideas how the world works, and then test those ideas: Loewenstein & Thompson, 2006, p. 90; they recommend this approach specifically for learning to negotiate.

27 Kuhn, 1989; People do not do well at distinguishing theories and evidence: Pasupathi, 2012, p. 92.

28 Peter Watson's 2–4–6 problem: Gorman & Gorman, 1984.

29 Strong opinions of complex issues … a biased manner: Lord, Ross, & Lepper, 1979 (in this classical experiment, participants confirmed their prior beliefs whether they were for

or against capital punishment; see Chapter 6); When we receive new information . . . with a critical eye: Sharot, 2017, p. 17; "Intuitive lawyers": Haidt, 2012, p. 67.

30 Sloman & Fernbach, 2017, p. 10.

31 Gorman & Gorman, 2017, p. 174.

32 This is what Maslow said: "I suppose it is tempting, if the only tool you have is a hammer, to treat everything as if it were a nail": Maslow, 1966, p. 15f.

33 People play the "Wall Street Game" differently from the "Community Game": Liberman, Samuels, & Ross, 2004.

34 Humans have the propensity to resonate emotionally with others: Yamada et al., 2011, p. 1336; Whitehouse.gov, 2017.

35 Empathy is not an automatic reflex of our brains: Pinker, 2012, p. 577; Trump: Whitehouse.gov, 2018.

36 Aderman & Unterberger, 1977.

37 Yamada et al., 2011.

38 When it was shown to American adults and children: Brugger & Brugger, 1993. "It is fundamentally unnatural and uncomfortable to change our minds, and this is reflected in the way our brains work": Gorman & Gorman, 2017, p. 251.

CHAPTER 5

1 Maxwell, 2012 (updated January 2018).

2 The "double curse of ignorance": Dunning, 2011, p. 260.

3 Putting theory into practice . . . major challenge: Wheeler, 2006; Ryle, 1945.

4 For skilled expertise to develop, learners need valid feedback: Kahneman & Klein, 2009, p. 519; high validity of feedback where there is a stable relationship between actions and outcomes: Kahneman & Klein, 2009, p. 524; "fractioned" expertise: Kahneman & Klein, 2009, p. 522.

5 Spitzer, 2002, p. 300; "lizard brain": Thaler & Sunstein, 2009, p. 21; humans predisposed for cooperation: Pasupathi, 2012, p. 44 and Spitzer, 2002, p. 300.

6 de Waal, 2009, p. 45.

7 Reaction machines: Ury, 1993, p. 8.

8 Ury, 1993, p. 8.

9 Memory is fallible . . . retrieval limitations: Levitin, 2014, p. xiv; "Inert Knowledge": Thompson, 2014, p. 171.

10 Experiment of revising a sales slump: Posavac, Kardes, & Brakus, 2010; Robert Cialdini summarized the outcome: Cialdini, 2016, p. 44.

11 Bruner, 2004, p. 347.

12 Maier, 1933.

13 Frank & Ramscar, 2003, p. 1345.

14 *The Simpsons* episode: Chabris & Simons, 2009, p. 169; Novella, 2012; p. 13.

15 The Shepard tone resembles the Escher staircase: Hartmann, 2004, p. 147. You can hear the Shepard tone on this YouTube link: www.youtube.com/watch?v=BzNzgsAE4F0.

CHAPTER 6

1 It is "devilishly" hard to learn the right lessons: Wheeler, 2013, p. 227.

2 Niels Bohr as quoted by Edward Teller in: Coughlan, 1954.

3 Stanovich, 2011, p. 39ff.
4 Dror, 2011.
5 Dinnar & Susskind, 2019, p. 43.
6 Learning is most likely if we get immediate clear feedback: Thaler & Sunstein, 2009, p. 82; feedback can be a great tool to prompt reflection and explanation: Loewenstein & Thompson, 2006, p. 83; Stone & Heen, 2015.
7 Wheeler, 2013, p. 222.
8 Thompson & DeHarpport, 1994, p. 273.
9 Wheeler, 2013, p. 227; Hogarth, 2001, p. 218; "wicked" and "kind" learning environment: Hogarth, Lejarraga, & Soyer, 2015, p. 278.
10 Raiffa, 1982; p. 221; it is hardly ever used: Thompson, 2008, p. 119.
11 Provide someone with new information: Sharot, 2017, p. 17; "Our brains are belief machines... want to believe": Novella, 2012, p. 44; "Confirmation bias": Thompson, 2014, p. 6; blissfully unaware of their own incompetence: Dunning, Johnson, Ehrlinger, & Kruger, 2003, p. 83; "we see what we expect to see": Chabris & Simons, 2009, p. 48.
12 Lord et al., 1979, p. 2100.
13 Substantial evidence-based research ... positive presentation of self: Korobkin & Guthrie, 2004, p. 800. We often consider data that supports our decision and ignore data that contradicts it: Bazerman & Neale, 1993, p. 14.
14 Biologists that replicated Thorndike's puzzle box experiments: Moore & Stuttard, 1979. They argued that the cats' behaviour was not learned in the puzzle box at all (reinforced or not). Rather, the cats exhibited their instinctive greeting behaviour. Cats greet each other and persons with a behaviour known as flank rubbing or head rubbing ("Köpfchengeben" in German): The target is brushed with head, arched back, and raised tail as the cat moves past. If the target is inaccessible, the behaviour might be redirected to a nearby inanimate object – such as the rod that opened the secret escape door. When no experimenter was in the room, the cats did not show that behaviour and did not escape the box. Moore and Stuttard concluded that "inadvertantly, the experimenters arranged to evoke the species-typical reactions which they, and many others, failed to recognize and which were construed as evidence for particular learning mechanisms" (p. 1033).
15 MBA students ... Mother Teresa: Diekmann & Galinsky, 2006.
16 Stanovich, 2011, p. 14.
17 Sloman & Fernbach, 2017, p. 261; Hoffman, 2019; Mercier & Sperber, 2017.
18 Gorman & Gorman, 2017, p. 251.
19 Simons & Chabris, 1999.
20 Dopamine spikes and learning: Frith, 2007; p. 95.
21 Polk, 2018, p. 115.
22 Schultz, 1998.

PART III

1 Niels Bohr, quoted in: Moore, 1966, p. 196; the human mind has an extraordinary capacity to reason and plan: Siegel, 2010, p. 10.

CHAPTER 7

1 "Deep work" is a term coined by Georgetown University professor Cal Newport. He describes it as one of the most important human skills, which is, regrettably, in ever rarer supply: Newport, 2016.
2 Plato, 1967.
3 The beneficial effect of aporia: (Plato, 380 B.C.E.).
4 Plato, 1967.
5 Plato, 2017, p. 155; Wilson et al., 2014.
6 It is a myth that when learning goes well it feels confident, successful and clear: Pasupathi, 2012, p. 24. "Learning is deeper . . . gone tomorrow": Brown et al., 2014, p. 3.
7 The phrases "steep learning curve" or "sharp learning curve" are often used backward: (Lilienfeld et al., 2015). Listen to a fascinating interview with the lead author of the study in episode 334 of the Freakonomics podcast: Lilienfeld, 2018.
8 Pursue a well-chosen goal when learning: Pasupathi, 2012, p. 26; the "Google effect": Sparrow, Liu, & Wegner, 2011.
9 Frugal learners: Wellen & Danks, 2014; expertise in categorizing useful versus distracting knowledge: Levitin, 2014, p. 33.
10 Doyle, 2003 [1887], p. 13.
11 Köhler, 1913; cited in Henle, 1971, p. 29.
12 Broad empirical support for the ELM: Benoit & Benoit, 2008, p. 29; Cacioppo & Petty, 1984.
13 Wilson, 2015.
14 Pasupathi, 2012, p. 76.
15 Ericsson & Pool, 2016, p. 56.
16 Roediger & McDermott, 1995; discussed in Pasupathi, 2012, p. 29.
17 A living organism organizes, and a human organism organizes meaning: Kegan, 1982, p. 11, paraphrasing William Perry. James Branch Cabell's definition of the optimist and the pessimist: "The optimist proclaims that we live in the best of all possible worlds; and the pessimist fears this is true": Cabell, 2009.
18 "When the ambiguous drawing was shown to American children as well as adults in the early 1990s, it was most frequently named a bunny on Easter and most often perceived as a bird in October": Brugger & Brugger, 1993.
19 What is unexpected is often much better learned than what was not; graduate student's office study: Lampinen, Copeland, & Neuschatz, 2001, described in: Gerrig, 2014, p. 223; purple cow: Godin, 2005; and indeed, a well-known German chocolate brand has a purple cow as its logo. Your chances of seeing one when driving on the motorway are therefore greater than you may have assumed.
20 False memory; graduate student's office study: Brewer & Treyens, 1981.
21 "Find the story behind the facts" recommends the Australian Science of Learning Research Centre: www.slrc.org.au/pen-principle-11/.
22 Configurations of jointly firing neurons: Monyer & Gessmann, 2017, p. 45. Hebb quoted in: Monyer & Gessmann, 2017, p. 41. Categorizing is a key function of memory: Gerrig, 2016, p. 264ff.
23 Two theories, data largely supports the exemplar view: Gerrig, 2014, p. 223.

24 Doeller: Max Planck Institute, 2018.
25 Bellmund, Gärdenfors, Moser, & Doeller, 2018, p. 654.
26 We look for differences ... differentiate and induce general rules: Brown et al., 2014, p. 85. So when we categorize information we rely on higher order ideas – an ancient idea going back to Plato's knowledge of the forms. This is not a coherent body of teaching. Rather, his thoughts about ideas that exist outside and separate from the realm of physical reality are dispersed all over his works. Plato often lets Socrates express these thoughts in his dialogues. For instance, in Meno he addresses the recollection of knowledge (we will return to this later); in Phaedo (73–80) he restates his theory of recollection as theory of the knowledge of forms (which he argues inhabit the soul prior to the birth of the body); and in the Republic (VI–VII) where he uses the famous "allegory of the cave," comparing the human struggle to understand forms with men in a cave guessing at shadows in firelight.
27 "Thinking about memory tends to activate other memories": Levitin, 2014, p. xvii.
28 Gentner, Loewenstein, Thompson, & Forbus, 2009, p. 1343ff (original italic).
29 "The Phenomenon of light from the sun": Kepler's theory as described in Gentner, 2002.
30 Epstein, 2019, p. 100f.
31 Dedre Gentner – the world's foremost authority on analogical thinking: Epstein, 2019, p. 102. Gentner emphasizes that when a learner is induced to compare two things, commonalities between the two become more salient and lead to a more abstract understanding of the object at hand: Gentner, 2002, p. 29. "Analogical reasoning conceptual change": Gentner, 2002, p. 21; Johannes Kepler quoted in: Gentner, 1980, p. 2.
32 Kopelman, 2014.
33 Wheeler, 2013, p. 215.
34 Loewenstein & Thompson, 2006, p. 87.
35 No known limit to the new knowledge you can acquire by integrating it with existing knowledge: Brown et al., 2014, p. 5; The Australian SLRC: www.slrc.org.au/pen-4-spacing-practice-enhances-memory/.
36 Godden & Baddeley, 1975.
37 Brown et al., 2014, p. 85.
38 "Mix up" your practice: www.slrc.org.au/pen-4-spacing-practice-enhances-memory/; Brown et al., 2014, p. 4.

CHAPTER 8

1 Aristotle, 1984, p. 1743. Wilson, 2015, p. 240,
2 The desire to cooperate to do it: Pasupathi, 2012, p. 44; saying that cooperation ... to speak: Spitzer, 2002, p. 318.
3 Pinker, 2012, pp. 571ff, 592ff, 642ff.
4 Genesis 3:7, as translated in Alter, 1996.
5 Cooperative behavior is reinforced while non-cooperative behavior is not: Wall Jr, 1977; reinforced behavior is repeated: Wall Jr, 1985, p. 98; tit for tat induces a perception of the strategist as both firm and fair: Pruitt, 1981, p. 117; as Axelrod emphasized, tit for tat can

never beat any other strategy in open contest: Axelrod, 1984 (revised 2006), p. 112; tit for tat elicits cooperative behavior from the other side: Pruitt, 1981, p. 116.

6 Pinker, 2012, pp. 291ff and 647ff.

7 "kin selection": Spitzer, 2002, p. 294; wild chimpanzees: Langergraber, Mitani, & Vigilant, 2007; "Because many hands ... few parasites": Sapolsky, 2017, p. 343f. Sapolsky cautions that the example of the vampire bats is rather controversial, in that colonies are often made up of somewhat related females, making way for a kin selection argument; "reciprocal altruism": Trivers, 1971.

8 Your friend cuts her finger: Bauer, 2015, p. 103; "mirror neurons": Collins, 2016, p. 94; empathy is not an automatic reflex of mirror neurons: Pinker, 2012, p. 577.

9 Girard, 2001; he argues further that both scapegoat mechanisms and human sacrifice were necessary consequences of mimetic conflicts, and that it is the supreme task of religion to overcome these; power of reciprocity: Strohmetz, Rind, Fisher, & Lynn, 2002; also discussed in: Haidt, 2006, p. 56.

10 Tangible advantages to having an honest reputation: SimanTov-Nachlieli, Moran, & Har-Vardi, 2017.

11 Vampire bats: Haidt, 2006, p. 50.

12 When human groups became too large for tit for tat, religious norms developed to enable cooperation within the group: Sacks, 2016, p. 38; Stevens & Hauser, 2004, p. 60.

13 Ability of human infants to differentiate their own beliefs: Martin & Santos, 2014, who argue that this ability is not shared by non-human primates, such as Rhesus macaque monkeys. More recent false-belief experiments with great apes, however, suggest that these animals may be able to attribute mental states to others: Kano, Krupenye, Hirata, Tomonaga, & Call, 2019. They may even anticipate that other individuals will act according to false beliefs: Krupenye, Kano, Hirata, Call, & Tomasello, 2016. The debate continues; fMRI: Rilling et al., 2002.

14 Homer, 2015, p. 1.

15 Homer, 2015, p. 541.

16 Hartman, 1926 (in German); von Thun, 2015 (in German). The "square of values" [*Wertequadrat*] is widely used in theory and practice in Germany, for instance in the field of leadership development, see e.g. Berkel, 2007 (in German). The square of values is also called the "square of development": von Thun, 2010, p. 54 (in German).

17 Dumas, 2019.

18 Babcock & Loewenstein, 1997.

19 We assume that others are affected by bias but we are not: Bohnet, 2016, p. 47.

20 "Boomerang effect": Sharot, 2017, p. 17.

21 Whitehead, 1929, p. 5.

22 Students were given a problem about how to destroy a patient's tumor: Gick & Holyoak, 1983.

23 Thompson & Lucas, 2014, p. 274.

24 Heidelberg University Hospital, n.d.

25 Beggs, 2014, p. 164.

26 Homer, 1996, p. 273.

27 Schelling, 1987, p. 46; Thaler, 2015, p. 104; Ersner-Hershfield, Wimmer, & Knutson, 2009.

28 Hershfield & Bartels, 2018, p. 93; Bryan & Hershfield, 2013; Hershfield, 2011.

29 Mischel, 2015, pp. 65, 256. The catchy title "Marshmallow Test" was invented decades after the experiment by a journalist. Note that the idea that children's ability to delay gratification would predict future achievement in school and life could not be replicated in recent experiments. Other factors, such as family background and intelligence, seem to play a major role too. However, the original experiment in the late 1980s was not about predicting future life success at all, but about how children develop the skill to delay gratification. Either way, the findings on self-control are undisputed – and they are what really interest us here. Such plans help people in a whole array of different domains: Gollwitzer & Crosby, 2018, p. 336.

30 Murakami, 2009, p. 56.

31 Clark & Chalmers, 1998, p. 12f.

32 Alter, 1996.

33 British reporter's comments cited in: Hastings, 2016.

34 Because we humans are often stubborn and no magical bullet has been found yet: Dubner, 2019. Practice is important . . . rarely true: Sousa, 2017, p. 111. Once a person reaches a level of acceptable performance . . . do not lead to any improvement: Ericsson & Pool, 2016, p. 13.

35 American Judges Association's white paper: Casey, Burke, & Leben, 2013. Learning is most likely if we receive immediate feedback after each attempt: Thaler & Sunstein, 2009, p. 82.

36 Learning is like a thermostat: Argyris, 1977. While he used the thermostat metaphor in this exploration of organizational learning, it (and the concept of double loop learning) are applicable also to individual learning. See also: Argyris, 1993.

37 Gladwell, 2008; Ericsson, Krampe, & Tesch-Römer, 1993; Ericsson & Pool, 2016, p. 112.

38 In *Peak*, Ericsson does not define "deliberate practice," but he characterizes it: Ericsson & Pool, 2016, p. 98ff; Sakakibara cited in: Ericsson & Pool, 2016, p. xii.

39 Ericsson & Pool, 2016, pp. xviii, 7.

40 The case of London taxi drivers: Ericsson & Pool, 2016, 32ff; "musical maps" and room for violin and trumpet sounds: Spitzer, 2002, p. 119; the brain can even "repurpose" neutrons: Ericsson & Pool, 2016, p. 35; Borgstein & Grootendorst, 2002.

41 Ericsson & Pool, 2016.

42 Authentic motivation: Ryan & Deci, 2000, p. 66.

43 Schäfer, 2012.

44 Ericsson & Pool, 2016, p. 9.

45 Duckworth, 2017, pp. 121–3.

46 Duckworth, 2017, pp. 132–3.

47 Ryan & Deci, 2000, p. 71.

48 "Internationalization . . . sense of self": Ryan & Deci, 2000, p. 71.

49 Ericsson & Ward, 2007, p. 349.

50 Elisabeth and Robert Björk quoted in: Brown et al., 2014, p. 98; we learn best when we are confused: Robson, 2019, p. 192; beneficial effect of difficulties can be compared to going to the gym: Robson, 2019, p. 197.

51 People who regard an upcoming negotiation as a threat experience more stress: O'Connor, Arnold, & Maurizio, 2010; for details of other studies indicating positive

affect, see: Carnevale, 2008, p. 53; Dweck, 2016; "They view failure . . . end of the road": Brown et al., 2014, p. 92; Dweck, 2016, p. 216.

52 Recent meta-analyses: Hambrick, Macnamara, Campitelli, Ullén, & Mosing, 2016; Duckworth, 2017; people differ in engagement with deliberate practice: Hambrick et al., 2016, p. 33; top skill level – everyone has practiced a lot, other factors determine super-elite level: Macnamara, Moreau, & Hambrick, 2016. This is indicated for music too by a recent attempt to replicate Ericsson and his colleague's original findings: The researchers studied the practice of violinists at the Cleveland Institute of Music. They found that while the less accomplished violinists had accumulated less practice alone than the more accomplished groups, there were no statistically significant differences in accumulated practice alone between the best and the good violinists: Macnamara & Maitra, 2019.

53 "The effect of deliberated practice . . . handling an aviation emergency": Macnamara, Hambrick, & Oswald, 2014, p. 1617; deliberate practice was found to benefit scripted, habitual activities in all fields: Wood, 2019, p. 114.

54 Beilock, 2013: Inverted-U relationship, p. 246; risk to "choke" under pressure, p. 209; "anti-choke techniques", p. 232.

55 McConigal, 2016, p. 111.

56 Studies indicate: O'Connor et al., 2010; negotiators who view stress as beneficial: Akinola, Fridman, Mor, Morris, & Crum, 2016.

CHAPTER 9

1 Robson, 2019, p. 136.

2 Kuperwasser, 2007.

3 Kaplan, 2017, p. 32.

4 Herzog & Hertwig, 2009, p. 231.

5 Herzog & Hertwig, 2009, p. 233.

6 Robson, 2019, pp. 3, 133ff.

7 For Silvia Mamede's review and interpretation, see: Mamede & Schmidt, 2017. Robson, 2019, p. 134.

CONCLUSION AND OUTLOOK

1 Franklin quoted in: Robson, 2019, p. 89.

2 Pope John XXIII quoted in: Esper, 2004, p. 153.

3 Kahneman, 2018.

4 Popper, 2000, p. 4.

5 Artificial intelligence better than humans at recognizing: Baldwin, 2019, p. 268; Garry Kasparov quoted in: Epstein, 2019, p. 22.

6 Zuckerman, 2019, p. xvii; Simons, 2014, starting at 49:08.

7 Early detection of cancer offers the greatest chance of cure, especially skin cancers: Tehrani & Miller, 2018; "CNN"system: Esteva et al., 2017; a full-time dermatologist will see 200,000 cases: Mukherjee, 2017.

8 Floridi, 2019.
9 Difference between constitutive and constraining rules: Floridi, 2019. AI is a disaster at finding the right strategy in a wicked environment: Epstein, 2019, p. 29; Vinay Prasad quoted in: Epstein, 2019, p. 29; Malone, 2019. AI is like a tractor, not a baby farmer: Baldwin, 2019, p. 152.
10 Epstein, 2019.
11 Baldwin, 2019, p. 269; Newport, 2016.
12 Facebook is experimenting with "negotiation bots": Lewis, Yarats, Dauphin, Parikh, & Batra, 2017; it had to shut the bots down: Maney, 2017; researchers are trying to program empathy and counterempathy: Chen & Wang, 2019.
13 We will incorporate these tools into "cyber-human" learning loops: Malone, 2018, p. 231ff.
14 The tractor's two main effects reinforced each other: Mann, 2019, p. 103.

Bibliography

Acemoglu, D. & Robinson, J. A. (2012). *Why Nations Fail: The Origins of Power, Prosperity, and Poverty*. New York: Crown Publishing Group.

Acemoglu, D. & Robinson, J. A. (2019). *The Narrow Corridor. States, Societies, and the Fate of Liberty*. New York: Penguin Press.

Aderman, D. & Unterberger, G. L. (1977). Contrast Empathy and Observer Modeling Behavior. *Journal of Personality*, 45(2), 267–80.

Adomeit, H. (2006). Gorbachev's Consent to Unified Germany's Membership in NATO. Paper presented at the "Europe and the End of the Cold War" conference, June 15–17, Sorbonne University, Paris.

Aiolfi, S. (2018, Mar. 2). Coop setzt Nestlé unter Druck – kann das gut gehen? *Neue Zürcher Zeitung (NZZ)*. Retrieved from www.nzz.ch/wirtschaft/nestle-spuert-die-geballte-macht-der-haendler-ld.1362093.

Akinola, M., Fridman, I., Mor, S., Morris, M. W., & Crum, A. J. (2016). Adaptive Appraisals of Anxiety Moderate the Association between Cortisol Reactivity and Performance in Salary Negotiations. *PLoS ONE*, 11(12), 1–10, e0167977. https://doi.org/10.1371/journal.pone.0167977.

Alemany, L. (2018). Valuation of New Ventures. In L. Alemany & J. J. Andreoli (eds.), *Entrepreneurial Finance: The Art and Science of Growing Ventures*, pp. 214–48. Cambridge University Press.

Alessi, C. (2015, Jan. 25). Siemens Chief Faces Tough Questions Over Dresser Price. Sharp Decline in Energy Prices Puts Harsh Light on $7.6 Billion Deal. *The Wall Street Journal*. Retrieved from www.wsj.com/articles/dresser-deal-price-likely-to-heat-up-siemens-meeting-1422237355.

Allemand, M., Steiger, A. E., & Hill, P. L. (2013). Stability of Personality Traits in Adulthood. *The Journal of Gerontopsychology and Geriatric Psychiatry*, 26, 5–13.

Alter, R. (1996). *Genesis. Translation and Commentary*. New York, London: W.W. Norton & Company, Inc.

Argyris, C. (1977). Double Loop Learning in Organizations. By Uncovering their own Hidden Theories of Action, Managers can Detect and Correct Errors. *Harvard Business Review*, September–October, 115–25.

Argyris, C. (1993). *Knowledge for Action: A Guide to Overcoming Barriers to Organizational Change*. San Francisco, CA: Jossey-Bass.

Ariely, D. (2009). *Predictably Irrational: The Hidden Forces That Shape Our Decisions*. New York: Harper.

Aristotle. (1938). *The Categories. On Interpretation. Prior Analytics.*

Cambridge, MA: Harvard University Press.

Aristotle. (1984). *The Complete Works of Aristotle*, vol. 2., J. Barnes (ed.). Princeton University Press.

Arnold, M. B. (1960). *Emotion and Personality*. New York: Columbia University Press.

Aaron, M. Corman (2007). *Negotiating Outcomes. Expert Solutions to Everyday Challanges*. Boston, MA: Harvard Business School Press.

Aumann, R. J. (2018, Dec. 12). Israeli-Palestinian Peace a Matter of Incentives, says Nobel laureate Aumann; Interviewer: M. Kalman. *The Times of Israel*.

Axelrod, R. (1984 (revised 2006)). *The Evolution of Cooperation*. New York: Basic Books.

Babcock, L. & Loewenstein, G. (1997). Explaining Bargaining Impasse: The Role of Self-Serving Biases. *Journal of Economic Perspectives*, 11(1), 109–26.

Bajari, P. & Tadelis, S. (2006). Incentives and Award Procedures: Competitive Tendering versus Negotiations in Procurement. In N. Dimitri, G. Piga, & G. Spagnolo (eds.), *Handbook of Procurement*, pp. 121–39. Cambridge University Press.

Baldwin, R. (2019). *The Globotics Upheaval. Globalisation, Robotics, and the Future of Work*. London: Weidenfeld & Nicolson.

Barkai, J. & Kent, E. (2014). Let's Stop Spreading Rumors About Settlement and Litigation: A Comparative Study of Settlement and Litigation in Hawaii Courts. *Ohio St. J. on Disp. Resol.*, 29, 85.

Barnier, M. (2019, Oct. 29). Brexit-Unterhändler Barnier "Viele haben die Konsequenzen unterschätzt"; Interviewer: K. Meta Beisel. *Süddeutsche Zeitung*. Retrieved from www.sueddeutsche.de/politik/brexit-eu-barnier-interview-1.4660829?reduced=true.

Barrett, D. (2001). *The Committee of Sleep. How Artists, Scientists, and Athletes use Dreams For Creative Problem-Solving – and How You Can Too*. N.p.: Oneiroi Press.

Bauer, J. (2015). *Selbststeuerung. Die Wiederentdeckung des freien Willens*. Munich: Karl Blessing Verlag.

Baumeister, R. (2005). *The Cultural Animal. Human Nature, Meaning, and Social Life*. New York: Oxford University Press.

Bayley, P. J. & Squire, L. R. (2005). Failure to Acquire New Semantic Knowledge in Patients With Large Medial Temporal Lobe Lesions. *Hippocampus*, 15(2), 273–80. https://doi.org/10.1002/hipo.20057.

Bazerman, M. H. (2013). Dealmaking: Why It's Tempting to Trust Your Gut. Knowing when to Employ Intuition in Dealmaking Negotiations. Harvard Law School. Retrieved from www.pon.harvard.edu/daily/dealmaking-daily/dealmaking-why-its-tempting-to-trust-your-gut/.

Bazerman, M. H. & Chugh, D. (2006). Bounded Awareness: Focusing Failures in Negotiation. In L. Thompson (ed.), *Negotiation Theory and Research*, pp. 7–26. New York: Psychology Press.

Bazerman, M. H. & Neale, M. A. (1993). *Negotiating Rationally*. New York: The Free Press.

BBC (2019, Oct. 22). *Brexit: All You Need to Know about the UK Leaving the EU.* Retrieved from www.bbc.com/news/uk-politics-32810887.

Beck, A. T. (1991 [1976]). *Cognitive Therapy and the Emotional Disorders.* London: Penguin Books.

Beggs, J. (2014). Homer Economicus or Homer Sapiens? Behavioral Economics in The Simpsons. In J. Hall (ed.), *Homer Economicus. The Simpsons and Economics*, pp. 161–76. Palo Alto, CA: Stanford University Press.

Beilock, S. (2013). *Choke. What the Secrets of the Brain Reveal about Getting it Right when You Have To.* New York, London: Atria Paperback.

Beilock, S. (2017). *How the Body Knows its Mind. The Surprising Power of the Physical Environment to Influence How You Think and Feel.* New York, London: Atria Paperback.

Bellmund, J. L., Gärdenfors, P., Moser, E. I., & Doeller, C. F. (2018). Navigating Cognition: Spatial Codes for Human Thinking. *Science*, 362(6415). 10.1126/science.aat6766.

Bennhold, K. (2019, Mar. 19). German Defense Spending Is Falling Even Shorter. The U.S. Isn't Happy. *The New York Times.* Retrieved from www.nytimes.com/2019/03/19/world/europe/germany-nato-spending-target.html.

Benoit, W. L. & Benoit, P. J. (2008). *Persuasive Messages. The Process of Influence.* Malden, MA: Blackwell Publishing.

Benoliel, M. (2013). Negotiating Successfully in Asia. *Eurasian Journal of Social Sciences*, 1(1), 1–18.

Berghoff, H. (2017). Shades of Green: A Business-History Perspective on Eco-Capitalism. In H. Berghoff & A. Rome (eds.), *Green Capitalism? Business and the Environment in the Twentieth Century*, pp. 13–32. Philadelphia, PA: University of Pennsylvania Press.

Berkel, K. (2007). Integratives Führen. Führung als Wertebalance. In F. Westernmann (ed.), *Entwicklungsquadrat. Theoretische Fundierung und praktische Anwendungen.* Göttingen: Hogrefe.

Berkel, G. (2015). Deal Mediation. Erfolgsfaktoren professioneller Vertragsverhandlungen. *Zeitschrift für Konfliktmanagement*, 1, 4–7.

Berkel, G. (2016). Contract Management. In M. Kleinaltenkamp, W. Plinke, & I. Geiger (eds.), *Business Project Management and Marketing. Mastering Business Markets*, pp. 159–206. Heidelberg: Springer.

Berkel, G. & Albers, S. (2015). Allianzen erfolgreich verhandeln. *Zeitschrift für Konfliktmanagement*, 4, 100–3.

Bernays, E. (2005). *Propaganda.* New York: Ig Publishing.

Blake, R. R. & Mouton, J. (1964). *The Managerial Grid.* Houston, TX: Gulf Publications.

Boffey, D., Henley, J., O'Carroll, L., & Mason, R. (2019, Oct. 15). Boris Johnson "on brink of Brexit deal" after Border Concessions. Negotiators Understood to Have Agreed in Principle to Customs Border down Irish Sea. *The Guardian.* Retrieved from www.theguardian.com/politics/2019/oct/15/boris-johnson-close-to-brexit-deal-after-border-concessions.

Bohnet, I. (2016). *What Works. Gender Equality by Design*. Cambridge, MA, London, England: The Belknap Press of Harvard University Press.

Bond, C. F. Jr. & DePaulo, B. M. (2006). Accuracy of Deception Judgments. *Personality and Social Psychology Review*, 10(3), 214–34.

Borgstein, J. & Grootendorst, C. (2002). Clinical Picture: Half a Brain. *The Lancet*, 359(9305), 473.

Bouncken, R. B., Gast, J., Kraus, S., & Bogers, M. (2015). Coopetition: A Systematic Review, Synthesis, and Future Research Directions. *Review of Managerial Science*, 9(3), 577–601.

Brams, S. J. (2003). *Negotiation Games*. New York: Routledge.

Brett, J. M. (2007). *Negotiating Globally. How to Negotiate Deals, Resolve Disputes, and Make Decisions Across Cultural Boundaries* (2nd ed.). San Francisco: Jossey-Bass.

Brett, J. M. (2014). *Negotiating Globally. How to Negotiate Deals, Resolve Disputes, and Make Decisions Across Cultural Boundaries* (3rd ed.). San Francisco: Jossey-Bass.

Brewer, W. F. & Treyens, J. C. (1981). Role of Schemata in Memory for Places. *Cognitive Psychology*, 13(2), 207–30.

Brown, P. C., Roediger, H. L., & McDaniel, M. A. (2014). *Make It Stick. The Science of Successful Learning*. Cambridge, MA: The Belknap Press of Harvard University Press.

Brugger, P. & Brugger, S. (1993). The Easter Bunny in October: Is it Disguised as a Duck? *Perceptual and Motor Skills*, 76 (2), 577–8. https://doi.org/10.2466/pms.1993.76.2.577.

Bruner, R. F. (2004). *Applied Mergers and Acquisitions*. Hoboken, NJ: John Wiley & Sons, Inc.

Bruner, R. F. (2005). *Deals from Hell. M & A Lessons that Rise Above the Ashes*. Hoboken, NJ: John Wiley & Sons, Inc.

Bryan, C. J. & Hershfield, H. E. (2013). You Owe It to Yourself: Boosting Retirement Saving with a Responsibility-Based Appeal. *Decision*, 1(S), 2–7. https://doi.org/10.1037/2325-9965.1.S.2.

Bühring-Uhle, C., Eidenmüller, H., & Nelle, A. (2017). *Verhandlungsmanagement. Analyse, Werkzeuge, Strategien* (2nd ed.). Munich: dtv Verlagsgesellschaft.

Bundesgerichtshof. (2014). BGH IZR 245/12: Civil Law Ruling.

Cabell, J. Branch (2009 [1953]). *The Silver Stallion*. Cabin John, MD: Wildside Press.

Cacioppo, J. T. & Petty, R. E. (1984). The Elaboration Likelihood Model of Persuasion. *ACR North American Advances*, 11, 673–5.

Cain, S. (2012). *Quiet. The Power of Introverts in a World that Can't Stop Talking*. London: Penguin Books.

Cairo, A. (2019). *How Charts Lie: Getting Smarter About Visual Information*. New York: W.W. Norton & Company, Inc.

Camp, J. (2002). *Start with No. The Negotiating Tools That the Pros Don't Want You to Know*. New York: Crown Business.

Carlson, P. (2009). *K Blows Top: A Cold War Comic Interlude Starring Nikita Khrushchev, America's Most Unlikely Tourist*. New York: Public Affairs.

Carnevale, P. J. (2008). Positive Affect and Decision Frame in Negotiation. *Group Decision and Negotiation*, 17(1), 51–63.

Carnevale, P. J. & De Dreu, C. K. (2006). Motive: The Negotiator's Raison D'Etre. In L. Thompson (ed.), *Negotiation Theory and Research*, pp. 55–76. New York, Hove: Psychology Press.

Caselli, S. (2009). *Private Equity and Venture Capital in Europe: Markets, Techniques, and Deals*. Burlington, MA: Academic Press.

Caselli, S. (2018). The Term Sheet and Negotiating with Investors. In L. Alemany & J. J. Andreoli (eds.), *Entrepreneurial Finance: The Art and Science of Growing Ventures*, pp. 249–77. Cambridge University Press.

Caselli, S., Gatti, S., & Visconti, M. (2006). Managing M&A Risk with Collars, Earn-Outs, and CVRs. *Journal of Applied Corporate Finance*, 18(4), 91–104.

Casey, P., Burke, K., & Leben, S. (2013). Minding the Court. Enhancing the Decision-Making Process. *International Journal for Court Administration*, 5(1), 45–54.

Cashmore, P. (2018, Feb. 27). The Power of Brexit Food Analogies – from Crisps and Cake to "Thick as Mince". Gastro-related phrases have infused the Brexit debate in recent days. But this type of political ribbing is nothing new. *The Guardian*. Retrieved from www.theguardian.com/lifeandstyle/shortcuts/2018/feb/27/crisps-full-fat-corbyn-rise-brexit-fod-analogies.

Chabris, C. F. & Simons, D. J. (2009). *The Invisible Gorilla. How Our Intuitions Deceive Us*. New York: Broadway Paperbacks.

Chen, J. & Wang, C. (2019). *Reaching Cooperation using Emerging Empathy and Counter-empathy*. Paper presented at the Proceedings of the 18th International Conference on Autonomous Agents and MultiAgent Systems.

Child, J., Faulkner, D., & Tallman, S. B. (2005). *Cooperative Strategy. Managing Alliances, Networks and Joint Ventures*. Oxford University Press.

Chua, H. F., Boland, J. E., & Nisbett, R. E. (2005). Cultural Variation in Eye Movements During Scene Perception. *Proceedings of the National Academy of Sciences*, 102(35), 12629–33.

Cialdini, R. (2016). *Pre-Suasion. A Revolutionary Way to Influence and Persuade*. London: Random House Books.

Clark, A. & Chalmers, D. (1998). The Extended Mind. *Analysis*, 58(1), 7–19.

Clark, C. (2012). *The Sleepwalkers: How Europe Went to War in 1914*. London: Allen Lande.

Cohen, N. (2018, July 14). Brexit Britain is Out of Options. *The Guardian*. Retrieved from www.theguardian.com/commentisfree/2018/jul/14/brexit-britain-out-of-options-humiliation-painful.

Cohen, T. R. (2010). Moral Emotions and Unethical Bargaining: The Differential Effects of Empathy and Perspective Taking in Deterring Deceitful Negotiation. *Journal of Business Ethics*, 94(4), 569–79.

Cohen, T. R., Leonardelli, G. J., & Thompson, L. (2014). Avoiding the Agreement Trap: Teams Facilitate Impasse in Negotiations with Negative Bargaining Zones. *Negotiation and Conflict Management Research*, 7(4), 232–42.

Cohen, Y. (1994). *Radicals, Reformers, and Reactionaries: The Prisoner's Dilemma and the Collapse of Democracy in Latin America*. University of Chicago Press.

Collins, S. (2016). *Neuroscience for Learning and Development. How to Apply Neuroscience & Psychology for Improved Learning & Training*. London: Kogan Page Ltd.

Cook, J. (1990, Nov. 8). Lemuel Ricketts Boulware, 95; Headed Labor Relations for G.E. (Obituary). *The New York Times*. Retrieved from www.nytimes.com/1990/11/08/us/lemuel-ricketts-boulware-95-headed-labor-relations-for-ge.html.

Cooper, C. & Myfanwy, C. (2018, Feb. 16). Merkel: Post-Brexit Trade Deal Need Not Mean 'Cherry-Picking'. *Politico*. Retrieved from www.politico.eu/article/brexit-trade-merkel-deal-need-not-mean-cherry-picking/.

Coughlan, R. (1954, Sept. 6). Dr. Edward Teller's Magnificent Obsession. *LIFE*. Retrieved from https://books.google.de/books?id=I1QEAAAAMBAJ&pg=PA62#v=onepage&q&f=false.

Cropanzano, R., Becker, W. J., & Feldman, J. (2012). The Effect of Moods and Discrete Emotions on Negotiator Behavior. In B. M. Goldman & D. L. Shapiro (eds.), *The Psychology of Negotiations in the 21st Century Workplace*, pp. 177–216. London and New York: Routledge.

Dale, R. & Plotnik, J. M. (2017). Elephants Know When Their Bodies Are Obstacles to Success in a Novel Transfer Task. *Scientific Reports*, 7, 46309.

De Dreu, C. K., Weingart, L. R., & Kwon, S. (2000). Influence of Social Motives on Integrative Negotiation: A Meta-Analytic Review and Test of Two Theories. *Journal of Personality and Social Psychology*, 78(5), 889.

de Waal, F. (2009). *The Age of Empathy. Nature's Lessons for a Kinder Society*. New York: Crown Publishing Group.

de Waal, F. (2019). *Mama's Last Hug. Animal Emotions and What They Tell Us About Ourselves*. New York, London: W.W. Norton & Company, Inc.

Debaty, P. A. G. (2014). Restoring Intuition to the Negotiation Table? Cognitive Processes in Negotiation Decision-Making. An Investigation of Negotiators in the EU Institutions. Unpublished PhD thesis, University of Leicester, School of Management.

Der Foo, M., Anger Elfenbein, H., Hoon Tan, H., & Chuan Aik, V. (2004). Emotional Intelligence and Negotiation: The Tension between Creating and Claiming Value. *International Journal of Conflict Management*, 15(4), 411–29.

Deutsch, D. (2011). *The Beginning of Infinity: Explanations that Transform the World*. New York: Viking Penguin.

Deutsch, M. (1960). The Effect of Motivational Orientation upon Trust and Suspicion. *Human Relations*, 13(2), 123–39.

Deutsch, M. (2014). *Cooperation, Competition, and Conflict*. San Francisco, CA: Jossey-Bass.

Diamond, J. (2019). *Upheaval. How Nations Cope With Crisis And Change*. London: Allen Lane, Penguin Random House.

Diekmann, K. & Galinsky, A. D. (2006). Overconfident, Underprepared: Why You May Not Be Ready to Negotiate. *Negotiation*, 9(10), 6–9.

Dinnar, S. & Susskind, L. (2019). *Entrepreneurial Negotiation: Understanding and Managing the Relationships that Determine your Entrepreneurial Success*. Switzerland AG: Palgrave Macmillan.

Dixit, A. K. & Nalebuff, B. J. (2008). *The Art of Strategy. A Game Theorist's Guide to Success in Business and Life*. New York, London: W.W. Norton & Company, Inc.

Dobelli, R. (2011). *Die Kunst des Klaren Denkens. 52 Denkfehler, die Sie besser anderen überlassen*. Munich: Carl Hanser Verlag.

Dörfler, T. & Roos, J. (2016). Foreword. In R. Gerrig, *Psychologie*. Hallbergmoos, Germany: Pearson Deuschland GmbH.

Dorn, S., Schweiger, B., & Albers, S. (2016). Levels, Phases and Themes of Coopetition: A Systematic Literature Review and Research Agenda. *European Management Journal*, 34(5), 484–500.

Doyle, A. C. (2003 [1887]). *A Study in Scarlet*. New York: The Modern Library.

Doyle, A. C. (2016 [1892]). *The Adventures of Sherlock Holmes*. London: Macmillan.

Dror, I. E. (2011). The Paradox of Human Expertise: Why Experts Get it Wrong. In N. Kapur (ed.), *The Paradoxical Brain*, pp. 177–88. Cambridge University Press.

Dubner, S. J. (2018, Nov. 28). Should America Be Run by . . . Trader Joe's? *The Freakonomics Radio Show* (ep. 359). Retrieved from https://freakonomics.com/podcast/trader-joes/.

Dubner, S. J. (2019, June 19). How Goes the Behavior-Change Revolution? *The Freakonomics Radio Show* (ep. 382). Retrieved from http://freakonomics.com/podcast/live-philadelphia/.

Duckworth, A. (2017). *Grit. Why Passion and Resilience are the Secrets to Success*. London: Penguin Random House.

Duguid, S., Wyman, E., Bullinger, A. F., Herfurth-Majstorovic, K., & Tomasello, M. (2014). Coordination Strategies of Chimpanzees and Human Children in a Stag Hunt Game. *Proceedings of the Royal Society Biological Sciences*, 281: 20141973. http://dx.doi.org/10.1098/rspb.2014.1973.

Duhigg, C. (2012). *The Power of Habit. Why We Do What We Do in Life and Business*. New York: Random House Trade Publishers.

Dumas, F. (2019, Nov. 9). When the Best Deal Is What You Give Away. My Father Taught Me that Negotiation is Not Always about Maximizing what You Can Get. *The New York Times*. Retrieved from www.nytimes.com/2019/11/09/opinion/sunday/parenting-ethics.html.

Dunning, D. (2011). The Dunning–Kruger Effect: On Being Ignorant of One's Own Ignorance. *Advances in Experimental Social Psychology*, 44, 247–96.

Dunning, D., Johnson, K., Ehrlinger, J., & Kruger, J. (2003). Why People Fail to Recognize their Own Incompetence. *Current Directions in Psychological Science*, 12(3), 83–7.

Dweck, C. (2016). *Mindset: The New Psychology of Success*. New York: Ballantine Books.

EFE-epa. (2018, Apr. 28). Germany's Merkel Open to Working with Trump to Contain Iran. Retrieved from www.efe.com/efe/english/world/germany-s-merkel-open-to-working-with-trump-contain-iran/50000262-3599435.

Ehrlinger, J., Mitchum, A. L., & Dweck, C. S. (2016). Understanding Overconfidence: Theories of Intelligence, Preferential Attention, and Distorted Self-Assessment. *Journal of Experimental Social Psychology*, 63, 94–100. https://doi.org/10.1016/j.jesp.2015.11.001.

Eidenmueller, H. (2016). Negotiating and Mediating Brexit. *Oxford Legal Studies Research Paper*, 29(2017).

Ekman, E. (2019, Oct. 22) Don't Think of a White Bear; Interviewer: L. R. Santos. *The Happiness Lab Podcast* (ep. 6). Retrieved from www.happinesslab.fm/season-1-episodes/dont-think-of-a-white-bear.

Elfenbein, H. A. (2015). Individual Differences in Negotiation: A Nearly Abandoned Pursuit Revived. *Current Directions in Psychological Science*, 24 (2), 131–6. https://doi.org/10.1177%2F0963721414558114.

Elfenbein, H. A., Curhan, J. R., Eisenkraft, N., Shirako, A., & Baccaro, L. (2008). Are Some Negotiators Better than Others? Individual Differences in Bargaining Outcomes. *Journal of Research in Personality*, 42(6), 1463–75.

Elgot, J. (2018, Feb. 27). Leaving Single Market "like swapping a meal for a packet of crisps", Warns Ex-Trade Chief. *The Guardian*. Retrieved from www.theguardian.com/politics/2018/feb/27/uk-economy-at-risk-outside-single-market-warns-former-trade-chief.

Ellingsen, T., Johannesson, M., Mollerstrom, J., & Munkhammar, S. (2012). Social Framing Effects: Preferences or Beliefs? *Games and Economic Behavior*, 76(1), 117–30. http://dx.doi.org/10.1016/j.geb.2012.05.007.

Enough, B. & Mussweiler, T. (2001). Sentencing Under Uncertainty: Anchoring Effects in the Courtroom. *Journal of Applied Social Psychology*, 31(7), 1535–51. https://doi.org/10.1111/j.1559-1816.2001.tb02687.x.

Epstein, D. (2019). *Range. How Generalists Triumph in a Specialized World.* London: Macmillan.

Ericsson, A. & Pool, R. (2016). *Peak. Secrets from the New Science of Expertise.* Boston, MA: Eamon Dolan.

Ericsson, K. A., Krampe, R. T., & Tesch-Römer, C. (1993). The Role of Deliberate Practice in the Acquisition of Expert Performance. *Psychological Review*, 100 (3), 363–406.

Ericsson, K. A. & Ward, P. (2007). Capturing the Naturally Occurring Superior Performance of Experts in the Laboratory: Toward a Science of Expert and Exceptional Performance. *Current Directions in Psychological Science*, 16 (6), 346–50.

Ersner-Hershfield, H., Wimmer, G. E., & Knutson, B. (2009). Saving for the Future Self: Neural Evidence for Self-Continuity in Temporal Discounting. *Social Cognitive and Affective Neuroscience*, 4(1), 85–92.

Esper, J. M. (2004). *More Saintly Solutions to Life's Common Problems.* Manchester, NH: Sophia Institute Press.

Esteva, A., Kuprel, B., Novoa, R. A., Ko, J., Swetter, S. M., Blau, H. M., & Thrun, S. (2017). Dermatologist-Level Classification of Skin Cancer with

Deep Neural Networks. *Nature*, 542 (7639), 115.

Evans, J. S. B. & Stanovich, K. E. (2013). Dual-Process Theories of Higher Cognition: Advancing the Debate. *Perspectives on Psychological Science*, 8(3), 223–41.

Evans, J. St. B. T. (2009). How Many Dual-Process Theories Do We Need? One, Two, or Many? In J. St. B. T. Evans & K. Frankish (eds.), *In Two Minds: Dual Processes and Beyond*, pp. 33–54. Oxford University Press.

Farrell, H. (2019, Oct. 23) Henry Farrell on Weaponized Interdependence, Big Tech, and Playing with Ideas; Interviewer: T. Cowen. *Conversations with Tyler* (ep. 78), Mercatus Center. Retrieved from https://conversationswithtyler.com/episodes/henry-farrell/.

Farrell, H. & Newman, A. L. (2019). *Of Privacy and Power: The Transatlantic Struggle Over Freedom and Security.* Princeton University Press.

Feldman Barrett, L. (2017). *How Emotions Are Made. The Secret Life of The Brain.* London: Macmillan.

Fisher, R. (1984). Comment on James J. White's "The Pros and Cons of Getting to YES". *Journal of Legal Education*, 34, 120–4.

Fisher, R. & Brown, S. (1989). *Getting Together. Building Relationships as We Negotiate.* New York: Penguin Books.

Fisher, R. & Shapiro, D. (2006). *Beyond Reason: Using Emotions as You Negotiate.* New York: Penguin Books.

Fisher, R., Ury, W. L., & Patton, B. (1999). *Getting to Yes. Negotiating Agreement Without Giving In* (updated and revised ed.). London: Penguin Books.

Fisher, R., Ury, W. L., & Patton, B. (2011). *Getting to Yes. Negotiating Agreement Without Giving In* (3rd ed., updated and revised). New York: Penguin Books.

Floridi, L. (2019). What the Near Future of Artificial Intelligence Could Be. *Philosophy & Technology*, 32(1), 1–15.

Frank, M. C. & Ramscar, M. (2003). *How Do Presentation and Context Influence Representation for Functional Fixedness Tasks?* Paper presented at the Proceedings of the Annual Meeting of the Cognitive Science Society.

Frey, S. (1998). Prejudice and Inferential Communication: A New Look at an Old Problem. In I. Eibl-Eibesfeldt & F. Kemp Salter (eds.), *Indoctrinability, Ideology and Warfare: Evolutionary Perspectives: Evolutionary Perpsectives*, pp. 189–220. New York and Oxford: Berghahn Books.

Friese, U. (2018, Mar. 14). Edeka weitet den Kampf gegen Nestlé aus. *Frankfurter Allgemeine Zeitung (FAZ)*. Retrieved from www.faz.net/aktuell/wirtschaft/unternehmen/edeka-und-nestle-streit-geht-in-die-naechste-runde-15492505.html.

Frith, C. (2007). *Making Up the Mind. How the Brain Creates our Mental World.* London: Blackwell.

Fröhlich, G. (2015). *Platon und die Grundfragen der Philosophie.* Göttingen: Vandenhoeck & Ruprecht.

Galinsky, A. D., Maddux, W. W., Gilin, D., & White, J. B. (2008). Why It Pays to Get Inside the Head of your Opponent: The Differential Effects of Perspective

Taking and Empathy in Negotiations. *Psychological Science*, 19(4), 378–84.

Galinsky, A. D. & Mussweiler, T. (2001). First Offers as Anchors: The Role of Perspective-Taking and Negotiator Focus. *Journal of Personality & Social Psychology*, 81(4), 657–69. https://doi.org/10.1037/0022-3514.81.4.657.

Galinsky, A. D. & Schweitzer, M. E. (2015). *Friend and Foe. When to Cooperate, When to Compete, and How to Succeed at Both*. New York: Crown Business.

Galinsky, A. D., Seiden, V. L., Kim, P. H., & Medvec, V. H. (2002). The Dissatisfaction of Having Your First Offer Accepted: The Role of Counterfactual Thinking in Negotiations. *Personality and Social Psychology Bulletin*, 28(2), 271–83.

Garrett, G. A. (2008). *Cost Estimating and Contract Pricing: Tools, Techniques and Best Practices*. Riverwood, IL: CCH Inc.

Geiger, I. & Hüffmeier, J. (2017). *The Impact of a Varying Number of Negotiation Issues: Economic and Socio-Emotional Outcomes*. Paper presented at the IACM International Association of Conflict Management, Berlin.

Gentner, D. (1980). *The Structure of Analogical Models in Science (No. BBN-4451)*. Cambridge, MA: Bolt Beranek And Newman Inc. Retrieved from https://apps.dtic.mil/docs/citations/ADA087625.

Gentner, D. (2002). Analogy in Scientific Discovery: The Case of Johannes Kepler. In L. Magnani & N. J. Nersessian (eds.), *Model-Based Reasoning* pp. 21–39. Boston, MA: Springer.

Gentner, D., Loewenstein, J., Thompson, L., & Forbus, K. D. (2009). Reviving Inert Knowledge: Analogical Abstraction Supports Relational Retrieval of Past Events. *Cognitive Science*, 33(8), 1343–82.

Gerrig, R. (2014). *Psychology and Life* (20th ed., international ed.). Harlow, Essex: Pearson Education Limited.

Gerrig, R. J. (2016). *Psychologie*. Hallbergmoos, Germany: Pearson Deutschland.

Gfrerer, N. & Taborsky, M. (2018). Working Dogs Transfer Different Tasks in Reciprocal Cooperation. *Biology Letters*, 14(2). https://doi.org/10.1098/rsbl.2017.0460.

Ghose, T. (2013). Autopsy Shows Why Famous Patient Couldn't Remember. *Live Science*. Retrieved from www.livescience.com/29341-amnesiac-patients-brain-autopsied.html.

Gick, M. L. & Holyoak, K. J. (1983). Schema Induction and Analogical Transfer. *Cognitive Psychology*, 15(1), 1–38.

Gigerenzer, G. (2007). *Gut Feelings. The Intelligence of the Unconscious*. New York: Penguin Books.

Gigerenzer, G. & Todd, P. M. (1999). *Simple Heuristics that Make Us Smart*. Oxford University Press.

Gilovich, T. & Ross, L. (2015). *The Wisest One in the Room: How You Can Benefit from Social Psychology's Most Powerful Insights*. New York: Free Press.

Gino, F. & Moore, D. (2008). Using Final Deadlines Strategically in Negotiation. *Negotiation and Conflict Management Research*, 1(4), 371–88.

Girard, R. (2001). *I See Satan Fall Like Lightning* (J. G. Williams, trans.). Ottawa: Novalis Saint Paul University.

Giridharadas, A. (2019). *Winners Take All. The Elite Charade of Changing the World*. New York: Vintage Books, Penguin Random House.

Gladwell, M. (2008). *Outliers. The Story of Success*. New York, Boston MA, London: Little, Brown and Company.

Globes (2012, Oct. 22). *Siemens to Exit Solar Business. The activity includes Israeli company Solel, bought three years ago for $418 million*. Retrieved from https://en.globes.co.il/en/article-1000791898.

Gnyawali, D. R. & Ryan Charleton, T. (2018). *Nuances in the Interplay of Competition and Cooperation: Towards a Theory of Coopetition*. Los Angeles, CA: SAGE Publications.

Godden, D. R. & Baddeley, A. D. (1975). Context-Dependent Memory in Two Natural Environments: On Land and Underwater. *British Journal of Psychology*, 66(3), 325–31.

Godin, S. (2005). *Purple Cow: Transform Your Business by Being Remarkable*. London: Penguin.

Goldberg, S. B. (2015). The Role of the Mediator. Professor Stephen B. Goldberg in conversation with Georg Berkel. *Zeitschrift für Konfliktmanagement*, 6, 196–8.

Gollwitzer, P. M. & Crosby, C. (2018). Planning Out Future Action, Affect, and Cognition. In G. Oettingen, A. T. Sevincer, & P. M. Gollwitzer (eds.), *The Psychology of Thinking about the Future*, pp. 335–61. New York: The Guilford Press.

Gorbachev, M. (2018, Oct. 25). Mikhail Gorbachev: A New Nuclear Arms Race Has Begun. *The New York Times*. Retrieved from www.nytimes.com/2018/10/25/opinion/mikhail-gorbachev-inf-treaty-trump-nuclear-arms.html.

Gorlick, A. (2011). Is Crime a Virus or a Beast? When Describing Crime, Stanford Study Shows the Word You Pick Can Frame the Debate on How to Fight It. *Stanford*. Retrieved from https://news.stanford.edu/news/2011/february/metaphors-crime-study-022311.html.

Gorman, M. E. & Gorman, M. E. (1984). A Comparison of Disconfirmatory, Confirmatory and Control Strategies on Watson's 2–4–6 task. *The Quarterly Journal of Experimental Psychology*, 36 (4), 629–48.

Gorman, S. E. & Gorman, J. M. (2017). *Denying to the Grave. Why We Ignore the Facts that Will Save Us*. Oxford University Press.

Gottlieb, P. (2015). Aristotle on Non-Contradiction. In E. N. Zalta (ed.), *The Stanford Encyclopedia of Philosophy* (Summer 2015 ed.). Stanford, CA: Metaphysics Research Lab, Stanford University. Retrieved from https://plato.stanford.edu/archives/sum2015/entries/aristotle-noncontradiction/.

Gracián, B. (2011 [1647]). *The Pocket Oracle and Art of Prudence* (J. Robbins, trans.). London: Penguin Books.

Grant, A. (2013). *Give and Take. A Revolutionary Approach to Success*. New York: Viking, Penguin Group.

Gu, F. & Lev, B. (2011). Overpriced Shares, Ill-Advised Acquisitions, and Goodwill

Impairment. *The Accounting Review*, 86 (6), 1995–2022.

Gunia, B. C. (2018). The Unreliability of Our Gut: Intuitions in Negotiation. Retrieved from https://briangunia.com/2018/06/13/the-unreliability-of-our-gut-intuitions-in-negotiation/.

Gunia, B. C. (2019). *The Bartering Mindset. A Mostly Forgotten Framework for Mastering Your Next Negotiation.* University of Toronto Press.

Haapio, H., Plewe, D., & deRooy, R. (2017). Contract Continuum: From Text to Images, Comics, and Code. In E. Schweighofer et al. (eds.), *Trends and Communities of Legal Informatics*, pp. 411–18. Proceedings of the 20th International Legal Informatics Symposium IRIS 2017. Vienna: Österreichische Computer Gesellschaft.

Haidt, J. (2006). *The Happiness Hypothesis. Putting Ancient Wisdom and Philosophy to the Test of Modern Science.* London: Arrow Books.

Haidt, J. (2012). *The Righteous Mind. Why Good People are Divided by Politics and Religion.* London: Allen Lane, Penguin.

Hambrick, D. Z., Macnamara, B. N., Campitelli, G., Ullén, F., & Mosing, M. A. (2016). Beyond Born versus Made: A New Look at Expertise. In B. H. Ross (ed.), *Psychology of Learning and Motivation*, vol. 64, pp. 1–55. San Diego: Elsevier.

Harris, P. (2015). *An Introduction to Law.* Cambridge University Press.

Hartman, N. (1926). *Ethik.* Berlin: De Gruyter.

Hartmann, W. M. (2004). *Signals, Sound, and Sensation.* New York: Springer Science & Business Media.

Harvey, S. (2018, May 2). Nestlé Reaches Agreement with European Retailer Alliance over Pricing Dispute. *Just Food.* Retrieved from www.just-food.com/news/nestle-reaches-agreement-with-european-retailer-alliance-over-pricing-dispute_id139172.aspx.

Haselgrove, M. (2016). *Learning. A Very Short Introduction.* Oxford University Press.

Hastings, R. (2016). Analysed: Nine Revealing Quotes from EU Chief Brexit Negotiator Michel Barnier. *iNews.* Retrieved from https://inews.co.uk/news/uk/eu-chief-brexit-negotiator-michel-barnier-talks-524117.

Haws, K. L. & Bearden, W. O. (2006). Dynamic Pricing and Consumer Fairness Perceptions. *Journal of Consumer Research*, 33(3), 304–11.

Heath, E. (1971). In *Britain and Europe in 10 speeches*, pp. 8–9. London: Europe House. Retrieved from www.europarl.europa.eu/unitedkingdom/resource/static/files/publications_ressources/ep_speeches_dps_final.pdf.

Heidelberg University Hospital. (n.d.). *Proton Therapy and Carbon Ion Therapy – High-Precision Cancer Treatment.* Retrieved from www.heidelberg-university-hospital.com/diseases-treatments/cancer-and-tumor-diseases/proton-therapy-and-carbon-ion-therapy/.

Hendon, D. W. (2007). Negotiation Concession Patterns: A Multi-Country, Multi-Period Study. *Journal of International Business Research*, 6(2), 123–39.

Henle, M. (1971). *The Selected Papers of Wolfgang Köhler.* New York: Liveright.

Herbst, U. & Voeth, M. (2016). So Verhandeln Deutsche Manager. *Harvard Business Manager*, 2016 (2), 32–7.

Herring, J. (2011). *How to Argue. Powerfully, Persuasively, Positively*. Upper Saddle River, NJ: Pearson Education Inc.

Hershfield, H. E. (2011). Future Self-Continuity: How Conceptions of the Future Self Transform Intertemporal Choice. *Annals of the New York Academy of Sciences*, 1235(1), 30–43. https://doi.org/10.1111/j.1749-6632.2011.06201.x.

Hershfield, H. E. & Bartels, D. M. (2018). The Future Self. In G. Oettingen, A. T. Sevincer, & P. M. Gollwitzer (eds.), *The Psychology of Thinking about the Future*, pp. 89–109. New York: Guilford Press.

Herzog, S. M. & Hertwig, R. (2009). The Wisdom of Many in One Mind. Improving Individual Judgements With Dialectical Bootstrapping. *Psychological Science*, 20(2), 231–7.

Hinds, P. J. (1999). The Curse of Expertise: The Effects of Expertise and Debiasing Methods on Prediction of Novice Performance. *Journal of Experimental Psychology: Applied*, 5(2), 205.

Hirschfeld Davis, J. (2018, Apr. 27). Trump and Merkel Meet One on One, but Still Don't See Eye to Eye. *The New York Times*. Retrieved from www.nytimes.com/2018/04/27/us/politics/trump-merkel.html.

Hochberg, F. P. (2020). *Trade Is Not a Four-Letter Word. How Six Everyday Products Make the Case for Trade*. New York: Avid Reader Press.

Hoffman, D. (2019). *The Case against Reality. Why Evolution Hid the Truth from Our Eyes*. New York, London: W.W. Norton & Company, Inc.

Hogarth, R. M. (2001). *Educating Intuition*. University of Chicago Press.

Hogarth, R. M., Lejarraga, T., & Soyer, E. (2015). The Two Settings of Kind and Wicked Learning Environments. *Current Directions in Psychological Science*, 24(5), 379–85.

Homer. (1996). *The Odyssey* (R. Fagles, trans.). New York: Penguin Classics.

Homer. (2015). *The Iliad. A New Translation by Caroline Alexander*. New York: Harper Collins.

Honig, D. (2018, July 4). Zero-Sum Tactics That Built Trump Inc. Could Backfire With World Leaders; Interviewer: A. Chang. *All Things Considered*, NPR. Retrieved from www.npr.org/2018/07/04/625980971/zero-sum-tactics-that-built-trump-inc-could-backfire-with-world-leaders.

Horch, W. (2018, Dec. 18). Lebensmittelhändler Edeka zettelt erneut Preiskampf an. *Hamburger Abendblatt*. Retrieved from www.abendblatt.de/wirtschaft/article216039157/Lebensmittelhaendler-Edeka-zettelt-erneut-Preiskampf-an.html.

Hüffmeier, J. & Hertel, G. (2012). Erfolgreich verhandeln: Das integrative Phasenmodell der Verhandlungsführung. *Psychologische Rundschau*, 63, 145–59. https://doi.org/10.1026/0033-3042/a000127.

Hukkanen, P. & Keloharju, M. (2015). *Initial Offer Precision and M&A Outcomes.*

Harvard Business School Research Paper 16-058.

Humphrey, N. (2015). Our Subjective Experience of the World May Be Like a Visit to a Gallery where the Artist is Our Brain. *Scientific American Mind.*, May, 64–9.

Hüther, G. (2016). *Mit Freude lernen – ein Leben lang. Weshalb wir ein neues Verständnis vom Lernen brauchen.* Göttingen: Vandenhoeck & Ruprecht.

Isaacson, W. (2003). *Benjamin Franklin: An American Life.* New York: Simon and Schuster.

Janiszewski, C. & Uy, D. (2008). Precision of the Anchor Influences the Amount of Adjustment. *Psychological Science*, 19 (2), 121–7.

Jap, S. D. (2007). The Impact of Online Reverse Auction Design on Buyer–Supplier Relationships. *Journal of Marketing*, 71(1), 146–59.

Jauernig, H. & Braun, K. (2019, May 14). Stationen des Niedergangs. Die Übernahme des Glyphosat-Herstellers Monsanto wird für Bayer zum Desaster. *Der Spiegel.* Retrieved from www.spiegel.de/wirtschaft/unternehmen/bayer-das-monsanto-desaster-und-seine-geschichte-a-1267399.html.

Jenkins, L. J., Yang, Y.-J., Goh, J., Hong, Y.-Y., & Park, D. C. (2010). Cultural Differences in the Lateral Occipital Complex while Viewing Incongruent Scenes. *Social Cognitive and Affective Neuroscience*, 5(2–3), 236–41.

Jensen, K. (2013). Why Negotiators Still Aren't "Getting To Yes". *Forbes.* Retrieved from www.forbes.com/sites/keldjensen/2013/02/05/why-negotiators-still-arent-getting-to-yes/#3f966fbf2640.

Johnson, S. (2010). *Where Good Ideas Come From. The Natural History of Innovation.* New York: Riverhead Books.

Jones, B. F. & Weinberg, B. A. (2011). Age Dynamics in Scientific Creativity. *Proceedings of the National Academy of Sciences*, 108(47), 18910–14.

Kaeser, J. (2015). *Unter Strom: Wohin steuern Sie Siemens, Joe Kaeser? Interview by Sigmund Gottlieb.* ARD. Retrieved from https://programm.ard.de/TV/Programm/Alle-Sender/?sendung=2810714983240375.

Kagan, R. (2007). Power and Weakness. *Policy Review*, 113(1), 10.

Kahneman, D. (2011). *Thinking, Fast And Slow.* London: Penguin Books.

Kahneman, D. (2018). Daniel Kahneman Wants You to Doubt Yourself. Here's Why. *The TED Interview.* Retrieved from www.ted.com/talks/the_ted_interview_daniel_kahneman_wants_you_to_doubt_yourself_here_s_why/transcript.

Kahneman, D. & Klein, G. (2009). Conditions for Intuitive Expertise: A Failure to Disagree. *American Psychologist*, 64(6), 515–26.

Kahneman, D. & Tversky, A. (1979). Prospect Theory: An Analysis of Decision under Risk. *Econometrica*, 47(2, Mar.), 263–92.

Kalisch, R. (2017). *Der resiliente Mensch. Wie wir Krisen erleben und bewältigen. Neueste Erkenntnisse aus Hirnforschung und Psychologie.* Berlin Verlag.

Kandasamy, N., Garfinkel, S. N., Page, L., Hardy, B., Critchley, H. D., Gurnell, M., & Coates, J. M. (2016). Interoceptive Ability Predicts Survival on a London Trading Floor. *Scientific Reports*, 6, 32986. https://doi.org/10.1038/srep32986.

Kandel, E. R. (2018). *The Disordered Mind: What Unusual Minds Tell Us about Ourselves*. New York: Farrar, Straus and Giroux.

Kano, F., Krupenye, C., Hirata, S., Tomonaga, M., & Call, J. (2019). Great Apes Use Self-Experience to Anticipate an Agent's Action in a False-Belief Test. *Proceedings of the National Academy of Sciences*, 116(42), 20904–9.

Kaplan, W. (2017). *Why Dissent Matters (Because Some People See Things the Rest of Us Miss)*. Montreal & Kingston, Ontario: McGill-Queen's University Press.

Kay, A. C. & Ross, L. (2003). The Perceptual Push: The Interplay of Implicit Cues and Explicit Situational Construals on Behavioral Intentions in the Prisoner's Dilemma. *Journal of Experimental Social Psychology*, 39(6), 634–43. https://doi.org/10.1016/S0022-1031(03)00057-X.

Kegan, R. (1982). *The Evolving Self. Problem and Process of Human Development*. Cambridge, MA and London, England: Harvard University Press.

Kennedy, P. (2017, Apr. 7). To Be a Genius, Think Like a 94-Year-Old. *The New York Times*. Retrieved from www.nytimes.com/2017/04/07/opinion/sunday/to-be-a-genius-think-like-a-94-year-old.html.

Kentish, B. (2017, Feb. 16). Theresa May says Britain Will Not 'Cherry Pick' which Parts of EU It Wants Access to after Brexit. *The Independent*. Retrieved from www.independent.co.uk/news/uk/politics/theresa-may-cherry-pick-brexit-single-market-european-union-downing-street-bernard-cazeneuve-a7584711.html.

Kerr, F., Wiechula, R., Feo, R., Schultz, T., & Kitson, A. (2016). The Neurophysiology of Human Touch and Eye Gaze and Its Effects on Therapeutic Relationships and Healing: A Scoping Review Protocol. *JBI Database of Systematic Reviews and Implementation Reports*, 14(4), 60–6.

Kirkner, R. M. (2018). Gene Therapy: Must Sky-High Prices 'Come on Down' Before the Price Is Right? *Managed Care*. Retrieved from www.managedcaremag.com/archives/2018/7/gene-therapy-must-sky-high-prices-come-down-price-right.

Kissinger, H. A. (2013 [1957]). *A World Restored: Metternich, Castlereagh and the Problems of Peace, 1812–22*. Brattleboro, VT: Echo Point Books & Media.

Kogan, E. B. (2019). Art of the Power Deal: The Four Negotiation Roles of Donald J. Trump. *Negotiation Journal*, 35(1), 65–83. https://doi.org/10.1111/nejo.12265.

Kohl, H. (1996). *Ich wollte Deutschlands Einheit. Dargestellt von Kai Diekmann und Ralf Georg Reuth*. Hamburg: Propyläen.

Kohl, H. (2003). *Helmut Kohl – Das Interview (I); Interviewer: S. Lamby & M. Rutz*. ARD German Television.

Koh, H. (2018). *The Trump Administration and International Law.* Oxford University Press.

Köhler, W. (1913). Über unbemerkte Empfindungen und Urteilstäuschungen. *Zeitschrift für Psychologie*, 66, 51–80.

Kolb, D. M. (1995). The Love for Three Oranges Or: What Did We Miss About Ms. Follett in the Library? *Negotiation Journal*, 11(4), 339–48.

Kopelman, S. (2014). *Negotiating Genuinely: Being Yourself in Business.* Palo Alto, CA: Stanford University Press.

Korobkin, R. & Guthrie, C. (2004). Heuristics and Biases at the Bargaining Table. *Marquette Law Review*, 87, 795–808.

Kreimeier, N. (2018). Wie Prevent der Autoindustrie einheizt. *Capital.* Retrieved from www.capital.de/wirtschaft-politik/wie-prevent-der-autoindustrie-einheizt.

Krupenye, C., Kano, F., Hirata, S., Call, J., & Tomasello, M. (2016). Great Apes Anticipate that Other Individuals Will Act According to False Beliefs. *Science*, 354(6308), 110–14.

Kryger, M. (2017). *The Mystery of Sleep. Why a Good Night's Sleep is Vital to a Better, Healthier Life.* New Haven, CT and London: Yale University Press.

Kuhn, D. (1989). Children and Adults as Intuitive Scientists. *Psychological Review*, 96(4), 674–89.

Kuhn, E. (1993). *Gorbatschow und die deutsche Einheit. Aussagen der wichtigsten russischen und deutschen Beteiligten.* Bonn: Bouvier Verlag.

Kuperwasser, Y. (2007). *Lessons from Israel's Intelligence Reforms.* Saban Center for Middle East Policy at the Brookings Institution (Analysis Paper No. 14). Retrieved from www.brookings.edu/wp-content/uploads/2016/06/10_intelligence_kuperwasser.pdf.

Lagace, M. (2004). Research & Ideas: Planning for Surprises. Harvard Business School. Retrieved from https://hbswk.hbs.edu/item/planning-for-surprises.

Lakoff, G. & Johnson, M. (2003). *Metaphors We Live By.* University of Chicago Press.

Lampinen, J. M., Copeland, S. M., & Neuschatz, J. S. (2001). Recollections of Things Schematic: Room Schemas Revisited. *Journal of Experimental Psychology: Learning, Memory, and Cognition*, 27(5), 1211–2.

Langergraber, K. E., Mitani, J. C., & Vigilant, L. (2007). The Limited Impact of Kinship on Cooperation in Wild Chimpanzees. *Proceedings of the National Academy of Sciences*, 104(19), 7786–90.

Lanzetta, J. T. & Englis, B. G. (1989). Expectations of Cooperation and Competition and Their Effects on Observers' Vicarious Emotional Responses. *Journal of Personality and Social Psychology*, 56(4), 543–54.

Lax, D. A. & Sebenius, J. K. (1986). *The Manager as Negotiator: Bargaining for Cooperation and Competitive Gain.* New York: Free Press.

Lax, D. A. & Sebenius, J. K. (2006). *3-D Negotiation: Powerful Tools to Change the Game in Your Most Important Deals.* Boston, MA: Harvard Business School Press.

Leary, K., Pillemer, J., & Wheeler, M. (2013). Negotiating with Emotion. *Harvard Business Review*, 91(1–2), 96–103.

Lee, D. (2017, May 26). Trump Wants to Cut Bilateral Trade Deals, But What if

Nobody Comes to the Table? *L.A. Times*. Retrieved from www.latimes.com/business/la-fi-trump-trade-strategy-20170526-story.html.

Lee, S., Brett, J., & Park, J. H. (2012). East Asians' Social Heterogeneity: Differences in Norms among Chinese, Japanese, and Korean Negotiators. *Negotiation Journal*, 28(4), 429–52.

Lev, B. & Gu, F. (2016). *The End of Accounting and the Path Forward for Investors and Managers*. Hoboken, NJ: John Wiley & Sons, Inc.

Levitin, D. J. (2014). *The Organized Mind. Thinking Straight in the Age of Information Overload*. New York: Plume, Penguin Books USA.

Levitin, D. J. (2017). *Weaponized Lies. How to Think Critically in the Post-Truth Era*. London: Penguin Books.

Levitsky, S. & Ziblatt, D. (2018). *How Democracies Die*. New York: Broadway Books, Penguin Random House.

Lewicki, P., Czyzewska, M., & Hoffman, H. (1987). Unconscious Acquisition of Complex Procedural Knowledge. *Journal of Experimental Psychology: Learning, Memory, and Cognition*, 13 (4), 523–30.

Lewicki, R. J., Saunders, D. M., & Barry, B. (2003). *Negotiation*. New York: McGraw-Hill.

Lewis, M., Yarats, D., Dauphin, Y. N., Parikh, D., & Batra, D. (2017). *Deal or No Deal? Training AI Bots to Negotiate*. Retrieved from Facebook Engineering, https://engineering.fb.com/ml-applications/deal-or-no-deal-training-ai-bots-to-negotiate/.

Li Ka-shing (2006, Dec. 29). Thoughts Of Li Ka-Shing. *Forbes*. Retrieved from www.forbes.com/2006/12/29/li-ka-shing-biz-cx_tf_vk_1229qanda.html#4d708576f792.

Liberman, V., Samuels, S. M., & Ross, L. (2004). The Name of the Game: Predictive Power of Reputations versus Situational Labels in Determining Prisoner's Dilemma Game Moves. *Personality and Social Psychology Bulletin*, 30(9), 1175–85. https://doi.org/10.1177/0146167204264004.

Lilienfeld, S. O. (2018, May 9). 5 Psychology Terms You're Probably Misusing; Interviewer: S. J. Dubner. *The Freakonomics Radio Show* (ep. 334). Retrieved from https://freakonomics.com/podcast/misused-psychology-terms/.

Lilienfeld, S. O., Sauvigné, K. C., Lynn, S. J., Cautin, R. L., Latzman, R. D., & Waldman, I. D. (2015). Fifty Psychological and Psychiatric Terms to Avoid: A List of Inaccurate, Misleading, Misused, Ambiguous, and Logically Confused Words and Phrases. *Frontiers in Psychology*, 6, 1–15. https://doi.org/10.3389/fpsyg.2015.01100.

Lindholst, M. (2015). *Complex Business Negotiation: Understanding Preparation and Planning*. PhD thesis, Copenhagen Business School.

Loewenstein, G., Issacharoff, S., Camerer, C., & Babcock, L. (1993). Self-Serving Assessments of Fairness and Pretrial Bargaining. *The Journal of Legal Studies*, 22(1), 135–59.

Loewenstein, J. & Thompson, L. (2006). Learning to Negotiate: Novice and Experienced Negotiators. In L. Thompson (ed.), *Negotiation Theory and*

Research, pp. 77–98. New York: Psychology Press.

Londono, E. & Motoko, R. (2018, Mar. 8). U.S. Allies Sign Sweeping Trade Deal in Challenge to Trump. *The New York Times*. Retrieved from www.nytimes.com/2018/03/08/world/asia/us-trump-tpp-signed.html.

Lord, C. G., Ross, L., & Lepper, M. R. (1979). Biased Assimilation and Attitude Polarization: The Effects of Prior Theories on Subsequently Considered Evidence. *Journal of Personality and Social Psychology*, 37(11), 2098–109.

Loschelder, D. D., Stuppi, J., & Trötschel, R. (2013). "€14,875?!": Precision Boosts the Anchoring Potency of First Offers. *Social Psychological and Personality Science*, 5(4), 491–9.

Low, P., Panksepp, J., Reiss, D., Edelman, D., Van Swinderen, B. & Koch, C. (2012). *The Cambridge Declaration on Consciousness*. Declaration signed at the Francis Crick Memorial Conference, July 7. Retrieved from http://fcmconference.org/img/Cambridge ? DeclarationOnConsciousness.pdf.

Macioszek, H.-G. (2005). *Chruschtschows dritter Schuh. Anregungen für geschäftliche Verhandlungen*. Hamburg: Ulysses.

Macnamara, B. N., Hambrick, D. Z., & Oswald, F. L. (2014). Deliberate Practice and Performance in Music, Games, Sports, Education, and Professions: A Meta-Analysis. *Psychological Science*, 25(8), 1608–18.

Macnamara, B. N. & Maitra, M. (2019). The Role of Deliberate Practice in Expert Performance: Revisiting Ericsson, Krampe & Tesch-Römer (1993). *The Royal Society Open Science*, 6(8), 1–19. https://doi.org/10.1098/rsos.190327.

Macnamara, B. N., Moreau, D., & Hambrick, D. Z. (2016). The Relationship Between Deliberate Practice and Performance in Sports: A Meta-Analysis. *Perspectives on Psychological Science*, 11(3), 333–50.

Macron, E. (2018, Jan. 20). *"Special" Deal Possible for UK, But It Can't "Cherry-Pick" Rules; Interviewer: A. Marr*. BBC. Retrieved from www.bbc.com/news/uk-politics-42757026.

Maier, N. R. (1933). An Aspect of Human Reasoning. *British Journal of Psychology*, 24(2), 144–55.

Malhotra, D. (2016). A Definitive Guide to the Brexit Negotiations. *Harvard Business Review*. Retrieved from https://hbr.org/2016/08/a-definitive-guide-to-the-brexit-negotiations.

Malone, T. W. (2018). *Superminds: The Surprising Power of People and Computers Thinking Together*. New York: Little, Brown and Company.

Malone, T. W. (2019, Aug. 31). *Open Phones with Thomas Malone; Interviewer: P. Slen*. C-SPAN, 19th Annual National Book Festival in Washington, DC. Retrieved from www.c-span.org/video/?463458-19/open-phones-thomas-malone&event=463458.

Mamede, S. & Schmidt, H. G. (2017). Reflection in Medical Diagnosis: A Literature Review. *Health Professions Education*, 3(1), 15–25.

Maney, K. (2017, July 5). How Facebook's AI Bots Learned Their Own Language and How to Lie. *Newsweek Magazine*. Retrieved from www.newsweek.com/2017/08/18/ai-facebook-artificial-intelligence-machine-learning-robots-robotics-646944.html.

Mann, C. (2019). *The Wizard and the Prophet. Two Remarkable Scientists and Their Dueling Visions to Shape Tomorrow's World.* New York: Alfred A. Knopf.

Mann, T. (1955). *Confessions of Felix Krull. Confidence Man. The Early Years.* New York: Alfred A. Knopf.

Margalit, A. (2011). *Über Kompromisse – und faule Kompromisse.* Berlin: Suhrkamp.

Marks, K. H., Slee, R. T., Blees, C. W., & Nall, M. R. (2012). *Middle Market M & A: Handbook for Investment Banking and Business Consulting.* Hoboken, NJ: John Wiley & Sons, Inc.

Marsden, G. J. & Siedel, G. J. (2017). The Duty to Negotiate in Good Faith: Are BATNA Strategies Legal? *Berkeley Business Law Journal*, 14, 127–56.

Martin, A. & Santos, L. R. (2014). The Origins of Belief Representation: Monkeys Fail to Automatically Represent Others' Beliefs. *Cognition*, 130(3), 300–8.

Maslow, A. H. (1966). *The Psychology of Science: A Reconnaissance.* New York: Harper & Row.

Max Planck Institute. (2018). *Navigating Our Thoughts: Fundamental Principles Of Thinking* [Press release]. Retrieved from www.mpg.de/12480215/navigating-our-thoughts-fundamental-principles-of-thinking?c=2249.

Maxwell, V. (2012 [updated Jan. 2018]). The Dying Art of Bargaining in Istanbul's Grand Bazaar. *Lonely Planet.* Retrieved from www.lonelyplanet.com/articles/the-dying-art-of-bargaining-in-istanbuls-grand-bazaar.

Mayer, B. (2015). *The Conflict Paradox: Seven Dilemmas at the Core of Disputes.* San Francisco, CA: Jossey-Bass and The American Bar Association.

McAdams, D. (2014). *Game-Changer: Game Theory and the Art of Transforming Strategic Situations.* New York: W.W. Norton & Company, Inc.

McAdams, R. H. (2008). Beyond the Prisoner's Dilemma: Coordination, Game Theory and the Law. *John M. Olin Law & Economics Working Paper, No. 437* (2nd series). The University of Chicago Law School.

McCloud, S. (1993). *Understanding Comics: The Invisible Art.* New York: HarperCollins.

McConigal, K. (2016). *The Upside of Stress: Why Stress Is Good for You, and How to Get Good at It* (reprint ed.). New York: Avery.

McEachrane, M. (2009). Emotion, Meaning, and Appraisal Theory. *Theory & Psychology*, 19(1), 33–53.

McGilchrist, I. (2019). *The Master and His Emissary. The Divided Brain and the Making of the Western World.* New Haven, CT and London, England: Yale University Press.

McKeown, T. (2013). Fisher and Ury's "Getting to Yes": A Critique: The Shortcomings of the Principled Bargaining Model. http://dx.doi.org/10.2139/ssrn.3054357.

McManus, I. C., Freegard, M., Moore, J., & Rawles, R. (2010). Science in the Making: Right Hand, Left Hand. II: The Duck–Rabbit Figure. *Laterality*, 15(1–2), 166–85.

Meissner, C. A. & Brigham, J. C. (2001). Thirty Years of Investigating the Own-Race Bias in Memory for Faces: A Meta-Analytic Review. *Psychology, Public Policy, and Law*, 7(1), 3–35. https://doi.org/10.1037/1076-8971.7.1.3.

Melo, M., Scarpin, D. J., Amaro Jr, E., Passos, R. B., Sato, J. R., Friston, K. J., & Price, C. J. (2011). How Doctors Generate Diagnostic Hypotheses: A Study of Radiological Diagnosis with Functional Magnetic Resonance Imaging. *PLoS ONE*, 6(12), e28752.

Menkel-Meadow, C. J., Love, L. P., & Schneider, A. K. (2006). *Mediation: Practice, Policy, and Ethics*. New York: Aspen Publishers.

Mercier, H. & Sperber, D. (2017). *The Enigma of Reason. A New Theory of Human Understanding*. London: Allen Lane, Penguin Books.

Merkel, A. (2019a). *Speech by Dr Angela Merkel, Chancellor of the Federal Republic of Germany, on the occasion of the 368th Harvard University Commencement, Cambridge, MA* [Press release]. Retrieved from www.bundeskanzlerin.de/bkin-en/news/speech-by-dr-angela-merkel-chancellor-of-the-federal-republic-of-germany-on-the-occasion-of-the-368th-harvard-university-commencement-on-may-30-2019-in-cambridge-ma-1634366.

Merkel, A. (2019b). *Speech by Chancellor Merkel at the 55th Munich Security Conference on February 16* [Press release]. Retrieved from www.bundesregierung.de/breg-en/news/speech-by-federal-chancellor-dr-angela-merkel-on-16-february-2019-at-the-55th-munich-security-conference-1582318.

Miller, E. L. (2008). *Mergers and Acquisitions. A Step-by-Step Legal and Practical Guide*. Hoboken, NJ: John Wiley & Sons, Inc.

Miltenberger, R. G. & Crosland, K. A. (2014). Parenting. In F. K. McSweeney & E. S. Murphy (eds.), *The Wiley Blackwell Handbook of Operant and Classical Conditioning*, pp. 509–31. Chichester, West Sussex: John Wiley & Sons, Ltd.

Mischel, W. (2015). *The Marshmallow Test. Understanding Self-Control and How to Master It*. London: Corgi Books.

Mnookin, R. H. & Kornhauser, L. (1979). Bargaining in the Shadow of the Law: The Case of Divorce. *Yale Law Journal*, 8(5), 950–97.

Monnet, J. (2015). *Memoirs*. London: Third Millennium, Profile Books Ltd.

Monyer, H. & Gessmann, M. (2017). *Das geniale Gedächtnis*. Munich: Penguin Verlag.

Moore, B. R. & Stuttard, S. (1979). Dr. Guthrie and Felis domesticus or: Tripping Over the Cat. *Science*, 205 (4410), 1031–3.

Moore, D. A. (2004). Deadline Pressure: Use It to Your Advantage. *Negotiation*, 7(8), 3–5. Retrieved from http://search.ebscohost.com/login.aspx?direct=true&db=bth&AN=14016783&site=ehost-live&scope=site.

Moore, R. (1966). *Niels Bohr: The Man, His Science, & the World They Changed*: New York: Alfred A. Knopf.

Mösing, A. & Steiner, C. (2013). *Im Herzen des Handels: Der Basar von Istanbul*.

Bayerischer Rundfunk [Bavarian Public Broadcasting], radioWissen. Retrieved from www.br.de/radio/bayern2/programmkalender/ausstrahlung-33600.html.

Moss, D. A. (2017). *Democracy. A Case Study*. Cambridge, MA: The Belknap Press of Harvard University Press.

Movius, H. & Susskind, L. (2009). *Built to Win. Creating a World-Class Negotiating Organization*. Boston, MA: Harvard Business Press.

Mukherjee, S. (2017, Apr. 3). A.I. versus M.D. What Happens when Diagnosis is Automated? *The New Yorker*. Retrieved from www.newyorker.com/magazine/2017/04/03/ai-versus-md.

Murakami, H. (2009). *What I Talk About When I Talk About Running*. London: Vintage.

Murnighan, J. K. (1991). *The Dynamics of Bargaining Games*. Englewood Cliffs, NJ: Prentice Hall.

Murnighan, J. K. (2015). Negotiation and Game Theory. Professor J. Keith Murnighan in conversation with Georg Berkel. *Zeitschrift für Konfliktmanagement*, 5, 164–5.

Murphy, S. T. & Zajonc, R. B. (1993). Affect, Cognition, and Awareness: Affective Priming with Optimal and Suboptimal Stimulus Exposures. *Journal of Personality and Social Psychology*, 64 (5), 723–9.

Nadler, J., Thompson, L., & Boven, L. V. (2003). Learning Negotiation Skills: Four Models of Knowledge Creation and Transfer. *Management Science*, 49 (4), 529–40.

Nakamura, D. & Parker, A. (2017, Nov. 11). Trump's "America first" looks more and more like "America alone". *The Washington Post*. Retrieved from www.washingtonpost.com/politics/trumps-america-first-looks-more-and-more-like-america-alone/2017/11/11/5cffa150-c666-11e7-aae0-cb18a8c29c65_story.htm.

Nalebuff, B. J. & Brandenburger, A. M. (2002). *Co-opetition*. London: Profile Books Ltd.

Neale, M. A. & Lys, T. Z. (2015). *Getting (More of) What You Want. How the Secrets of Economics and Psychology Can Help You Negotiate Anything, in Business and in Life*. New York: Basic Books.

Newport, C. (2016). *Deep Work. Rules for Focused Success in a Distracted World*. New York, Boston MA: Grand Central Publishing.

Nisbett, R. E. (2015). *Mindware. Tools for Smart Thinking*. New York: Farrar, Straus and Giroux.

Nisbett, R. E. & Masuda, T. (2003). Culture and Point of View. *Proceedings of the National Academy of Sciences*, 100(19), 11163–70.

Nisbett, R. E., Peng, K., Choi, I., & Norenzayan, A. (2001). Culture and Systems of Thought: Holistic versus Analytic Cognition. *Psychological Review*, 108(2), 291–310.

North, A. C., Hargreaves, D. J., & McKendrick, J. (1999). The Influence of In-Store Music on Wine Selections. *Journal of Applied Psychology*, 84(2), 271–6.

Novella, S. (2012). *Your Deceptive Mind: A Scientific Guide to Critical Thinking Skills – Course Guidebook*, Course No. 9344. Chantilly, VA: The Teaching Company.

Nutt, P. C. (2002). *Why Decisions Fail: Avoiding the Blunders and Traps That Lead to Debacles*. San Francisco: Berrett-Koehler.

O'Connor, K. M., Arnold, J. A., & Maurizio, A. M. (2010). The Prospect of Negotiating: Stress, Cognitive Appraisal, and Performance. *Journal of Experimental Social Psychology*, 46(5), 729–35.

Osborne, M. J. & Rubinstein, A. (1994). *A Course in Game Theory*. Cambridge, MA: The MIT Press.

Packer, G. (2014, Dec. 1). The Quiet German. The Astonishing Rise of Angela Merkel, the Most Powerful Woman in the World. *The New Yorker*. Retrieved from www.newyorker.com/magazine/2014/12/01/quiet-german.

Pape, R. (2019, Oct. 30). Speak Softly and Carry Big Data; Interviewer: S. J. Dubner. *The Freakonomics Radio Show* (ep. 395). Retrieved from https://freakonomics.com/podcast/chicago-live/.

Parker Follett, M. (1994 [1925]). Constructive Conflict. In P. Graham (ed.), *Mary Parker Follett – Prophet of Management: A Celebration of Writings from the 1920s*. Washington DC: Beard Books.

Pasupathi, M. (2012). *How We Learn. Course Guidebook*, Course No. 1691. Chantilly, VA: The Teaching Company.

Paul, L. A. (2014a). *Transformative Experience*. Oxford University Press.

Paul, L. A. (2014b). *Vampires and Life Decisions*. OUPblog. Retrieved from https://blog.oup.com/2014/11/vampires-transformative-experience/.

Pedersen, P. J. & Pytlikova, M. (2008). *EU Enlargement: Migration Flows from Central and Eastern Europe into the Nordic Countries – Exploiting a natural experiment*. Working Paper, Department of Economics, Aarhus School of Business, University of Aarhus.

Peng, K. & Nisbett, R. E. (1999). Culture, Dialectics, and Reasoning about Contradiction. *American Psychologist*, 54(9), 741–54.

Peppet, S. R. & Moffitt, M. L. (2006). Learning How to Learn to Negotiate. In C. Honeyman & A. K. Schneider, *The Negotiator's Fieldbook: The Desk Reference for the Experienced Negotiator*, pp. 615–26. Washington DC: American Bar Association, Section of Dispute Resolution.

Peters, S. (2012). *The Mind Management. Programme for Confidence, Success and Happiness*. London: Vermilion.

Philippe, J. M. (2004). French and American Approaches to Contract Formation and Enforceability: A Comparative Perspective. *Tulsa Journal of Comparative & International Law*, 12 (2), 357–99.

Pinker, S. (2012). *The Better Angels of our Nature. Why Violence has Declined*. New York: Penguin Books.

Plato. (1967). *Plato in Twelve Volumes*, vol. 3 (W. R. M. Lamb, trans.). Cambridge, MA: Harvard University Press; London: William Heinemann Ltd. Retrieved from www.perseus.tufts.edu/hopper/text?doc=Perseus%3Atext%3A1999.01.0178%3Atext%3DMeno%3Apage%3D85.

Plato (1976). *The Portable Plato* (S. Buchanan, ed.). New York: The Viking Press.

Plato (2017). *Apology* (C. Emlyn-Jones & W. Preddy, eds. and trans.). Cambridge, MA and London: Harvard University Press, Loeb Classical Library.

Plett Usher, B. (2018, Apr. 27). *Merkel Lobbies Trump on Trade and Iran.* BBC. Retrieved from www.bbc.com/news/world-us-canada-43925422.

Plotnik, J. M., Lair, R., Suphachoksahakun, W., & De Waal, F. B. (2011). Elephants Know when They Need a Helping Trunk in a Cooperative Task. *Proceedings of the National Academy of Sciences*, 108 (12), 5116–21.

Polk, T. A. (2018). *The Learning Brain – Coursebook*, Course No. 1569. Chantilly, VA: The Teaching Company.

PON. (2012, Dec. 5). Are You an Overconfident Negotiator? *Business Negotiations.* Retrieved from www.pon.harvard.edu/daily/business-negotiations/are-you-an-overconfident-negotiator/.

Popper, K. (2000). *In Search of a Better World: Lectures and Essays from Thirty Years.* London and New York: Routledge.

Posavac, S. S., Kardes, F. R., & Brakus, J. J. (2010). Focus Induced Tunnel Vision in Managerial Judgment and Decision Making: The Peril and the Antidote. *Organizational Behavior and Human Decision Processes*, 113(2), 102–11.

Post, J. (2019). *Dangerous Charisma. The Political Psychology of Donald Trump and His Followers.* New York: Pegasus Books.

Povaly, S. (2007). *Private Equity Exits: Divestment Process Management for Leveraged Buyouts.* Berlin Heidelberg: Springer Science & Business Media.

Press, W. H. & Dyson, F. J. (2012). Iterated Prisoner's Dilemma Contains Strategies that Dominate any Evolutionary Opponent. *Proceedings of the National Academy of Sciences*, 109(26), 10409–13.

Pruitt, D. G. (1981). *Negotiation Behavior.* New York: Academic Press.

Pruitt, D. G. & Rubin, J. Z. (1986). *Social Conflict. Escalation, Stalemate, and Settlement.* New York: Random House.

Raiffa, H. (1982). *The Art and Science of Negotiation.* Cambridge, MA: The Belknap Press of Harvard University Press.

Raiffa, H., Richardson, J., & Metcalfe, D. (2002). *Negotiation Analysis. The Science and Art of Collaborative Decision Making.* Cambridge, MA: The Belknap Press of Harvard University Press.

Reyes, V. M. (2015). The False Promise of Principled Negotiations. *Journal of Global Initiatives: Policy, Pedagogy, Perspective*, 9(2), 3–18.

Rilling, J. K., Gutman, D. A., Zeh, T. R., Pagnoni, G., Berns, G. S., & Kilts, C. D. (2002). A Neural Basis for Social Cooperation. *Neuron*, 35(2), 395–405.

Robson, D. (2019). *The Intelligence Trap. Why Smart People Make Stupid Mistakes – and How to Make Wiser Decisions.* London: Hodder & Stoughton.

Roediger, H. L. & McDermott, K. B. (1995). Creating False Memories: Remembering

Words not Presented in Lists. *Journal of Experimental Psychology: Learning, Memory, and Cognition*, 21(4), 803–14.

Rogers, C. R. (1967 [2004]). *On Becoming a Person. A Therapist's View of Psychotherapy*. Lancaster: Constable & Robinson Ltd.

Rogers, I. (2018, Dec. 13). *Brexit. What's Next?* Paper presented at the University of Liverpool's Heseltine Institute for Public Policy, Practice and Place.

Rogers, I. (2019). *9 Lessons in Brexit*. London: Short Books.

Rosen, D. (2016). *99 Negotiation Strategies. Tips, Tactics & Techniques Used by Wall Street's Toughest Dealmakers*. New York: Ross & Rubin.

Ross, L. & Stillinger, C. (1991). Barriers to Conflict Resolution. *Negotiation Journal*, 7(4), 389–404.

Rozental, S. (ed.) (1967). *Niels Bohr: His Life and Work as Seen by His Friends and Colleagues*. Amsterdam: Elsevier.

Russett, B. & Oneal, J. R. (2001). *Triangulating Peace: Democracy, Interdependence, and International Organizations*. New York: W.W. Norton & Company, Inc.

Ryan, R. M. & Deci, E. L. (2000). Self-Determination Theory and the Facilitation of Intrinsic Motivation, Social Development, and Well-Being. *American Psychologist*, 55(1), 68-78.

Ryle, G. (1945). Knowing How and Knowing That: The Presidential Address. *Proceedings of the Aristotelian Society*, 46 (1945–1946), 1–16.

Sachs, O. (2017). *The River of Consciousness*. New York: Picador.

Sacks, J. (2016). *Not in God's Name. Confronting Religious Violence*. Jerusalem: Maggid.

Sadler-Smith, E. (2015). Wallas' Four-Stage Model of the Creative Process: More than Meets the Eye? *Creativity Research Journal*, 27(4), 342–52.

Safina, C. (2015). *Beyond Words. What Animals Think and Feel*. New York: Picador.

Sagy, S. & Mana, A. (2017). The Relevance of Salutogenesis to Social Issues Besides Health: The Case of Sense of Coherence and Intergroup Relations. In M. B. Mittelmark, S. Sagy, M. Eriksson, G. F. Bauer, J. M. Pelikan, B. Lindström, & G. A. Espnes (eds.), *The Handbook of Salutogenesis*, pp. 77–81. Switzerland: Springer.

Salacuse, J. W. (2017). *Real Leaders Negotiate! Gaining, Using, and Keeping the Power to Lead Through Negotiation*. New York: Palgrave Macmillan.

Sapolsky, R. M. (2017). *Behave: The Biology of Humans at Our Best and Worst*. London: Vintage.

Saulton, A., Bülthoff, H. H., De La Rosa, S., & Dodds, T. J. (2017). Cultural Differences in Room Size Perception. *PLoS ONE*, 12 (4), e0176115.

Schäfer, A. (writer and director). (2012). *John Irving und wie er die Welt sieht*. Florianfilm GmbH. Retrieved from www.wfilm.de/john-irving-und-wie-er-die-welt-sieht/inhalt/.

Schelling, T. C. (1980 [1960]). *The Strategy of Conflict*. Cambridge, MA: Harvard University Press.

Schelling, T. C. (1987). Ethics, Law, and the Exercise of Self-Command. In R. John

& S. M. McMurrin (eds.), *Liberty, Equality, and Law: Selected Tanner Lectures on Moral Philosophy*. Salt Lake City, UT: University of Utah Press. Retrieved from https://tannerlectures.utah.edu/_documents/a-to-z/s/schelling83.pdf.

Schmelz, M., Duguid, S., Bohn, M., & Völter, C. J. (2017). Cooperative Problem Solving in Giant Otters (Pteronura Brasiliensis) and Asian Small-Clawed Otters (Aonyx Cinerea). *Animal Cognition*, 20(6), 1107–14.

Schmidt, S. & Eisend, M. (2015). Advertising Repetition: A Meta-Analysis on Effective Frequency in Advertising. *Journal of Advertising*, 44(4), 415–28.

Schneider, A. K. (2002). Shattering Negotiation Myths: Empirical Evidence on the Effectiveness of Negotiation Style. *Harvard Negotiation Law Review*, 7, 143–233.

Schneider, C. J. (2009). *Conflict, Negotiation and European Union Enlargement*. Cambridge University Press.

Schock, K. R. (2013). Getting to Yes: Remembering Roger Fisher. *Arbitration Law Review*, 5(1), 422–38.

Schonfield, E. (2008). *Art and its Uses in Thomas Mann's Felix Krull*, Bithell Series of Dissertations, 32. Cambridge, UK: MHRA.

Schott. (2016). *SCHOTT to close CSP deal with Rioglass Solar* [Press release]. Retrieved from www.schott.com/english/news/press.html?NID=com4944.

Schroth, H. A. (2015). *Negotiations & Influence Workshop*. University of California at Berkeley, Haas School of Business. Retrieved from https://executive.berkeley.edu/programs/negotiation-and-influence.

Schuh, C., Raudabaugh, J. L., Kromoser, R., Strohmer, M. F., Triplat, A. T., & Pearce, J. (2017). *The Purchasing Chessboard: 64 Methods to Reduce Costs and Increase Value with Suppliers*. New York: Springer.

Schultz, W. (1998). Predictive Reward Signal of Dopamine Neurons. *Journal of Neurophysiology*, 80(1), 1–27.

Schwartz, B. (2004). *The Paradox of Choice: Why More Is Less*. New York: Harper Perennial.

Shackle, S. (2018, July 24). Should We Treat Crime as Something to be Cured Rather than Punished? Scotland's Police Force has Adopted a Public Health Model to Tackle Violence. *The Guardian*. Retrieved from www.theguardian.com/news/2018/jul/24/violent-crime-cured-rather-than-punished-scottish-violence-reduction-unit.

Sharot, T. (2017). *The Influential Mind. What the Brain Reveals About Our Power to Change Others*. London: Little, Brown and Company.

Shaw, J. & Porter, S. (2015). Constructing Rich False Memories of Committing Crime. *Psychological Science*, 26(3), 291–301. https://doi.org/10.1177%2F0956797614562862.

Shell, G. R. (2001). Bargaining Styles and Negotiation. *Negotiation Journal*, 17 (April), 155–74.

Shell, G. R. (2006). *Bargaining for Advantage: Negotiation Strategies for Reasonable People* (2nd ed.). New York: Penguin Books.

Shultz, G. P. (2018, Oct. 25). George Shultz: We Must Preserve this Nuclear Treaty.

The New York Times. Retrieved from www.nytimes.com/2018/10/25/opinion/george-shultz-nuclear-treaty.html.

Siegel, R. D. (2010). *The Mindfulness Solution: Everyday Practices for Everyday Problems*. New York, London: Guilford Press.

Siemens (2015). *Siemens Awarded Record Energy Orders that Will Boost Egypt's Power Generation by 50%* [Press release]. Retrieved from https://press.siemens.com/middleeast/en/pressrelease/siemens-awarded-record-energy-orders-will-boost-egypts-power-generation-50.

SimanTov-Nachlieli, I., Moran, S., & Har-Vardi, L. (2017). The Advantage of Having an Honest Reputation: The "Big Two" Agency and Communion Dimensions in Negotiations. *Academy of Management Proceedings*, 2017(1), 15110.

Simon, F. (2002). Paradoxien in der Psychologie. In R. Hagenbüchle & P. Geyer (eds.), *Das Paradox. Eine Herausforderung des abendländischen Denkens*, pp. 71–88. Würzburg: Königshausen & Neumann.

Simons, D. J. & Chabris, C. F. (1999). Gorillas in Our Midst: Sustained Inattentional Blindness for Dynamic Events. *Perception*, 28(9), 1059–74.

Simons, J. H. (2014). *Mathematics, Common Sense and Good Luck*. The American Mathematical Society and the Mathematical Sciences Research Institute 2014 AMS Einstein Public Lecture in Mathematics. San Francisco State University. Retrieved from www.youtube.com/watch?v=Tj1NyJHLvWA.

Sisario, B. (2015, June 21). Taylor Swift Criticism Spurs Apple to Change Royalties Policy. *The New York Times*. Retrieved from https://www.nytimes.com/2015/06/22/business/media/taylor-swift-criticizes-apples-terms-for-streaming-music-service.html.

Skyrms, B. (2001). *The Stag Hunt*. Paper presented at the Proceedings and Addresses of the American Philosophical Association.

Sloman, S. & Fernbach, P. (2017). *The Knowledge Illusion. Why We Never Think Alone*. New York: Penguin Random House.

Smith, J. (2019, June 12). If Trump Wants to Take On China, He Needs Allies. And he should start with Europe. *The New York Times*. Retrieved from www.nytimes.com/2019/06/12/opinion/china-europe-trump.html.

Solís, M. (2017). *'America First' is a Losing Strategy on Trade*. Brookings. Retrieved from www.brookings.edu/blog/order-from-chaos/2017/10/24/america-first-is-a-losing-strategy-on-trade/.

Spaniel, W. (2014). *Game Theory 101: Bargaining*. Leipzig: CreateSpace Independent Publishing Platform.

Sparrow, B., Liu, J., & Wegner, D. M. (2011). Google Effects on Memory: Cognitive Consequences of Having Information at Our Fingertips. *Science*, 333 (6043), 776–78.

Spiegel Economy. (2018). *Zulieferstreit: Prevent kauft wichtige Gießerei – und erhöht Preise für VW offenbar um das Zehnfache*. Retrieved from www.spiegel.de/wirtschaft/unternehmen/volkswagen-zulieferrebell-preventerhoeht-preise-um-das-zehnfache-a-1210233.html.

Spitzer, M. (2002). *Lernen: Gehirnforschung und Schule des Lebens*. Heidelberg: Spektrum Akad. Verlag.

Standing, L. (1973). Learning 10000 Pictures. *The Quarterly Journal of Experimental Psychology*, 25(2), 207–22.

Stanovich, K. E. (1999). *Who is Rational? Studies of Individual Differences in Reasoning*. New York and London: Psychology Press.

Stanovich, K. E. (2009). Distinguishing the Reflective, Algorithmic, and Autonomous Minds: Is it Time for a Tri-Process Theory? In J. S. B. T. Evans & K. Frankish (eds.), *In Two Minds: Dual Processes and Beyond*, pp. 55–88. Oxford University Press.

Stanovich, K. E. (2011). *Rationality & the Reflective Mind*. Oxford University Press.

Stanovich, K. E. (2018). Miserliness in Human Cognition: The Interaction of Detection, Override and Mindware. *Thinking & Reasoning*, 24(4), 423–44. https://doi.org/10.1080/13546783.2018.1459314.

Stearns Johnson, J. (2018, June 7). How Artful Is Trump's Dealmaking? Interviewer: S. Horsley. *Morning Edition*, NPR. Retrieved from www.npr.org/2018/06/07/617677566/how-artful-is-trumps-dealmaking.

Steinberg, G. (2011, Dec. 9). *From Ron Arad to Gilad Shalit: Germany's Role in the Middle Eastern Prisoner Exchanges*. American Institute for Contemporary German Studies at Johns Hopkins University. Retrieved from www.aicgs.org/2011/12/from-ron-arad-to-gilad-shalit-germanys-role-in-the-middle-eastern-prisoner-exchanges/.

Stevens, J. R. & Hauser, M. D. (2004). Why Be Nice? Psychological Constraints on the Evolution of Cooperation. *Trends in Cognitive Sciences*, 8(2), 60–5.

Stone, D. & Heen, S. (2015). *Thanks for the Feedback. The Science and Art of Receiving Feedback Well*. New York: Penguin Books.

Strohmetz, D. B., Rind, B., Fisher, R., & Lynn, M. (2002). Sweetening the Till: The Use of Candy to Increase Restaurant Tipping. *Journal of Applied Social Psychology*, 32(2), 300–9.

Subramanian, G. (2010). *Negotiauctions. Deal Making Strategies for a Competitive Marketplace*. New York: W. W. Norton & Company, Inc.

Sullivan, A. (2018, Apr. 4). The Strange Tale of Volkswagen and its Bosnian Supplier. *Deutsche Welle*. Retrieved from www.dw.com/en/the-strange-tale-of-volkswagen-and-its-bosnian-supplier/a-43251412.

Susskind, L. (2014). *Good for You, Great for Me. Finding the Trading Zone and Winning at Win–Win Negotiation*. New York: Public Affairs.

Swift, T. (2015). *Taylor Swift's Letter to Apple Inc.* [Press release]. Retrieved from www.forbes.com/sites/hughmcintyre/2015/06/21/taylor-swifts-letter-to-apple-stern-polite-and-necessary/#d9c86a9113d4.

Taylor, P. (2013). *The Thirty-Six Stratagems: A Modern Interpretation Of A Strategy Classic*. Oxford: Infinite Ideas Limited.

Tehrani, N. & Miller, D. (2018). The Impact of Artificial Intelligence on Cancer. *Global*

Journal of Advanced Research, 5(1), 1–3.

Teitelman, R. (2019, Mar. 22). Bayer's Deal for Monsanto Looked Like a Winer. Now it looks like a Lesson in How Not to Do M&A. *Barron's*. Retrieved from www.barrons.com/articles/bayers-acquisition-of-monsanto-how-not-to-do-m-a-51553296373.

ten Kate, G. (2017). *Obscure Retail Buying Groups Mapped* [Press release]. Centre for Research on Multinational Corporations (SOMO), Amsterdam. Retrieved from www.somo.nl/obscure-retail-buying-groups-mapped/.

Tendler, A. & Wagner, S. (2015). Different Types of Theta Rhythmicity Are Induced by Social and Fearful Stimuli in a Network Associated with Social Memory. *Elife*, 4, e03614. Retrieved from https://cdn.elifesciences.org/articles/03614/elife-03614-v2.pdf.

Thaler, R. H. (2015). *Misbehaving. The Making of Behavioral Economics*. London: Penguin Books.

Thaler, R. H. & Sunstein, C. R. (2009). *Nudge. Improving Decisions about Health, Wealth and Happiness*. London: Penguin Books.

The Economist (2017, July 22). *The Six Flavours of Brexit*. Retrieved from www.economist.com/britain/2017/07/22/the-six-flavours-of-brexit.

The Economist (2019, Oct. 24). *IPOs are a Racket. But Try Finding Something Better*. Retrieved from www.economist.com/business/2019/10/24/ipos-are-a-racket-but-try-finding-something-better.

Thibodeau, P. H. & Boroditsky, L. (2011). Metaphors We Think With: The Role of Metaphor in Reasoning. *PLoS ONE*, 6 (2), e16782. https://doi.org/10.1371/journal.pone.0016782.

Thomas, K. W. (1992). Conflict and Conflict Management: Reflections and Update. *Journal of Organizational Behavior*, 13(3), 265–74.

Thompson, L. (2008). *The Truth About Negotiations*. Harlow, Essex: Pearson Prentice Hall Business.

Thompson, L. (2014). *The Mind and Heart of the Negotiator* (5th ed.). London: Pearson.

Thompson, L. & DeHarpport, T. (1994). Social Judgment, Feedback, and Interpersonal Learning in Negotiation. *Organizational Behavior and Human Decision Processes*, 58(3), 327–45.

Thompson, L. & Hrebec, D. (1996). Lose–Lose Agreements in Interdependent Decision Making. *Psychological Bulletin*, 120(3), 396–409.

Thompson, L. L. & Lucas, B. J. (eds.). (2014). *Judgmental Biases in Conflict Resolution and How to Overcome Them*. San Francisco, CA: Jossey-Bass.

Tirrell, M. (2018). *A US Drugmaker Offers to Cure Rare Blindness for $850,000*. CNBC. Retrieved from www.cnbc.com/2018/01/03/spark-therapeutics-luxturna-gene-therapy-will-cost-about-850000.html.

Trivers, R. L. (1971). The Evolution of Reciprocal Altruism. *The Quarterly Review of Biology*, 46(1), 35–57. https://doi.org/10.1086/406755.

Trötschel, R., Loschelder, D. D., Höhne, B. P., & Majer, J. M. (2015). Procedural Frames in Negotiations: How Offering My Resources versus Requesting Yours Impacts Perception, Behavior, and

Outcomes. *Journal of Personality and Social Psychology*, 108(3), 417–35.

Trump, D. J. (2019, July 25). Memorandum Of Telephone Conversation. Subject: Telephone Conversation with President Zelensky of Ukraine. Participants: President Zelensky of Ukraine. Retrieved from www.whitehouse.gov/wp-content/uploads/2019/09/Unclassified09.2019.pdf.

Tsay, C. J. & Bazerman, M. H. (2009). A Decision-Making Perspective to Negotiation: A Review of the Past and a Look to the Future. *Negotiation Journal*, 25(4), 467–80.

Turnwald, B. P., Bertoldo, J. D., Perry, M. A. [and nine others]. (2019). Increasing Vegetable Intake by Emphasizing Tasty and Enjoyable Attributes: A Randomized Controlled Multisite Intervention for Taste-Focused Labeling. *Psychological Science*, 30(11), 1603–15. https://doi.org/10.1177/0956797619872191.

Tversky, A. & Kahneman, D. (1974). Judgment under Uncertainty: Heuristics and Biases. *Science*, 185(4157), 1124–31. https://doi.org/10.1126/science.185.4157.1124.

Tversky, A. and Kahneman, D. (1986). Rational Choice and the Framing of Decisions. *Journal of Business*, 59, 251–78.

Twain, M. (1897). *Following the Equator: A Journey Around the World*. Hartford, CT: American Publishing Company.

Ury, W. L. (2007 [1993]). *Getting Past No. Negotiating in Difficult Situations* (reissued revised ed.). New York: Bantam Dell.

Ury, W. L. (2015). *Getting to Yes with Yourself (and Other Worthy Opponents)*. New York: HarperCollins.

Ury, W. L., Brett, J. M., & Goldberg, S. B. (1993). *Getting Disputes Resolved. Designing Systems to Cut the Costs of Conflict*. Cambridge, MA: PON Books, Harvard Law School.

van der Wal, S. & ten Kate, G. (2017). *Eyes on the Price: International Supermarket Buying Groups in Europe*. SOMO, Amsterdam. Retrieved from www.somo.nl/international-supermarket-buying-groups-in-europe/.

Voeth, M., Herbst, U., Haggenmüller, S., & Weber, M.-C. (2020). Wie verhandeln deutsche Manager? *Zeitschrift für Konfliktmanagement*, February.

von Hellfeld, M. & Chase, J. (2010). *German Reunification: How Kohl and Gorbachev sealed the deal on German reunification*. DW. Retrieved from www.dw.com/en/how-kohl-and-gorbachev-sealed-the-deal-on-german-reunification/a-5788998.

von Neumann, J. (1928). Zur Theorie der Gesellschaftsspiele. *Mathematische Annalen*, 100(1), 295–320.

von Neumann, J. & Morgenstern, O. (1944). *Theory of Games and Economic Behavior*. Princeton University Press.

von Senger, H. (2004). *36 Strategeme für Manager*. Munich: Hanser.

von Thun, F. S. (2015). Von wem stammt das Werte – und Entwicklungsquadrat? SyStemischer. *Die Zeitschrift für systemische Strukturaufstellungen* 7, 88–98.

von Thun, F. S. (2010). *Miteinander reden 2: Stile, Werte und*

Persönlichkeitsentwicklung. Differentielle Psychologie der Kommunikation. Reinbek bei Hamburg: Rowohlt.

Voss, C. & Raz, T. (2016). *Never Split the Difference. Negotiating as if Your Life Depended on It*. London: Random House.

Wade, K. A., Garry, M., Don Read, J., & Lindsay, D. S. (2002). A Picture is Worth a Thousand Lies: Using False Photographs to Create False Childhood Memories. *Psychonomic Bulletin & Review*, 9(3), 597–603. https://doi.org/10.3758/BF03196318.

Wainer, H. & Zwerling, H. L. (2006). Evidence that Smaller Schools Do Not Improve Student Achievement. *Phi Delta Kappan*, 88(4), 300–3. Retrieved from www.pdkmembers.org/members_online/publications/Archive/pdf/k0612wai.pdf.

Walch, K. S., Mardyks, S. M., & Schmitz, J. (2018). *Quantum Negotiation: The Art of Getting What You Need*. Hoboken, NJ: John Wiley & Sons, Inc.

Wall Jr., J. A. (1977). Operantly Conditioning a Negotiator's Concession Making. *Journal of Experimental Social Psychology*, 13(5), 431–40.

Wall Jr, J. A. (1985). *Negotiation: Theory and Practice*. Glenview, IL: Scott, Foresman and Company.

Wallas, G. (1926). *The Art of Thought*. London: Jonathan Cape.

Walsh, J. (2018, Feb. 27). "It's still pie in the sky": Remain voters on Corbyn and Brexit. *The Guardian*. Retrieved from www.theguardian.com/politics/2018/feb/27/its-still-pie-in-the-sky-remain-voters-on-corbyn-and-brexit.

Walsh, J. P. & Nagaoka, S. (2009). *Who Invents? Evidence from the Japan–US Inventor Survey*. RIETI Discussion Paper Series 09-E-034, Research Institute of Economy, Trade and Industry, Japan. Retrieved from www.rieti.go.jp/jp/publications/dp/09e034.pdf.

Walker, M. (2018). *Why We Sleep. The New Science of Sleep and Dreams*. London: Penguin Books.

Walton, R. E. & McKersie, R. B. (1965). *A Behavioral Theory of Labor Negotiations. An Analysis of a Social Interaction System* (2nd ed. 1991). Ithaca, New York: Cornell University Press.

Wammes, J. (2017). *On the Mnemonic Benefits of Drawing. UWSpace*. Retrieved from http://hdl.handle.net/10012/12114.

Warsitzka, M. & Trötschel, R. (2017). *Focusing on Different Issues: Stumbling Block or Strong Point for Successful Negotiations?* Paper presented at the IACM International Association of Conflict Management, Berlin, Germany.

Watzlawick, P., Beavin Bavelas, J., & Jackson, D. D. (1967 [reissued 2014]). *Pragmatics of Human Communication. A Study of Interactional Patterns, Pathologies, and Paradoxes*. New York: W.W. Norton & Company Inc.

Wellen, S. & Danks, D. (2014). Learning with a Purpose: The Influence of Goals. *Proceedings of the Annual Meeting of the Cognitive Science Society*, 36(36), 1766–71.

Wetlaufer, G. B. (2004). The Limits of Integrative Bargaining. In C. Menkel-Meadow & M. Wheeler, *What's Fair. Ethics for Negotiators*, pp. 30–56. San Francisco, CA: Jossey-Bass.

Wheeler, M. (2006). Is Teaching Negotiation Too Easy, Too Hard, or Both? *Negotiation Journal*, 22(2), 187–97.

Wheeler, M. (2013). *The Art of Negotiation: How to Improvise Agreement in a Chaotic World*. New York: Simon and Schuster.

White, J. J. (1984). The Pros and Cons of Getting to YES. *Journal of Legal Education*, 34, 115–24.

Whitehead, A. North (1967 [1929]). *The Aims of Education and Other Essays*. New York: Macmillan, The Free Press.

Whitehouse.gov. (2017). *Joint Press Conference with President Trump and German Chancellor Merkel* [Press release]. Retrieved from www.whitehouse.gov/briefings-statements/joint-press-conference-president-trump-german-chancellor-merkel/.

Whitehouse.gov. (2018). *President Trump Hosts a Joint Press Conference with Chancellor Merkel of Germany*. Retrieved from www.youtube.com/watch?v=yye0_Y1cgWs.

Wilson, T. (2015). *Redirect: Changing the Stories We Live By*. New York, Boston, London: Back Bay Books.

Wilson, T. D., Reinhard, D. A., Westgate, E. C. [and five others]. (2014). Just Think: The Challenges of the Disengaged Mind. *Science*, 345(6192), 75–7.

Wood, W. (2019). *Good Habits, Bad Habits. The Science of Making Positive Changes that Stick*. New York: Farrar, Straus and Giroux.

Wyatt, D. (2016). *Why 'Cherry Picking' is a Bad Description of the UK's Aims in the Brexit Negotiations*. Paper presented at the Talk at The European University Institute on November 4, 2016. Retrieved from www.law.ox.ac.uk/research-and-subject-groups/research-collection-brexit/blog/2016/11/why-cherry-picking-bad.

Wyn Jones, R. (2019, Oct. 24). *Future of England Survey Reveals Public Attitudes towards Brexit and the Union*. Cardiff University. Retrieved from www.cardiff.ac.uk/news/view/1709008-future-of-england-survey-reveals-public-attitudes-towards-brexit-and-the-union.

Yamada, M., Lamm, C., & Decety, J. (2011). Pleasing Frowns, Disappointing Smiles: An ERP Investigation of Counterempathy. *Emotion*, 11(6), 1336.

Young, H. P. (1994). *Equity in Theory and Practice*. Princeton University Press.

Young, M. (2016). Games People Play: And How to Change Them . . . *Journal of Mediation & Applied Conflict Analysis*, 3(1), 330–41.

Yurtsever, G. (2008). Negotiators' Profit Predicted by Cognitive Reappraisal, Suppression of Emotions, Misrepresentation of Information, and Tolerance of Ambiguity. *Perceptual and Motor Skills*, 106(2), 590–608.

Zhang, J.-D. & Brett, J. (2017). *The Effect of Trust on Anchoring in Negotiation*. Paper presented at the IACM International Association of Conflict Management Berlin, Germany.

Zimmerman, L. (2016). Deception Detection. *Monitor on Psychology of the American Psychological Association*, 47(3), 46.

Zlatev, J., Daniels, D., Kim, H., & Neale, M. (2017). Default Neglect in Attempts at Social Influence. *Proceedings of the National Academy of Sciences*, 114(52), 13643–8.

Zuckerman, G. (2019). *The Man Who Solved the Market. How Jim Simons Launched the Quant Revolution.* New York: Portfolio/Penguin.

Index